ENGLISH EPISCOPAL ACTA
21

NORWICH 1215–1243

ENGLISH EPISCOPAL ACTA

1. LINCOLN 1067–1185. Edited by David M. Smith. 1980.
2. CANTERBURY 1162–1191. Edited by C. R. Cheney and Bridget E. A. Jones. 1986.
3. CANTERBURY 1193–1205. Edited by C. R. Cheney and E. John. 1986.
4. LINCOLN 1186–1206. Edited by David M. Smith. 1986.
5. YORK 1070–1154. Edited by Janet E. Burton. 1988.
6. NORWICH 1070–1214. Edited by Christopher Harper-Bill. 1990.
7. HEREFORD 1079–1234. Edited by Julia Barrow. 1993.
8. WINCHESTER 1070–1204. Edited by M. J. Franklin. 1993.
9. WINCHESTER 1205–1238. Edited by Nicholas Vincent. 1994.
10. BATH AND WELLS 1061–1205. Edited by Frances M. R. Ramsey. 1995.
11. EXETER 1046–1184. Edited by Frank Barlow. 1996.
12. EXETER 1186–1257. Edited by Frank Barlow. 1996.
13. WORCESTER 1218–1268. Edited by Philippa M. Hoskin. 1997.
14. COVENTRY AND LICHFIELD 1072–1159. Edited by M. J. Franklin. 1997.
15. LONDON 1076–1187. Edited by Falko Neininger. 1999.
16. COVENTRY AND LICHFIELD 1160–1182. Edited by M. J. Franklin. 1998.
17. COVENTRY AND LICHFIELD 1183–1208. Edited by M. J. Franklin. 1998.
18. SALISBURY 1078–1217. Edited by Brian Kemp. 1999.
19. SALISBURY 1218–1228. Edited by Brian Kemp. 2000.
20. YORK 1154–1181. Edited by Marie Lovatt. 2000.
21. NORWICH 1215–1243. Edited by Christopher Harper-Bill. 2000.

ENGLISH EPISCOPAL ACTA

21

NORWICH 1215–1243

EDITED BY
CHRISTOPHER HARPER-BILL

Published for THE BRITISH ACADEMY
by OXFORD UNIVERSITY PRESS

Oxford University Press, Great Clarendon Street, Oxford OX2 6DP
Oxford   New York
Athens   Auckland   Bangkok   Bogotá   Buenos Aires   Calcutta
Cape Town   Chennai   Dar es Salaam   Delhi   Florence   Hong Kong   Istanbul
Karachi   Kuala Lumpur   Madrid   Melbourne   Mexico City   Mumbai
Nairobi   Paris   São Paulo   Shanghai   Singapore
Taipei   Tokyo   Toronto   Warsaw

with associated companies in
Berlin   Ibadan

Published in the United States by
Oxford University Press Inc., New York

© The British Academy, 2000

All rights reserved. No part of this publication may be reproduced,
stored in a retrieval system, or transmitted, in any form or by any means,
without the prior permission in writing of the British Academy

British Library Cataloguing in Publication Data
Data available

ISBN 0-19-726212-0

Typeset by Wyvern 21 Ltd, Bristol
Printed in Great Britain
on acid-free paper by
Antony Rowe Limited
Chippenham, Wiltshire

In fond memory of my mother
Violet Dearden Harper-Bill
1909–1995

CONTENTS

LIST OF PLATES	viii
ACKNOWLEDGEMENTS	ix
MANUSCRIPT SOURCES CITED	xi
PRINTED BOOKS AND ARTICLES CITED, WITH ABBREVIATED REFERENCES	xiii
OTHER ABBREVIATIONS	xviii
INTRODUCTION	
The Early Thirteenth-Century Bishops	xix
Pandulph Verracclo	xx
Thomas Blundeville	xxiv
The vacancy of the see, 1236–39	xxviii
William Raleigh	xxx
The Bishops of Norwich and the Crown	xxxvii
The Bishops' Officers and *Familia*	xliii
The Acta	liv
Contents of the acta	liv
Diplomatic of the acta	lxiii
Format and script	lxx
Sealing	lxxi
Editorial Method	lxxiii
THE ACTA	1
Pandulph Verracclo nos. 1–27	1
Thomas Blundeville nos. 28–123	23
William Raleigh nos. 124–154	113
APPENDICES	147
I. Additional acta of the Bishops of Norwich, 1070–1214	147
II. References to acts of the bishops 1215–1243	158
III. Itineraries	175
IV. Corrigenda to *Fasti* ii: Monastic Cathedrals, 1066–1300	182
INDEX OF PERSONS	183
INDEX OF SUBJECTS	210

LIST OF PLATES
(between page lxiv *and page* lxv*)*

I. ACTUM OF BISHOP PANDULPH VERRACCLO (no. 4)
II. ACTUM OF BISHOP THOMAS BLUNDEVILLE (no. 69)
III. ACTUM OF BISHOP WILLIAM RALEIGH (no. 140)
IV. SEALS AND COUNTERSEALS OF BISHOPS THOMAS BLUNDEVILLE AND WILLIAM RALEIGH (nos. 38, 69, 138)

ACKNOWLEDGEMENTS

It is once again a pleasure to acknowledge the debts incurred during the preparation of this second volume of Norwich episcopal acta. I am deeply indebted to the Leverhulme Trust for the funding of a semester's sabbatical during which the final stages of this work were almost completed. Thanks are expressed to all those who have allowed access to and permitted publication of manuscripts in their ownership or custody, that is, the authorities of all those national, ecclesiastical, collegiate and local repositories which are recorded in the list of manuscript sources. Transcripts of Crown copyright material in the Public Record Office appear by permission of the Controller of HM Stationery Office, and of material in the British Library by permission of the Trustees. To the list of archivists who have provided me with help recorded in the first volume, I would wish to add Mr S. Dixon at Strood, Mrs Angela Doughty at Exeter and Dr Kate Harris at Longleat. The staff of all the archives which I have used have been unfailingly helpful and courteous.

Many scholars have given me help and advice over the years. I would like to thank specifically Dr Mark Bailey and Dr Dorothy Owen for assistance with particular texts, Professor Diana Greenway for her observations on the palaeography of original charters, Dr Michael Franklin for checking the transcription of texts at Cambridge, and Professor Brian Kemp, Mr Nicholas Karn and Professor Nicholas Vincent for bringing to my attention *acta* which they found in unexpected locations. Along with all editors of English episcopal *acta*, I am extraordinarily grateful to Professors Christopher Brooke and David Smith and Dr Philippa Hoskin for the time and care devoted to the meticulous checking of this text; needless to say, the errors which undoubtedly remain are entirely my own.

The production of work such as this requires a stable environment. As ever, I wish to express my thanks to my wife, Dr Ruth Harvey, for providing both love and intellectual stimulus at home. To the whole School of History at Norwich, and most especially to Professor Colin Davis, who rescued me from a very difficult situation, I could not be more grateful; and I wish to thank particularly Professor John Charmley, Dr Stephen Church, Professor Michael John, Dr Carole Rawcliffe, Mrs Jenni Tanimoto, Dr Tom Williamson and Dr Richard Wilson for receiving me so warmly into their society.

The dedication of this volume is a final expression of a longer standing debt.

School of History   Christopher Harper-Bill
University of East Anglia
Norwich

MANUSCRIPT SOURCES

ORIGINAL CHARTERS OF THE BISHOPS OF NORWICH

Auxerre, Archives-Départementales de la Yonne
—H1406: *145A*
Canterbury, Dean and Chapter Archives
—*Chartae Antiquae*, C115/165, *28*; D14, *38*; D16, *39*
Gloucester, Gloucestershire Record Office
—D225/T10: *Appx I 12*
London, British Library
—Additional Charter 75321: *Appx I 5*
London, Public Record Office
—E40/13997: *74*; E40/14104, *18*; E40/14117, *73;* E42/302 (duplicate): *69*; E42/459: *120*; E42/460 (duplicate): *69*; E210/7639: *30*; E315/53/9: *31*; E327/533: *4*
Ipswich, Suffolk Record Office
—HD1538/269/3: *137A*
Norwich, Norfolk Record Office

—DCN 43/36: *85*; DCN 43/37: *95*; DCN 43/38: *88*; DCN 43/39: *87*; DCN 43/40: *78*; DCN 43/41: *140*; DCN 43/42: *144*; DCN 43/43: *145*; DCN 45/24/1: *96*; DCN 84/3: *142*
—Flitcham 703: *Appx I 10A*
Oxford, Bodleian Library
—Norfolk Charter 505: *152*
Oxford, New College (Newington Longville Charters)
—muniments 12046: *138*
Sens, cathedral treasury. Pontigny archive
—H3: *145B*
Wells cathedral, Dean and Chapter
—Charter 40: *124A*
Windsor, St George's Chapel
—X G 23: *125*

COPIES, TRANSCRIPTS AND MENTIONS OF CHARTERS OF THE BISHOPS OF NORWICH

Caen, Bibliothèque Municipale
—ms. 323: *Appx I 4*
Cambridge, Christ's College
—Creake Abbey Muniments 7: *130*
Cambridge, Emmanuel College
—Muniments box 20/A1, no. 4: *70, Appx I 9*
Cambridge, King's College
—GBR 290, *60*
—GBR 291, *60*
—KER 638, *70–1, Appx II 11*
Cambridge, University Library
—Additional Manuscript 4220: *5*
—Ely Diocesan Registry, G3/28: *13–14, 53–4*
—ms. Ee v 31: *140*
—ms. Ff ii 33: *5*
—ms. Mm iv 19: *5*
Canterbury, Dean and Chapter Archives

—Chartae Antiquae: D9: *39*; D12: *38*; N1: *78, 95*; N24: *107–9*; N26: *140*
—Register A: *28, 124*
—Register B: *38–9*
—Register E: *38–9*
Chelmsford, Essex Record Office
—D/D By Q 19: *55–8, 132–4*
Colchester, Essex Record Office
—Acc. 38 pt. 1: *49–50*
—Acc. 38 pt. 2: *49A–B*
Evreux, Archives Départementales
—H711: *146*
Exeter, Devon Record Office
—Dean and Chapter of Exeter ms. 2089: *131*
Gloucester, Cathedral Library
—Register A: *59*
Ipswich, Suffolk Record Office

—HD1538/169/19: *36*
—HD1538/222/3: *Appx II 54*
—HD1538/345: *105–6*
London, British Library
—Additional Manuscripts: 5516: *75*; 7096: *5*; 46353: *117–9, 154*; 47677: *Appx I x*
—Cotton Charter ii 21: *140*
—Cotton Manuscripts: *Appx xxi: 150–1*; Claudius D xiii, *34, Appx II 27, 39*; Faustina A iv: *102–4, 149*; Faustina B i: *29*; Galba E ii: *15–16, 65–8, 136–7*; Julius D ii: *6*; Nero E vii: *26, 114–5*; Tiberius C ix: *116*; Tiberius E vi: *Appx I, vi–viii, xii*; Titus C viii: *27, 121–3, Appx I 1, Appx II 27*; Vespasian E xiv: *37*; Vespasian F xv: *17*
—Cotton Rolls: ii 19: *95*; iv 57: *15, 65–6, 68*
—Egerton Manuscript 3137: *35*
—Harley Manuscripts: 391: *153*; 2110: *7–11, 40–48, 127–8, 152*; 3697: *24–5*
London, Lambeth Palace Library
—Manuscript 241: *12*
—Register of archbp Warham: *38*
London, Lincoln's Inn Library
—Hale Manuscript 87: *2, 30–1*
London, Public Record Office
—C150/1: *59*
—CP25/1/156/57/9: *Appx II 41A*; /213/7/90: *Appx II 26*
—DL 42/5: *6*
—E135/15/17: *111–12*
—E210/1483: *32*
—E315/54/140: *30*
Norwich, Norfolk Record Office
—DCN 40/1: *80-1, 85–6, 88–9, 91–5, 139–40, 142, 145*; DCN 40/2/1: *20, 76–8, 80–1, 83, 85–6, 88–9, 91–4, 140, 142, 145*; DCN 40/2/2: *77, 79–80, 84, 87, 89, 92, 94*; DCN 40/4: *76–83, 85–6, 88–9, 91–5, 140, 142, 144–5, 152*; DCN 40/5: *19, 76, 78, 82, 85–6, 91, 93, 152*; DCN 40/7: *81, 83, 88, 140–2, 145*; DCN 40/8: *15, 65–8*; DCN 40/11: *140*; DCN 42/1/4: *140*; DCN 43/36: *Appx II 36*; DCN 44/78/11: *90*; DCN 44/154/1: *Appx II 23*
—FEL 31: *96A*
—SUN 8: *51–2, Appx II 50A*
Oxford, Bodleian Library
—Essex Charter 220: *Appx II 2*
—Laud Misc. 647: *13–14, 53–4A, Appx I 2A*
—Norfolk Charters, 195: *Appx II 24*; 228: *Appx II 43*; 249: *Appx II 38*
—Suffolk Charter 190: *126*
—Suffolk Roll 2: *36*
—Tanner 425: *63–4*
—Top. Lincs. d. 1: *Appx I 3*
—Top. Suff. d. 15: *148*
Rome, Archivo Segreto Vaticano
—Reg. Vat. 18 (Gregory IX): *23*
—Reg. Vat. 24 (Alexander IV): *23*
San Marino, California, H.E. Huntington Library
—Battle Abbey Papers vol. 29: *1–3, 30–1, 33*
Shrewsbury Borough Library
—Haughmond Abbey Cartulary: *61–2, 135–6*
Spalding, Gentlemen's Society
—Crowland Cartulary: *Appx I 2*
Strood, Rochester, Medway Archives
—DRc/L4: *58A*
Warminster, Longleat
—North Muniment Room 1163: *120*
Windsor, St George's Chapel
—IV B 1: *125*

PRINTED BOOKS AND ARTICLES CITED, WITH ABBREVIATED REFERENCES

Acta Langton	K. Major, ed., *Acta Stephani Langton Cantuariensis Archiepiscopi, A.D. 1207–1228* (CYS 50, 1950)
Anglia Sacra	H. Wharton ed., 2 vols (London 1691)
Ann. mon.	H. R. Luard, ed., *Annales monastici*, 5 vols (Rolls Series, 1864–9)
Banfield, T. G.	'A descriptive Catalogue of the Seals of the Bishops of Norwich', *Norfolk Archaeology* i (1847), 305–23
Bec Documents	M. Chibnall, ed., *Select Documents of the English Lands of the Abbey of Bec* (Camden 3rd series 73, 1951)
Bk Fees	H. C. Maxwell-Lyte, ed., *Liber Feodorum: the Book of Fees commonly called Testa de Nevill*, 3 vols (London, 1920–31)
Blomefield, *Norfolk*	F. Blomefield and C. Parkin, *An Essay towards a Topographical History of the County of Norfolk*, 2nd edn, 11 vols (London, 1805–10)
Blythburgh Cartulary	C. Harper-Bill, ed., *Blythburgh Priory Cartulary*, 2 vols (Suffolk Record Society, Suffolk Charters 2–3, 1980–1)
BM Seals	W. de G. Birch, *Catalogue of Seals in the Department of Manuscripts in the British Museum*, 6 vols (London, 1887–1900)
Bracton	G. E. Woodbine, ed., *Bracton: de Legibus et consuetudinibus Angliae*, trans. with revisions and notes by S. E. Thorne, 4 vols (Cambridge, Mass., 1968–77)
Bracton's Notebook	F. W. Maitland, ed., *Bracton's Notebook: a Collection of Cases Decided in the King's Courts during the Reign of Henry the Third, Annotated by a Lawyer of that Time, seemingly by Henry of Bratton*, 3 vols (London, 1887)
BRUO	A. B. Emden, *A Biographical Register of the University of Oxford to A.D. 1500*, 3 vols (Oxford, 1957–9)
Bury Chron.	A. Gransden, ed., *The Chronicle of Bury St Edmunds, 1212–1301* (NMT, 1964)
Bury Hospital Charters	C. Harper-Bill, ed., *Charters of the Medieval Hospitals of Bury St Edmunds* (Suffolk Record Society, Suffolk Charters 14, 1994)
CACW	J. G. Edwards, ed., *Calendar of Ancient Correspondence concerning Wales* (Board of Celtic Studies, Cardiff, 1935)
Cal. Ch. R.	*Calendar of Charter Rolls preserved in the Public Record Office*, 6 vols (1903–27)
Cal. Docs. Scotland	J. Bain, ed., *Calendar of Documents relating to Scotland*, i, *1108–1272* (1881)
Cal. Lib. R.	*Calendar of Liberate Rolls*, 6 vols (1917–64)
Canterbury Professions	M. Richter, ed. (CYS 67, 1973)
Carpenter, D. A.	*The Minority of Henry III* (London, 1990)
Cheney, C. R.	*English Synodalia of the Thirteenth Century* (Oxford, 1941)
	From Becket to Langton: English Church Government, 1170–1213 (Manchester, 1956)
	Notaries Public in the Thirteenth and Fourteenth Centuries (Oxford, 1972)
	'A Papal Privilege for Tonbridge Priory', *Bulletin of the Institute of Historical Research* 38 (1965), 192–200; repr. in *Medieval Texts and Studies* (Oxford, 1973), 66–77.
	Pope Innocent III and England (Päpste und Papsttum, band 9, Stuttgart, 1976)

Chron. Maj.	H. R. Luard, ed., *Matthaei Parisiensis Chronica Majora*, 7 vols (Rolls Series, 1872–84)
Churchill, I. J.	*Canterbury Administration*, 2 vols (London, 1933)
Cirencester Cartulary	C. D. Ross and M. Devine, eds, *The Cartulary of Cirencester Abbey*, 3 vols (Oxford, 1964–77)
Clay, C. T.	*York Minster Fasti*, 2 vols (Yorkshire Archaeological Society Record Series 123–4, 1958–9)
Close Rolls	*Close Rolls of the Reign of Henry III*, 14 vols (1902–38)
Coggeshall	J. Stevenson, ed., *Radulphi de Coggeshall Chronicon Anglicanum* (Rolls Series, 1875)
Colchester Cartulary	S. A. Moore, ed., *Cartularium monasterii sancti Johannis Baptiste de Colecestria*, 2 vols (Roxburghe Club, 1897)
Colne Cartulary	J. L. Fisher, ed., *Cartularium Prioratus de Colne* (Essex Archaeological Society Occasional Publications 1, 1946)
Colvin, H. M.	*The White Canons in England* (Oxford, 1951)
Cotton	H. R. Luard, ed., *Bartholomaei de Cotton Historia Anglicana (449–1298) necnon ejusdem Liber de Archiepiscopis et Episcopis Angliae* (Rolls Series, 1859)
CPL	W. H. Bliss, C. Johnson and J. A. Twemlow, eds, *Entries in the Papal Registers relating to Great Britain and Ireland, 1198–* (London and Dublin, 1894–)
CPR	*Calendar of Patent Rolls* (London 1981–)
CRR	*Curia Regis Rolls . . . preserved in the Public Record Office* (1922–)
Creake Cartulary	A. L. Bedingfield, ed., *A Cartulary of Creake Abbey* (Norfolk Record Society 35, 1966)
D. Crook	*Records of the General Eyre* (Public Record Office Handbooks 20, London 1982)
C. & S.	*Councils and Synods, with other Documents relating to the English Church*; i, *A.D. 871–1204*, ed. D. Whitelock, M. Brett and C. N. L. Brooke, 2 parts; ii, *1205–1313*, ed. F. M. Powicke and C. R. Cheney, 2 parts (Oxford, 1964–81)
CYS	Canterbury and York Society
DD	P. Chaplais, ed., *Diplomatic Documents preserved in the Public Record Office, 1101–1272* (London, 1964)
DNB	*Dictionary of National Biography*
Dodnash Charters	C. Harper-Bill, ed., *Dodnash Priory Charters* (Suffolk Record Society, Suffolk Charters 16, 1998)
EBC	C. R. Cheney, *English Bishops' Chanceries, 1100–1250* (Manchester, 1950)
EEA	*English Episcopal Acta*, 1– ((British Academy, 1980–)
English Baronies	I. J. Sanders, *English Baronies; a Study of their Origins and Descent, 1086–1327* (Oxford, 1960)
Exc. Rot. Fin.	C. Roberts, ed., *Excerpta e Rotulis Finium in Turri Londinensi asservatis, Henry III, 1216–1272*, 2 vols (Record Commission, 1835–6)
EYC	*Early Yorkshire Charters*; i–iii, ed. W. Farrer, 1914–16; iv–xii and index of i–iii, ed. C. T. Clay (Yorkshire Archaeological Society Record Series, extra series, 1935–65)
Eye Cartulary	V. Brown, ed., *Eye Priory Cartulary and Charters*, 2 vols (Suffolk Record Society, Suffolk Charters 11–12, 1992–4)
Farrer, W.	*Honors and Knights' Fees*, 3 vols (London, 1923–5)
Fasti	D. E. Greenway, ed., *Fasti Ecclesiae Anglicanae, 1066–1300* by John le Neve, i– (London, 1968–)
Fines i, ii	B. Dodwell, ed., *Feet of Fines for the County of Norfolk (1198–1202); Feet of Fines for the County of Norfolk (1202–15) and of Suffolk (1199–1214)*, PRS ns xxvii, xxxii (1950–8)
First Register	H. W. Saunders, ed., *The First Register of Norwich Cathedral Priory* (Norfolk Record Society 11, 1939)

BOOKS AND ARTICLES CITED

Fisher, J. L.	'The Leger Book of St John's Abbey, Colchester', *Transactions of the Essex Archaeological Society* ns 24 (1951), 77–127
Flores Hist.	H. R. Luard, ed., *Flores Historiarum*, 3 vols. (Rolls Series, 1890)
Foedera	T. Rymer, ed., *Foedera, Conventiones, Litterae et cujuscumque generis Acta Publica*, new edn, 3 vols in 6, ed. A. Clark *et al.* (Record Commission, 1816–30)
Formulare Anglicanum	T. Madox, ed. (London, 1702)
Furness Coucher Bk.	J. C. Atkinson, ed., *The Coucher Book of Furness Abbey*, 3 vols (Chetham Society ns 9, 11, 14 (1886–8)
Gesta Abbatum	H. T. Riley, ed., *Gesta Abbatum Monasterii S. Albani a Thoma Walsingham (A.D. 793–1401)*, 3 vols (Rolls Series, 1867–9)
Gibbs, M. and Lang, J.	*Bishops and Reform, 1215–1272* (Oxford, 1934)
Gloucester Cartulary	W. H. Hart, ed., *Historia et Cartularium Monasterii S. Petri Gloucestriae*, 3 vols (Rolls Series, 1863–7)
Grosseteste's Letters	H. R. Luard, ed., *Letters of Robert Grosseteste, illustrative of the Social Conditions of his Time* (Rolls Series, 1861)
Guala's Letters	N. Vincent, ed., *The Letters and Charters of Cardinal Guala Bicchieri, Papal Legate in England, 1216–1218* (CYS 83, 1996)
Harper-Bill, C.	'Battle Abbey and its East Anglian Churches', in *Studies in Medieval History presented to R. Allen Brown*, ed. C. Harper-Bill, C. J. Holdsworth and J. L. Nelson (Woodbridge, 1988), 159–72
Harper-Bill, C.	'The Diocese of Norwich in the Early Thirteenth Century: Sources and Themes', in *Counties and Communities: Essays on East Anglian History presented to Hassell Smith*, ed. C. Rawcliffe, R. Virgoe and R. Wilson (Norwich, 1996), 21–36
Harper-Bill, C.	'The Diocese of Norwich and the Italian Connection, 1198–1261', in *England and the Continent. Essays dedicated to the Memory of Andrew Martindale*, ed. J. Mitchell (Stamford, 2000)
Haughmond Cartulary	U. Rees, ed., *The Cartulary of Haughmond Abbey* (Shropshire Archaeological Society and University of Wales Press, Cardiff, 1985)
Hist. Maréchal	P. Meyer, ed., *L'Histoire de Guillaume le Maréchal*, 3 vols (Société de l'Histoire de France, Paris, 1891–1901)
HMC Various Collections	Historical Manuscripts Commission, *Report on Manuscripts in Various Collections*, 8 parts (HMC, 1903–13)
HMC Wells	Historical Manuscripts Commission, *Calendar of Manuscripts of the Dean and Chapter of Wells*, 2 vols (HMC, 1907–14)
HRH	D. Knowles, C. N. L. Brooke and V. C. M. London, *The Heads of Religious Houses: England and Wales, 940–1216* (Cambridge, 1972)
H & S	A. W. Haddan and W. Stubbs, eds, *Councils and Ecclesiastical Documents relating to Great Britain and Ireland, edited after Spelman and Wilkins*, 3 vols (Oxford, 1869–78)
King's Lynn	D. M. Owen, ed., *The Making of King's Lynn: a Documentary Survey* (Records of the Social and Economic History of England and Wales, ns 9, 1984)
Lawrence, C. H.	*St Edmund of Abingdon* (Oxford, 1960)
Leiston Cartulary	R. Mortimer, ed., *Leiston Abbey Cartulary and Butley Priory Charters* (Suffolk Record Society, Suffolk Charters 1, 1979)
Letters of Innocent III	C. R. and M. G. Cheney, eds, *The Letters of Pope Innocent III (1198–1216) concerning England and Wales* (Oxford, 1967)
Lewes Cartulary: Norfolk Portion	J. H. Bullock, ed., *The Norfolk Portion of the Cartulary of the Priory of St Pancras at Lewes* (Norfolk Record Society 12, 1939)
Liber Censuum	P. Fabre and L. Duchesne, eds, *Le Liber Censuum de l'Église Romaine*, 3 vols (Paris, 1905–10)
Liber Eliensis	E. O. Blake, ed. (Camden Society 3rd series 92, 1962)
Lipman, V. D.	*The Jews of Medieval Norwich* (London, 1967)
Lunt, W. E.	*Financial Relations of the Papacy with England to 1327* (Medieval Academy of America, Cambridge, Mass., 1939)

Meekings, *Studies*	C. A. F. Meekings, *Studies in Thirteenth-Century Justice and Administration* (London, 1981)
Memorials of St Edmunds	T. Arnold, ed., *Memorials of St Edmund's Abbey*, 3 vols (Rolls Series, 1890–6)
Monasticon	W. Dugdale, *Monasticon Anglicanum*, J. Caley, H. Ellis and B. Bandinel, eds, 6 vols in 8 (London, 1817–30)
MRH	D. Knowles and R.N. Hadcock, *Medieval Religious Houses: England and Wales*, 2nd edn (London, 1971)
Newington Longville Charters	H. E. Salter, ed. (Oxfordshire Record Society 3, 1921)
NMT	Nelsons Medieval Texts
Norwich Cathedral 1096–1996	I. Atherton, E. Fernie, C. Harper-Bill and A. H. Smith, eds, *Norwich Cathedral: Church, City and Diocese, 1096–1996* (London, 1996)
Norwich Cathedral Charters	B. Dodwell, ed., *The Charters of Norwich Cathedral Priory*, 2 vols (PRS ns 40, 46, 1974–85)
ns	new series
OMT	Oxford Medieval Texts
os	old series
Patent Rolls	2 vols (London, 1901–3) (after 1232, *CPR*)
Powicke, F. M.	*Henry III and the Lord Edward* (Oxford, repr. 1966)
PRS	Pipe Roll Society
Prynne, *Records* iii	W. Prynne, *The Third Tome of an Exact Chronological Vindication . . . of the Supreme Ecclesiastical Jurisdiction of our . . . English Kings* (London, 1668)
PSIA	*Proceedings of the Suffolk Institute of Archaeology and History*
PUE	W. Holtzmann, ed., *Papsturkunden in England*, 3 vols (Abhandlungen der Gesellschaft der Wissenschaften zu Göttingen. phil.-hist. Klasse, neue Folge 25 (1930–1), 3 Folge 14–15 (1935–6), 33 (1952))
Reg. Alex. IV	B. de la Roncière *et al.*, eds, *Les Régistres d'Alexandre IV*, 3 vols (Paris, 1902–59)
Reg. Ant.	C. W. Foster and K. Major, eds, *The Registrum Antiquissimum of the Cathedral Church of Lincoln*, 10 vols and 2 vols of facsimiles (Lincoln Record Society, 27–9, 32, 34, 41–2, 46, 51, 62, 67–8, 1931–73)
Reg. Bateman	P. E. Pobst, ed., *The Register of William Bateman, Bishop of Norwich, 1344–55*, 2 vols (CYS, 84, 1996–)
Regesta	H. W. C. Davis, C. Johnson, H. A. Cronne and R. H. C. Davis, eds, *Regesta Regum Anglo-Normannorum, 1066–1154*, 4 vols (Oxford, 1913–69)
Reg. Greg. IX	L. Auvray, ed., *Les Régistres de Gregoire IX*, 4 vols (Paris, 1896–1910)
Reg. Hon. III	P. Pressutti, ed., *Regesta Honorii Papae III*, 2 vols (Rome, 1888–95)
Reg. Inn. IV	E. Berger, ed., *Les Régistres d'Innocent IV*, 4 vols (Paris, 1884–1911)
RL	W. W. Shirley, ed., *Royal and other Historical Letters illustrative of the Reign of Henry III*, 2 vols (Rolls Series, 1862–6)
Rot. Chart.	T. D. Hardy, ed., *Rotuli Chartarum in Turri Londinensi asservati, 1199–1216* (Record Commission, 1837)
Rot. Grosseteste	F. N. Davis, ed., *Rotuli Roberti Grosseteste, Episcopi Lincolniensis, A.D. mccxxxv–mccliii* (CYS 10, 1913, and Lincoln Record Society 11, 1914)
Rot. H. de Welles	F. N. Davis, W. P. W. Phillimore *et al.* eds, *Rotuli Hugonis de Welles, Episcopi Lincolniensis, A.D. mccix–mccxxxv* (CYS 1, 3, 4, 1907–9; Lincoln Record Society 3, 6, 9, 1912–14)
Rot. Litt. Claus.	T. D. Hardy, ed., *Rotuli Litterarum Clausarum in Turri Londinensi asservati*, 2 vols (Record Commission, 1833–44)
Rot. Litt. Pat.	T. D. Hardy, ed., *Rotuli Litterarum Patentium in Turri Londinensi asservati, 1201–16* (Record Commission, 1835)
Rye, *Norfolk Fines*	W. Rye, ed., *A Short Calendar of the Feet of Fines for Norfolk* (Norwich, 1885)

BOOKS AND ARTICLES CITED

Rye, *Suffolk Fines*	W. Rye, ed., *A Calendar of the Feet of Fines for Suffolk* (Ipswich, 1900)
St Benet of Holme	J. R. West, ed., *St Benet of Holme, 1020–1210* (Norfolk Record Society 2–3, 1932)
St Frideswide's Cartulary	S. R. Wigram, ed., *The Cartulary of the Monastery of St Frideswide at Oxford*, 2 vols (Oxford Historical Society 28, 31, 1895–6)
Saltman, *Theobald*	A. Saltman, *Theobald, Archbishop of Canterbury* (University of London Historical Studies 2, 1956)
Saunders, 'Coxford Priory'	H. W. Saunders, 'A History of Coxford Priory', *Norfolk Archaeology* 17 (1910), 284–372
Saunders, H. W.	*An Introduction to the Obedientiary and Manor Rolls of Norwich Cathedral Priory* (Norwich, 1930)
Sayers, *Papal Government*	J. E. Sayers, *Papal Government and England during the Pontificate of Honorius III (1216–1227)* (Cambridge, 1984)
Sayers, *Papal Judges-Delegate*	J. E. Sayers, *Papal Judges-Delegate in the Province of Canterbury, 1198–1254* (Oxford, 1971)
Scott, J. R.	'Charters of Monks Horton Priory', *Archaeologia Cantiana* 10 (1876), 269–81
Sibton Charters	P. Brown, ed., *Sibton Abbey Cartularies and Charters* (Suffolk Record Society, Suffolk Charters 7–10, 1985–8)
Stacey, R. C.	*Politics, Policy and Finance under Henry III, 1216–1245* (Oxford, 1987)
Stoke by Clare Cartulary	C. Harper-Bill and R. Mortimer, eds (Suffolk Record Society, Suffolk Charters 4–6, 1982–4)
Taxatio	S. Ayscough and J. Caley, eds, *Taxatio Ecclesiastica Angliae et Walliae auctoritate Papae Nicholai IV circa 1291* (Record Commission, 1802)
Thorne	*Chronica Guillelmi Thorne ... de Gestis Abbatum S. Augustini Cantuariae*, in R. Twysden, ed., *Historiae Anglicanae Scriptores Decem* (London, 1652)
Tout, *Chapters*	T. F. Tout, *Chapters in the Administrative History of Medieval England*, 6 vols (Manchester, 1920–33)
TRHS	*Transactions of the Royal Historical Society*
Trivet	T. Hog, ed., *Annales F. Nicholai de Triveti* (English Historical Society, 1845)
Turner, R. V.	*The English Judiciary in the Age of Glanvill and Bracton, c. 1176–1239* (Cambridge, 1985)
Vincent, 'Election'	N. C. Vincent, 'The Election of Pandulph Verracclo as Bishop of Norwich (1215)', *Historical Research* 68 (no. 166)(1995), 143–63
Vincent, N. C.	*Peter des Roches. An Alien in English Politics, 1205–1238* (Cambridge, 1996)
VN	W. E. Lunt, ed., *The Valuation of Norwich* (Oxford, 1926)
Walker, D.	'A Register of the Churches of the Monastery of St Peter's, Gloucester', in *An Ecclesiastical Miscellany* (Publications of the Bristol and Gloucestershire Archaeological Society, Records Section, 2, 1976)
Walter of Coventry	W. Stubbs, ed., *Memoriale Fratris Walteri de Coventria. The Historical Collections of Walter of Coventry*, 2 vols (Rolls Series, 1872–3)
Waltham Charters	R. Ransford, ed., *The Early Charters of the Augustinian Canons of Waltham Abbey, Essex, 1062–1230* (Woodbridge, 1989)
Wendover, *Flores*	H. O. Coxe, ed., *Rogeri de Wendover Chronica sive Flores Historiarum*, 5 vols (English Historical Society, 1841–4)

OTHER ABBREVIATIONS

Add.	Additional
Appx	Appendix
archbp(s)	archbishop(s)
archdn(s)	archdeacons
BL	British Library
BN	Bibliothèque Nationale, Paris
Bodl.	Bodleian Library, Oxford
bp(s)	bishop(s)
Ch.	Charter
Ch. Ant	Charta Antiqua
D. & C.	Dean and Chapter
fo.	folio
m.	membrane
misc.	miscellanea, miscellaneous
om.	omitted
pd	printed
PRO	Public Record Office, London
repd	reprinted
RO	Record Office
s. -ex.	late-century
s. -in	early-century
s. -med.	mid-century
ser.	series
Trans.	Transactions
transl.	translated

INTRODUCTION

THE EARLY THIRTEENTH-CENTURY BISHOPS

By 1215 the boundaries and the administrative structure of the diocese of Norwich were long established.[1] At the centre, bishop John de Gray (1200–14) had done much to resolve the acrimonious conflict between his predecessor, John of Oxford (1175–1200), and the Benedictine chapter of the cathedral church,[2] and had also appointed the first known official to act as his jurisdictional *alter ego*; the extent of the reconciliation is illustrated by the fact that this most important of episcopal officers was, most unusually, a monk and subsequently prior of Norwich.[3] The ecclesiastical geography of the diocese had been transformed since the late 1080s by the foundation of well over forty male religious houses of varying size and wealth and of eight nunneries. Between 1215 and 1243 there were only eight small Augustinian foundations,[4] and a few hospitals,[5] although by the time of bishop Raleigh's translation the Dominicans were established at Norwich and the Franciscans at Norwich, Ipswich and Lynn.[6] Four territorial archdeaconries were administered either by the archdeacons in person, or in the case of absentees or those with wider diocesan responsibilities, by their own officials. The creation of parishes, already well advanced at the time of Domesday Book, had continued, probably at a slower pace, and very many of these local churches had already passed into the hands of religious communities, a process which was to continue in this period and beyond.

Between 1215 and 1243 three bishops presided over this very large diocese. All three were, in strictly legal terms, freely elected, but the influence

---

[1] For discussion, see *EEA* 6 pp. xxv–xxvii.
[2] For the conflict, see C. Harper-Bill, 'John of Oxford, Diplomat and Bishop', in M. J. Franklin and C. Harper-Bill, eds., *Medieval Ecclesiastical Studies in Honour of Dorothy M. Owen* (Woodbridge, 1995) 83–106, at 97–101; for the resolution, *EEA* 6 nos. 380, 383–4, 386–7, 389–93, 407–10; and also *Norwich Cathedral 1096–1996* 291–5.
[3] *EEA* 6 p. xxxviii.
[4] Beeston, *c.* 1216; Chipley, before 1235; Flitcham, after 1216; Kersey, *c.* 1218; North Creake, converted from hospital to abbey, 1231; St Olave's, Herringfleet, *c.* 1216; Spinney, *c.* 1227–28; Weybridge, before 1225; see *MRH* 137–82 passim.
[5] For example, Beck at Billingford and Great Hautbois, both *c.* 1216; *MRH* 341, 361.
[6] *MRH* 214, 222–3.

of the crown was paramount in each appointment—somewhat paradoxically, since Pandulph had first come to England as the agent of pope Innocent III at a time of bitter conflict between Rome and the Angevin monarchy, while William Raleigh, once Henry III's most trusted counsellor, was before his departure from Norwich reviled as the king's great enemy. Of the three bishops, it was Pandulph, the papal legate whose consecration was long delayed, who was hardly ever in the diocese because of his legation and his notable service to the minority government both in England and overseas. Both Blundeville and Raleigh appear to have been frequently present, in the case of the former probably and the latter certainly in part at least because of loss of royal favour. What is notable, however, is that throughout this period the administration of the diocese apparently continued to operate effectively, and that the ecclesiastical policies of the so-called 'curialist' bishops differed very little from those of renowned reformers such as St Edmund Rich at Canterbury and Robert Grosseteste at Lincoln.

PANDULPH VERRACCLO

Pandulph's family name has only recently been conclusively established;[7] in most historical works he is called Pandulph Masca, which represents a confusion with an older contemporary, who was cardinal deacon of the basilica of the Twelve Apostles from 1182 to the early years of the thirteenth century, and who was dead by 1213. It is clear now that the Pandulph who eventually became bishop of Norwich was one of three known brothers who came from the region of Monte Cassino, probably from San Germano, where both he and his brother Giles made gifts to the Cassinese monks. Both Pandulph and Giles entered the papal administration, and Giles was active therein until the 1230s.

Pandulph, a papal subdeacon, was sufficiently senior and trusted by pope Innocent III to be despatched to England in 1211 as one of two envoys commissioned to ratify the draft terms of a peace between pope and king; with limited room for manoeuvre and faced by the king's intransigence, they failed completely.[8] He returned to England in May 1213 to accept John's submission to the apostolic see, and thereafter negotiated with the king's enemies in

---

[7] Vincent, 'Election' 153–6.
[8] For Pandulph's activities in England from 1211 to 1216, see Cheney, *Pope Innocent III and England* 323–91 *passim*.

France and in Wales. He was heavily involved in the collection of Peter's Pence and the annual subsidy promised by the king to the papacy; he advanced the promotion of papal clerks to English benefices and acted as a judge-delegate, and he took a leading part in arranging compensation for returning bishops. Pandulph attended negotiations between king John and the dissident barons at Runnymede, his name appears in the preamble to Magna Carta, and it was suggested that thereafter he and Nicholas of Tusculum, the papal legate, were indirectly responsible for the breakdown in relations which led to civil war.[9]

The circumstances of Pandulph's election to the bishopric of Norwich have only recently been elucidated.[10] In the vacancy of the see following the death of his trusted servant John de Gray on 18 October 1214, king John, eager now for accommodation with pope Innocent III, had until March 1215 allowed Gray's official to have custody of the temporalities. On 18 July the king despatched a delegation to Norwich to supervise the election of a new bishop; its members, the bishops of Worcester and Exeter and the precentor of York, had almost certainly been nominated by the pope. The monks, no doubt in accordance with papal wishes transmitted by the commissioners, unanimously elected Pandulph on 25 July 1215.[11] The temporalities were restored to him by the king on 9 August.[12] Because of his role as papal *nuncio*, his consecration was delayed so that he would not have to give a profession of obedience to archbishop Stephen Langton, which would have been particularly embarrassing in view of the growing tension between primate and pope over the unfolding political situation in England, and would have been no more appropriate when he returned to England in summer 1218 and shortly afterwards received a legatine commission, dated 12 September. In fact, Pandulph was not consecrated until after the termination of his legation in summer 1221, and then at Rome in May 1222.[13]

It was inevitable that Pandulph should spend little time in his diocese. From his election until his departure for Rome in September 1215 he was

---

[9] *DD* no. 21.
[10] Vincent, 'Election' 144–53, 161. At the time of his election Pandulph had benefices in Chichester and Salisbury dioceses, the bps of which were ordered by the pope on 4 Sept. 1218 not to dispose of them before his consecration; these two, with the bp of Winchester, were on the same day instructed to revoke certain papal letters surreptitiously obtained to the detriment of Pandulph and his church (*CPL* i 58; *Reg. Hon. III* nos. 1612–13).
[11] Vincent, 'Election' 161; *EEA* 12 no. 219A.
[12] *Rot. Litt. Pat.* 152; the king committed custody to mr Ranulf of Warham and whomsoever Pandulph might appoint.
[13] *CPL* i 58, *Reg. Hon. III* no. 1621 for appointment as legate; *Fasti* ii 56, citing *Ann. mon.* ii (Waverley) 296 for consecration.

busy with the affairs of the pope and of the royal court. He then attended the Fourth Lateran Council, where he was expected to represent the king's interests. After the death of Innocent III, the favour with which he was regarded by the new pope, Honorius III, is reflected in the conferment of the title of papal chamberlain.[14] In the summer of 1218, before 7 June, he returned to England with a commission to raise papal taxation for the projected crusade, and in the autumn he succeeded Guala Bicchieri as legate, being officially received at St Paul's on 3 December.[15] After the resignation of William Marshal as regent on 9 April 1219 and his death a month later, Pandulph became, with Hubert de Burgh the justiciar and Peter des Roches, bishop of Winchester, a member of the 'triumvirate' which directed the young king's government and attempted to restore both good order and the rights of the crown.[16] His energy in these tasks is revealed both by his correspondence and his itinerary,[17] but this took him more often to the west and the north of England than to East Anglia. He can only be demonstrated to have been in his diocese once, in April 1220 (nos. 7–9), in the period until he resigned his legatine commission on 26 July 1221, and the following October he set out on a governmental mission to Poitou before returning again to Rome.[18] He was in England again from summer 1223 to November 1224, and was certainly in his diocese in June 1223 and September 1224 (nos. 24–5, 27). On 30 December 1223 it was ordered that Norwich and Orford castles should be transferred from the custody of Hubert de Burgh to that of Pandulph.[19] On 11 November 1224 he issued his last episcopal *actum* dated in England (no. 25), and about the same time his accounts, extending back over several years, were audited at the Exchequer.[20] He arrived back at Rome apparently on 17 February 1225,[21] and although he issued four more *acta* for his diocese in Italy (nos. 2–4, 14), he did not return again to England before his death on 16 September 1226. Bartholomew Cotton, writing many years later, records that

---

[14] See Vincent, 'Election' 158 n. 79 for his appearance with this title.
[15] *C. & S.* II i 51–2; *CPL* i 58; *Reg. Hon. III* nos. 1609, 1621 (1 and 5 Sept.); for his legation in its wider context, see Sayers, *Papal Government*, index *s.n.* Pandulf (Masca).
[16] For the latest and fullest analysis, see D. A. Carpenter, *The Minority of Henry III* (1990), 128–262 and index *s.n.* Pandulph; also F. A. Cazel, 'The Legates Guala and Pandulf', in P. R. Coss and S.␣D. Lloyd, eds., *Thirteenth-Century England* 2, *1987* (Woodbridge 1988) 15–22, where it is argued that Pandulph failed in his aim of dominating the government, but then worked fairly harmoniously as one of the 'triumvirate'.
[17] An edition of Pandulph's legatine letters and charters is being prepared by Prof. N. Vincent; many are printed in *RL* and *DD*, and for others see Vincent, 'Election' 158–9 n. 82.
[18] For references, see below Appx III, Itinerary.
[19] *Patent Rolls 1216–25* 418.
[20] *Rot. Litt. Claus.* ii 4b, 7b–8b, 149–b.
[21] *DD* nos. 162, 177.

he gave a chest of relics to his cathedral church, and the notice of his will in the papal register confirms that he made gifts to his successor and to the church of Norwich.[22] Cotton also states that he was buried at Norwich, but there is no physical evidence of this, and it seems improbable.

The records of the royal chancery and the *curia regis* provide much incidental evidence for the active role in the governance of the diocese taken by Pandulph's officials. The sacramental functions of a bishop, which even when rarely present he could not exercise until his consecration, were on one occasion at least, in 1225, fulfilled by William bishop of Llandaff when commissioned by the official.[23] Doubtless because of his peculiar relationship to the *curia*, Pandulph obtained several papal indults. That authorising him to recall to his see what the bishop of Chichester, when his official, had alienated, is probably a reflection of concessions extracted from Ranulf of Warham when he had been captured by rebels against the crown in 1216–17.[24] On 11 May 1220 it was conceded that Pandulph should not be liable to pay arrears of the papal twentieth, as his church was in need of repair, and later in the same month he received licence to present clerks in his service to more than one benefice, since those in his gift were few and of little value[25]—a perennial problem for bishops with monastic cathedral chapters which did not have prebends for episcopal clerks, but exacerbated by the wider responsibilities of his legatine office. In fact, only one of Pandulph's clerks can be demonstrated to have been beneficed in the diocese (nos. 8–9), although in September 1218 he obtained an indult to grant his brother Giles, now archdeacon of Thessalonica, a benefice in Norwich diocese,[26] and in September 1225 he collated the newly and well endowed vicarage of Aylsham to his nephew Roffridus (no. 4). Far more significant was the indult granted to the bishop-elect on 16 November 1219, and renewed on 28 May 1220, that during the pope's pleasure, because of the debts of his church, he might take for a period of two years the proceeds of non-conventual churches in his diocese which became vacant, as long as this might be done without scandal and he should provide for proper ministry therein.[27] This right, reduced to one year, was claimed by Pandulph's successors, and the indults were the origin of the custom, unique

---

[22] *Cotton* 394; *Reg. Hon. III* no. 6032.
[23] *Stoke by Clare Cartulary* i no. 103.
[24] *CPL* i 68; *Reg. Hon. III* no. 2236; cf. Vincent, 'Election' 157.
[25] *CPL* i 71; *Reg. Hon. III* no. 2428 (11 May), no. 2463 (30 May).
[26] *CPL* i 58; *Reg. Hon. III* no. 1618. Giles subsequently became archdn of Ely (*Fasti* ii 51; Vincent, 'Election' 155, 162).
[27] *CPL* i 68; *Reg. Hon. III* no. 2257 (16 Nov. 1219); *CPL* i 71; *Reg. Hon. III* no. 2456 (28 May 1220).

in English dioceses, whereby the bishop of Norwich took the first year's revenue of newly instituted incumbents. This led to a bitter dispute between bishop John Salmon and archbishop Winchelsey, who after his visitation of 1304 challenged the diocesan's right to first fruits, claimed by long usage.[28] The archbishop eventually lost his case at the papal *curia* in 1310, and the custom prevailed until the Reformation, as is revealed in the registers both of archbishop Morton's *sede vacante* administration in 1499 and of bishop Richard Nix.[29]

It is impossible to make any meaningful assessment of Pandulph's record at Norwich, although there is every indication that the diocese was well governed during his almost continual absence. He had wider responsibilities both to the pope and to the young king Henry III. Honorius III, when appointing him legate, had referred not only to his own unshakable confidence in him, but also to Pandulph's own love for England, and behind the rhetoric there may be a considerable element of truth.[30] The English government continued to place trust in him after he had resigned as legate, and even Matthew Paris, no lover of Italians or of papal agents, passed a favourable verdict on him.[31] The latest historian of Henry III's minority, too, is highly respectful of Pandulph's role in the governance of the realm in this very difficult period for the English crown.[32]

THOMAS BLUNDEVILLE

Blundeville[33] came from a family who were tenants of the de Ria lordship of Hockering in Norfolk. There is no mention of a Blundeville in Hubert de Ria's *carta* of 1166, but Robert, father of Thomas, held a manor in Newton Flotman in the 1190s, and in 1302 this was assessed at a quarter of a knight's

---

[28] For an account of this dispute see J. H. Denton, *Robert Winchelsey and the Crown, 1294–1313* (Cambridge 1980) 46–7 and refs. there given.

[29] C. Harper-Bill, ed., *The Register of John Morton, Archbishop of Canterbury, 1486–1500* iii (CYS 89, 2000) no. 232; P. Heath, *The English Parish Clergy on the Eve of the Reformation* (London, 1969) 43, 197–9.

[30] *CPL* i 58; *Reg. Hon. III* nos. 1609, 1620–1.

[31] *Flores Hist.* ii 173.

[32] Carpenter, *Minority of Henry III* 254–6.

[33] Variants of the name are Blumvile, Blunville. 'Flamvilla' (*Ann. mon.* iii (Dunstable) 100) is obviously an error.

fee.[34] The family also held a manor in Deopham, with part of the advowson; in 1283 this was listed as half a knight's fee.[35] Thomas was the nephew of Hubert de Burgh, Justiciar from 1215 to 1232,[36] and thus also of Geoffrey de Burgh, senior Exchequer clerk, archdeacon of Norwich and ultimately, after an earlier unsuccessful candidature, from 1225 bishop of Ely. Thomas's elder brother William was constable of Corfe castle in John's reign.[37]

Thomas first occurs in 1205 as an agent of royal government in his native East Anglia, where he was still based in 1216.[38] In September 1218 he received collation of the church of Ryston, Norfolk, from the legate Guala.[39] A clerk of the Exchequer,[40] on 16 September 1222 he was appointed custodian of the vacant bishopric of Chichester, and on 28 November 1223 was granted custody of Colchester castle.[41] In 1224 he was one of those commissioned to ensure the effective fortification of the Cinque Ports.[42] By April 1225 he was constable of the Tower of London.[43] On 10 May 1225 he was made keeper of the vacant bishopric of Ely,[44] and on 30 September 1226 was granted the deanery of the royal free chapel of Tettenhall, Staffordshire.[45]

Blundeville was granted custody of the temporalities of the see of Norwich on 24 October 1226, probably as soon as the news of Pandulph's death reached England. Three days later the licence to elect was issued, royal assent to his election was given on 5 November and the temporalities restored on 21 November. Thomas was ordained priest on 19 December and consecrated the next day by archbishop Langton in St Katherine's chapel, Westminster.[46]

In September 1227 the bishop was despatched to Antwerp as one of a distinguished delegation sent to meet imperial ambassadors;[47] but otherwise, for one of his background, he appears to have played remarkably little part in politics or in royal administration, even before the decline in Hubert de

---

[34] Blomefield, *Norfolk* v 64; Farrer, *Honors and Knights' Fees* iii 109.
[35] Blomefield, *Norfolk* ii 491–2; Farrer, *Honors and Knights' Fees* iii 151.
[36] *Ann. mon.* i (Tewkesbury) 69.
[37] *Rot. Litt. Pat.* 33b (1203), 55b (1205).
[38] *Rot. Litt. Claus.* i 59b, 60b, 244, 256b.
[39] *Lewes Cartulary: Norfolk Portion* no. 67; *Guala's Letters* no. 59. He was also presented to the church of Plumstead, Kent, but did not obtain possession (*CRR* xiii no. 2300).
[40] Wendover, *Flores* iv 138.
[41] *Patent Rolls 1216–25* 340, 416.
[42] *Patent Rolls 1216–25* 418; *Rot. Litt. Claus.* 614, 620, 625, 638b, 639, 640.
[43] *Patent Rolls 1216–25* 524; still on 31 Oct. 1225 (*Patent Rolls 1225–32* 1).
[44] *Patent Rolls 1216–25* 525.
[45] *Patent Rolls 1225–32* 63.
[46] For references, see *Fasti* ii 56–7; the Bury Chronicle places his consecration on 21 Dec. 1226.
[47] *Patent Rolls 1225–32* 161–2.

Burgh's influence from late 1229 or his fall in Summer 1232.[48] In September 1227 the bishop was granted by the king weekly markets at his manors of Hoxne and Langham and an annual fair at Homersfield on St Nicholas's day.[49] Within twelve months, however, there are indications of tension between Thomas and the crown. On 7 August 1228 a writ was despatched to the sheriff of Norfolk and Suffolk ordering him to restore full seisin to the bishop, notwithstanding the previous royal mandate to take the episcopal barony into his hands;[50] but a month later on 7 September Thomas was ordered to render to the king the castle at Norwich, of which he had previously had custody.[51]

Thereafter, apart from his commission in 1230 as one of four lords instructed with the sheriff to take the assize of arms in Norfolk and Suffolk,[52] and his raising of loans for the crown in 1231 (Appx II 35),[53] he appears free from involvement in secular government, and apart from his attendance at a council where on 12 October 1234 the law of bastardy was debated,[54] he hardly appeared on the national stage. In 1231 he was challenged by the crown to show by what warrant he held the manor of Wicks Bishop, near Ipswich, and the case was heard before the barons of the Exchequer.[55] Although Thomas was successful in his plea, and in July received a charter granting the manor in free alms to the church of Norwich, it may have been this experience which prompted him in May 1232 to obtain confirmation of four charters of Henry II and John, and also the grant to the bishop and the prior of all amercements of their demesne and of their immediate tenants.[56] For these concessions the bishop paid a fine of 2500 marks, which he was permitted by the crown to recover from the knights and tenants of the bishop-

---

[48] It was at the bp's house, probably at Terling, that de Burgh stayed just before his arrest at Brentwood in Sept. 1232; see Powicke, *Henry III and the Lord Edward* 82 n. 1; Vincent, *Peter des Roches* 315.
[49] *Cal. Ch. R. 1226–57* 58.
[50] *Close Rolls 1227–31* 73. The reason for this temporary confiscation is not known. It is tempting, although there is no evidence, to relate it to the minor jurisdictional dispute concerning amercements (see below pp. xxxvii–xxxviii).
[51] *Close Rolls 1227–31* 79. On 19 June 1228 a writ had been directed to the bailiffs of Norwich ordering them to allow the bp materials for the repair of the castle (ibid. 59).
[52] *Close Rolls 1227–31* 401.
[53] *Patent Rolls 1225–32* 440.
[54] *C. & S.* II i 200; *CRR* xv no. 1178.
[55] *CRR* xiv no. 1793; *Close Rolls 1227–31* 503, 524; *Cal. Ch. R. 1226–57*, 136; *Norwich Cathedral Charters* i no. 85.
[56] *Norwich Cathedral Charters* i nos. 41–3, 45; *Close Rolls 1227–31* 57; *Cal. Ch. R. 1226–57* 152–3.

ric.[57] The citations of the bishop to answer the royal justices on various matters, discussed below, are common form and do not indicate particular royal hostility, but tension with the king's regional representative is suggested by Blundeville's complaint to the crown around November 1234 that the sheriff was releasing captured excommunicates before they had made satisfaction to the church (Appx II 42).[58]

The place dates of Blundeville's *acta*, if correctly identified, indicate that he was habitually in his diocese (Appx III), and the number of surviving *acta* and references thereto (101, plus thirty further references in Appx II) indicate a high level of activity. In 1233 he conducted a visitation of non-exempt religious houses, in accordance with the mandate of pope Gregory IX to the English bishops (Appx II 41). He offered support to the new Augustinian communities of Kersey and Spinney (nos. 70, 107). His dispute with the priors of Binham and Wymondham over their relationship with the diocesan and his rights in their parish churches was eventually in November 1228 settled before papal judges-delegate (Appx II 27). A concerted campaign was conducted to increase the bishop's ecclesiastical patronage, both by acquisition of the advowsons of Great Massingham and Terling (the latter in London diocese) (Appx II 23, 38), and also by the extensive employment of the stratagem first used by Pandulph of granting appropriation of parish churches on condition that the religious should present a vicar chosen by himself and his successors.[59] Although, because the cathedral priory was already well endowed, bishop Thomas was naturally less generous than some of his predecessors to his own monks, he was regarded by them as having performed many good deeds and was commemorated as a benefactor.[60] The only glimpse which we have of his own religious feelings is the devotion to St Thomas Becket expressed in two *acta* for Christ Church, Canterbury (nos. 38–9) and to the Blessed Virgin Mary, as indicated by his counterseal.

Blundeville obviously had a keen eye for his personal finances. In the year before his consecration he made fine with the king for the custody and mar-

---

[57] *Patent Rolls 1225–32* 476–7. For the amount of the fine, see Vincent, *Peter des Roches* 284, 291, citing PRO C60/31 m. 5 and E372/76 m. 11d for the payment in full of the fine by the end of the year. Des Roches obtained greater privileges for the church of Winchester at no cost.
[58] C. R. Cheney, *Episcopal Visitation of Monasteries in the Thirteenth Century* (Manchester 1931) 33–4.
[59] See below pp. lviii–lix, and Harper-Bill, 'The Diocese of Norwich in the Early Thirteenth Century' 25–6.
[60] *First Register* 110; H. W. Saunders, *An Introduction to the Obedientiary and Manor Rolls of Norwich Cathedral Priory* (Norwich, 1930) 177–8.

riage of the heiress of Ralph of Killingthorp and for custody of the lands of Oliver Avenel and the marriage of his heirs and widow.[61] Twice while bishop he was impleaded by widows claiming their dower from the estates of minors in his wardship.[62] He built up a small personal estate. On 12 November 1236 a royal writ instructed that his executors should be allowed full seisin of his goods in Wicks Bishop, Bacton and Glemham.[63] Some land at Glemham was held by him of Roger de Cressi, and a further 160 acres, a mill and rent of £4 11s had been acquired by enfeoffment of the prior of Thetford.[64] Blundeville had also in 1228 secured by assize of *mort d'ancestor* against Robert son of William a very small estate in Playford (Appx II 26).[65]

It is probable that the bishop's health declined in his last few months. His last extant *actum* is dated 18 November 1235 (no. 37), and there is a reference in a case in the *curia regis* to the need to prove that a fine made with him concerning a wardship was executed while he was of sound mind and could speak (Appx II 45).[66] He eventually died on 16 August 1236.[67]

THE VACANCY OF THE SEE, 1236–39

The royal licence to elect was issued six days after Blundeville's death, on 22 August 1236,[68] and the monks elected their own prior, Simon of Elmham. The crown objected and appealed to the pope on 9 November 1236,[69] and on

---

[61] *Exc. Rot. Fin.* i 135, 143.

[62] At Trinity term 1231 Juliana, widow of William Ruffus, sued for her dower; her son William was a ward in the bp's custody (*CRR* xv no. 73; cf. *CRR* xiv no. 1661; *Bracton's Notebook* ii no. 578). At Trinity term 1234 Muriel de Sumeri sought her dower from the lands of Peter of Melton, a ward in the custody of the bp and William Bardolf (*CRR* xv no. 1016).

[63] *Close Rolls 1234–37* 389.

[64] *Close Rolls 1234–37* 390; *CRR* xvi no. 1788; xvii no. 878. In the latter of these cases, in 1241, Robert of Boyton, *consanguineus* of the bp, claimed against Ralph de Blundeville, archdn of Norfolk.

[65] PRO, CP25/1/213/7/90.

[66] *CRR* xv no. 1929.

[67] *Bury Chron.* 9; *Chron. Maj.* iii 378.

[68] *CPR 1232–47* 156.

[69] *Chron. Maj.* iii 389; *CPR 1232–47* 167. The king notified the archbp of Canterbury that, having heard and understood from his proctor the reasons for which John of Ferentino, archdn of Norwich, was appealing to the pope against royal assent being given to Simon's election, he had thought it right to defer to this appeal. On 27 Nov. 1236 the king appointed master William of Kilkenny to appear before the archbp on 1 Dec. at Bromley to lodge the royal objection to election, electors and elect, granting him authority to appeal to the papacy should it be necessary

16 June 1237 Gregory IX delegated the case to the legate Otto,[70] who heard it on 15 January 1238.[71] The election was finally quashed by the pope on 17 January 1239, when the mandate for a new election was issued.[72] William Raleigh was elected on 10 April 1239, but not consecrated until 25 September.[73]

In the previous two vacancies, administration of the spiritualities had been exercised by the officials of the deceased bishops, by master Ranulf of Warham in 1214–15 and by master Alan of Beccles in 1226.[74] In this vacancy of three years, arrangements were more complex. In Hilary term 1237 master Walter of Suffield is mentioned in the *curia regis* rolls as official of the archbishop of Canterbury in Norwich diocese,[75] but on 7 March 1237, in an actum recording his ordination of a vicarage in Cretingham church, Anger abbot of West Dereham describes himself as 'vicegerent of the archbishop of Canterbury and of the archdeacons'.[76] On 25 September 1237 Ralph Blundeville, archdeacon of Norfolk, granted to Creake abbey a mediety of All Saints church, Wreningham, which had been resigned into his hands during the vacancy of the see by its incumbent; among the witnesses was master Richard of Shipton, who had been bishop Blundeville's official but now has no title.[77] James of Ferentino, rural dean of Holt, was commissioned by his kinsman

---

(*CPR 1232–47* 169), and on 23 Jan. 1237 he was appointed as the king's proctor at Rome in this matter (ibid. 174). For royal rejection of several monastic candidates for sees, see Gibbs and Lang, *Bishops and Reform* 80.

[70] *CPL* i 163; *Reg. Greg. IX* nos. 3758–9; cf. *CPR 1232–47* 193, 199, 223. Otto was instructed to hear the case between Simon, bp-elect, represented by master Thomas, clerk of the convent of Norwich, and Kilkenny, king's clerk. It was alleged that the elect was of servile status; that his incontinence was demonstrated by the testimony of his own daughter; and that elect and electors had committed simony by admitting persons to the convent for money and in buying from the abbot of Bon Repos the patronage of the churches of Bawburgh, Hindringham and Costessy. In the case of Bawburgh at least, this was in fact a straightforward transaction by final concord in the *curia regis* while Simon was prior (see below, no. 140n).

[71] *C. Lib. R.* i 299.

[72] *CPL* i 178; *Reg. Greg. IX* no. 4714; *Chron. Maj.* iii 525.

[73] *Fasti* ii 57.

[74] For Warham, who also acted for part of the vacancy of 1214–15 as royal custodian, see Vincent, 'Election', 148–50; for Beccles as official *sede vacante*, see *Patent Rolls 1225–32* 65, 92.

[75] *CRR* xvi no. 318.

[76] PRO, E40/14021; see also *CRR* xvi no. 78 (Trinity term 1237). An indulgence for benefactors of the chapel of St Mary, Haverhill, indicates that episcopal functions were for at least part of this vacancy exercised by John, formerly bp of Ardfert, now bp in the universal church, who describes himself as 'domini E. Cant' vicarius in Norwicensi diocesi' (BL ms. Harley 2110, fo. 124r–v); for him, see Lawrence, *St Edmund of Abingdon* 149.

[77] Christ's College, Cambridge, Muniments ms. At 32, also witnessed by mr Peter of Ware, official of the archdn of Norfolk.

John, the archdeacon of Norwich, to conduct institutions *sede vacante* in that archdeaconry, and in October 1238 he ordained vicarages in the churches of Guestwick, Guist and Scarning.[78]

WILLIAM RALEIGH

Nothing is known of Raleigh's life before 1212, except that he sprung from one of the branches of the extended Devon family of that name.[79] It has been shown that he is to be distinguished from the William de Ralegh, *miles*, who was sheriff of Devon, 1225–28.[80] William, the clerk, was on 8 August 1212 presented by the crown to the living of Bratton Fleming, Devon, saving the perpetual vicarage of Odo of Bratton.[81] He first occurs in the context of secular judicial administration when in 1214 he is noted as holding a chirograph, and at Michaelmas 1219 he was keeping the notes of final concords and chirographs.[82] Hereafter he figures regularly in judicial records, and it has now been made clear that he did so in his capacity as senior clerk to Martin of Pattishall, chief justice of the Bench, to whom, after his death, Raleigh referred as 'of good memory, my sometime lord'.[83] He accompanied Pattishall on eyre in 1221 and 1226–27,[84] and in the late 1220s 'he seems to have been the equal, if not the superior, of several junior justices'.[85]

On Pattishall's retirement in 1229, Raleigh was himself promoted to the Bench, and by Michaelmas term 1233 he was regarded as the senior judge of that court.[86] He served as senior justice on the eyres of Middlesex in 1229, Kent and the Midland counties in 1232 and Cornwall in 1233.[87] Aside from his judicial work, he was appointed as keeper for his lifetime of Rockingham castle.[88] In May 1234 Raleigh was moved to the newly revived court *coram*

---

[78] BL ms. Harley 391 fos. 114v–15r.
[79] For a study of his judicial career, see Meekings, *Studies* XI, 'Martin Pateshull and William Raleigh'; also Turner, *The English Judiciary* ch. 5.
[80] Meekings, *Studies* XI 172–5; for William the sheriff, see *Patent Rolls 1216–25* 554.
[81] *Rot. Litt. Pat.* 93b.
[82] Meekings, *Studies* XI 161–2.
[83] Meekings, *Studies* XII, 'Martin de Pateshull of Good Memory, my Sometime Lord'.
[84] Meekings, *Studies* XI 163, 167–8; Crook, *General Eyre* 163, 167–8.
[85] Meekings, *Studies* XI 160. Apart from his judicial activities, he was appointed to tax commissions in 1225 and 1227 (ibid. 158–9, 165).
[86] Meekings, *Studies* XI 171.
[87] Crook, *General Eyre* 86–9.
[88] *Patent Rolls 1225–32* 490; *Close Rolls 1231–34* 88.

rege, and he remained the senior judge in the kingdom until his elevation to the episcopate. With the suspension of the office of justiciar in 1234, he enjoyed enhanced status both in judicial work and in the council, and was the king's principal adviser in legal matters,[89] as is illustrated by his role in the making of the Statute of Merton in 1236.[90] In effect, after the fall of the Poitevins, Raleigh acted as the king's chief minister; his reforms increased royal revenue and built up a reserve of treasure.[91] An obvious manifestation of such activity occurred when in January 1236 he demanded a grant of taxation from the great council, and in denouncing him for this Matthew Paris calls him 'clericus ac domini regis familiaris'.[92] The chronicler disapproved equally when in November 1237 Raleigh remained as a royal observer at the legatine council at St Paul's, which he had inhibited from any action contrary to the king's dignity.[93] While deprecating his role as a principal agent of royal authority, however, Paris admitted that he was 'a discreet man and very learned in the law of England',[94] a judgement which is certainly echoed by modern legal historians, among whom there now seems to be agreement that in the complex evolution of the treatise commonly known as *Bracton* he played a key part. Nearly all the references therein to suits are from the rolls of Pattishall and Raleigh, the additions made in the 1230s were all connected with cases which Raleigh heard,[95] and it has become clear that Raleigh was 'the prime mover behind the *De Legibus*'.[96] This attribution, and the respect and even affection with which he was treated by Edmund Rich and Robert Grosseteste,[97] has led one authority to suggest the likelihood that he had attended Oxford or some other centre of legal learning as a young man.[98]

As was natural for a royal servant whose career was in the ascendant,

---

[89] *CRR* xv pp. xxvii–xxviii; Powicke, *Thirteenth Century* 68–9; Turner, *The English Judiciary* 201–3.

[90] *Grosseteste's Letters* 95, no. 24; Powicke, *Henry III and the Lord Edward* 151–2.

[91] R. Stacey, *Politics, Policy and Finance under Henry III* 104, 116, 130, and index *s.n.* Stacey considers that had Raleigh's fiscal policy, based on the concept that baronial consent was essential for the effective conduct of government, prevailed, many of Henry III's later problems would have been averted (ibid. 259).

[92] *Chron. Maj.* iii 380.

[93] *Chron. Maj.* iii 417.

[94] *Chron. Maj.* iii 525. In the context of the Winchester election, Paris has Henry III say that Raleigh had killed more men by the sharpness of his tongue than had William of Savoy with his sword (ibid. 493–4).

[95] Meekings, *Studies* XII 157, 164, 178–9; Turner, *The English Judiciary* 235.

[96] *Bracton* iii pp. xxx, xxxv.

[97] For correspondence between Grosseteste and Raleigh, see *Grosseteste's Letters* 63–5, no. 17; 76–94, no. 23; 95–7, no. 24; 333, no. 113. Archbp Edmund on his deathbed addressed his last letter to Raleigh (Lawrence, *St Edmund* 267–8).

[98] Turner, *The English Judiciary* 237.

Raleigh was granted two papal indults for plurality, in July 1225 and February 1238.[99] The accumulation of benefices had begun before the earlier of these. By 1219 he had been presented to Norton sub Hamdon, Somerset, a church of Grestain abbey,[100] and in 1220 to Blatherwycke, Northamptonshire, by Viel Engayne.[101] Probably in 1224 he succeeded Martin of Pattishall in his benefice of King's Somborne, Hampshire, in the gift of Mottisfont priory,[102] and two years later he was rector of Whaplode, Lincolnshire, a Crowland abbey church.[103] By the late 1230s he was a canon of Lichfield,[104] a canon of St Paul's,[105] for a short time archdeacon of Berkshire,[106] and treasurer of Exeter.[107]

On 24 February 1239 the monks of Coventry, having negotiated a composition with the canons of Lichfield, elected Raleigh as their bishop. According to Paris, this was done because the king was impeding elections and would only consent to an elect whom he favoured.[108] Raleigh hesitated, and when on 10 April the monks of Norwich, following the quashing of the election of their own prior Simon of Elmham, also elected him,[109] he accepted, according again to Paris, because he preferred to remain in England with the English rather than to go to the borders of Wales.[110] The temporalities of the see of Norwich were restored to him in June or July, and he was consecrated at St Paul's by archbishop Edmund on 25 September 1239.[111] Paris reports that the prognostic was: 'There is joy in the presence of the angels of God over one sinner that repenteth' (Luke 15.10), and hoped that Raleigh, like St Matthew who had abandoned the tax-collector's desk for the apostolic life, would

---

[99] On 8 July 1225 Raleigh received a dispensation that, provided he were of legitimate birth, he might hold another benefice, even with cure of souls, in addition to those which he already held (*Reg. Hon. III* no. 5546). On 26 Feb. 1238 pope Gregory IX, at the king's petition, granted licence to the legate Otto to grant such dispensation as he might see fit to Raleigh, treasurer of Exeter, to hold a plurality of benefices with cure of souls (*CPL* i 168; *Reg. Greg. IX* no. 4098).
[100] *Bracton's Notebook* iii no. 1189; cf. Meekings, *Studies* XII 228–9.
[101] *Rot. H. de Welles* ii 99; *Rot. Grosseteste* 193; cf. Meekings, *Studies* XI 165.
[102] Meekings, *Studies* XII 229.
[103] *Rot. H. de Welles* iii 187; *Rot. Grosseteste* 24, 36, 122.
[104] *CPR 1232–47* 274.
[105] *Chron. Maj.* iii 417; *Fasti* i 37.
[106] *Fasti* iv 30. In 1249 he is referred to as former archdn of Berkshire; his tenure must fall between Feb. 1236 and Dec. 1237.
[107] *CPR 1232–47* 177; M. Gibbs, ed., *Early Charters of the Cathedral Church of St Paul, London* (Camden 3rd series 63, 1939) no. 300.
[108] *Chron. Maj.* iii 525.
[109] *Bury Chron.* 10.
[110] *Chron. Maj.* iii 531–2.
[111] *Fasti* ii 57.

escape from the business of the court to the heights of sanctity — a wish which in the chronicler's eyes was to be fulfilled.[112]

Matthew Paris credited the new bishop with the long-delayed execution by hanging in 1240 of three Norwich Jews, accused of the circumcision of a Christian boy ten years before, stating that Raleigh belatedly claimed the alleged perpetrators of this outrage for the court Christian.[113] Since the bishop is not mentioned in the proceedings in the *curia regis* relating to this case, and the penalty was unknown to canon law, this is extremely unlikely, although it is highly possible that the eminent jurist was consulted in a matter relating to his own diocese.

Between April and July 1240 Raleigh obtained a series of papal indults.[114] On 20 April he received a dispensation that he should not be compelled by apostolic mandate to grant either benefices in his gift or annual pensions to any clerk, unless specific mention was made in the mandate of this indult; this was surely primarily an attempt to protect episcopal patronage from the not inconsiderable number of Italians whose interest in the diocese had been awakened during Pandulph's tenure.[115] On the same day Raleigh received licence to grant dispensation to five clerks who assisted him when attending the royal council or engaged in the affairs of the realm[116] — a clear indication that at this stage he envisaged continuing employment at the highest levels of royal government. An indult of 12 June allowed him to remove from their benefices those who had obtained them by the collusive resignation of their predecessors, so as to ensure the succession of son to father or nephew to uncle; three days later it was conceded that he might refuse licence even to those who had obtained papal permission for the establishment of private chapels, if he were not sure that the founder had made adequate provision for endowment extending beyond his own death.[117] On 19 July the bishop received an indult to give a benefice without cure of souls to each of the rural deans of his diocese, providing that they should surrender those livings with

---

[112] *Chron. Maj.* iii 617–8.

[113] *Chron. Maj.* iv 30–1; for proceedings in the *curia regis*, see *CRR* xv nos. 1320, 1385. For a judicious review of this matter, see V. D. Lipman, *The Jews of Medieval Norwich* (1967) 59–62.

[114] Although the royal licence to elect to Winchester was not issued until 1 May 1240 (see below), Raleigh must have known of the intention of a party within the chapter to postulate him, and it is likely that a proctor was at the *curia* from April 1240 to represent him in a matter already contentious.

[115] *CPL* i 191; *Reg. Greg. IX* no. 5270. For a reassessment of the extent of Italian occupation of English benefices, see *Guala's Letters* lxvii–lxxiv, and specifically within the diocese, Harper-Bill, 'The Diocese of Norwich and the Italian Connection'.

[116] *CPL* i 191; *Reg. Greg. IX* no. 5271.

[117] *CPL* i 190; *Reg. Greg. IX* nos. 5215, 5217.

cure which they might hold.[118] This appears to be the formal origin of the custom, unique in England, whereby the rural deans of Norwich diocese were administrative officers of the bishop and archdeacons without responsibility for a parish of their own, and the indult is perhaps a reflection of the very active jurisdictional role of these officers in the diocese, which led in the 1230s and 1240s to their frequent citation by litigants before the royal courts, and eventually to the crisis of 1286.[119]

The most notable contribution made to the development of the diocese of Norwich by Raleigh during his brief episcopate was, if Professor Cheney's attribution is correct, the promulgation of a series of synodal statutes, based on those of Robert Grosseteste for Lincoln.[120] Despite their different stance on various matters, the two men obviously felt mutual respect, and it seems entirely likely that the experienced jurist would wish to introduce in his diocese a written code which would promote sound practice in religion and facilitate orderly ecclesiastical governance.

The convoluted story of Raleigh's translation to Winchester belongs to the history of that see and will be fully treated in another volume of this series; but it cannot be ignored here, as the conflict which it generated overshadowed almost the entire period of his episcopate at Norwich.[121] The monks of Winchester had intended to elect Raleigh after the death of Peter des Roches on 9 June 1238, but were frustrated by the king, who proposed the promotion of William of Savoy, his wife's uncle.[122] The chapter refused to be intimidated, and shortly before 28 August 1238 postulated Ralph de Neville, bishop of Chichester and royal chancellor. Henry III's determination was signalled when he deprived Neville of the great seal, and on 17 February 1239 the bishop's postulation was quashed by the pope.[123] The monks now failed to elect within the prescribed period and had to seek renewed papal permission to proceed. By the time this was granted on 11 January 1240, William

---

[118] *CPL* i 191; *Reg. Greg. IX* no. 5265. It was stated that some deans could not reside in person in their benefices with cure.

[119] Harper-Bill, 'Diocese of Norwich in the Early Thirteenth Century', 30–1; P. R. Hyams, 'Deans and their Doings: the Norwich Inquiry of 1286', *Proceedings of the Sixth International Congress of Medieval Canon Law* (Vatican City, 1985), 619–46.

[120] *C. & S.* II i 342–57; cf. Cheney, *English Synodalia* 135–6.

[121] For brief accounts of this dispute, see *Bracton* iii pp. xl–xliii; Powicke, *Henry III and the Lord Edward* 271–3; and R. W. Southern, *Western Society and the Church in the Middle Ages* (Harmondsworth, 1970) 127–9. The last of these minimises the significance of what might be interpreted by others as an extraordinarily bitter conflict; cf. Stacey, *Politics, Policy and Finance under Henry III* 221: 'there is no doubt that relations between Henry and Raleigh after 1240 were hostile in an unusually personal way'.

[122] *Chron. Maj.* iii 494.

[123] *Chron. Maj.* iii 495, 525; *Close Rolls 1237–42* 95; *Reg. Greg. IX* no. 4278.

of Savoy was dead.[124] When the king granted licence to elect on 1 May 1240, he was determined that the see should now be filled by Boniface of Savoy, another of the queen's uncles.[125] The community, under a new prior and with new obedientiaries appointed by the crown *sede vacante*, was now split, and of the committee of monks appointed to choose by way of *compromissio*, three opted for Boniface while four reverted to the original choice of Raleigh, now of course bishop of Norwich.[126] In May relations between king and bishop were still good. On 15 May Raleigh acted as one of the arbiters appointed by the crown in negotiations with David son of Llewellyn at Gloucester,[127] and on 27 May Henry sent the bishops ten oaks for the enclosure of the episcopal park at Gaywood.[128] By the next year, however, according to Matthew Paris, the king had begun to manifest his fury against those Winchester monks who had advocated Raleigh's translation, some of whom were eventually imprisoned and maltreated,[129] and his anger was extended to Raleigh himself, from whom he demanded a charter of renunciation, which the bishop refused to concede.[130] By now proceedings were under way at the papal *curia*, but these were interrupted by the death of pope Gregory IX on 22 August 1241. The first manifest sign of active royal hostility to Raleigh is a writ of 25 September 1241 to the sheriff of Norfolk and Suffolk ordering him to release the bishop of Norwich's men captured and detained on the king's orders because of the contention between them; the sheriff was to do no injury to the bishop or his men without specific royal instructions.[131]

[124] First mandate for new election, 23 Feb. 1239, *Reg. Greg. IX* no. 4727; cf. *Chron. Maj.* iii 630; second mandate, 11 Jan. 1240, *Reg. Greg. IX* no. 5019, cf. no. 5021.
[125] *Fasti* ii 86 and n. 1, with refs. there given.
[126] *Chron. Maj.* iv 107–8. An appeal by the king and his monastic supporters at Winchester was planned by 16 August 1240 (*Close Rolls 1237–42* 215).
[127] *Close Rolls 1237–42* 240–1.
[128] *Close Rolls 1237–42* 193.
[129] *Chron. Maj.* iv 159–60.
[130] *Chron. Maj.* iv 159–60. Raleigh was out of the country for much of 1241. Matthew Paris, immediately after his recitation of pope Gregory IX's summons of 15 Oct. 1240 to a council, states that the bp of Norwich and other English prelates did not attend, but rather delayed their departure and sought a safer path (*Chron. Maj.* iv 98). At some time between February and 24 March 1241 Raleigh, with William Brewer, bp of Exeter, and Walter Cantilupe, bp of Worcester, was at Pontigny (nos. 145A–B). The records of the *curia regis* reveal that in June and July he was *in partibus transmarinis* (*CRR* xvi nos. 1664, 1862); it is possible, although there is no evidence, that he went to the papal *curia*. On his return to England, and probably at a council of the clergy at Oxford on 30 Nov. 1241, he joined with the archbp of York and the bps of Lincoln and Carlisle in writing to the emperor Frederick II, urging him to abandon his hostility to the church of Rome (*Chron. Maj.* iv 173; *C. & S.* II i 338–9).
[131] *Close Rolls 1237–42* 334. One case merits special mention, since it is linked by Paris with the conflict between the king and Raleigh. According to the chronicler a royal scribe, noted in the margin as Thomas Dairel, was wounded because of his 'rash usurpation', and from this

In 1243 the new pope, Innocent IV, took cognizance of the case and on 17 September confirmed Raleigh's postulation to Winchester.[132] On the same day the king requested papal confirmation of the election of his former rival, Boniface of Savoy, to the archbishopric of Canterbury.[133] The papal ruling arrived in England on 11 November, and according to the Waverley annals, Raleigh now resigned the see of Norwich in accordance with the papal mandate, and regarded himself as translated to Winchester.[134] His last extant *actum* for his first diocese is dated 16 November 1243 (no. 137A). Paris states that Raleigh was now held to be the public enemy of the king, who forbade the sale of provisions to him and wrote to the *curia*, and also to the university of Oxford, stating that he had been postulated by *suggestio falsi*. The see of Norwich was taken into royal custody (*infiscari*).[135] Subsequent hostilities are not relevant to the present purpose, but in short the barring of the city gates against Raleigh was answered by an interdict on Winchester and the excommunication of his opponents.[136] As regards Norwich, on 3 December 1243 the king refused the monks licence to elect,[137] as it did not seem to him that the see was vacant—the postulation to Winchester had been obtained by *suppressio veri* and *suggestio falsi*, and they should not elect until the king should know the pope's will, for he was renewing his appeal to Rome.[138] The dispute continued with mounting bitterness, and Matthew Paris, who had been so suspicious of Raleigh's curial background, now compared his stance and his

---

incident much trouble ensued in Norwich diocese; many clerks and laymen were beaten, wounded and suffered much at the hands of the secular power, which excesses the king refused to restrain unless Raleigh would seal a charter of renunciation (*Chron. Maj.* iv 159). In the records of the *curia regis* it appears that a Thomas Darel sued the bp from Michaelmas term 1240 to Michaelmas term 1241 as to why the bp had seized his goods and chattels; on five occasions the bp failed to appear (*CRR* xvi nos. 1267, 1374, 1456, 1664, 1862, 2525). At Hilary term 1241 the sheriff was ordered to investigate which laymen were present when Dayrel's house at Hethersett was broken into and his goods removed, against the king's peace and royal letters of protection. The sheriff returned a list of eighteen names, headed by Alan, *serviens* of Thorpe, elsewhere identified as the bp's servant. The sheriff was instructed to produce these, and also Ingelram the bp's marshal, before the king's justices, if they could be found (*CRR* xvi no. 1474, cf. no. 1862).

[132] *Reg. Inn. IV* no. 113; *Chron. Maj.* iv 259.

[133] *CPR 1232–47* 400. Boniface was still described as postulant of Winchester on 22 Feb. and 2 July 1243 (ibid. 365, 384).

[134] *Ann. mon.* ii 330.

[135] *Chron. Maj.* iv 263–5. Much of this is substantiated by royal records; see especially *CPR 1232–47* 409–14.

[136] *Chron. Maj.* iv 266; *Ann. mon.* ii 332.

[137] *CPR 1232–47* 409. Two days later custody of the diocese was committed to the abbot of St Benet of Holme and the Cluniac prior of Thetford (ibid.).

[138] The appeal had been despatched by 18 Dec. 1243 (*CPR 1232–47* 413; cf. *Chron. Maj.* iv 265).

plight to that of Becket.[139] Raleigh retreated to the continent on 20 or 21 February 1244.[140] Eventually, after mediation by the pope, archbishop Boniface, Louis IX of France and the count of Flanders, peace was at last made at Windsor on 9 September 1244.[141] Before then, Raleigh had temporarily returned to England for negotiations on 5 April 1244,[142] and it was surely after this meeting that Henry III accepted that the see of Norwich was indeed vacant, for Walter Suffield was elected before 9 July 1244, when he received royal assent. The temporalities were restored eight days later.[143] Thus ended an extremely bitter electoral dispute, which must have preoccupied Raleigh throughout the greater part of his tenure of the bishopric of Norwich.

THE BISHOPS OF NORWICH AND THE CROWN

The inauguration of the various rolls produced by the royal chancery and the *curia regis* from the turn of the twelfth and thirteenth centuries provides information concerning the interaction of royal and episcopal administrations rarely available in an earlier period.[144] With regard to secular jurisdiction, there was accommodation between bishop and crown, normally and naturally in favour of the king. At the beginning of the eyre of Norfolk and Suffolk in 1228 bishop Blundeville conceded that crown pleas concerning land and fees, which he claimed for his court, should on this occasion be heard by the royal justices, saving the liberties of the church of Norwich. A royal writ of 18 June instructed that assizes of *novel disseisin*, *mort d'ancestor* and others which were disputed should on this occasion be heard by the king's judges in the bishop's court. Amercements were not to be collected until Michaelmas, and after a roll of the proceedings had been sent to the Exchequer, there should be discussion as to whether these were due to king or bishop.[145] The dispute continued in the *curia regis* in Hilary term 1230 when the bishop sought, by reason of his liberty, amercements levied both in the shire court and by the

---

[139] *Chron. Maj.* iv 286.
[140] *Chron. Maj.* iv 295.
[141] *Chron. Maj.* iv 346–53.
[142] *Chron. Maj.* iv 359–60.
[143] *Fasti* ii 57.
[144] Harper-Bill, 'The Diocese of Norwich in the Early Thirteenth Century', 29–31.
[145] Appx II 25; *Close Rolls 1227–31* 56, 65.

justices in eyre.[146] Eventually, in May 1232, the king granted to the bishop, prior and church of Norwich all amercements of their demesnes and their fees, saving to the crown the amercements of men of their fees who did not hold of them in chief.[147] A large fine, however, was payable for this and for the confirmation of the charters of the king's predecessors.[148]

The interaction of royal and episcopal jurisdiction in temporal matters may be seen most clearly in relation to the town of Lynn. The bishop was, of course, expected to implement governmental policy in his town. Twice, in March 1227 and April 1234, bishop Blundeville was authorised to tallage the town, as the king was tallaging the royal demesne, because of urgent necessity.[149] In May 1228 the chief justice, Martin of Pattishall, was instructed to go in person to Lynn and, with the bailiffs of the bishop and of the earl of Arundel[150] to investigate a case of piracy in which some sailors of the town were implicated. In December 1229 the justices in eyre were ordered to hold an assize of *novel disseisin* concerning a tenement there, but only with the consent of the bishop and of Hubert de Burgh as guardian of the young earl.[151] In 1220 Pandulph's seneschal had undertaken to produce in the *curia regis*, notwithstanding the episcopal liberty of Lynn, a defendant accused of proceeding in the church courts contrary to a writ of prohibition.[152] Of far wider consequence, Raleigh was in July 1242 ordered to arrest all merchants of the kingdom of France currently at Lynn, in retaliation for the detention of the persons and goods of merchants subject to Henry III by the French government.[153] The bishop and his bailiffs in the port were themselves sued in the king's courts at least twice between 1229 and 1240 in relation to allegedly wrongful extortion of tolls and customs.[154]

The bishop was involved in two major and long-running disputes at Lynn in this period. The first was with the burgesses over various jurisdictional matters, most especially their freedom to elect a mayor, and after their complaint to the *curia regis* that the bishop had excommunicated them, this was eventually in July 1234 settled by a final concord made by royal authority

---

[146] Appx II 32; *CRR* xiii no. 2612; *Bracton's Notebook* ii no. 391.
[147] *Cal. Ch. R. 1226–57* 152; *Close Rolls 1227–31* 57.
[148] See above, p. xxvi.
[149] *Patent Rolls 1225–32* 114; *Close Rolls 1231–34* 411.
[150] *Close Rolls 1227–31* 105.
[151] *Patent Rolls 1225–32* 350–1.
[152] *CRR* viii 311.
[153] *CPR 1232–47* 300.
[154] By Hugh Dod in 1229 (Appx II 29; *CRR* xiii no. 1416) and by Richard of Hadstock, who initiated his action in 1240 and withdrew in 1242 (*CRR* xvi nos. 1319, 1398, 1527: xvii no. 219).

after the payment by the town of a fine (Appx II 41A).[155] The second conflict, which had been simmering at least from the time of bishop John of Oxford, was between the bishop and the earl of Arundel over their respective rights of toll.[156] An attempt to resolve this issue was made before Martin of Pattishall in 1224,[157] but there is no obvious sign of royal intervention to secure the agreement of 1243 recounted in the somewhat opaque concord between bishop Raleigh and the earl (Appx II 55). In another dispute between the bishop and one of his comital neighbours, in this case with Earl Roger Bigod over fishing rights between Homersfield and Bungay, the crown did intervene, and on 18 May 1242 a jury of twelve knights was summoned to testify on this matter.[158]

There is even more information available in the early thirteenth century on the interaction of the royal and the ecclesiastical courts, and the pressure which had certainly been exercised by the crown in the previous century is now clearly documented. It was not always a matter of conflict, but the royal justices did have the right to insist on the cooperation of the diocesan and his officers. When cases judicable in the *curia regis* turned on a related matter within the purview of the church courts, the bishop or his official was required to conduct enquiries and to provide information. Thus, when the defendant in an assize of *mort d'ancestor* alleged that her opponent was a bastard, bishop Blundeville was ordered to investigate the truth of the matter (no. 98). Claims for dower might depend on the disputed validity of the widow's marriage, on which the bishop's verdict was essential (nos. 21, 100).[159] A particularly interesting instance of the interaction of the two jurisdictions is provided by a claim in 1243 for *maritagium*.[160] In one case of 1221 concerning dower, the bishop-elect certified that the marriage of the claimant had indeed been valid, but that she was now excommunicate and thus disqualified from pleading in the royal court (Appx II 37). Pleas against one of the bishop's officers in 1223 (no. 22) and against an ecclesiastical judge in 1242 (no. 147) were adjourned

---

[155] Appx II 26; cf. *Close Rolls 1231–34* 465.
[156] Harper-Bill, 'John of Oxford' (as n. 2), 94.
[157] *CRR* xi no. 544; cf. no. 2147.
[158] *CPR 1232–47* 305.
[159] See also *CRR* viii 174, ix 367 (to Pandulph's official); *CRR* xvii no. 2086 (to bp Raleigh).
[160] At Easter 1243 Simon de Blavigny and Muriel his wife sued Hamo son of Hamo Chevere for her *maritagium* in Heckingham. The land had been promised to Hamo by Alan of Heckingham, Muriel's father, on condition that he should marry her. Simon and Muriel alleged that Hamo, while not having married her, had the land, whereby they had lost £20. Hamo did not deny that he held the land, but was claiming before the bp of Norwich that Muriel was indeed his wife. The royal justices decreed that Simon was in seisin of Muriel as his wife and should recover seisin of the land until Hamo might establish his claim to her (*CRR* xvii no. 2145).

sine die after the bishop certified that the plaintiffs were excommunicate. Two cases were also terminated in 1231 when the bishop claimed for his own jurisdiction three clerks and a monastic superior (nos. 99, 101).

The bishops' officials were on occasion cited to appear in the *curia regis* to answer as to why they had heard in the episcopal court a case pertaining to royal jurisdiction in contravention of a writ of prohibition. If the official failed initially to appear, and he did not have lay fee on which the sheriff might distrain, the bishop was required to ensure his presence by confiscation of his ecclesiastical revenues.[161] Master Alan of Beccles was thus summoned five times between 1219 and 1223,[162] master Robert of Bilney in 1229,[163] master Richard of Shipton twice in separate cases in 1232,[164] and master Hervey of Fakenham in 1241.[165]

The bishop or his official was similarly required to compel the attendance at the royal court of other ecclesiastical judges. In Blundeville's episcopate, between 1229 and 1234 six rural deans were required to appear in four separate cases.[166] In 1223 the official was ordered to ensure the appearance of the prior of Bricett, the archdeacon of Ipswich and the dean of Sampford, who must have been acting as papal judges delegate,[167] as surely were the archdeacon of Bedford and the chancellor of Cambridge, on whose ecclesiastical revenues in the diocese of Norwich the official was ordered by the king's justices to distrain at Trinity term 1225.[168]

Similarly, the diocesan authorities were required to ensure the attendance in the *curia regis* of clerks who had no lay fee who were impleaded for initiating litigation in the church courts.[169] Usually these charges related to proceedings in the court of the diocese, but in 1233 the bishop was required to distrain upon the benefice of Roger of Willington, because the sheriff of

---

[161] At Michaelmas 1219 one litigant in the *curia regis* withdrew from a plea against mr Alan of Beccles because the sheriff stated that he had no lay fee, but at Hilary term 1223 it was stated that the sheriff had seized Beccles's houses in Norwich to compel his appearance (*CRR* viii 63; x 439).

[162] *CRR* viii 63, 311, 314, 368, 380; x 298; xi nos. 39, 1342.

[163] *CRR* xiii no. 2037.

[164] *CRR* xiv nos. 2109, 2125, 2390; *Bracton's Notebook* ii no. 865.

[165] *CRR* xvi no. 1602.

[166] Easter term 1229: Robert dean of Holt, Henry dean of Burnham, Ralph dean of Walsingham (*CRR* xiii nos. 2000, 2734); Hilary term 1230: William dean of Sparham (*CRR* xiii no. 2693; xiv no. 233); Trinity term 1230: Richard dean of Coddenham (Appx II 20); Trinity term 1234: Philip dean of Dunwich (*CRR* xv no. 1002).

[167] *CRR* xi no. 498.

[168] *CRR* xii no. 646.

[169] *CRR* ix 264; x 91; xi no. 1812; xii no. 1521; xiii no. 2137; xiv no. 403; xv nos. 288, 366, 403, 1602.

Bedfordshire, where he had lay fee, could not locate him.[170] In 1230 the bishop's proctor in the *curia regis* gave an undertaking that Blundeville would not allow Jocelin the chaplain to prosecute Hamo Ruffus in an ecclesiastical court contrary to a writ of prohibition.[171]

There was a great deal of interaction between royal and episcopal jurisdictions in regard to advowsons. Not only did the king, like any other patron, present to the bishop clerks to fill vacant benefices in his gift, both crown livings and those which came into his hands by reason of the minority or the forfeiture of a tenant-in-chief or of the vacancy of a bishopric or abbey.[172] The diocesan authorities also received numerous writs ordering institution at the presentation of a litigant who had established or recovered seisin of an advowson in the *curia regis*,[173] and the bishop's failure to comply occasionally led to further litigation, as when in 1229 Robert FitzWalter impleaded Thomas Blundeville as to why he would not institute at his presentation to Barningham church, of which he had recently recovered seisin in the king's court,[174] or in

---

[170] *CRR* xv no. 541.

[171] Appx II 31.

[172] Royal presentations include: 1224, to a mediety of Ingworth (*Patent Rolls 1216–25* 427); to two unidentified Ipswich churches (ibid. 434); to Kettleburgh, normally earl of Richmond (ibid. 441); to Orford (ibid. 531); 1226, to Keningham, normally Bigod (*Patent Rolls 1225–32* 65); to Langham, normally bp of Norwich (ibid. 92); to Easton, normally Guy de Valle (ibid. 93); 1229, to Wetheringsett, normally bp of Ely (ibid. 247); to Coney Weston, normally abbot of Bury (ibid. 269); to Weston (ibid. 272); to Worlingham (ibid. 272); 1235, to Nettlestead (*CPR 1232–47* 121); 1237, to Cressingham, normally bp of Norwich (ibid. 190); 1242, Fransham, normally Tosni (ibid. 303); 1243, Edingthorpe, normally Warenne (ibid. 376). In 1226 the crown contested the right of William de Warenne and Matilda his wife, widow of Hugh Bigod, to present to the Bigod church of Hethel; subsequently a writ was directed to the bp to institute at the king's presentation (*CRR* xii no. 2616).

[173] In 1220, to a third part of St Mary, Itteringham, at presentation of Walter of Wolterton (*CRR* viii 395); mediety of Hillington, Sarra de Candos (*CRR* ix 158; cf. ibid. 3); 1221, Syderstone, Matilda de Valognes (*CRR* x 66); 1225, mediety of Boxford, abbot of Bury (*CRR* xii no. 316); Helmingham, Bartholomew of Creake (ibid. no. 672); Rougham, prior of Westacre (ibid. no. 675); Felmingham, abbot of St Benet of Holme (ibid. no. 1071); 1228, two-thirds of East Beckham, prior of Weybourne (*Close Rolls 1227–31* 53); 1230, Alderford, Constantia widow of William Bataille (*CRR* xiii no. 2752); two-thirds of Kirby Cane, Walter de Caen and others (*CRR* xiv no. 381); Great Thurlow, abbot of Battle (ibid. no. 456); 1231, Bodham, William de Meynilwaring and wife (ibid. no. 1496); St Mary, Saxlingham Nethergate, Guy de Verdun (ibid. no. 1507); 1232, Calthorpe, Peter de Alto Bosco (ibid. no. 2385); 1233, Morley, William Bardolf (*CRR* xv no. 349); mediety of Saxlingham, Simon de Nuiers (ibid. no. 453); 1242, Panxford, Ralph of Timworth (*CRR* xvi no. 1960); Creeting St Peter, John of Tuddenham (ibid. no. 1971); Wickhampton, Geoffrey de Monasteriis (*CRR* xvii no. 1900).

[174] *CRR* xiii no. 2029; *Bracton's Notebook* ii no. 355. Previously William Gernun had been summoned to answer Robert FitzWalter as to why he had impleaded him in an ecclesiastical court concerning the advowson, and the papal judges-delegate as to why they had heard this plea in contravention of a writ of prohibition; the defence was that the judges had in fact heard a plea concerning the murder of a clerk (*CRR* xiii no. 252).

1232 William of Felmingham sued the bishop for his failure to institute at his presentation to East Beckham (Appx II 40). On one occasion, a claimant successfully demonstrated that an institution by Pandulph had been effected unjustly, because it was implemented after she had obtained a royal writ (Appx II 1). On the one hand, an assize of *darrein presentment* might be terminated by episcopal certification that the benefice was not, in fact, vacant (no. 97); on the other, at Michaelmas 1232 a writ was despatched to bishop Blundeville forbidding him to collate the church of Wells Next-the-Sea in accordance with the decree of the Lateran Council, because it had long been vacant, since it was not the fault of the claimant, Richard earl of Cornwall, that the assize of *darrein presentment* had been abortive, and because he was a minor in the king's custody.[175] The bishop was himself cited to the king's court to answer litigants contesting advowsons held or claimed by the church of Norwich (Appx II 16–17).

In a wide variety of other and miscellaneous ways governmental directions impinged on diocesan administration. On 10 May 1228 a writ was directed to the bishops of Norwich and Ely ordering them to excommunicate any persons who might come to a planned clandestine tournament in Suffolk.[176] Blundeville was instructed some time before 26 May 1234 to sequestrate revenues from the benefices of Richard of St John, chaplain, because of his debts to the crown, and subsequently, when he regained royal favour, to restore them to him.[177] Raleigh, in May 1242, was required to relax his sequestration of part of the revenues of R. Brito's church of Cawston, because this made payment of the incumbent's debt to the crown less likely.[178] In some cases commands were disguised as requests, as when in December 1235 the king asked the bishop to unite the church of Nettlestead, to which he had recently presented William de Rupella, to that of Blakenham, currently held by another royal clerk, and to permit William to hold both;[179] or when in March 1235 Henry III informed Blundeville that if the bishop should choose to confer the church of Bawburgh on the monks of Bon Repos (Morbihan, France), it would please him well, notwithstanding his recent presentation of John Mansel, king's clerk, who was in fact presented once again within six weeks by the

---

[175] *CRR* xiv no. 2349; *Bracton's Notebook* ii no. 883). Earl Richard and Isabelle his wife claimed against the abbot of St Etienne, Fontenay.
[176] *Close Rolls 1227–31* 106.
[177] *Close Rolls 1231–34* 431, 570.
[178] *Close Rolls 1234–37* 422.
[179] *CPR 1232–47* 131.

abbot and convent.[180] Within four months, by a fine made in the *curia regis*, it was agreed that the prior and convent of Norwich should hold the church of the monks of Bon Repos.[181]

THE BISHOPS' OFFICERS AND *FAMILIA*

THE OFFICIALS

The first known official, appointed by bishop John de Gray by 1202, was Ranulf of Warham, a monk of the cathedral priory but also styled *magister*. Documents in his name surviving in cartulary copies and the records of the *curia regis* and Chancery show him to have been in effective control of the diocese during Gray's almost perennial absence on king John's business.[182] Quite remarkably, he was granted custody of the temporalities of the see following Gray's death on 18 October 1214, until the appointment of the normal brace of royal officials around 29 March 1215.[183] After the election of Pandulph on 25 July 1215, the crown on 9 August 1215 granted custody of the see to Warham and to whomsoever else the bishop-elect might appoint.[184] When in September Pandulph set out for Rome to attend the Fourth Lateran Council, not only administration of the diocese but also enforcement of the papal sentence of excommunication against rebels fell, in East Anglia, to Warham.[185] Around Pentecost (29 May) 1216 he was captured by the king's enemies, but was free again by August 1217 and presided at Hoxne over the Michaelmas synod for the southern archdeaconries. Probably in 1217 he became prior of Norwich, but later in the same year he was elected bishop of Chichester, and was consecrated in January 1218.[186]

He was succeeded as official by master Ranulf of Harpley, who had been

---

[180] *Close Rolls 1234–37* 58; cf. *CPR 1232–47* 101.

[181] *Norwich Cathedral Charters* i no. 231.

[182] *EEA* 6 pp. xxxviii, xliii, lix; *Fasti* ii 60. In 1220, as bp of Chichester, he referred to 'eo tempore curam episcopatus Norwicensis gerebamus nomine bone memorie Iohannis de Gray tunc episcopi Norwicensis' (*Blythburgh Cartulary* i no. 206). For references to his work under Gray, see Vincent, 'Election' 144 n. 5.

[183] Vincent, 'Election' 143–50.

[184] *Rot. Litt. Pat.* 152.

[185] *Rot. Litt. Claus.* i 229b; *Rot. Litt. Pat.* 166, 168, 170; *Letters of Innocent III* no. 1029.

[186] Vincent, 'Election' 157–8, 161; *Fasti* v 4.

instituted by bishop John of Oxford to Haverhill, a church in the patronage of Castle Acre priory apparently reserved for episcopal clerks, and by bishop Gray, for whom he attested twenty *acta*, to Threxton church.[187] He held land at Little Plumstead and had a son, Geoffrey.[188] He occurs, probably in May 1218, as joint official with master William of Calne, who had attested *acta* of John of Oxford.[189] In 1219 papal judges-delegate addressed a notification to Harpley apparently as sole official.[190] By Michaelmas 1219, however, he had been drawn by Pandulph into the wider sphere of royal and legatine administration. On 18 September 1220 master Ranulf, clerk of Pandulph, was granted custody of the English lands of the recently deceased abbot of Fécamp, and in January 1221 received joint custody both of the vacant bishopric of London and of Bristol castle.[191]

Alan of Beccles first occurs as official by Michaelmas 1219 and continued in that role throughout Pandulph's episcopate and into the first few months of Blundeville's.[192] He was *magister*, possibly of Oxford, and subsequently, according to Matthew Paris, studied and taught at Paris;[193] but if the chronicler is correct in stating that he returned thence with other English *magistri* on the dispersal of the university in 1229, he must have either gone or returned there after he ceased to be official of Norwich in the course of 1227. He was rector of Bunwell, another church in the gift of the monks of Castle Acre, with whom he came into dispute (no. 10), and was also granted Haughley church by the legate Guala when he deposed Richard de Camera for adherence to the king's enemies.[194] By 19 September 1224 he was archdeacon of Sudbury

---

[187] *EEA* 6 nos. 197, 342, and index *sub nomine*.
[188] Bodl. ms. Norfolk ch. 360, 363.
[189] For biographical details of Calne, see *Guala's Letters* no. 7n. He had attested *acta* of William de Vere, bp of Hereford, and of archbp Hubert Walter, as well as of bp John of Oxford; he was *persona* of Little Melton (below, Appx I 9). His occurrence as joint official is in San Marino, Battle Abbey Papers vol. 29, fo. 80r–v, a letter of Harpley and Calne, using no title, to archbp Langton informing him that they had admitted Guy the clerk to the perpetual vicarage of Exning, and another, in which they are described as 'officiales Norwic' ', to the rural dean of Fordham, ordering him to induct. Langton returned to England in May 1218, Pandulph a few weeks later, by 7 June, and it is therefore tempting to date this notification to May–June 1218.
[190] *Lewes Cartulary: Norfolk Portion* no. 135.
[191] *Patent Rolls 1216–25* 253, 277, 282.
[192] His first dated occurrence as official is *CRR* viii 63, his last *actum* no. 88. For brief biographies see *DNB*, *BRUO* and *Guala's Letters* no. 1n. Before 13 May 1217 the legate had written to the pope testifying to his learning and morals, and this resulted in a dispensation to hold more than one benefice with cure of souls (*Guala's Letters* nos. 1, 176; *Reg. Hon. III* no. 922).
[193] *Chron. Maj.* iii 168.
[194] *Guala's Letters* no. 49; *Lewes Cartulary: Norfolk Portion* no. 67. By 1219 he also held the church of Shelland *per dominum legatum* (*Bk Fees* 282); by 1330 Shelland had been reduced to a chapel of Haughley.

(no. 1). His *acta* as official occur in several monastic cartularies, and in Pandulph's almost continuous absence he was often addressed by name in royal writs relating to the diocese.[195] In 1225 he commissioned William bishop of Llandaff to perform the episcopal function of dedicating the infirmary chapel at Stoke by Clare.[196] He lived some fourteen years after ceasing to act as official. His last public appearance was in 1240 as one of the papally appointed arbiters between bishop Grosseteste and his cathedral chapter of Lincoln, and he was dead by 25 March 1241.[197] His career, both academic and administrative, was very little different from those of men who became respected diocesan bishops, and provides an excellent early example of the more than adequate provision made for the governance of dioceses where bishops were seldom resident.

Master Robert of Bilney was instituted by Pandulph, in succession to Ranulf of Harpley, to the church of Haverhill (no. 11). He first occurs as official under Blundeville on 16 October 1227 (no. 89), having earlier that year been described as bishop's clerk (no. 78). He first occurs as archdeacon of Norfolk in late May 1229 (nos. 61–2)[198] and he continued to act as official (nos. 73–4). He last occurs as archdeacon on 29 March 1232 (no. 66). By Michaelmas 1232 he had been succeeded as official by master Richard of Shipton,[199] who had previously been official of the archdeacon of Sudbury, Alan of Beccles, occurring in 1227 and 1229 (nos. 31, 39n.). It is possible, although probably unlikely, that Shipton succeeded Bilney too as archdeacon

---

[195] For examples of his *acta*, see *Stoke by Clare Cartulary* i no. 103; BL ms. Cotton Titus viii (Wymondham cartulary) fos. 55v, 97v–8r. For examples of writs addressed to him, see *Rot. Litt. Claus.* ii 55b, 101b; *Patent Rolls 1216–25* 506; *Patent Rolls 1225–32* 39, 65, 92; the last two references demonstrate that he remained official *sede vacante* in the vacancy between Pandulph and Blundeville.

[196] *Stoke by Clare Cartulary* i no. 103. The narrative at the beginning of the *Creake Cartulary* (no. 1) states that Geoffrey, bp of Ely, acted as suffragan for Pandulph in 1221, but this is impossible since Geoffrey, although first elected to Ely in 1215, did not obtain possession or consecration until after his second election in 1225; possibly this is an error for John of Fountains, bp of Ely 1219–25 (*Fasti* ii 46).

[197] *Grosseteste's Letters* 259 no. 80; *CPR 1232–47* 248; *Fasti* ii 70. He had acted as papal judge-delegate in 1226 and 1231 and as a papal mandatory in 1236 (*CPL* i 113, 126; *Reg. Hon. III* no. 6070; *Reg. Greg. IX* nos. 642, 3266).

[198] His predecessor, Martin of Pattishall, was dean of St Paul's by 24 Sept. 1228 and died on 14 Nov. 1229 (*Fasti* ii 65). Bilney himself held land in Wyngate, Bishop's Lynn, which he granted to Blackborough priory (*King's Lynn* 79 no. 17).

[199] *CRR* xiv nos. 2059, 2109, 2125, 2390. The identification is uncertain — perhaps one of the many Shiptons in various counties (but not in East Anglia), but also possibly Shipden or Shipdham, Nf., or Sibton, Sf.

of Norfolk, but the reference to 'R. archydiaconum Norfolch' officialem nostrum' in March 1233 (no. 117) probably refers back to Bilney.[200]

The first official to serve bishop Raleigh was master Geoffrey of Ferring,[201] who had been in the service of archbishop Edmund Rich from before his consecration in April 1234; he was rector of Denham, Bucks., and held a portion of the church of Elham, Kent, for life. By 1239 he had entered Raleigh's service, and he occurs as official at Norwich on 30 December 1239 and in an undated *actum* (nos. 130, 132). After Raleigh's translation to Winchester he was despatched there, and suffered harassment from royal officers for exercising the bishop-postulant's disputed jurisdiction there.[202] He remained Raleigh's official until the bishop of Winchester's death, and following a papal indult of 1245 allowing him to hold three benefices with cure of souls and with royal support, he acquired prebends at St Paul's and Beverley, by 1254 he was precentor of Chichester, and he was dean of St Paul's, probably from 11 December 1262 to his death in 1268.

Ferring was succeeded as official in Norwich diocese by master William of Clare, who occurs on 8 January 1241 (no. 140), having previously attested three of Raleigh's *acta* (nos. 128, 135, 150). Master William first occurs as archdeacon of Sudbury on 3 December 1242, succeeding master Roger Pincerna, who was translated to Suffolk; he continued in office as archdeacon until at least 1256.[203] At Easter 1241 master Hervey of Fakenham occurs in the records of the *curia regis* as official, but two years later, in a document in the Castle Acre cartulary, he is described as 'official of the consistory'.[204] It appears that this is a distinct position, for although there is no other occurrence of Clare as official, and certainly within a year of bishop Suffield's consecration, in May 1245, master William of Horham was described as official,[205] Fakenham appears still as official of the consistory c. 1258, under bishop Simon of Walton, attesting after John of Alvechurch, the bishop's

---

[200] *Fasti* ii 66.
[201] For references, see Lawrence, *St Edmund* 150 and notes; *Fasti* v 13.
[202] *Close Rolls 1242–47* 238.
[203] *Fasti* ii 70 and Appx. 4 below. On 2 Nov. 1244 he was granted an indult to hold two additional benefices beyond those that he then had (*CPL* i 210; *Reg. Inn. IV* no. 751). On 23 Dec. 1244 papal authority was granted to William Raleigh, now bp of Winchester, to grant dispensation to the archdn of Suffolk to hold another benefice with cure in addition to his church of Redenhall (*CPL* i 210; *Reg. Inn. IV* no. 825).
[204] *CRR* xvi no. 1602; BL ms. Harley 2110 (Castle Acre cartulary) fo. 124v; see also below, Appx II 50A.
[205] BL ms. Harley 2110 fo. 131v.

official.[206] It is perhaps unsurprising that this specialisation of function should apparently have been introduced at Norwich by William Raleigh, the greatest English jurist of his generation.

ARCHDEACONS

There is a sharp distinction to be drawn between those archdeacons — Beccles, Bilney and Clare — who acted also as bishop's official, and also master Roger de Pincerna, successively archdeacon of Sudbury (1241–2) and of Suffolk (1242–6), who frequently acted as datary of bishop Raleigh's *acta*, and those other archdeacons who held office between 1215 and 1243 but who hardly figure at all in episcopal *acta*. Geoffrey de Burgh, who had been appointed by the crown in 1200, *sede vacante*, to the archdeaconry of Norwich, continued in office, despite his abortive election to the bishopric of Ely in 1215, until he was eventually elevated to that same see in 1225.[207] His main occupation was in the royal Exchequer, and he does not occur once after May 1205 as a witness to episcopal *acta*.[208] He was succeeded on 9 November 1226 by Luke the chaplain, again inserted by the crown *sede vacante*; a senior clerk of the royal wardrobe, and also chancellor of Lichfield and dean of St Martin le Grand in London, he was elected to the archbishopric of Dublin before 13 December 1228, and consecrated on 30 April 1230;[209] he attests no Norwich *acta* as archdeacon. The archdeaconry of Norwich had been contested by master John of Ferentino, who had been provided thereto by the pope, and who occupied the office without royal opposition after Luke's elevation to Dublin.[210] He first appears in England in January 1222, as a servant both of the pope and the king,[211] and subsequently he is described as

---

[206] Bodl. ms. Gough Norfolk 18, fos. 35v–36r. For discussion of the distinction, see D. M. Smith, 'The "*Officialis*" of the Bishop in Twelfth- and Thirteenth-Century England' in *Medieval Ecclesiastical Studies in Honour of Dorothy M. Owen* (as n. 2 above) 201–20, especially 219.
[207] *Fasti* ii 64.
[208] *EEA* 6 no. 390.
[209] *Fasti* ii 64; *Guala's Letters* no. 76n.
[210] *Fasti* ii 64; *Patent Rolls 1225–32* 191; *Reg. Greg. IX* no. 271.
[211] In Jan. 1222 he acted as intermediary in a transfer of an instalment of the royal tribute to Pandulph (*Rot. Litt. Claus.* i 486b; cf. Lunt, *Financial Relations* 143). In Dec. 1222 and Jan. 1223 he was acting as constable of Bristol castle (*Rot. Litt. Claus.* i 523b, 530). See also ibid. 492b, 521, 525b.

papal subdeacon and chamberlain.[212] Pandulph had attempted unsuccessfully to institute him to the church of Sproughton (Appx II 1). On several occasions he acted as executor of papal provisions in England, and on at least one occasion as judge-delegate.[213] When in England, he was probably habitually resident in London; he never attested episcopal *acta*, and on 23 August 1236 he was granted a papal indult to visit his archdeaconry by deputy, but nevertheless to receive the proceeds of visitation.[214] His deputy was most probably his kinsman James of Ferentino, dean of Holt, whom he commissioned to institute to churches in the archdeaconry during the vacancy of the see.[215]

In the archdeaconry of Norfolk Geoffrey of Buckland, clerk of Hubert Walter and kinsman of Hubert's successor as Justiciar, Geoffrey FitzPeter, had been appointed before 1200 and probably continued in office until his death in autumn 1225,[216] but his one appearance in this collection is as a royal justice rather than archdeacon (no. 19). He was succeeded by Martin of Pattishall, another and more eminent royal justice,[217] who visited East Anglia at the head of a judicial eyre in 1228,[218] but again does not attest any *acta*. Pattishall was succeeded, probably before his death, by Robert of Bilney, bishop's official,[219] and Bilney was possibly succeeded by the next official, master Richard of Shipton;[220] but if indeed Shipton was ever archdeacon of Norfolk, he had been replaced by 7 November 1236 by Ralph de Blundeville, certainly a kinsman of bishop Thomas, from whom he received a legacy.[221] Blundeville's tenure was, however, challenged on the grounds that after his promotion to the archdeaconry he had obtained the unification to his *personatus* of Thornham (which was in fact a small annual pension) of the vicar-

---

[212] As papal subdeacon first on 17 Feb. 1229 (*CPL* i 120; *Reg. Greg. IX* no. 271); as papal subdeacon and chaplain on 5 Nov. 1232 (*CPL* i 130; *Reg. Greg. IX* no. 946); as papal chamberlain first on 23 Aug. 1236 (*CPL* i 157; *Reg. Greg. IX* nos. 3302–3).

[213] *CPL* i 125, 147, 236; *Reg. Greg. IX* nos. 552–3, 2590, 3822.

[214] *CPL* i 157; *Reg. Greg. IX* no. 3302. He had been in England in Dec. 1231, when at St Albans he had escaped attack by a crowd hostile to Italian incumbents (Wendover, *Flores* iv 231). He was in Italy between May and Oct. 1234, when he acted as papal emissary to the Lombard League (*Reg. Greg. IX* nos. 1937–40, 2168). He was back in England on 31 May 1235 (*CPL* i 147; *Reg. Greg. IX* no. 2590), but at the *curia* in Nov. 1237 (*Reg. Greg. IX* no. 3541).

[215] BL ms. Harley 391 (Waltham cartulary) fo. 114v; see note to *actum* no. 153 below.

[216] *Fasti* ii 65; Turner, *The English Judiciary* 76, 128.

[217] See Meekings, *Studies* XII, and Turner, *The English Judiciary* index *s.n.* Martin of Pattishall.

[218] Crook, *General Eyre* 83.

[219] *Fasti* ii 66 and above, pp. xlv–vi.

[220] Above, p. xlv–xlvi.

[221] *Close Rolls 1234–37* 384; see also *CRR* xvi no. 1788, where it is recorded that on 31 July 1241 he was sued in the *curia regis* by Robert of Boyton, who claimed to be bp Blundeville's heir, for land at Glemham held of the prior of Thetford; the reference to Ralph as archdn here is surely retrospective.

age of that church, and had thus obtained a benefice with cure of souls which was incompatible with the archidiaconal office. In Trinity term 1237 he was challenged by the crown, which claimed the advowson of Thornham church *sede vacante*, but on 18 November 1237 he produced in court both the late bishop's charter recording the collation to him of the *personatus* (no. 110) and also a charter of Anger, abbot of Dereham, acting as vicar of the archbishop of Canterbury during the prolonged episcopal vacancy, consolidating parsonage and vicarage.[222] The English government, moreover, clearly regarded the archdeaconry as vacant. Thomas de Lecche, who was or subsequently became keeper of the queen's wardrobe, occurs once as archdeacon of Norfolk on 5 May 1237.[223] On 31 May, however, the crown appointed master Simon the Norman, king's clerk and also papal subdeacon and chaplain, but the writ was not delivered,[224] and on 25 September 1237 Ralph de Blundeville was exercising archidiaconal authority, appropriating a mediety of Wreningham church to Creake abbey (no. 130n.).[225] A second royal writ collating the archdeaconry to master Simon was issued on 7 December 1237.[226] A papal letter of 4 March 1239 records that master Simon brought a case against Ralph in the court of the legate Otto. The issue turned on the exact nature of Ralph's benefice at Thornham and its compatibility with the office of archdeacon; the matter was so complex that the legate felt it necessary to refer it to the *curia*. The eventual verdict was that master Simon had not proved his case, and that the archdeaconry could not be considered vacant *de iure*; but on the other hand, by Ralph's own confession and from the legate's report, it was obvious that, contrary to the statute of the Lateran Council, he had attempted to hold archdeaconry and a benefice with cure together, and therefore the pope, in consultation with his cardinals, deprived him of the archdeaconry.[227] Despite his failure to obtain an unequivocal verdict at Rome, master Simon was still regarded by the English crown as archdeacon until in 1240, when he dramatically fell from royal favour, he was deprived of this office by the king.[228] Mr Walter de Salerne (or of London) won a case at the papal *curia* against master Simon

---

[222] *CRR* xvi no. 78.
[223] *CPR 1232–47* 181; cf. *Fasti* ii 66.
[224] *CPR 1232–47* 183. For mr Simon the Norman, see Powicke, *Henry III and the Lord Edward*, Appx E, 772–84.
[225] Christ's College, Cambridge, Muniments ms. At. 32.
[226] *CPR 1232–47* 206.
[227] *CPL* i 179; *Reg. Greg. IX* no. 4738. Ralph was still alive in January 1245 when, described as deacon, he was granted an indult to hold an additional benefice with cure (*CPL* i 210; *Reg. Inn. IV* no. 898).
[228] *Chron. Maj.* iv 63; cf. Powicke, *Henry III and the Lord Edward* 781.

for the archdeaconry on 18 June 1244,[229] but there is no evidence in this collection of *acta* of either of them exercising the office of archdeacon of Norfolk.[230]

The tenure of the two southern archdeaconries is rather less complex. A master R. of Tew, who occurs as archdeacon of Suffolk (Ipswich) in 1214 is probably the same man as the master Robert of Tew who frequently attested bishop Gray's *acta*, and also the master Robert of Tew who first certainly occurs as archdeacon on 6 April 1227 and last on 1 April 1235—although he does occur without title until 24 January 1227.[231] He was followed in succession by master Alexander of Walpole[232] and master Roger Pincerna, translated from Sudbury, in which archdeaconry master Robert of Gloucester, king's clerk, dead by 28 October 1222, was succeeded in turn by three diocesan administrators, Beccles, Pincerna and Clare.[233]

OTHERS EXERCISING JURISDICTION

In a notification of a judgement, *c.* 1230, master Alan of Beccles referred to an earlier hearing of the case before master Maurice, *tunc tempore vices officialis Norwicensis*;[234] it appears, therefore, that he was vice-official. It is possible that the same function was fulfilled by master Richard of Stowe, who in Hilary term 1224 was cited, with the deans of Hoxne and Redenhall, to answer why they had heard a plea in the court Christian relating to the advowson of the chapel of St Giles at Topcroft; he appeared and stated that he had heard no plea after the bishop of Norwich had revoked the jurisdiction which he had committed to him.[235] It is more likely that master Robert of Wendling, cited to the *curia regis* in 1220 to answer why he had heard a plea in contravention of a writ of prohibition at the suit of a man identified elsewhere as an inhabit-

---

[229] *CPL* i 210; *Reg. Inn. IV* no 746; for references to his subsequent career, see *Fasti* ii 66.

[230] Two references to him as archdn in *Fasti* ii 66 are in fact misleading. CUL ms. G. 3. 28 is an *actum* of bp William Turbe (*EEA* 6 no. 87), in which 'Walc' ' is archdn Walkelin; and Eye cartulary fo. 28v (*EEA* 6 no. 93; *Eye Cartulary* no. 43) is also an *actum* of bp Turbe, where 'Waltero' is in error for 'Walkelino'.

[231] *Fasti* ii 67–8.

[232] Walpole attested three acta of bp Blundeville (nos. 67, 73, 93). He had acted as proctor of Lewes priory in 1219, and occurs as archdn only in the records of that house (*Fasti* ii 68).

[233] *Fasti* ii 70.

[234] BL ms. Cotton Titus C viii (Wymondham cartulary) fo. 55v.

[235] *CRR* xi no. 2803; xii no. 168; he occurs as a witness to *actum* no. 19, 27 Sept. 1219.

ant of Lynn, was exercising the bishop's jurisdiction in that town.[236] The function of master R. of Somerton, similarly cited to the king's court at Michaelmas 1242, cannot be determined, but it is probable that he too was acting as a delegate of the diocesan.[237]

In the *acta* and in other documents there are now references to the officials of archdeacons. Master Richard of Shipton exercised this function for the archdeacon of Sudbury before he became bishop's official (nos. 31, 39n), and he was succeeded by November 1229 by Gilbert of Yaxley (no. 32). In 1238 Henry of Holkham was official of the archdeacon of Norwich, and during the vacancy of the see instituted to at least one benefice (no. 127n), and during the same vacancy master Peter of Ware occurs as official of the archdeacon of Norfolk.[238]

THE *FAMILIA*

It is extremely difficult to distinguish between those who served in Pandulph's household as he moved across England in his legatine capacity and those who contributed to the governance of the diocese of Norwich. The submission to the pope by Reginald, king of the Isles, is attested by thirteen members of the legate's *familia*,[239] but only one of his episcopal *acta*, as transmitted, has a witness list. This charter (no. 1) is dated 19 September 1224, almost exactly five years after the king's submission, and of the six bishop's clerks who attest in September 1224 only one, Rusticus, had occurred also in 1219. Master Lando, certainly an Italian, who attests no. 1, acted as the bishop's proctor in England after Pandulph returned to Italy, was commissioned to act in conjunction with the official (no. 3) and as one of a group charged to negotiate with the earl of Arundel (Appx II 15), and finally the pope requested the king to allow him administration of the deceased bishop's goods in his domains (Appx II 18). Of the four other clerks who attest no. 1, Peter de Lucca is certainly Italian and Peter de Iull' probably so; it is impossible to determine the nationality of Lawrence or of William the chaplain. Of the thirteen witnesses of the 1219 submission, eight were certainly Italian;[240] but

---

[236] *CRR* viii 264; cf. ibid. 8, 311.
[237] *CRR* xvii no. 736.
[238] Christ's College, Cambridge, Muniments ms. At. 32.
[239] *CPL* i 69–70.
[240] Sayers, *Papal Government* 185–6.

that Pandulph did have in his household Englishmen is demonstrated by the occurrence of John of London, legate's scribe, in 1219,[241] and John Bacun, clerk to the legate, in 1221.[242] Nicholas Rueland represented him in the *curia regis* (Appx II 7). One chaplain neither English nor Italian was Luke of Wissant (Pas de Calais), who had, however, been in receipt of a pension of five marks from the English crown from 1206,[243] and is to be distinguished from Luke the chaplain (of Hubert de Burgh), who subsequently became archdeacon of Norfolk and archbishop of Dublin.[244] The most interesting reference to one of Pandulph's clerks concerns master James (probably in fact Giacomo), who had been instituted to the vicarage of South Creake, in the gift of Castle Acre priory. A papal scribe who had been seconded to Pandulph's service before 1219, he was, because of some unspecified transgression, deprived of his benefice at the Norwich synod of Easter 1220, and subsequently of his papal office, although he was later restored to the latter by Honorius III in August 1220, when he was required to make satisfaction to the legate and to obey his commands; but by this time his Norfolk vicarage had been granted to another Italian (nos. 8–9).[245]

Despite the large number of extant *acta*, the regular witnesses of bishop Blundeville's charters are few. Master Robert of Bilney was bishop's clerk (no. 78) before he became official and archdeacon, and master Alan of Beccles continued to attest after he ceased to be official, as archdeacon of Sudbury (nos. 93, 95); but of the other *magistri*, Nicholas of Houghton, Alexander de Munci and Michael of Ringsfield attest only *acta* in favour of the cathedral priory issued in the first months of the episcopate (nos. 76–7, 80–2), and there is no evidence that they were members of the *familia*.[246] The only masters, apart from Bilney, who may be presumed to have been members of the household are Alexander of Walpole, who attests *acta* in favour of three different beneficiaries between 1227 and 1235 (nos. 69, 73, 93), and Andrew of Croydon, who witnesses four *acta* for three different beneficiaries from April 1230

---

[241] *CPL* i 70.
[242] *Patent Rolls 1216–25*. It may have been either John Bacon or John of London for whom Pandulph as legate requested the grant by the prior and convent of Coventry of the church of Newnham (BL ms. Add. 47677 fo. 325r (314r)).
[243] *Rot. Litt. Pat.* 68; he also received a gift from the crown in 1224 (*Rot. Litt. Claus.* i 585).
[244] For the distinction between the two see *Guala's Letters* no. 76n. It is just possible that Luke of Wissant was the canon of Chichester who occurs several times 1215 –1245 × 53, although this is more likely to have been Luke des Roches, archdn of Surrey (*Fasti* v 62–3).
[245] *CPL* i 69–70; *Reg. Hon. III* nos. 1159, 1307, 2008; cf. Sayers, *Papal Government* 42–3, 199.
[246] For mr Alexander de Munci, see *Sibton Charters* i 75–6. He was rural dean of Waynford, a benefactor of Bungay, Langley and Sibton, and was dead by 1242. Michael of Ringsfield was rector of a mediety of Scottow (no. 66).

to March 1232 (nos. 34, 66, 73–4). Master Thomas of Huntingdon, who represented the bishop in the *curia regis* in 1234 (Appx II 26), was probably the same man who was vicar of Crimplesham, in the gift of Stoke by Clare priory, in 1229.[247]

The most frequent witnesses of Blundeville's *acta* were Denis of Catton or Cotton, almost certainly the same man as Denis the bishop's clerk, who attests eleven times between early 1227 and 1235, and John Terry, three times described as bishop's clerk (nos. 78, 80–2), who also attested eleven times throughout the episcopate and who represented the bishop in the *curia regis* (Appx II 33). Reginald of Ringstead, bishop's clerk, who attested two *acta* for Lewes priory (nos. 73–4), also represented Blundeville in the king's court in 1229 (Appx II 30), and on 24 April 1224 paid £80 into the Wardrobe at Portsmouth as pledged by the bishop to the king for his first crossing.[248] Richard of Gayton, described once as bishop's clerk, attests only in 1227 (nos. 76, 78, 81–2, 87, 89), while Henry, the bishop's chaplain, witnesses on eleven occasions between 1227 and 1230 (nos. 39, 49, 74, 76, 78, 81, 87–9, 95).

Under William Raleigh there is a clear distinction between natives of East Anglia and those introduced from outside the diocese. In the former category were master William of Clare (nos. 128, 135, 150), subsequently official (no. 140) and archdeacon of Sudbury (nos. 129, 144–5), Thomas of Breckles (nos. 128, 132, 140) and Richard of Fritton, clerk (nos. 128, 140). From Raleigh's native Devon came Philip of Sydenham, his own kinsman, who was also a servant of the crown, rector of Lilford and Bugbrooke, Northants., and dispensed by the papacy in 1238 to hold an additional benefice with cure of souls;[249] he is described as bishop's chaplain, and acted as datary of seven of Raleigh's *acta* (nos. 125, 128, 132, 135, 138, 140–1). Also from Devon were Walter of Exeter, chaplain (no. 145), clerk (no. 132) and from December 1240 *magister* (nos. 128, 132, 135, 140, 145), and William of Dunkeswell, clerk (nos. 128–9, 132, 140, 145, 149). From divers quarters came John of Leominster, clerk (nos. 128–9, 132, 140, 145, 149), John of Chilbolton, chaplain (nos. 129, 145, 149) or clerk (nos. 128, 132, 140) and Philip of Godalming, chaplain (nos. 129, 145, 149). Roger Hautesce, clerk, who attests only once (no. 145), was rector of Thornham (no. 143) and acted with Ralph of Gayton as the bishop's attorney in the *curia regis* (Appx II 51). Another attorney was Roger of Boyland, who in 1243 claimed a case for the bishop's court at Lynn.[250]

---

[247] *Patent Rolls 1225–32* 290.
[248] *C. Lib. R.* i 246.
[249] *CPL* i 169; *Reg. Greg. IX* no. 4167; for Bugbrooke, *Rot. Grosseteste* 196.
[250] *CRR* xvii no. 2207.

SECULAR OFFICERS

There are only two references in these *acta* to the bishop's secular officers, both to the same man, and not as witness. Alexander of Bassingbourn was Pandulph's seneschal in 1219 and 1220 (nos. 5, 15),[251] but was no longer serving in that capacity by the end of the episcopate, as there is a reference in a legal case to Bartholomew of Brancaster serving as seneschal at the time after the bishop had gone to Rome and never returned.[252] It is probable that Bartholomew was already seneschal when he was one of those commissioned at Trinity term 1224 by the bishop to hear testimony relating to the making of peace with the earl of Arundel at Lynn.[253] Also on this commission was Simon of Scarning, certainly an episcopal servant, against whom a complaint was made in the *curia regis* by an inhabitant of Lynn, declared by the bishop to be excommunicate, that he had distrained his animals.[254] Martin, who attests the submission of the king of the Isles as Pandulph's steward,[255] almost certainly travelled in the legate's itinerant household, and would therefore seldom have been in East Anglia. The only other reference to a secular officer, Ingelram, marshal of bishop Raleigh, occurs in the records of the royal court.[256]

THE *ACTA*

CONTENTS OF THE *ACTA*

The largest category of *acta* is provided by confirmations — a total of fifty-six, of which twenty-six are in the form of *inspeximus* charters.[257] The *inspeximus*

---

[251] See also *CRR* viii 311. In Dec. 1222 he was acting as constable of the king's castle of Marlborough (*Rot. Litt. Claus.* i 523b).

[252] Alexander of Bassingbourn was, however, still alive in Feb. 1231, when a royal writ ordered bp Blundeville not to distrain upon him, as previously ordered, because he had been pardoned £2 18s demanded by summons of the Exchequer for the issues of the manor of Costessy when it was in the king's hands (*Close Rolls 1227–31* 480).

[253] *CRR* xi no. 2709.

[254] *CRR* xi no. 884.

[255] *CPL* i 70.

[256] *CRR* xvi no. 1457.

[257] A further four *inspeximus* charters do not specify confirmation, but three of these do not refer to diocesan matters (nos. 20, 128, 145A–B). In seven *inspeximus* charters the text of the previous charter is not recited (nos. 74, 77, 84, 128, 134–5, 137A).

was most commonly of previous episcopal *acta*, to which on three occasions was added new provision for a vicarage (nos. 61, 70, 105), while twice previous provision for a vicar was modified (nos. 128, 135); but it was also occasionally used to confirm grants by an ecclesiastic (no. 134), by lay persons (nos. 19–20, where *vidimus* is used), or agreements relating to tithes (nos. 109, 122, 137). Of the other confirmation charters not using the *inspeximus* format, three are very long documents, recording in detail the extensive possessions in the diocese of Norwich of St John's Colchester, Lewes and Wymondham and their confirmation by bishop Blundeville (nos. 49, 74, 121). Those for Lewes and Wymondham repeat in large measure earlier general confirmations by bishops William Turbe and John of Oxford, although in the case of Wymondham no specific reference is made to the earlier *actum*. Other general confirmations were given in favour of Bec, Eye, Longueville, Préaux, St Paul's hospital in Norwich and Rumburgh priory (nos. 95, 123, 133, 138, 146, 148), and that they were sought by two Norman houses and two daughters of monasteries in the duchy may reflect insecurity after the end of the Anglo-Norman realm. Several general confirmations of tithes and pensions due to the cathedral priory and its obedientiaries were issued in the name of bishop Blundeville (nos. 76, 78–9, 84), while in a far more terse form a confirmation was issued for St Benet of Holme of the tithes of its own manors, which were not enumerated (no. 68). There were few new foundations in this period, but bishop Blundeville did confirm in some detail the endowment of the Augustinian community at Spinney (nos. 107–9) and far more briefly that of Kersey (nos. 71–2) — both fledgling institutions were taken under episcopal protection.

Other confirmations were more specific—of particular grants by laymen ranging from the king (no. 23) through the earl of Gloucester and Hertford (nos. 26, 111) to lesser grantors (no. 72), of a church, pension or tithes which had been long held and were probably now under threat (nos. 49A, 59, 75, 80, 150), of the lease of tithes to a vicar for his lifetime (no. 57), or of the endowment of an early chantry chapel (no. 137A). Particularly interesting are the reference in a confirmation of a pension from the church of St Peter Mancroft to the *matricula* of the church of Norwich, an earlier version of the Great Domesday of Norwich, which lists the valuation of all churches, pensions and portions in the diocese (no. 59),[258] and the confirmation by bishop Raleigh of vicarages ordained by the rural dean of Holt during the long vacancy of the see (no. 153).

Turning to grants, the three bishops alienated remarkably little from the

---

[258] Cheney, *English Bishops' Chanceries* 112–3.

episcopal demesne — only a grant *in proprios usus* of a church previously of the bishop's advowson (no. 145),[259] and a third part of the tithes of the episcopal assarts at Thorpe to St Paul's hospital (Appx II 47). A very different form of grant was that made in the bishop's capacity of diocesan. There are three instances of the bishop detaching a certain sum of money from a church's revenues to create therein a benefice to be held by a religious house (nos. 50, 52, 102), while certain portions of the church of Stradishall were diverted to the canons of Tonbridge at the request of the earl of Gloucester (no. 112).

A large group of documents refer to the appropriation of parish churches, or medieties thereof, to religious communities. Twenty-six *acta* or pairs of *acta* (nos. 30–1, 38–9, 144–5) and also four notifications by beneficiaries, record new grants *in proprios usus* by the current diocesan. A further three *acta* are reiterations of earlier grants of appropriation, but do not mention the bishop's predecessor (nos. 44, 102, 119). The surviving evidence records the appropriation authorised for the first time in the period 1215–43 of thirty churches, six medieties and a chapel. As for the period 1175–1215, this annual average of approximately 1.5 appropriations must be an indeterminate but fairly small fraction of those actually conceded, to judge from the Valuation of 1254. Five new grants *in proprios usus* are recorded for Pandulph, twenty-seven for Blundeville and five for Raleigh. A further twenty *inspeximus* charters refer to such grants by the bishop's predecessor, almost always John of Oxford or John de Gray, although in one case by William Turbe (no. 136). These are usually straightforward confirmations, but occasionally a slight modification is made, such as provision for a vicar (no. 105), or recognition that the church could not sustain within it two benefices, and that therefore the vicar should merely pay a pension to the monastic rector (no. 128).

There is clear evidence that after a grant *in proprios usus*, the acquisition of the parochial revenues by the monastic beneficiary might in fact be long delayed. The monks of Bury were, indeed, fortunate in taking possession in 1219 of the rectory of Mildenhall, appropriated to them by John de Gray in 1205 (no. 5).[260] Often the delay was much longer, and several appropriations initially authorised by John of Oxford before 1200 were reiterated by Blundeville because they had not yet been implemented, normally due to the longevity of the *persona* on whose death or resignation they were to take effect (nos. 44, 61–2, 70, 102, 105–6). Castle Acre priory had to wait many years for some churches originally appropriated by bishop John I. His appropriation of

---

[259] Cf. *EEA* 6 nos. 373, 391.
[260] Cf. *EEA* 6 no. 332.

Herringby was repeated by Blundeville (no. 46)[261] but was only finally effected by Raleigh in 1240 because Robert Haltein, instituted before 1196, had only just died (no. 128). Despite the appropriation of Kempstone before 1200,[262] Blundeville instituted a new *persona* (no. 41) and the monks only finally acquired the rectory in 1249.[263] John I's appropriation of Methwold[264] was reiterated by Blundeville, but the monks were still not in possession in 1249.[265] At St Neots' church of Barton Bendish, John of Oxford had authorised appropriation on the death or resignation of the *persona*,[266] but this award had been ineffectual, and Blundeville similarly ordered appropriation to take effect when the church should be vacated by a different rector (no. 103).

In the great majority of cases appropriation was accompanied by the ordination of a vicarage. There are thirty-one such instances, and a further four recorded in *acta* the main purpose of which is to record an institution to a vicarage. In two cases the vicar was to receive the revenues of the church and to pay a pension to the monastic rector—a very large one at All Saints, Dunwich (no. 132), and a small one, because of the poverty of the church, at Herringby (no. 128). In all other cases the vicar was assigned a benefice from the revenues of the church. In many instances, when the appropriation was not to take effect immediately, it was merely stated that the provision made for the vicar should be honourable and suitable or competent, but in others the monetary value of the vicarage was stipulated (nos. 15, 31, 38, 52, 61, 114, 118–9; Appx II 24, 43), and in others still the sources of the vicar's income were enumerated in varying degrees of detail (nos. 2, 5, 29, 44, 102, 105–6; Appx II 2). Sometimes both the monetary value and the detailed sources of revenue were expressed, usually in two distinct *acta* (nos. 15, 30–1, 38–9, 61–2, 114–5). In some *acta* it was stated that the component parts of the vicar's income had been assessed and established by various subordinates of the bishop—the official (nos. 61, 104, 117), in conjunction with the bishop's proctor (no. 3) or seneschal (nos. 5, 15), or the archdeacon's official (no. 31). The values of vicarages varied considerably: where it is expressed in the *acta* themselves, from five marks (the minimum laid down by the Council of Oxford of 1222)[267] at Stradsett (no. 118) to a generous twenty-five marks

---

[261] Cf. *EEA* 6 no. 202.
[262] *EEA* 6 nos. 199–200.
[263] BL ms. Harley 2110 fos. 131v–33r.
[264] *EEA* 6 nos. 199–200.
[265] BL ms. Harley 2110 fo. 133r.
[266] *EEA* 6 no. 277.
[267] *C. & S.* II i 112 (cap. 21).

at Ludham and Exning (nos. 15, 30). For other vicarages ordained in these *acta*, the *Valuation of Norwich* shows even wider discrepancies, from the very low £1 of Deopham and Oulton,[268] which must have been supplemented from other sources, to £20 at Aylsham and Mildenhall.[269] These latter were valuable benefices, far better endowed than most neighbouring rectories; and indeed the vicarage of Aylsham was collated by Pandulph to his own nephew (no. 4).

Both vicars and vicarages are frequently described as perpetual,[270] indicating that security of tenure demanded by canon XXXII of the Fourth Lateran Council. Only twice is the obligation to minister in person specifically mentioned (nos. 129, 132), but on thirteen occasions it is stipulated that the vicar should discharge the ecclesiastical (that is, financial) obligations of the church. Three times it is decreed that he should bear one third of the costs of the repair of books and ornaments (nos. 30, 39, 116).[271] It is interesting to note that now, in the early thirteenth century, in the diocese of Norwich at least, *persona* was frequently used to refer to a vicar (see Index, *s.v. persona*), whereas in the twelfth century it almost always means 'rector'.

The most notable feature of episcopal ordination of vicarages in this period is the determination of the bishops to reserve to themselves the choice of vicars.[272] It seems certain that in the late twelfth century bishop John of Oxford granted the appropriation of some parish churches at the next vacancy in return for the immediate presentation by the monastic patrons of one of his own clerks.[273] His successors sought a more permanent arrangement which would secure the extension of their own patronage. Pandulph, who complained to pope Honorius III that the churches in his gift were few and of little value,[274] was the first to stipulate, in all four appropriations authorised by him of which record survives, that the monastic rector and patron of the vicarage should present to the diocesan for institution the man whom the bishop himself wished (nos. 2, 5, 15; Appx II 2), and episcopal nomination of vicars was imposed on religious communities by bishop Blundeville on nine recorded occasions (nos. 29–31, 52, 61–2, 66, 103, 114–6, 119), and once by bishop Raleigh (no. 132). These vicarages, now effectively at the bishop's disposal, included some of the best endowed, such as Aylsham,

---

[268] *VN* 367, 399.
[269] *VN* 367, 432.
[270] See Index *s.v.* vicar, vicarage.
[271] The most detailed ordinations of vicarages are those made by James of Ferentino, dean of Holt, in the vacancy of the see, 1236–39; see *actum* no. 153 n.
[272] See Harper-Bill, 'Diocese of Norwich in the Early Thirteenth Century' 25–6.
[273] Harper-Bill, 'Struggle for Benefices' 129–32.
[274] *CPL* i 71; *Reg. Hon. III* no. 2643.

Exning, Ludham and Mildenhall. It is certain that there was a concerted campaign to extend episcopal patronage, of which another aspect was Blundeville's acquisition of the advowsons of Terling (Essex) and Great Massingham from, respectively, the canons of St Paul's, London, and the Norman monastery of Hambye (Appx I 23, 38). The condition imposed, however, also ensured that the bishop would be able to select suitable pastors for the parishes, and this was probably most important when the patrons were far-distant houses such as Battle and Haughmond.

Twenty-four of the *acta* record institutions to benefices. That this must be a tiny proportion of such documents issued is suggested by the fact that eight, a third of the recorded total, refer to churches in the gift of Castle Acre priory, in the cartulary of which are copied these documents of ephemeral interest omitted from most others because they did not pertain to the rights of the community. Under Pandulph the verb used for the act of institution varies; no. 3, which omits any reference to presentation by the normal patrons, is almost certainly a collation in the sense of the bishop himself presenting, but 'contulisse' or 'contulerimus' is used on its own (nos. 7, 9) or in conjunction with 'instituisse' (nos. 13, 18) in cases where institution is stated to be at the presentation of the patrons. Once only 'admisimus' is used (no. 24). Under Blundeville and Raleigh 'instituisse' is the invariable norm, even when the bishop did collate according to the ruling of the Fourth Lateran Council (no. 58). Four institutions to vicarages were supplemented by a brief statement of the portion of the church to be ceded to the vicar (nos. 104, 106, 127, 129) and another by a stipulation of the money to be paid from the church by the vicar to the monastic patron (no. 132).

A small group of *acta* illustrate what can only be described as miscellaneous episcopal functions in regard to the churches and persons under the bishop's jurisdiction. The unification of a rectory and a vicarage (no. 17) and of a vicarage with a pension from a church (no. 56) reveal the desire of diocesans, so often rendered impossible by vested interests, to create unitary benefices. Blundeville clarified the proportions of a long-established pension due to Lewes priory to be paid by each of two rectors on whom it had been imposed (no. 73). At the institution of the first chaplain, very brief regulations were laid down by Raleigh for an early chantry chapel at Ilketshall St John (no. 137A). Pandulph was acting in both legatine and diocesan capacities when he announced the expulsion of a papal scribe on his own staff from a Norfolk vicarage and issued a mandate to his proctors, the prior and convent of Westacre, to refrain from any interference in the revenues of the benefice (nos. 8–9). A more spiritual aspect of the bishop's role is illustrated by the grant of four indulgences, three of them by Pandulph, none of them for the maximum of forty days (nos. 6, 12; Appx II 9), and one by Raleigh (no. 131), but none of them for churches within the diocese.

The great majority of surviving *acta* are general notifications, but the bishop also addressed mandates to his subordinates. There are only five in this collection, all of them mandates to induct into corporal possession of a church or pension, one directed from abroad to the bishop's official and proctor (no. 3), three to the archdeacon's official (nos. 32–3, 67), and one to the local rural dean (no. 90). This must be a very small proportion of the administrative mandates which were despatched to the bishop's officers and local judicial representatives and which, because of their ephemeral nature, were rapidly discarded.

Although none survive, there are references to eight letters sent by the bishops to the king's justices, and again this is certainly a small proportion of the total, as often the rolls of the *curia regis* refer only to information received from the bishop, which was probably by letter but may have been communicated verbally by his proctor in the court. Twice the bishop claimed clerks (on one occasion the prior of Horsham St Faith) for the ecclesiastical courts (nos. 99, 101). Twice, too, he sought to protect one of his servants and an ecclesiastical judge by stating that the plaintiff who had brought a case against them in the *curia regis* was excommunicate, and thus debarred from pleading (nos. 22, 147).[275] Other letters record the bishop's response to the justices' demands for information, testifying that a church was not in fact vacant (no. 97), to a legitimate marriage (nos. 21, 100) or to legitimate birth (no. 98).

A small number of *acta* refer to the judicial activities of the bishop and his official. The regular jurisdictional role of the official is reflected by bishop Blundeville's notification of a settlement concerning the tithes of Flitcham (no. 122) and his ratification of the delineation of the Wiggenhall parishes (Appx II 36) made by the authority of his official. In the last year of Raleigh's episcopate at Norwich, master Hervey of Fakenham is described as official of the consistory of Norwich, now adjudicating in a permanently constituted court rather than in the diocesan synod, as had his predecessor at the beginning of the century.[276] The bishop himself did, however, still give judgement at time of synod, although perhaps not in it, as when Blundeville heard a dispute concerning Binham priory's claim to a benefice in the church of Bacton (Sf.), which had already been ventilated before his official (Appx II

---

[275] These letters are a reflection of the large number of actions brought against ecclesiastical judges in the diocese; see above pp. xxxix–xlii.
[276] BL ms. Harley 2110 fo. 124v; cf. *EEA* 6 p. lix. See C. Morris, 'From Synod to Consistory: the Bishops' Courts in England, 1150–1250', *Journal of Ecclesiastical History* xxii (1971) 115–33.

39). The nature of the tribunal in which Pandulph in 1224 imposed a composition on Battle abbey and the archdeacon of Richmond (no. 1) is not clear, as neither is that of the forum in which Blundeville heard an appeal by a man excommunicated by the rural dean of Coddenham (Appx II 20) or Raleigh with the counsel of prudent men adjudicated in a tithe dispute (no. 152), although the latter at least was presumably the emerging court of Audience. Perhaps the most unusual *actum* in the whole collection is the account of the proceedings before the bishop between the monks of Colchester and the rector of Eriswell; this records two hearings before Blundeville, between which the rural dean, having summoned a jury of twelve local men, conducted an inquisition (no. 49B). The narrative of these proceedings is verbose and full of grammatical errors, but it gives a far better impression of the litigiousness of medieval clerical society than more polished *acta*.

With regard to delegated papal jurisdiction, the position of Pandulph was anomalous, since for much of the time that he was bishop-elect he was also papal legate. It was as such, certainly, that he confirmed the statutes of the abbey of Bury St Edmunds (Appx II 6), for the monks would never have admitted the intrusion of the diocesan; and although judgement on his own clerk master James was passed in the diocesan synod, the consequences for the miscreant were certainly more serious because of Pandulph's special relationship with the pope (no. 8).[277] There is little evidence of his successors' activity as papal judges-delegate. Blundeville occurs in this capacity on two recorded occasions, once in association with the dean of Norwich and the prior of Horsham St Faith in a dispute between the twin foundations of Butley and Leiston (no. 37) and once in a major matrimonial cause beyond the bounds of his own diocese (Appx II 43). Blundeville's own dispute with the priors of Binham and Wymondham was resolved before papal judges-delegate in 1228 (Appx II 27), and the bishop occasionally issued a notification of decisions reached by papal judges (nos. 10, 96), or indeed informed the judges of facts germane to a case being heard by them (no. 65).

A group of *acta* refer to the relationship between the bishop and his monastic cathedral chapter.[278] Among these are the only two grants which involved the alienation of episcopal assets—a third part of the tithes of the bishop's assarts at Thorpe to St Paul's hospital (Appx II 47) and the grant to the cathedral priory *in proprios usus* of the church of Catton, from which the monks had previously received only certain tithes and a pension of 5s (no.

---

[277] *CPL* i 75.
[278] See *Norwich Cathedral 1096–1996* 281–300.

145).[279] The church of Martham, mentioned at a later date as having been granted by Blundeville, had in fact been of the monks' advowson before it was initially appropriated to them by bishop Gray in 1205 (no. 90),[280] and the church of Bawburgh, appropriated to them by Raleigh, had recently been acquired from the abbey of Bon Repos (no. 140).[281] Bishop Blundeville issued several general confirmations for the monks of Norwich (nos. 76, 78–9, 95), confirmed specific grants (nos. 80, 86, 89, 92–4), and also ratified many of John de Gray's *acta* in their favour (nos. 77, 81–5, 87–8). Raleigh imitated Gray in attempting to resolve any remaining issues which might cause discord between bishop and monks, rationalising their respective rights at Thorpe and Plumstead (no. 139), exchanging land at Thornham and finally settling the long-standing altercation between the cathedral priory and the rector there (nos. 143–4), delineating the revenues of monastic *persona* and vicar at North Elmham (no. 142), and establishing the office of dean, with somewhat limited powers, for the convent's manors, where the monks already exercised some spiritual jurisdiction (no. 141). Compared with the munificence shown by the bishops during the first eighty years of the cathedral's existence, this was little enough, and the monks now had to look elsewhere for small-scale augmentation of their endowment.

In one respect, however, the early thirteenth-century bishops continued to show special favour to their own monks, for they maintained the practice established by bishop Gray of allowing them to serve many of their appropriated churches through the agency of chaplains who did not have to be presented to the bishop for institution and might be unilaterally removed;[282] the normal obligation to establish a vicarage in an appropriated church was waived (nos. 81–2, 85, 87–8, 92). In the case of the poorly endowed city churches this was perhaps justifiable, but more revealing is the case of Wighton. Here, in a church appropriated by Gray, Pandulph insisted that a vicarage should be established. The monks complained to Blundeville that this vicarage could not be sustained and was to their prejudice and injury, and although Blundeville decreed that a vicarage should be maintained, its revenues were much reduced (no. 91). Assessed at forty marks in 1254 and 1291, Wighton was hardly a poorly endowed church, and here the special consideration of the cathedral priory's interests appears an exception to the bishops' generally sustained policy of balancing the financial advantage of monasteries with a concern for the welfare of incumbents.

---

[279] Cf. *EEA* 6 nos. 373, 391.
[280] Cf. *EEA* 6 nos. 390–1, 400, 406.
[281] See above pp. xlii–xliii.
[282] *EEA* 6 nos. 381, 388, 391, 395, 405.

Apart from compositions with the monks of Norwich, there are very few documents relating to the episcopal estates. In 1243 Raleigh entered into an agreement with the custodians of the lands of Bartholomew of Creake relating to view of frankpledge and the assize of ale at Flixton (Appx II 54). Of wider significance are two agreements made by the bishops in relation to their town of Lynn. In July 1234 Blundeville entered into a final concord with the mayor and burgesses, who had complained to the crown that they had been excommunicated for the making of a mayor without the bishop's consent. He now conceded that they might elect whomsoever they wished, as long as he might take an oath of loyalty from the new mayor to the bishop and church of Norwich (Appx II 26). The long-standing dispute between the bishop and the earl of Arundel, of which there is evidence from the time of bishop John of Oxford and which had continued under Pandulph, was resolved by Raleigh in an agreement of April 1243 concerning their respective rights in the town, particularly in relation to the Tolbooth (Appx II 55).

DIPLOMATIC OF THE *ACTA*

INTITULATIO

Before his belated consecration, Pandulph used the title *Dei gratia Norwicensis electus domini pape camerarius apostolice sedis legatus*, omitting the legatine element in the one surviving actum issued between his surrender of the legation and his consecration (no. 10). Thereafter his title was given as *Dei gratia Norwicensis episcopus* or *episcopus Norwicensis*, except in one instance, an indulgence, where he is styled *permissione divina Norwicensis episcopus* (no. 12).

There is only one variation from Blundeville's title *Thomas Dei gratia Norwicensis episcopus*; in no. 121, a long general confirmation for Wymondham, he is styled *Thomas permissione divina Norwicensis ecclesie minister humilis*—this is the title used in a similar charter of bishop John of Oxford, on which Thomas's actum is very closely based.[283] William Raleigh also universally used the formula *Dei gratia episcopus Norwicensis*; on three

---

[283] *EEA* 6 no. 316.

occasions, however, he did unusually use his full name before his title (nos. 125, 131, 145).

INSCRIPTIO

The great majority of the surviving *acta* are addressed universally. Under Pandulph the most common form of address was *universis presentes litteras inspecturis* (eleven instances), and in a further five *acta*, *has* was substituted for *presentes*. Twice *Cristi fidelibus* was added after *universis* (nos. 7, 15). In two *acta* the address was *omnibus has litteras inspecturis* (nos. 2, 13), and once in an indulgence the more elaborate *universis sancte matris ecclesie filiis ad quos presentes littere pervenerint* (no. 12).

Under Blundeville there was increasing standardisation. The formula *omnibus Cristi fidelibus ad quos presens scriptum pervenerit* was used sixty-one times, and in other *acta* there were numerous minor variations: *omnibus Cristi fidelibus has* (or *presentes*) *litteras* (or *presens* or *hoc scriptum*) *inspecturis* (or *visuris*), occasionally with the addition of *et* or *vel audituris*. There are six such minor variations in all, but none of them was used on more than three occasions. *Cristi fidelibus* was occasionally omitted. *Omnibus sancte matris ecclesie filiis* was used in a confirmation for Wymondham based largely on an actum of John of Oxford (no. 121) and in three documents for St John's Colchester, which continue *presentem paginam inspecturis vel audituris* or *ad quos presentes littere pervenerint* (nos. 49–49B).

The standard formula of the *inscriptio* under Raleigh was, as under Blundeville, *omnibus Cristi fidelibus ad quos presens scriptum pervenerit*, with twenty-one instances. Minor variations were *presens scriptum visuris vel audituris* (nos. 145, 154) or *presentes litteras inspecturis* (no. 153). On two occasions the announcement of an agreement was introduced directly by the *notificatio* (nos. 139, 144).

Under Pandulph the *intitulatio* preceded the *inscriptio* on nine occasions and followed it in twelve *acta*. Thereafter the *intitulatio* invariably followed the *inscriptio*.

There are extant only six *acta* addressed specifically, although very many more must have been produced. In four instances the title precedes the address (nos. 3, 9, 53, 67) and twice follows it (nos. 33, 65).

ACTUM OF BISHOP PANDULPH VERRACCLO

ACTUM OF BISHOP THOMAS BLUNDEVILLE

ACTUM OF BISHOP WILLIAM RALEIGH

SEALS AND COUNTERSEALS OF
BISHOPS THOMAS BLUNDERVILLE AND WILLIAM RALEIGH

No. 38   *Canterbury Dean & Chapter*    No. 69   *Public Record Office*

No. 138   *New College, Oxford*    No. 138   *New College, Oxford*

PLATE IV

SALUTATIO

The simple greeting *salutem in Domino* was used almost universally throughout the three episcopates; *salutem* alone in no. 41 is possibly a scribal omission. *Salutem eternam in Domino* is used in four of Blundeville's *acta* (nos. 37, 73–4, 96) and one of Raleigh's (no. 131), and *salutem in Domino sempiternam* in five of Blundeville's, including three in favour of St John's Colchester (nos. 49–49B, 53, 71). *Salutem et benedictionem* was used on one occasion when Pandulph addressed his official and proctor (no. 3).

ARENGA

The pious preamble had fallen into relative disuse in the episcopates of John of Oxford and especially of John de Gray.[284] It continued to be employed occasionally under Pandulph (four instances) and Blundeville (seven instances), and more frequently, proportionately, under Raleigh (again seven instances). It is interesting that of these eighteen occurrences, all but two (nos. 130–1) are *acta* in favour of Benedictine houses or their dependencies. Except in the case of two indulgences (nos. 12, 131), and one long report of court proceedings which began with a reflection on the bishop's duty to enforce justice (no. 49B), the theme was invariably the special episcopal obligation to care for the welfare of religious houses in the diocese where God is well served, amplified occasionally by the observation that this is especially the case when they are immediately subject to Rome—a reference in an *actum* for Bury to Pandulph's legatine status (no. 5)—or are his own cathedral church (nos. 91, 140), or are in straitened circumstances (no. 130).

The *arenga* was normally a complete sentence, only once being a dependent clause introduced by *cum* (no. 148). In four instances it was followed by a notificatory clause (nos. 86, 95, 125, 140), twice introduced in papal style by *eapropter* (nos. 86, 95). More often, however, the *arenga* was followed immediately by the text of the *dispositio*, introduced by *hinc est quod* (nos. 5, 15, 49–49B), *cum igitur* (nos. 2, 130, 150–1), *sunt autem* (no. 121) or *sane cum* (no. 91).

---

[284] *EEA* 6 pp. lxv.

NOTIFICATIO

The notification clause was a very common component of episcopal *acta* in this period, although not as near universal as it had been under John of Oxford, due to the increasing use of the *inspeximus* charter, which often did not include it. Of the 142 complete texts here, eighty-seven include the *notificatio*.

Under Pandulph the most common form was *noverit universitas vestra*, with eight instances, of which seven are followed by accusative and infinitive. There also occur, once each, *notum sit universitati vestre quod*, *ad vestram volumus pervenire notitiam*, and *universitati vestre volumus esse notum*. In Blundeville's episcopate, while *noverit universitas vestra* occurs thirteen times, nine of these are in favour of the cathedral priory. Far more frequent, with thirty-nine instances, are variations, in the order of words, of *ad universorum notitiam volumus pervenire*. *Universitati vestre notum fieri volumus* occurs twice, *ad omnium volumus pervenire notitiam* once, and a simple *noveritis* on six occasions. Under Raleigh *noverit universitas vestra* becomes the most common formula, occurring eleven times, but five other forms occur once or twice each.

NARRATIO AND DISPOSITIO

As was noted of earlier Norwich episcopal *acta*, the form of the central part of the text varies almost infinitely, and no meaningful generalisations can be made.[285] Some *acta* provide a brief statement of the virtues of the religious community which is the beneficiary (nos. 2, 49, 49A, 86, 148) or the desirability of helping it in its need (nos. 5, 15, 39, 130). Sometimes there is a brief account of the recent history of a church, for example, the circumstances which now allowed the bishop to unite *personatus* and vicarage (nos. 17, 56), caused a vacancy by deprivation (no. 8), necessitated collation because of a long vacancy (no. 58) or resulted in the modification of a predecessor's provisions (nos. 91, 128). There might be a reference to the grant by a lay person which had prompted the bishop's action (nos. 26, 72, 111–2, 118), or to the request for episcopal confirmation by the beneficiaries (nos. 31, 133, 150–1)

---

[285] *EEA* 6 p. lxvii.

or by an episcopal colleague (no. 53). In the case of one new community, the story of its foundation is rehearsed (nos. 107, 109). In judicial decisions, the course of dispute and litigation is often recorded in various degrees of detail (nos. 1, 10, 37, 49B, 96, 122, 152). The bishop might specify that he had learned certain things from the *acta* of his predecessors (nos. 62, 73–4) or, most interestingly, from the *matricula* of the church of Norwich (no. 59).

The *narratio* was normally followed by the *dispositio*, the effective core of the *actum*. In cases of the confirmation of a single church or property this might be extremely terse, but general confirmations rehearsed at length all the possessions, or certain categories such as tithes or pensions, within the diocese (nos. 49, 74, 76–9, 95, 121, 125, 133, 138, 148), which might include confirmation of assets legitimately acquired in the future. The establishment of a vicarage upon the appropriation of a church could vary from the stipulation merely that it should be honourable and competent, through the specification of its financial value, to a very detailed statement of the sources from which the vicar's revenues should be derived.

Clauses reserving the rights of the church of Norwich and of the bishop and his successors occur frequently, as does reference to the consent of the prior and cathedral chapter to the bishop's *acta*.

THE INSPEXIMUS

The charter by which the *actum* or *acta* of the bishop's predecessors was inspected, normally recited, and confirmed came into frequent usage in the episcopate of John de Gray (1200–1214).[286] Under Pandulph the verb used was *vidimus*, and there are three such *acta*, two reciting grants by lay persons to the cathedral priory (nos. 19–20), one confirming a charter of bishop Gray for Walden (no. 25).

From the episcopate of Thomas de Blundeville there are extant twenty-two *inspeximus* charters, in twelve of which the charter inspected is recited, in the remainder of which reference is merely made to the inspection. In twelve cases the *inspeximus* was noted immediately after the salutation, in the other ten *inspexisse* follows a notification clause. Under Raleigh, *inspeximus* occurs twice, as compared with four instances of the notification of an inspection.

---

[286] *EEA* 6 p. lxviii.

INIUNCTIO

By the early thirteenth century the injunctive clause was confined almost entirely to mandates directed to subordinates (nos. 3, 9, 33, 67), although it occurs in the course of the *narratio* of no. 1.

SANCTIO

This clause too was almost redundant. It occurs only once in a solemn charter in favour of Wymondham, based on an earlier model (no. 121). This is balanced by a single benediction in a general confirmation for Lewes priory (no. 74).

CORROBORATIO

The great majority of episcopal grants and confirmations have after the *dispositio* or *inspeximus* a corroborative clause. Most of these, in all three episcopates, begin *in cuius* (or less frequently *huius*) *rei testimonium*, but many others are introduced by a wide variety of conjunctive clauses. There is frequent reference to the desire that a grant or confirmation should not be doubted in the future. Almost universally they refer to the making, as testimony, of a written record (*litteras*, *scriptum*), and the affixing of the bishop's seal (*sigillum*, or in two cases for St Benet's, *signum* (nos. 136–7)).

ESCHATOCOL

At the conclusion of episcopal *acta*, a dating clause had now become the norm, although the survival of four original charters without a date (nos. 39, 78, 96, 145) reveals quite clearly that this was not invariable. It is interesting that of sixteen *acta* which might be expected to have a dating clause but do not (that is, excluding indulgences or mandates to individuals), ten, including three originals, are in favour of the cathedral priory. The place is normally expressed by *apud* with the accusative, but occasionally by the locative case.

Where the day and month is given, which is in the great majority of cases, under both Pandulph Verracclo and William Raleigh it is invariably according to the Roman calendar. Under Thomas Blundeville, there is greater variety; on forty occasions the Roman calendar is used, but in sixteen *acta* the liturgical calendar is employed, and in three cases dating is by modern usage (nos. 31, 69, 92). Three of Blundeville's *acta* are dated by month and year, either of grace or pontifical, only (nos. 74–5, 106), and three by the year of grace only (nos. 73, 87, 93). More generally, as for the year, Pandulph's scribes on nine occasions used the pope's pontifical year, twice the year of grace, and five times his own pontifical year, once in conjunction with the year of grace (no. 25).[287] Under Blundeville, the bishop's pontifical year was the norm, the year of grace being used only six times, four times in conjunction with the pontifical year (nos. 37, 49B, 73–4, 87, 93). Under William Raleigh, too, *acta* were normally dated by the pontifical year, but three times by the year of grace, once with the pontifical year also (nos. 135, 138–9). The use of a datary, and of the *per manum* clause, almost habitual under bishop John de Gray but not occurring under his two successors, resurfaced more sporadically during the pontificate of William Raleigh; Philip of Sydenham, the bishop's chaplain, acted as datary on six occasions between 30 December 1239 and 9 January 1241 (nos. 128, 132, 135, 138, 140–1), and Roger Pincerna, archdeacon of Sudbury and then of Suffolk, five times between 20 November 1241 and 21 October 1243 (nos. 129, 133, 142, 151–2).

There are, of course, problems relating to the calculation of the year, either of grace or by pontifical years. The evidence for the reckoning of the year of grace in the twelfth and early thirteenth centuries is ambiguous, although indications are accumulating for the early to mid thirteenth century of its commencement on the feast of the Annunciation (25 March). The problem rarely arises in this collection, but the one crucial text is no. 74, an *actum* of bishop Blundeville dated March '1230' in the fifth year of his pontificate. Whether dated from election, restoration of temporalities or consecration, this must be March 1231 by the modern reckoning. No. 73 points in the same way, and nos. 49B and 93, also dated by the year of grace and pontifical year, are not incompatible with the year beginning on 25 March. Therefore, in this edition, on the rare occasions where the year of grace is the sole criterion for dating, it is assumed to have begun on the feast of the Annunciation (25 March).

As for pontifical year, it appears clear that Pandulph dated his from his

---

[287] In three instances Pandulph's acta have day and month only (nos. 9, 13, 19), but this may represent abbreviation by the cartulary scribe.

consecration, delayed almost seven years after his election (no. 25). A slight problem is caused by no. 14, which if correctly dated in the transcript would indicate a reckoning of the pontifical year from some date before his consecration, but long after election or restoration of temporalities; it seems more logical to assume that this was a mistranscription. For Thomas Blundeville, nos. 36 and 41, dated 5 and 17 December in the first year of his pontificate, demonstrate that he was not, at least in these instances, dating from his election in October 1226, royal assent on 5 November or the restoration of temporalities on 21 November 1226, since he is not therein described as elect, and therefore the only conceivable date for reckoning of his pontifical year is his consecration on 20 December 1226. As for Raleigh, since it is certain from his itinerary that his indulgence for Exeter cathedral (no. 131) was granted in June 1242, his third year, his pontifical year cannot be dated from his election (10 April 1239), and thus is most likely dated from his consecration on 25 September 1239. The evidence is not altogether conclusive, but it has been assumed in this edition that the pontifical year is dated from the consecration of the bishop.

There remains the problem of dating those few undated *acta* of William Raleigh, due to the litigious circumstances of his translation to Winchester. The Waverley Annals state that Innocent IV's confirmation of his postulation to Winchester arrived in England on 11 November 1243, and that thereafter he regarded himself as translated to that see (above, p. xxxvi). In view of the highly contentious nature of this matter, it seems unlikely that he would continue thereafter to use his Norwich title, and indeed his last dated *actum* as bishop of Norwich was issued on 16 November 1243 (no. 137A). The terminal date of undated *acta* has therefore been given as November 1243 (nos. 126, 136, 145). There must, however, be a remote possibility that he continued to use the title until royal assent was given on 9 July 1244 to the election at Norwich of Walter Suffield, or even until the temporalities of Winchester were restored to him on 10 September 1244.[288]

FORMAT AND SCRIPT

The majority of the extant original *acta* are in such a format that the vertical measurement of the parchment (including the turn-up) is between half and

---

[288] *Fasti* ii 57, 86.

two thirds than that of the horizontal measurement. Of this group, the shortest horizontal measurement is 130 mm., the longest 230 mm., and the average 170 mm. The shortest vertical measurement is 68 mm., the longest 137 mm., the average 102 mm. Apart from these, a small group of three *acta*, all for the cathedral priory or its dependent hospital of St Paul's, are almost square, with an average measurement of 147 × 140 mm. (nos. 78, 95, 140), and one *actum* for the monks of Norwich is longer than wide (140 × 185 mm., no. 142). The most notable variation from the norm is the elongated pancarte of bishop Blundeville for Lewes priory, in which the vertical measurement is almost twice the horizontal (no. 74). Four of these originals, one of Blundeville and three of Raleigh, are in the form of a chirograph (nos. 96, 142, 144, 152).

As for script, it is difficult to make any intelligent remarks. The two extant original *acta* of Pandulph are in different hands, both probably Italian (nos. 4, 18). Blundeville's *acta* are written in a multiplicity of different, but very similar hands. Nos. 30 and 31, for Battle abbey, are in different hands, as are nos. 38 and 39, for Christ Church Canterbury. Nos. 73 and 74, for Lewes priory, are written by the same scribe; as are nos. 78 and 87, for Norwich cathedral priory. The remaining originals are all in different, but very similar and standardised, hands. Particularly interesting are the two versions of no. 69–one in a standard hand, the other in a very polished charter hand, almost a book hand (Pl. II). Of the nine originals in the name of bishop William Raleigh, it appears that nos. 140, 142 and 152 are in the same hand,[289] but these all relate to the cathedral priory. It is impossible to say with certainty that any two *acta* for different beneficiaries were written in the same hand, and therefore these originals cannot contribute to our knowledge of how many *acta* were produced in the bishop's chancery, and how many by scribes of the beneficiaries.

SEALING

The normal means of affixing the seal, which was almost universally used for these *acta*, was by a parchment tag.[290] The attachment was strengthened

---

[289] From the angle of the writing, the abbreviation signs, the form of 'g' and the heavy shading in 'a' and 'd'. It would almost be possible to match up the 'CYROGRAPHUM' of nos. 142 and 152.

[290] For methods of sealing, see *EEA* 2 pp. xlvi–xlvii.

by a turn-up at the foot of the charter, a single slit was cut through the two thicknesses of parchment, and the tag drawn through the slit to carry the seal. This method is almost invariable—no. 31 is doubtful, but it is likely that the turn-up has been cut off. The only exception is bishop Raleigh's confirmation for Bec, to which the seal is attached by red cords (no. 125). The wax of extant seals and fragments is normally green; the only exceptions are no. 38 (red) and nos. 131 and 138 (natural wax varnished light brown).

No example of Pandulph's seal has been found. Of Blundeville's there are nine surviving examples of which only two are in reasonably complete form; there is also a sulphur cast of both seal and counterseal in the British Library's collection.[291] The seal is pointed oval, measuring approx. 80 × 50 mm. It shows a conventional full-length representation of the bishop standing on a carved corbel, dressed in mass vestments, a pastoral staff in his left hand, his right hand raised in benediction. The legend is: + THOMAS DEI GRATIA NORWICENSIS EPISCOPVS. The counterseal, which is invariably applied, is a smaller pointed oval, approx. 40 × 30 mm. It shows the Virgin, seated on a throne set on a corbel, holding the Christ child on her knees, to the right; to the left the bishop is kneeling before her, holding a scroll inscribed AVE. Overhead, a hand of blessing issues from the clouds. To the scroll and hand of blessing is attached the impression of a small antique gem, set in the metal of the matrix, showing the sign of the Zodiac Virgo. The legend is + EST THOME SIGNUM VIRGO. FAC HUNC TIBI DIGN(UM).

There are extant only three damaged examples of the seal of William Raleigh as bishop of Norwich, and again a sulphur cast of the seal, but not of the counterseal.[292] It is pointed oval, approx. 80 × 40 mm. It shows the bishop full length, standing on a corbel or platform, vested for mass, a crozier in his left hand, his right hand raised in benediction. The background is diapered faintly with a double reticulated pattern, lozengy with a small indistinct ornament in each space. In the field on either side at hip level there is a small carved opening enclosing a (saint's) head, and below these the characters W . . . II. Of the legend, only . . . ORWIC EP . . . remains. The counterseal, oval, approx. 55 × 35 mm., shows a conventional representation of the Trinity, and the legend can be conjecturally reconstructed from the two examples where part of it remains as: + TE WILLELME ROGO TRINI[TAS ET] VNVS EGO.

---

[291] BL seal lvii 92, 93.
[292] BL seal lvii 95.

EDITORIAL METHOD

These *acta* of the early thirteenth-century bishops of Norwich have been edited in accordance with the plan described in Professor Smith's introduction to the first volume of the series, except that now all texts, including copies printed elsewhere in modern editions, are here presented in full.

Original *acta* are given the siglum A (or A^1 and A^2 in the case of duplicates). Where an original is extant, it has not normally been collated with copies; but where there survive only transcripts, these have been collated and most variants noted — and most especially this principle has been applied to personal and place names. Any *actum* of which the text has been lost, but the existence of which is certain, is noted as a mention and included in the main numerical sequence with an asterisk preceding its number. It should be noted, however, that very many of the references included in Appendix II, where there is mention of an action rather than a written *actum*, by the early thirteenth century almost certainly represent documents now lost.

Within each episcopate the *acta* are printed in alphabetical sequence according to beneficiary or addressee, or the person or corporation primarily affected by judicial mandates or decisions. Under each beneficiary an attempt has normally been made to arrange documents in chronological order.

The majority of these *acta* are dated. Where they are not, or where the date in the text is not precise, the dating limits are placed in square brackets after the caption, and where these are narrower than the dates of the pontificate, they are justified in the notes appended to individual documents. The modern practice of beginning the year on January 1 has been used throughout.

The usual aids to chronology have been employed throughout, most especially the new edition of Le Neve's *Fasti*, *Medieval Religious Houses: England and Wales*, the *Handbook of British Chronology* and the *Handbook of Dates for Students of English History*. Wherever dating criteria are given without reference, one of these invaluable works may be assumed to have provided the essential information.

PANDULPH VERRACCLO

1. Battle Abbey

Settlement, at the request of the parties, of a dispute between the monks and William of Rotherfield, archdeacon of Richmond, concerning the church of Aylsham. They have agreed that the bishop's award should be observed, on penalty of £300 to be exacted from their benefices within his diocese. Perpetual silence is imposed on William in this matter, and he is to swear to withdraw from any action against the monks and to renounce all claim in the church. The monks are to provide him with annual revenue of £12, either from a lay fee or an ecclesiastical benefice, for his lifetime only; it is not to be alienated and shall revert to Battle after his death.

Thetford, 19 September 1224

B = San Marino, Huntington Library, Battle Abbey Papers vol. 29 (Battle cartulary) fo. 84r–v (73r–v). s. xiii ex.

Pandulphus[a] Dei gratia episcopus Norwicensis universis presentes litteras inspecturis salutem in Domino. Notum sit universitati vestre quod cum inter dilectos filios abbatem et conventum de Bello ex una parte et Willelmum de Redhenfeld' archidiaconum Richemund' ex altera super ecclesia de Elesham questio fuisset diutius agitata et ab utraque parte super ea processum, tandem mutuo volentes parcere laboribus et expensis super tota causa ipsa, provisioni nostre se absolute et libere supposuerunt, in manibus nostris ab utraque parte corporali prestito iuramento quod arbitrio et provisioni nostre super hoc sine aliqua reclamatione parerent; et ad hoc firmius observandum, pena .ccc. librarum si committetur in pios usus convertendarum de assensu partium fuit adiecta, ita ut absque contradictione partium, si aliqua earum ab arbitrio et provisione nostra aliquatenus resiliret, per beneficia [fo. 84v] que habent in episcopatu nostro absque contradictione ipsorum eos ad arbitrium observandum plenius cogere debemus. Nos igitur, ipsius cause meritis plenius consideratis[b] et solum Deum habentes pre oculis in hac parte, de consilio prudentium virorum archidiacono ipsi perpetuum silentium imposuimus super ecclesia memorata, sub debito prestiti iuramenti iniungentes eidem ut monasterio de Bello super ecclesia predicta nullam de cetero moveat questionem et renuntiet omni liti et actioni et quicquid iuris se credidit in ea posse habere, et super hoc litteras suas patentes abbati et conventui de Bello concedat; et quia gratiam venerabilis patris W. archiepiscopi Eboracensis fratris nostri[c] et devotionem ipsius archidiaconi abbati et conventui de Bello credimus fructuosam, eisdem dedimus in mandatis ut ipsi archidiacono in redditibus duodecim libras sive in feodo seculari sive in ecclesiastico beneficio debeant providere et eidem suis patentibus litteris confirmare, ita tamen quod beneficium ipsum post mortem archidiaconi sine diminutione ad monasterium de Bello libere revertatur, omni sibi sublata potestate beneficium ipsum ab[d] iurisdictione monasterii alienandi. De quibus omnibus ne possit in posterum dubitari, has proinde litteras fieri fecimus et sigillo nostro muniri. Actum apud Teford' in domo canonicorum sancti Sepulchri .xiii. kalendas Octobris anno Domini m°. cc°. xxiiii°. Hiis testibus: Ada[e] de Buttel' et sancti Sepulchri de Theford' prioribus, magistro A. archidiacono Sudbir' officiali nostro, Willelmo capellano, Landone, Rustico, Laurentio, Petro de Iull' et Petro de Luca clericis nostris.

[a] Pand' B [b] *There follow eleven words struck through.* [c] sui B [d] a B [e] Adam B

The vicarage (then first mentioned for the first time) had been granted to William of Rotherfield, royal clerk, during the vacancy of the abbey and before 22 April 1213, when it was confirmed to him by the crown (*Rot. Chart.* i 199; the roll is damaged at this point, and the beneficiary's name is printed as 'William de P.', but the confirmation immediately following is to Rotherfield of Walsoken church); for him, see *York Minster Fasti*, ed. C. T. Clay, 2 vols (Yorkshire Archaeological Society Record Series cxxiii–iv, 1958–9) i 46. Two documents issued at the papal *curia* late in 1220 almost certainly reflect an earlier stage of this litigation. On 4 December a dispensation was granted to the archdn to hold all the benefices which he had before the Fourth Lateran Council, and four days later the abbot and convent of Battle were inhibited from giving to anyone churches granted to them for the sustenance of the monks, in which vicars were to be instituted—this injunction was surely issued at their own request (*Reg. Honorius III* nos. 2828, 2842; *CPL* i 77). For the wider context, see Harper-Bill, 'Battle Abbey'.

2. Battle Abbey

Grant in proprios usus *for the monks, with the consent of his cathedral chapter, of the church of Aylsham, saving a vicarage assessed by his official and here detailed. To this vicarage when it is vacant the abbot and convent shall present for institution whom the bishop wishes, and if they fail so to do the bishop and his successors may nevertheless ordain as they will.*

Tivoli, 29 May 1225

B = Lincoln's Inn, ms. Hale 87 (Battle cartulary) fo. 30r–v. s. xiii med. C = San Marino, Huntington Library, Battle Abbey Papers vol. 29 (Battle cartulary) fos. 84v–85r (73v–74r). s. xiii ex. D = ibid. fos. 85v–86r (74v–75r) (*inspeximus* by prior William and convent of Norwich, 30 July 1225).

Omnibus has litteras inspecturis Pandulfus[a] Dei gratia episcopus Norwicensis[b] etc. Licet omnium ecclesiarum nostre diocesis[c] teneamur utilitatibus invigilare, illarum tamen presertim propensius procurare tenemur in quibus Deo devotius deservitur et viri religiosi commorantes in eisdem divino mancipati obsequio bone opinionis et conversationis honeste testimonio commendantur. Cum igitur monasterium de Bello religionis commendabilis censeatur et ibidem Deo laudabiliter serviatur, divine pietatis intuitu et abbatis et fratrum ipsius loci devotione inducti, ecclesiam de Eylesham[d] nostre diocesis[c] ad ipsorum donationem spectantem in proprios usus, de assensu capituli nostri, duximus concedendam, salva vicaria quam per officialem nostrum taxari fecimus in eadem, ad quam quotiens[e] vacare contigerit nobis et successoribus nostris quem voluerimus predicti abbas et conventus de Bello presentabunt, et nos et successores nostri absque contradictione aliquorum instituemus eundem. Et ne de portione vicarie possit inposterum dubitari, presentibus litteris universa que vicariam contingunt duximus exprimenda, videlicet altaragium[f] totum cum minutis decimis et primitiis ac omnibus oblationibus, domum cum parco et gardino, redditus assisos, molendinum et pretium consuetudinum, et campum quod vocatur campus ultra aquam, et campum sub parco de Causton', cum omnibus utilitatibus et pertinentiis eorum. Vicarius autem qui pro tempore fuerit canonicam reverentiam et obedientiam[g] nobis et successoribus nostris prestabit secundum morem et consuetudinem ecclesie Norwicensis.[b] Et si in aliquo excesserit pro quo debeat corrigi vel removeri, per nos et successores nostros removebitur et corrigetur. Et si forte vacante vicaria abbas et conventus de Bello neglexerint prout dictum est de voluntate nostra personam ydoneam presentare, nos nichilominus et successores nostri libere ordinabimus de eadem, reservata nobis potestate addendi vel corrigendi circa factum ipsius vicarie si quid viderimus corrigendum. Preterea sciendum est quod vicarius ipse omnia onera canonica ad ipsam ecclesiam spectantia sustinebit. Et ne de hoc possit inposterum dubitari, has litteras fieri fecimus et sigillo nostro muniri. Actum[h] apud Tybure quarto kalendas Iunii [j]pontificatus domini Honorii pape tertii anno nono.[j]

[a] Pand' C, D   [b] Nortwicensis B   [c] dyocesis B   [d] Eilesham B; Eylisham D   [e] cum B   [f] altalagium C, D   [g] obedientiam et reverentiam C, D   [h] Act' B   [j-j] *struck through* C, D

In 1254 the monks' portion in the church was valued at £33 6s 8d and the vicarage at £20 (*VN* 367); the vicar received in addition a portion of 6s 8d in Stiffkey St John (ibid. 373). In 1291 the rectory and vicarage were assessed respectively at £46 13s. 4d. and £18 13s. 4d. (*Taxatio* 83). The manor of Aylsham was held by Bury St Edmunds (*VN* 48, 541–42).

3. Battle Abbey

Mandate to master A[lan] of Beccles, archdeacon of Sudbury and his official, and to Lando the clerk, his proctor. Having received their assessment of a vicarage in the church of Aylsham, he has accordingly ordained it as stated in letters to the abbot and convent [no. 2], whom he hereby orders them to induct into corporal possession of the church. Tivoli, 31 May 1225

> B = San Marino, Huntington Library, Battle Abbey Papers vol. 29 (Battle cartulary) fo. 86r (75r). s. xiii ex.

Pandulphus[a] Dei gratia episcopus Norwicensis dilectis filiis magistro A. archidiacono Subir' officiali suo et Landoni clerico et procuratori suo salutem et benedictionem. Litteras quas nobis misistis super taxatione vicarie ecclesie de Eylesham vidimus et intelleximus diligenter, et consideratis universis que continebantur in eis, vicariam ipsam sic duximus ordinandam prout in litteris quas abbati et conventui de Bello fecimus de ecclesia ipsa in proprios usus concessa videatis contineri. Quare monemus discretionem vestram et mandamus ut abbatem predictum in possessionem ipsius ecclesie secundum formam concessionis nostre inducatis et faciatis pacifice possidere. Et si ambo hiis exequendis non poteritis interesse, tu fili Lando ea nichilominus exequeris. Dat' apud Tybure pridie kalendas Iunii [b-] (pontificatus domini Honorii pape tertii anno nono).[-b]

> [a] Pand' B [b-b] *struck through and illegible in* B, *supplied from no. 2.*

4. Battle Abbey

Collation to Roffridus, the bishop's nephew, of the vicarage of the church of Aylsham. Rieti, 27 December 1225

> A = PRO, E327/533. Endorsed: Pandulfus, de ecclesia de Eylesham (s. xiii); approx. 130 × 66 + 12 mm.; parchment tag, seal missing.
> Pd from A in Madox, *Formulare* no. 533.

Universis presentes litteras inspecturis Pandulfus[a] Dei gratia episcopus Norwicensis salutem in Domino. Noverit universitas vestra nos divine pietatis intuitu contulisse vicariam ecclesie de Helisham dilecto filio Roffrido nepoti nostro ipsumque canonice instituisse vicarium in eadem, salvis nobis et successoribus nostris consuetudinibus et dignitatibus episcopalibus. In cuius rei testimonium has litteras sibi duximus concedendas. Act' Reate .vi. kalendas Ianuarii pontificatus domini Honorii tertii pape anno decimo.

> [a] Pandl' A

'Contulisse' is used in some of Pandulph's *acta* when he is certainly admitting at the presentation of a patron (nos. 7, 13, 18, in the latter two cases in conjunction with 'instituisse'). The absence here of any mention of presentation by the abbot and convent suggests that the bp is collating in the later canonical sense, in accordance with the terms of no. 2, although this need in no way imply Battle's opposition to Roffridus.

5. Bury, St Edmund's Abbey

Grant to the monks in proprios usus, *with the assent of the prior and convent of Norwich, for the increase of hospitality and alms, of the church of St Mary, Mildenhall, saving a vicarage of twenty-five marks taxed by master Alan his official and Alexander of Bassingbourn his seneschal, to which at each vacancy they shall present that suitable* persona *whom the bishop and his successors may wish. If at a vacancy of the vicarage the abbot and convent should fail to present, the bishop and his successors may institute without their consent. The vicarage shall consist of all the altarage, estimated at twelve marks, except for the tithes of the hall; the tithes of various tofts (specified); and the abbot and convent have granted to the vicar the houses of the* persona, *with an inner court and a dovecote therein. The vicar shall swear loyalty to the bishop and his successors, and that he will faithfully serve the church and alienate nothing from it, nor will he defraud the churches of Norwich and Bury St Edmunds of their rights, but rather will serve honestly to the best of his ability and will discharge all canonical obligations. If he is delinquent, he will submit to episcopal correction, and even to removal by the bishop should his faults so demand.*

Downton [Wilts.], 20 December 1219

B = CUL ms. Ff ii 33 (sacrist's register) fos. 74v–75r. s. xiii ex. C = PRO, DL42/5 (cellarer's cartulary) fo. 26r–v (16r–v). s. xiii ex. D = CUL ms. Mm iv 19 (vestry register) fos. 233v–34r. s. xiii ex. E = BL ms. Add. 7096 (abbot Curteys's register) fos. 106r–v. s. xv med. F = CUL ms. Add. 4220 (cellarer's register) fos. 102v–103r. s. xv med.

Universis has litteras inspecturis Pandulphus[a] Dei gratia Norwicensis[b] electus domini pape camerarius[c] apostolice sedis legatus salutem in Domino. Licet universa loca religiosa pro reverentia Dei diligere teneamur, monasteria tamen immediate ad sacrosancte ecclesie Romane iurisdictionem spectantia in quibus divino sunt mancipati obsequio tenemur uberiore caritate amplecti et in quibus secundum Deum possumus confovere quo specialius tuitioni beati Petri subesse noscuntur et nos ex legationis nostre[d] officio sumus eisdem artius obligati. Hinc est quod[e] monasterium sancti Eadmundi[f] Norwicensis[b] diocesis tanquam ecclesie Romane filiam specialem pia volentes consideratione fovere et eiusdem profectibus in posterum providere, ecclesiam sancte Marie de

Mildenhale^g Norwicensis^b diocesis^h cum omnibus pertinentiis suis abbati et conventui monasterii prefati in proprios usus ad hospitalitatis et elemosinarum ac alia pia opera uberius exercenda de consensu filiorum dilectorum prioris et conventus Norwicensis^b perpetuo duximus concedendam, salva vicaria viginti quinque marcarum quam de assensu et voluntate dictorum abbatis et conventus per dilectos filios magistrum^j Alanum officialem et Alexandrum de Basingeburn'^k senescallum fideles nostros taxari fecimus in eadem, ad quam quotiens^l ipsam vacare contigerit^m nobis et successoribus nostris personam idoneam quam nos et successores nostri voluerimus sine difficultate seu alicuius pravitatis et contradictionis obstaculo presentabunt, ^n-et nos et successores nostri libere et quiete auctoritate diocesana ^o-in prefata ecclesia^-o vicarium instituemus eundem.^-n Et si abbas et conventus prefati omiserint vel neglexerint aliquem nobis vel successoribus nostris ut dictum est cum vacaverit presentare, nos et successores nostri eis irrequisitis vicarium instituemus ibidem. Et ne inter ipsos et vicarium qui^p postquam a Norwicensi^b episcopo fuerit institutus materia possit scandali^q suboriri, universa que ad vicariam pertinent de voluntate ipsorum taxata^r litteris presentibus duximus exprimenda, totum videlicet altaragium estimatum^s duodecim^t marcis^u cedet vicarie, exceptis decimis aule; item decime toftarum, exceptis toftis forinsecis in campo^v de Tremhowe^w a dominico ad capud^x fossati per viam de Tremhowe^y versus meridiem usque ad dominicum aule ad Cadehowes usque in mariscum, salvo dominico; in campis de Stapehowe^z a dominico aule usque ad Shinemer'^aa inter viam de Stapehowe^z et mariscum versus aquilonem usque ad viam de Fulforde^bb et in longitudine eiusdem vie usque ad Bradehowe,^cc salvo dominico; et per viam de Staphowe^z semper per mariscum usque ad culturam predicti Shinemer'^aa ad pretium tresdecim^dd marcarum. Preterea concesserunt abbas et conventus vicario domos in quibus persona habitabit et curiam interiorem et columbarium infra curiam situm, secundum terminos a predictis clericis nostris in predicta taxatione distinctos. Ipse autem vicarius in presentia nostra vel officialis nostri vel coram alio cui hoc duxerit committendum nobis et successoribus nostris fidelitatem secundum consuetudinem ecclesie Norwicensis^b prestabit et iurabit quod ecclesie deserviet bona fide et quod de hiis que ad vicariam et ecclesiam ipsam pertinent nichil alienabit nec defraudabit iura ecclesie Norwicensis^b nec monasterii sancti Eadmundi,^f sed potius quantum cum Deo poterit et honestate meliorare curabit et omnia onera canonica sustinebit. Ipse autem^ee vicarius si deliquerit^ff correctioni episcopi subiacebit et removebitur etiam per eundem si tales fuerint ipsius excessus quod merito debeat amoveri.^gg Et ne super hiis possit aliquatenus in posterum dubitari, has literas fieri fecimus et sigillo nostro muniri. Dat' apud Dunton'^hh .xiii. kalendas Ianuarii pontificatus domini Honorii .iii. pape anno quarto.^ij

^{a} Pandulfus B; Pandulf' D; Pandulff' F ^{b} Norwyc' F ^{c} et *inserted* B ^{d} nostre *om.* F ^{e} quoddam F ^{f} Edmundi B ^{g} Mildenhal' BCD; Mildenhalie F ^{h} dyocesis B ^{j} D *inserts* et ^{k} Bassingburn B; Besingburnn F ^{l} cum E ^{m} vacare contigerit ipsam B $^{n-n}$ *om.*C $^{o-o}$ *om.* B ^{p} qui *interlined* d, *om* C,F ^{q} scandali possit F ^{r} taxati C,F ^{s} extimatum F ^{t} .xii. B ^{u} marcarum F ^{v} campis C,F ^{w} Tremhow F ^{x} caput F ^{y} Thremhowe B ^{z} Stapehow B ^{aa} Schinemere B; Schinemer' F ^{bb} Fulford E,F ^{cc} Badehowe B ^{dd} .xiii. B, F ^{ee} etiam B ^{ff} dereliquerit B; delinquit C ^{gg} ammoveri F ^{hh} Doneton' C,E; Doniton F ^{ji} F *adds* ab incarnatione auctor' m° cc° xx°.

The church had been appropriated to Bury by bp John de Gray in 1205 (*EEA* 6 no. 332). For its complex history before then, see ibid., note. In 1211 bp Gray instructed that when the church was vacated by the present *persona* the monks might enter into possession (ibid. no. 333). The vicarage was a valuable one, assessed at £20 both in 1254 and 1291; the monks of Battle continued to receive their portion of £13 6s. 8d. (*VN* 432; *Taxatio* 121).

That this *actum* was given at Downton in Wiltshire, rather than another Downton or Dunton, is strongly suggested by Pandulph's itinerary; see Appx III, p. 176.

*6. Canterbury, St Augustine's Abbey

Indulgence of twenty days granted to benefactors of the abbey.
[29 May 1222 × 16 September 1226]

Indulgentia P. Dei gratia Norwicensis episcopi viginti dierum.

Mentioned in BL Cotton Julius D ii (St Augustine's register) fo. 68r (list of indulgences). s. xiv in.

After Pandulph's consecration. This indulgence was possibly granted as he returned to England before 4 June 1223, or more likely as he departed for what was to be the last time in November 1224; see also no. 12.

7. Castle Acre Priory

Institution, at the presentation of the monks, of William of Newton, priest, to the vicarage of [West] Barsham.   Gaywood, 17 April 1221

B = BL ms. Harley 2110 (Castle Acre cartulary) fo. 128v (122v). s. xiii med.

Universis Cristi fidelibus presentes litteras inspecturis Pandulphus^a Dei gratia Norwicensis electus domini pape camerarius apostolice sedis legatus salutem in Domino. Noverit universitas vestra nos divine pietatis intuitu vicariam ecclesie de Westbarsh' vacantem cum omnibus pertinentiis et rationibus suis ad presentationem dilectorum filiorum prioris et monachorum de Castellacra patronorum verorum ipsius ecclesie dilecto filio Willelmo de Neuton' presbitero canonice contulisse. In cuius rei testimonium has litteras fieri fecimus et sigillo nostro muniri. Dat' apud Gath'[b] .xv. kalendas Maii pontificatus domini Honorii pape .iii. anno .v.

[a] Pand' B   [b] *sic* B, *rectius* Gaywde, Gawde (cf. nos. 8–9)

This is the first mention of a vicarage established in this church. In 1254 the church was valued at £15 and the vicarage at £2 (*VN* 420).

8. Castle Acre Priory

Notification that following the deprivation in the Easter synod of 1220 of James, once his clerk, after his conviction for many transgressions, and his grant at the presentation of the monks of the vicarage of South Creake to J[ohn] Iudicis de Urbe, clerk, he granted the farm of the vicarage to the monks for fifteen marks p.a., to be paid at Pentecost to J[ohn] or his representative in the sacristy of Bury St Edmunds.   Gaywood, 20 April 1221

B = BL ms. Harley 2110 (Castle Acre cartulary) fo. 128v (122v). s. xiii med.

Universis has litteras inspecturis Pandulphus[a] Dei gratia Norwicensis electus domini pape camerarius apostolice sedis legatus salutem in Domino. Ad vestram volumus pervenire notitiam quod cum vicariam de Sudcrec dilecto filio I. iudicis clerico de Urbe contulerimus ad presentationem dilectorum filiorum prioris et monachorum de Castelacra, qua Iacobum quondam clericum nostrum cui contuleramus eandem privavimus in sinodo Norwicensi Pasche pontificatus domini Honorii .iii. pape anno .iiii., exigentibus culpis suis et pro multibus excessibus quibus fuit in presentia nostra convictus, nos vicariam ipsam dictis priori et monachis ad firmam concessimus pro .xv. marcis eidem clerico vel certo nuntio suo in festo Pentecoste apud Sanctum Edmundum in sacristaria sancti Edmundi singulis annis solvendis. In cuius rei testimonium has litteras fieri fecimus et eas sigillo nostro muniri. Dat' apud Gaywde .xii. kalendas Maii anno domini Honorii .iii. pape quinto.

[a] P. B

Mr James was a papal scribe and *familiaris*, probably but not certainly Italian. On 16 March 1218 the provost of St Omer was ordered to confer a prebend on him (a mandate which had not yet been put into effect on 17 April 1219). On 11 May 1218 bp-elect Robert of Ely was ordered to provide him with a benefice (Sayers, *Papal Government* 199). He probably came to England with Pandulph in summer 1218, and was certainly in his household on 22 April 1219 (*CPL* i 70). The unspecified transgressions which led to the loss of this vicarage partially explains his temporary deprivation of the office of papal scribe, but he was absolved by the pope on 18 August 1220 and was required to make satisfaction to the legate and be obedient to him (ibid. 75). He signs again as papal scribe from 1224 and continued in that office under pope Gregory IX (Sayers, *Papal Government* 43). For the de Iudice family, see F. Gregorov-

9. Castle Acre Priory

Mandate to the prior and canons of Westacre. Since James, his own clerk, has been deprived of South Creake on account of his transgressions, he has collated the vicarage to John Iudicis de Urbe, clerk, at the presentation of the monks of Castle Acre, to whom he has granted it at farm. The canons, as James's proctors, are prohibited on pain of excommunication from molesting the monks nor demanding anything from them in relation to the vicarage.

Gaywood, 20 April [1221]

B = BL ms. Harley 2110 (Castle Acre cartulary) fo. 128v (122v). s. xiii med.

Pandulfus Dei gratia Norwicensis electus domini pape camerarius apostolice sedis legatus dilectis filiis priori et canonicis de Westacra salutem in Domino. Cum vicariam de Sudcrec ad presentationem dilectorum filiorum prioris et monachorum de Castelacra contulerimus dilecto filio Iohanni iudicis de Urbe clerico, qua vicaria Iacobum quondam clericum nostrum cui contuleramus eandem privavimus exigentibus culpis suis et pro multis excessibus quibus fuit in presentia nostra convictus, nos eam prefatis priori et monachis ad firmam concessimus, verumque vos sicut dicitur ipsius Iacobi procuratores fuistis, monemus discretionem vestram districte vobis sub pena excommunicationis precipiendo mandantes quatinus dictos priorem et monachos occasione illius procurationis nullatenus molestetis nec aliquid exigatis ab ipsis nec ulterius de procuratione ipsa vos aliquatenus intromittatis. Dat' apud Gawde .xii. kalendas Maii.

The mandate was obviously issued on the same day as no. 8.

10. Castle Acre Priory

Notification of the settlement before papal judges-delegate, the priors of Thetford and Ixworth and the sacrist of Bury, of a dispute between master Alan of Beccles, rector of Bunwell, and the monks, concerning tithes which he claimed should pertain to his church. The rector and his successors shall hold the tithes of the monks for an annual payment of 5s.

[19 July 1221 × 29 May 1222]

B = BL ms. Harley 2110 (Castle Acre cartulary) fo. 128v (122v). s. xiii med.

Universis has litteras inspecturis Pandulphus[a] Dei gratia Norwicensis electus domini pape camerarius salutem in Domino. Cum dilectus filius noster magister Alanus de Becles rector ecclesie de Bunewell' dilectos filios priorem et conventum monachorum de Acra coram de Theford' et de Yxewrth' prioribus et sacrista sancti Edmundi super quibusdam decimis quas ad ecclesiam suam de Bunewell' spectare contendebat de iure auctoritate apostolica traxisset in causam, lis tandem inter eos in hunc modum coram dictis iudicibus conquievit, videlicet quod predictus magister et successores sui tenebunt dictas decimas inperpetuum nomine dictorum prioris et conventus, solvendo inde annuatim eisdem priori et conventui .v. solidos ad duas sinodos Norwicenses, scilicet .xxx. denarios in una sinodo et .xxx. denarios in alia sinodo. Et ne hoc deceterro possit in dubium revocari, nos ad instantiam utriusque partis conventionem ipsam sicut legitime ac provide facta est ab utraque parte sponte recepta auctoritate presentium confirmamus.

[a] Pand' B

Issued between the resignation of the legatine commission and Pandulph's consecration (see Appx III, 177–8). Mr Alan of Beccles was the bp's official. In 1254 the monks received only a portion of 5s. *p.a.* from the church; the rectory was assessed at £13 13s. 4d., the portion of the monks of Lewes at £4 and that of the monks of Sées at 10s. (*VN* 411–12).

It is impossible to determine which of the priors of Thetford was judge-delegate in this case; both were commissioned by pope Honorius III (Sayers, *Papal Judges Delegate* 30, 323).

11. Castle Acre Priory

Institution of master Robert of Bilney as persona *of the church of St Mary, Haverhill, with the chapel in the marketplace, at the presentation of the monks.* [29 May 1222 × 16 September 1226]

B = BL ms. Harley 2110 (Castle Acre cartulary) fo. 128v (122v). s. xiii med.

Pandulphus[a] Dei gratia episcopus Norwicensis universis presentes litteras inspecturis salutem in Domino. Noverit universitas vestra nos ecclesiam sancte Marie Haverhille cum capella ad forum cum omnibus pertinentiis et rationibus suis dilecto filio magistro Roberto de Bylneia clerico canonice concessisse, ipsumque in eis ad presentationem prioris et monachorum de Acra instituisse personam, salvis consuetudinibus et rationibus episcopalibus et dignitatibus ecclesie Norwicensis. In cuius rei testimonium has litteras nostro sigillo munitas sibi ducimus concedendas.

[a] Pand' B

The monks had previously presented mr Ranulf of Harpley in the time of bp John of Oxford, who had granted them the church *in proprios usus* on his death or resignation (*EEA* 6 nos.

197–98). Harpley and Bilney were both episcopal clerks who subsequently served as official (see pp. xliii–vi).

12. Dover Priory

Indulgence of twenty days granted to those of his diocese, and of other dioceses whose diocesans ratify this grant, whenever penitent and confessed they shall grant alms to, or shall devoutly visit, the altar of St Thomas the Martyr in the priory church. [29 May 1222 × 16 September 1226]

B = Lambeth Palace Library ms. 241 (Dover priory cartulary) fos. 55v–56r. s. xiv ex.

Universis sancte matris ecclesie filiis ad quos presentes litere pervenerint Pandulphus permissione divina Norwycensis episcopus[a] salutem in Domino sempiternam. Gratum, obsequium et Deo acceptum totiens impendere [fo. 56r] opinamur quotiens mentes fidelium ad caritatis et devotionis opera excitamus, ut exinde reddantur divine gratie aptiores. De Dei igitur misericordia, beate Marie virginis gloriose, beatorum apostolorum Petri et Pauli atque sancti Thome martiris meritis confidentes, omnibus parochianis nostris et aliis Cristi fidelibus de peccatis suis penitentibus et confessis, quorum diocesani hanc nostram indulgentiam ratam habuerint, qui altare sancti Thome predicti in prioratu Dovorr' per pias elemosinarum elargitiones vel devotis precibus in honore Dei et ipsius martiris duxerint quandocumque visitandis viginti dies de iniuncta sibi penitentia misericorditer relaxamus. Valete.

[a] episcopus *interlined*

After Pandulph's consecration. This indulgence was possibly granted as he returned to England before 4 June 1223, or more likely as he departed for what was to be the last time in November 1224; see also no. 6.

The terms of this indulgence are not entirely clear, but it appears most probable that it was granted to those properly shriven who either gave alms or visited in person; such terms, designed not to exclude those with no pecuniary resources who might make a personal visit, are common in later medieval episcopal indulgences.

13. Ely Cathedral Priory

Institution of master Richard of Barking as persona *of the church of Melton, at the presentation of the prior and convent.* Botley, 1 February [1220]

B = CUL, EDR ms. G3/28 (Ely cartulary) p. 206a–b. s. xiii ex. C = Bodl. ms. Laud misc. 647 (*Liber Eliensis*) fo. 126r. s. xiv in.

Pandulfus Dei gratia Norwicensis[a] electus domini pape camerarius apostolice sedis legatus omnibus has litteras inspecturis salutem in Domino. Universitati vestre volumus esse notum nos intuitu Dei dilecto filio magistro Richardo de Berking' ad presentationem dilectorum filiorum[b] prioris et monachorum Elyensium ecclesiam de Melton'[c] cum omnibus pertinentiis et rationibus suis contulisse ipsumque in ea instituisse personam. In cuius rei testimonium presentes litteras fieri fecimus et nostro sigillo muniri. Dat' Botel' kalendas Februarii.

[a] Norwycensis B   [b] B *has space for an initial*   [c] Melton' C

Botley is now in the city of Oxford; Pandulph was at Eynsham on the previous day.

14. Ely Cathedral Priory

Institution of John of Horsey, clerk, as persona *of the church of Orford, at the presentation of the prior and convent.*

Santa Maria de Palladio, Rome, 17 March [? 1226]

B = CUL, EDR ms. G3/28 (Ely cartulary) p. 206b. s. xiii ex. C = Bodl. ms. Laud misc. 647 (*Liber Eliensis*) fo. 126r. s. xiv in.

Pandulfus Dei gratia Norwicensis episcopus universis presentes litteras inspecturis salutem in Domino. Noverit universitas vestra nos divine pietatis intuitu admisisse dilectum filium Iohannem de Horshae clericum ad ecclesiam de Orford'[a] cum omnibus pertinentiis et rationibus suis, ipsumque in ea ad presentationem dilectorum filiorum[b] nostrorum[c] prioris et conventus Elyensis eiusdem ecclesie verorum ut dicitur patronorum canonice instituisse personam, salvis consuetudinibus et rationibus episcopalibus et dignitatibus ecclesie Norwicensis. In cuius rei testimonium has litteras nostras sibi duximus concedendas. Actum Rome apud sanctam Mariam de Palladia .xvi. kalendas Aprilis pontificatus nostri anno quinto.[d]

[a] Oreford' B   [b] filiorum *om*. B   [c] B *has space for an initial*   [d] .v°. C

The fifth year of Pandulph's pontificate gives a date of 17 March 1227, but the bp died on 16 September 1226. It is probable that the cartulary scribes mistranscribed *quarto*, although it must remain possible that the date of Pandulph's consecration, attested only by the Waverley annals, is incorrect.

15. Holme, St Benet's Abbey

Grant in proprios usus *to the monks, with the consent of the prior and convent of Norwich, for the increase of hospitality and alms, of the church of St Katherine, Ludham, with the chapels of St Mary and St John, saving a vicarage of twenty-five marks assessed by master Alan of Beccles, his official, and*

Alexander of Bassingbourn, his seneschal; to which at each vacancy the monks shall present that suitable persona *whom the bishop and his successors may wish; and if at a vacancy they fail to present, the bishop and his successors may institute without their consent. To prevent dissent in the future, the revenues of the vicarage are detailed: the altarage with oblations and lesser tithes, that is of flax, wool, hemp, dairy produce, lambs, piglets, oxen, ganders and hens, with other obventions and with the appurtenances of the free lands, the chapel of St Mary with its appurtenances, the chapel of St John with the tithes of 'Redescroft' from the house of William Puncelot to the marsh and from the king's highway towards the east, and an acre of land in 'Brunescroft' near the church, for the vicar's house. The vicar shall swear fealty to the bishop, that he will serve the church, and that he will alienate nothing from vicarage or church, but will seek rather to augment their resources. He will bear all the burdens of the church, and will not defraud the monks of their rights. If he is delinquent he will submit to episcopal correction, even to removal should his faults so demand.*

London, 8 February 1220

B = BL ms. Cotton Galba E ii (St Benet cartulary) fo. 48r. s. xiii ex. C = Bodl. ms. Norfolk roll 82 (St Benet roll, damaged) a. s. xiv in. D = ibid. b (*inspeximus* by prior William and convent of Norwich, 24 July 1219 × 23 July 1220). E = BL ms. Cotton roll iv 57 (St Benet roll, damaged) no. i. s. xiv. F = Norfolk R.O., DCN 40/8 (St Benet cartulary) fos. 4v–5r (5v–6r). s. xiv ex.

Pandulphus[a] Dei gratia Norwicensis electus domini pape camerarius apostolice sedis legatus universis Cristi fidelibus presentes litteras inspecturis salutem in Domino. Licet universa loca religiosa pro reverentia Dei diligere teneamur, monasteria tamen que ad nostram iurisdictionem spectare noscuntur in quibus viri religiosi Domino famulantur tenemur eo uberiori caritate amplecti et in quibus possumus secundum Deum confovere, quo cure nostre specialius sunt commissa et nos ex regiminis debito eis sumus artius obligati. Hinc est quod monasterium sancti Benedicti de Hulmo, quod ad iurisdictionem Norwicensis ecclesie immediate pertinet, pia consideratione fovere volentes et eiusdem profectibus in posterum providere, ecclesiam sancte Caterine de Ludham cum capellis sancte Marie et beati Iohannis adiacentibus eidem, in quibus abbas et conventus ipsius monasterii ius optinent patronatus, in proprios usus ut hospitalitatis et elemosinarum ac alia pia opera uberius exercere possint, eis de assensu dilectorum filiorum prioris et conventus Norwicensis perpetuo duximus concedendam, salva vicaria viginti quinque marcarum quam de assensu et voluntate predictorum abbatis et fratrum sancti Benedicti de Hulmo per dilectos filios magistrum Alanum de Becles[b] officialem et Alexandrum de Bassingburne[c] senescallum nostros taxari fecimus in eadem; ad quam vicariam quotiens ipsam vacare contigerit nobis et successoribus nostris personam idoneam[d] quam nos et successores nostri voluerimus sine difficultate ac alicuius pravitatis et contradictionis obstaculo presentabunt, et nos et successores nostri libere et absolute auctoritate diocesana in eadem vicarium instituemus eandem. Et si dicti abbas et fratres omiserint vel neglexerint aliquem nobis et successoribus nostris ut dictum est cum vacaverit presentare, nos et successores nostri eis irrequisitis vicarium instituemus ibidem. Et ne inter ipsos et vicarium postquam a Norwicensi episcopo fuerit institutus materia possit scandali suboriri, universa que vicarie competunt auctoritate nostra ut dictum est de assensu ipsorum taxate presentibus duximus litteris exprimenda, videlicet alteragium cum oblationibus et minutis decimis, scilicet cum lino, lano, canabo, lacte, agnis,[e] porcellis, bobus, anceribus,[f] gallinis et ceteris obventionibus et cum pertinentiis liberarum terrarum, et capellam sancte Marie cum pertinentiis et capellam beati Iohannis cum decimis de Redecroft[g] a domo Willelmi Puncelot[h] usque ad mariscum et a via regia versus orientem; item unam acram terre in crofta que vocatur Brunecroft[j] iuxta pratum abbatis prope ecclesiam quam ad edificium vicarii qui pro tempore fuerit abbas et conventus assignaverunt de dominico suo. Ipse autem vicarius nobis et successoribus nostris fidelitatem faciet secundum consuetudinem ecclesie Norwicensis et iurabit etiam quod ecclesie deserviet bona fide et quod de hiis que ad vicariam et ecclesiam ipsam pertinent nichil alienabit, sed potius quantum cum Deo poterit et honestate meliorare curabit. Omnia honera canonica sustinebit. Iura et rationes predictorum fratrum nullatenus defraudabit. Ipse etiam vicarius si deliquerit correctioni episcopi subiacebit et removebitur etiam per eundem si tales fuerint excessus ipsius pro quibus merito debeat ammoveri. Et ne super hiis possit aliquid in posterum dubitari, has litteras fieri fecimus et nostro sigillo muniri. Dat' [l] London' .vi[to]. Idus Februarii pontificatus domini Honorii pape anno quarto.

[a] Pandulfus C D F   [b] Bekles C D   [c] Bassingeburne C; Bassingburn D   [d] ydoneam B D   [e] angnis C D   [f] ancis C D F   [g] Ridecroft B; Redecrofth F   [h] Punceloth F   [j] Brunestoft B; Brunecroft F   [k] ecclesiam ipsam et vicariam B   [l] B *ends here with* etc.

The *inspeximus* by the prior and convent (D) was given in the fourth year of pope Honorius III, and was witnessed by mr Alan of Beccles, Alexander of Bassingbourn and others.

In 1254 the church was valued at £26 13s. 4d. and the vicarage at £5 6s. 8d. (*VN* 414); in 1291 at £28 13s. 4d. and £5 6s. 8d. respectively (*Taxatio* 86b).

16. Holme, St Benet's Abbey

Institution, at the presentation of Abbot R[eginald] and the convent, of Stephen of Ludham, clerk, to the church of Swanton [Abbot].

Stratford, 9 March 1224

B = BL ms. Cotton Galba E ii (St Benet cartulary) fo. 48r. s. xiii ex.

Pandulphus Dei gratia Norwicensis episcopus universis presentes litteras inspecturis salutem in Domino. Noverit universitas vestra nos divine intuitu pietatis admisisse dilectum filium Stephanum de Ludham clericum ad ecclesiam de Swaneton' iuxta Scothowe cum omnibus pertinentiis et rationibus suis, ipsumque in ea ad presentationem R. abbatis et conventus sancti Benedicti de Hulmo eiusdem ecclesie ut dicitur verorum patronorum canonice instituisse personam, salvis consuetudinibus et rationibus episcopalibus et dignitatibus ecclesie Norwicensis. In huius rei testimonium has litteras nostras sibi duximus concedendas. Act' apud Strafford .vii. Idus Martii pontificatus nostri (anno) secundo.

This *actum* was probably issued at the Cistercian monastery of Stratford Langthorne (Ess.), but Stratford St Mary (Sf.) is also possible.

17. Lewes Priory

Unification of the personatus *and vicarage of the church of Letton, and institution of Richard of Kenilworth, the vicar, to the vacant* personatus.

London, 18 October 1218

B = BL ms. Cotton Vesp. F xv (Lewes cartulary) fo. 254v (283v). s. xv med.
Pd (abstract), *Lewes Cartulary Norfolk Portion* no. 118.

Universis has literas inspecturis Pandulphus Dei gratia Norwicensis electus domini pape camerarius apostolice sedis legatus salutem in Domino. Cum dilectus filius Ricardus de Kenilwurthe clericus vicariam in ecclesia de Letton' Norwicensis diocesis canonice possideret et vacaret eiusdem ecclesie personatus, nos personatum et vicariam ipsius ecclesie unientes prefato R. clerico de gratia liberaliter duximus conferendum, salvis in omnibus episcopalibus consuetudinibus et Norwicensis ecclesie dignitate. In cuius rei testimonium presentes literas nostro sigillo munitas sibi duximus concedendas. Dat' London' .xv. kalendas Novembris anno Domini millesimo cc^{mo} xviii^o.

Richard of Kenilworth (then called *magister*) had been instituted to the vicarage on 31 May 1213 (*EEA* 6 nos. 365–66). The church was in 1254 valued at £10 (*VN* 400).

18. Lewes Priory

Institution of Roger of Rising, priest, as persona *of the church of Castle Rising, at the presentation of the prior and convent.*

London, 27 September 1219

A = PRO, E40/14104. Endorsed: Pandulfi Norwicensis electi de ecclesia de Risingges (s. xiii); pressmark; approx. 135 × 65 + 9 mm.; seal missing, parchment tag.

Universis presentes litteras inspecturis Pandulfus Dei gratia Norwicensis electus domini pape camerarius apostolice sedis legatus salutem in Domino. Noverit universitas vestra nos intuitu Dei dilecto filio Rogero de Rising' presbitero ecclesiam de Rising' Norwicensis diocesis cum omnibus pertinentiis et rationibus suis liberaliter contulisse ipsumque in ea ad presentationem dilectorum filiorum prioris et conventus de Lewes ipsius ecclesie sicut dicitur verorum patronorum canonice instituisse personam, salvis in omnibus episcopalibus rationibus et Norwicensis ecclesie dignitatibus. In cuius rei testimonium presentes litteras nostro sigillo signatas sibi duximus concedendas. Dat' London' .v. kalendas Octobris pontificatus domini Honorii pape iii anno quarto.

19. Norwich Cathedral Priory

Vidimus and confirmation of the charter of Robert son of Richard of Worstead, recording his gift in free alms to the monks of the advowson of the church of St Mary, Worstead, with the chapel of St Andrew.

London, 27 September [1219]

B = Norfolk R.O., DCN 405 (cellarer's cartulary) fo. 20 (19v). s. xiii ex.

Universis presentes litteras inspecturis Pandulfus Dei gratia Norwicensis electus domini pape camerarius apostolice sedis legatus salutem in Domino. Vidimus litteras Roberti filiii Ricardi de Wrstede sub hac forma: Notum sit omnibus presentibus et futuris quod ego Robertus filius Ricardi de Wrstede divine pietatis intuitu et pro salute anime mee et·omnium antecessorum meorum et successorum concessi et dedi et hac presenti carta mea confirmavi Deo et ecclesie sancte Trinitatis de Norwico et monachis ibidem Deo servientibus advocationem ecclesie sancte Marie de Wrstede cum capella sancti Andree eiusdem ville et cum omnibus ad eas pertinentibus et omne ius quod habui in eisdem in liberam, puram et perpetuam elemosinam, solutam et quietam inperpetuum de me et heredibus meis. Et ut hec mea concessio et donatio firma et stabilis inperpetuum perseveret, eam presenti scripto et sigilli mei appositione corroboravi. Hiis testibus: domino G. de Bochland, Iohanne de Wrstede, Ricardo de Seng', Iordano de Saukevill' tunc iusticiariis itinerantibus Norff', magistro Alano de Becles, Fulcone Bainyad, Willelmo le Enveyse, Hardrico de Claverham, Adam de Rathlesdane, Ricardo Colet, magistro Ricardo de Stowe, Ricardo de Ingewrth et aliis. Nos igitur donationem ipsam sicut iuste ac rationabiliter facta est ratam et gratam habentes intuitu Dei confirmavimus et presentis scripti patrocinio communivimus. Dat' Londoniis .v. kalendas Octobris.

> The royal justices who attest Robert's charter conducted an eyre in East Anglia in 1219 and were at Norwich between 19 January and 12 March (Crook, *General Eyre* 74–5). The church was appropriated to the monks by bp Blundeville in 1227 and they were inducted into corporal possession in 1235 (nos. 86, 93).
>
> An *inspeximus* by prior Nicholas and the convent of Canterbury, 1249, refers to *acta* of Pandulph, among other bishops, which granted and confirmed *in proprios usus* to the monks of Norwich various churches (*Norwich Cathedral Charters* i no. 271). No general confirmation by Pandulph survives in the Norwich registers, and it is probably nos. 19–20 which were inspected.

20. Norwich Cathedral Priory

Vidimus *of the charter of Agnes de Reflei, recording her gift to the monks of a mediety of the church of All Saints, Wicklewood.*

[October 1218 × 26 July 1221]

> B = Norfolk R.O., DCN 40/2/2 (almoner's cartulary) fo. 42v (33v, 105v). s. xiv in.

Universis has litteras inspecturis Pandulphus Dei gratia Norwicensis episcopus electus domini pape camerarius apostolice sedis legatus salutem in Domino. Vidimus litteras Agnetis mulieris de Reflei sub hac forma: Omnibus sancte matris ecclesie filiis ad quorum notitiam presens scriptum pervenerit Agnes de Reflei salutem in Domino. Noscat universitas vestra me caritatis intuitu pro animabus patris et matris mee et antecessorum meorum concessisse et dedisse et presenti carta confirmasse Deo et ecclesie sancte Trinitatis Norwici et monachis ibidem Deo servientibus ius advocationis medietatis ecclesie omnium sanctorum de Wiclewode in puram et perpetuam elemosinam. Et ut ista mea donatio perpetuum robur optineat, eam presenti scripto et sigilli mei appositione communivi. Testibus etc.

> The date is determined by Pandulph's legation, granted by the pope at Rome on 1 September 1218, but news of which would not have reached England before early October. The donor was the wife of Gilbert Malet; their charter, witnessed by Geoffrey, archdn of Suffolk, and therefore before 30 September 1214, is on fo. 42v of B. The quitclaim by Nigel de Reflei of the mediety granted by his grandmother states that the monks say that the advowson of this mediety pertains to the bp (fos. 42v–43r of B), but bp Blundeville appropriated it to the use of the almoner after the death of *persona* and vicar (no. 89). The advowson of the other

mediety was granted to the monks by Nigel of Happisburgh, chaplain, and was appropriated to the almoner's use by bp Blundeville in 1235 (no. 94).

*21. Royal Justices

Letter testifying that Ascelina, widow of Robert Chevre, has proved that she had been legitimately married to him. Michaelmas term, 1220

Mention of a letter produced in the *curia regis*.
Pd in *CRR* ix 367.

A case was brought by Ascelina against Hamo Chevre concerning a third part of thirty acres with appurtenances in Wixoe, which she successfully claimed as her dower.

*22. Royal Justices

Letter notifying them that Ralph Cosman is excommunicate.

Michaelmas term 1223

Mention of letter produced in the *curia regis*.
Pd in *CRR* xi no. 884.

A case was brought by Ralph Cosman against Simon of Scarning (probably an ecclesiastical official) *de averiis captis*; on production of the bp's letter the case was adjourned *sine die*.

23. Viterbo, Abbey of S. Martino del Monte

Grant in alms to the monks of a mediety of the church of Holkham, the advowson of which they had obtained by the grant of king Henry of England, henceforth to be held in proprios usus, *saving a vicarage assessed at ten marks. According to local custom the monks shall present a vicar to the bishop of Norwich, and after his admission the vicar shall serve [the cure] himself, and be responsible for synodals and all canonical obligations of the mediety.*

Reading, 11 April 1219

B = Rome, Archivo Segreto Vaticano, Reg. Vat. 18 (register of Gregory IX) fo. 315v. s. xiii med. C = ibid., Reg. Vat. 24 (register of Alexander IV) fo. 210v. s. xiii med.
Pd from C in *Reg. Alex. IV* no 1568; (cal.) *Reg. Greg. IX* no. 3834; *CPL* i 165, 339.

Universis Cristi fidelibus ad quos littere iste pervenerint Pandulphus[a] Dei gratia Norwicensis electus domini pape camerarius apostolice sedis legatus, salutem in Domino. Noverit universitas vestra quod nos, considerata honestate et religione abbatis monasterii sancti Martini de monte Viterbii, ordinis Cisterciensis, et fratrum ibidem Deo servientium, medietatem ecclesie de Holcham,

Norwicensis diocesis, cum pertinentiis suis, in qua medietate dictum monasterium ius obtinet patronatus ex donatione domini Henrici regis Anglie illustris, concessimus et donavimus de consensu capituli nostri prefato monasterio in puram et perpetuam elemosinam, habendam et tenendam perpetuo in proprios usus ad paupertatem ipsius monasterii sublevandam, salva vicaria quam taxavimus in proventibus tantum decem marcarum; in qua vicaria vicarius secundum consuetudinem loci ex parte dicti monasterii Norwicensi episcopo presentatus cum admissus fuerit ab eodem deserviet semper in propria persona; et synodalia et alia omnia canonica onera pro medietate ipsius ecclesie sustinebit. In cuius rei testimonium has litteras fieri fecimus et sigillo nostro muniri. Dat' Rading' .iii. idus Aprilis pontificatus domini Honorii pape .iii. anno tertio.

[a] Pand' B, C

For the background to the two medieties of the church, and the grant of the other mediety by William de Montchesney to the Premonstratensian canons of West Dereham, see *EEA* 6 no. 427. On 26 May 1214 king John granted to the Cistercians of Viterbo an annual pension of thirty marks from the royal mediety (*Rot. Chart.* 198b); this grant was confirmed by the legate, Nicholas of Tusculum, and approved by the prior and convent of Norwich, and was subsequently on 20 April 1217 confirmed by pope Honorius III (*CPL* i 45; *Reg. Hon. III* no. 350). The grant of the advowson by the minority government was probably determined upon around William Marshal's deathbed; it was repeated by king Henry III on 13 August 1233, and both appropriation and royal confirmation were confirmed by popes Gregory IX and Alexander IV (as above). By 1254 the canons of Walsingham were farming Viterbo's mediety. In that year the portions of the abbot of Dereham and the prior of Walsingham were valued at £53 6s. 8d., the vicarage at £3 and the tithes pertaining to Castle Acre priory at £1 10s. (*VN* 373; Blomefield, *Norfolk* ix 243). In 1291 the portions of both Viterbo and West Dereham were assessed at £23 6s. 8d. and the vicarage at £4 6s. 8d. (*Taxatio* 81).

On the death of Denise de Montchesney, wife of Hugh de Vere, in 1313, the lands and rights of Montchesney passed to Aymer de Valence, earl of Pembroke (J. R. S. Phillips, *Aymer de Valence, Earl of Pembroke, 1307–1324* (Oxford, 1972) 15, 242, 260), who very soon, doubtless at the instance of the West Dereham community, attempted to reunite the two medieties of Holkham church. On 6 March 1319 he wrote to the Chancellor asking him not to issue a writ of warranty of the advowson to the abbot of Viterbo. He recovered seisin of the advowson in June 1319 due to the abbot's default, and execution of the judgement in his favour was ordered in October 1321 (Phillips, *Aymer de Valence* 182–3, and sources there cited). On 5 May 1323 a royal licence for alienation of this mediety in mortmain to West Dereham and for it appropriation was issued (*CPR 1321–24* 290). In 1347 the canons of West Dereham complained to bp Bateman of Norwich that, although bp Salmon (d. 1325) had appropriated to them the whole church of Holkham, one mediety had been lost through the action of the lay power. Bateman granted them the whole church *in proprios usus*, to take effect on the death or resignation of the vicar of the mediety now restored to them (*Reg. Bateman* no. 4). In October 1351 a Chancery writ recorded that the abbey of Viterbo was attempting to reverse in the papal court the verdict delivered by the justices of the Bench in Edward II's reign in favour of the earl, who had granted the advowson of the mediety to West Dereham (*CPR 1350–54* 201). Viterbo was still attempting to obtain restitution at the papal *curia* in 1369 (*CPR 1367-70* 259). On both occasions the crown ordered the arrest of any prosecuting such appeals outside the realm. In November 1405 the crown claimed the revenues of the mediety formerly held by Viterbo until, it was stated, 21 Edward III, with arrears amounting to £1089, on the grounds that the abbot and convent of Viterbo were aliens, and that there had been war between the king and the parts of Viterbo from then to now (did the royal lawyers really believe that Viterbo was in France?). When at an inquisition nobody appeared to give information to support the king's case, the crown withdrew the claim (*CCR 1405-1409* 14). For other refs., see W. Hassall and J. Beauroy, eds, *Lordship and Landscape in Norfolk, 1250-1350: the Early Records of Holkham* (British Academy Records of Social and Economic History n.s. 20) index, *s.v.* Holkham, church, and Viterbo.

24. Walden Abbey

Institution of Thomas of Walden, clerk, to the vicarage of Chippenham, at the presentation of the abbot. Gaywood, 4 June 1223

B = BL ms. Harley 3697 (Walden cartulary) fo. 50r (35r). s. xiv ex.

Pandulphus Dei gratia episcopus Norwicensis universis presentes literas inspecturis salutem in Domino. Noverit universitas vestra quod cum dilectus filius abbas de Waleden' patronus ecclesie de Chippenham nobis presentasset Thomam de Waleden' clericum ad ipsius ecclesie vicariam, nos clericum ipsum tanquam a patrono presentatum admisimus ad eandem, salvo nobis et successoribus nostris omni iure quod in dicta ecclesia nos quocumque modo contingit. In cuius rei testimonium has literas fieri fecimus et sigillo nostro muniri. Act' apud Gayod' .ii. nonas Iunii pontificatus nostri anno secundo.

The church, originally the gift of Geoffrey II de Mandeville, had been appropriated to the monks by bp John of Oxford (*EEA* 6 no. 302). In 1254 the church was valued at £30 13s. 4d. and the vicarage at £5 (*VN* 432).

25. Walden Abbey

Vidimus *and confirmation of the* inspeximus *and confirmation by bishop John II [de Gray] of the grant by bishop John [of Oxford] to the monks* in proprios usus *of the church of Chippenham, with provision to be made for a vicar* [*EEA* 6 no 421; also no. 302]. London, 10 November 1224

B = BL ms. Harley 3697 (Walden cartulary) fos. 40v–41r (23v–24r). s. xiv ex. C = ibid. fo. 41r (24r) (*inspeximus* by prior William and convent of Norwich).

Pandulfus Dei gratia episcopus Norwicensis universis presentes litteras inspecturis salutem in Domino. Vidimus litteras bone memorie Iohannis secundi predecessoris nostri episcopi Norwicensis in hec verba: [*EEA* 6 no. 421; also no. 302]. Nos vero dictas predecessorum nostrorum concessiones et confirmationes sicut iuste ac sine pravitate provide facte sunt ratas habentes, ipsas presentis scripti patrocinio confirmamus, salva per omnia obedientia, reverentia et honore et consuetudinibus nobis et successoribus nostris debitis et sancte ecclesie Norwicensi. In cuius[a] rei testimonium has literas fieri fecimus et sigillo nostro muniri.[b] Dat' London' .iiii. idus Novembris anno Domini m.cc.xxiiii pontificatus nostri anno tertio.

[a] huius C   [b] *C ends here.*

At the end of the transcript is noted: *exhibitum archiepiscopo v*. This refers probably to archbp Pecham's visitation of 1281, possibly to that of archbp Winchelsey in 1304.

26. Walsingham Priory

Confirmation for the canons of the church of St Peter, Great Walsingham, the gift of Richard, earl of Hertford. [26 July 1221 × 29 May 1222]

B = BL ms. Cotton Nero E vii (Walsingham cartulary) fo. 31r (26r, 29r). s. xiii ex.

Universis presentes litteras inspecturis Pandulfus Dei gratia Norwicensis electus domini pape camerarius salutem in Domino. Cum bone memorie Ricardus comes de Herford' ius patronatus quod in ecclesia sancti Petri de Magna Walsingham habebat dilectis filiis priori et canonicis sancte Marie de Walsingham duxerit misericorditer concedendum, nos concessionem ipsam ratam et gratam habentes eandem auctoritate presentium confirmamus et in huius rei testimonium has litteras nostras ipsis duximus concedendas.

There had been a long-running dispute, since the reign of Henry I, concerning a mediety of this church, which the monks of Binham claimed against the lords of Clare (*EEA* 6 nos. 25, 324, 371A). Following an inconclusive plea brought by Binham in 1210 (*CRR* vi 3), earl Richard granted the whole church to Walsingham, as here confirmed. Before this grant, bp Gray had collated the church by devolution (*EEA* 6 no. 371A), probably to Richard Marsh, who was certainly rector at the time of his appointment to the bpric of Durham, when the legate Guala collated the church to a certain Thomas (*Guala's Letters* no. 32). Earl Richard's grant was probably made between his capture at the battle of Lincoln in May 1217 and his death between 30 October and 28 November 1217; his charter is on fo. 31r of B. In 1237 the crown brought a case against the canons, claiming the advowson by reason of the minority of Richard of Clare, grandson of the grantor; from the pleading in this case the history of the church can be reconstructed (*Bracton's Notebook* iii no. 1238). Walsingham priory in 1264 received licence to appropriate on the death or resignation of Bartholomew of Ferentino, the current incumbent (fos. 31r, 41v of B).

Pandulph's confirmation was probably given before early October 1221, when he departed for Poitou; but since he subsequently issued episcopal *acta* from the papal *curia*, this cannot be certain (see Appx III, p. 178).

27. Wymondham Priory

Institution of John of Southwood, deacon, as persona *of the church of Carleton [Forehoe], at the presentation of the monks.*

Thetford, 18 September 1224

B = BL ms. Cotton Titus C viii (Wymondham cartulary) fo. 98r. s. xiii med.

Pandulphus[a] Dei gratia episcopus Norwycensis universis presentes literas inspecturis salutem in Domino. Noverit universitas vestra nos divine pietatis intuitu admisisse dilectum filium Iohannem de Sowode diaconum ad ecclesiam de Karltun' vacantem ipsumque in ea ad presentationem dilectorum filiorum monachorum de Wymundham canonice instituisse personam, salvis in omnibus rationibus et consuetudinibus episcopalibus et dignitatibus ecclesie Norwicensis. In cuius rei testimonium has literas fieri fecimus et nostro sigillo muniri. Actum apud[b] Tefordiam .xiiii°. kalendas Octobris pontificatus nostri anno tertio.

[a] Pand' B   [b] apud actum B

THOMAS BLUNDEVILLE

28. Profession

Profession of obedience made to Stephen [Langton] archbishop of Canterbury. 20 December 1226

> A = Canterbury D. & C. Ch. Ant. C115/165. No endorsement; approx. 133 × 47mm.
> B = Canterbury D. & C. register A (prior's register) fo. 230r. s. xiv med.
> Pd from A and B in *Canterbury Professions* no. 165; cf. nos. 122, 155.

Ego Thomas Norwicensis ecclesie electus et a te, venerande pater Stephane sancte Cantuariensis ecclesie episcope et totius Anglie primas, consecrandus antistes, tibi et sancte Cantuariensi ecclesie et successoribus tuis canonice substituendis debitam et canonicam obedientiam et subiectionem me per omnia exhibiturum profiteor et promitto, et propria manu subscribendo confirmo. +

29. Barlings Abbey

Grant to the canons in proprios usus *of the church of Holy Trinity, Bungay, saving the perpetual vicarage of Ranulf the chaplain for his lifetime and of other vicars to be instituted by the bishop and his successors, who shall discharge all the canonical obligations of the church. At each vacancy the bishop shall nominate a* persona *to the abbot and canons, who shall present him to the bishop, and if they fail so to do, the bishop may nevertheless institute whomsoever he wishes. The vicar shall have all the altarage, with rents and tithes of hay, flax and hemp, and other lesser tithes pertaining to the altarage; he shall also have the great tithe of various named tenements. He shall have all the buildings, except for a plot to the south and half the garden. The abbot and convent shall have all other tithes, including the tithe of mills, the plot to the south and half the garden and the buildings thereon.*

East Bergholt (?), 8 March 1229

> B = BL ms. Cotton Faust. B i (Barlings cartulary) fos. 43v–44r. s. xiii ex. C = ibid. fo. 44r (*inspeximus* by prior William and convent of Norwich). s. xiii ex.

Omnibus Cristi fidelibus ad quos presens scriptum pervenerit Thomas Dei gratia Norwicensis episcopus salutem in Domino. Ad universorum notitiam volumus pervenire nos Dei causa et religionis favore concessisse et dedisse dilectis nobis in Cristo abbati et canonicis de Barl' ecclesiam sancte Trinitatis de Bungeia, habendam in proprios usus et perpetuo possidendam, salva perpetua vicaria Ranulpho capellano quoad vixerit et aliis vicariis a nobis et successoribus nostris pro tempore instituendis qui in eadem ecclesia ministrabunt et omnia honera canonica sustinebunt, ad quam vicariam quotiens vacare contigerit predicti abbas et canonici personam a nobis vel successoribus nostris quemcumque volumus nominandam nobis vel successoribus nostris presentabunt et ipsum presentatum admittemus, vel si presentare omiserint personam a nobis vel successoribus nostris nominandam, nos nichilominus personam quam voluerimus in predicta ecclesia instituemus. Et ne futuris [temporibus] inter prefatos abbatem et canonicos et vicarium pro tempore dicte ecclesie super portionibus eisdem per nos assignatis oriatur dissensio, ipsas portiones presentibus duximus distinguendas, videlicet quod vicarius pro tempore habebit totum altaragium cum redditibus et fenis [fo. 44r] et lino[a] et canabio et aliis minutis decimis ad altaragium spectantibus. Idem vicarius habebit decimas garbarum de subscriptis terris provenientium,[b] videlicet de toto dominico Hugonis filii Radulfi, scilicet novies .xx. acrarum et quatuor, cum dote domine Agnetis quondam uxoris fratris ipsius Hugonis; item decimas de terra Willelmi filii Reginaldi, videlicet .x. acrarum; item decimas de tota terra que fuit Willelmi Turkil, videlicet .xxiiii. acrarum; et omnia edificia remanebunt vicario, exceptis uno placio versus austrum et dimidio orto. Dicti autem abbas et conventus de Barl' omnes decimas alias a prescriptis, cum decimis molendinorum, et placium versus austrum et dimidium ortum ad edificia ibidem construenda habebunt, salvis etiam in omnibus nobis et successoribus nostris reverentia et obedientia et sacrosancte Norwicensis ecclesie consuetudinibus debitis vel consuetis. In cuius rei testimonium presentes literas fieri fecimus et sigillo nostro muniri. Dat' apud Berch' octavo Idus Martii pontificatus nostri anno tertio.

[a] et lino *om.* C   [b] supervenientium C

For confirmation by bp John II of the grant of the church by Hamelin Bardolf, see *EEA* 6 no. 321. In 1254 the church was valued at £10 and the vicarage at £3 6s. 8d., in 1291 at £10 13s. 4d. and £4 6s. 8d. respectively (*VN* 459; *Taxatio* 118).

30. Battle Abbey

Grant, with the consent of his chapter, to the monks in proprios usus *of the church of Exning, to take effect after the death of George of Vercelli the rector and Guy the vicar, saving a vicarage of twenty-five marks to be assigned to a vicar to be nominated to the monks by the bishop or his successors and to be presented by them to the bishop; if the monks fail to present, the bishop may nevertheless institute a vicar. The vicar shall discharge all the obligations of the church, that is, the procurations of archdeacon and dean. Defects in books and ornaments shall be supplied by the monks and the vicar in the proportion of two parts of the cost to one.* London, 9 October 1227

   A = PRO E210/7639. Endorsed: Confirmatio Thome Norwicensis episcopi super ecclesia de Ixning iiii^a (s. xiii); approx. 164 × 87 + 18 mm.; parchment tag, seal missing.
   B = PRO E315/54/140 (*inspeximus* by prior William and convent of Norwich) s. xiii med. C = Lincoln's Inn ms. Hale 87 (Battle cartulary) fo. 29v. s. xiii med. D = San Marino, Huntington Library, Battle Abbey Papers vol. 29 (Battle cartulary) fos. 80v–81r (69v–70r).s. xiii ex. E = ibid. fo. 81r–v (70r–v) (as B). s. xiii ex.

Omnibus Cristi fidelibus ad quos presens scriptum pervenerit Thomas Dei gratia Norwicensis episcopus salutem in Domino. Ad universorum notitiam volumus pervenire nos causa Dei et religionis favore et assensu capituli Norwicensis concessisse et presenti carta nostra confirmasse dilectis filiis in Cristo abbati et conventui de Bello ecclesiam de Ixning nostre diocesis cum omnibus ad ipsam pertinentibus, habendam in proprios usus et perpetuo possidendam post decessum Georgii Vercellens' rectoris et Wydonis vicarii eiusdem ecclesie, salva vicaria viginti quinque marcarum, ad quam vicariam quotiens vacare contigerit nobis et successoribus nostris predicti abbas et conventus de Bello personam ydoneam quam nos et successores nostri voluerimus sine difficultate ac alicuius pravitatis ac contradictionis obstaculo presentabunt, et nos et successores nostri libere et absolute auctoritate diocesana in vicaria predicta eundem instituemus; et si dicti abbas et conventus omiserint vel neglexerint presentare, nos et successores nostri ipsis irrequisitis vicarium instituemus ibidem; salvis etiam in omnibus reverentia et obedientia nobis et successoribus nostris et sacrosancte Norwicensis ecclesie consuetudinibus debitis vel consuetis. Dictus autem vicarius omnia onera canonica prefate ecclesie sustinebit, videlicet in procurationibus archidiaconorum et decanorum. Dicti autem abbas et conventus omnes deffectus ecclesie predicte tam in libris quam in ornamentis ecclesiasticis quoad duas partes et vicarius quoad tertiam partem sustinebunt. In cuius rei testimonium presentes literas fieri fecimus et sigillo nostro muniri. Dat' Lond' septimo idus Octobris pontificatus nostri anno primo.

   In the early thirteenth century the *persona* of Exning was Richard de Camera, also canon of St Paul's and rector of Haughley, Sf., who in 1217–18, in conjunction with the monks' proctor, presented Guy the chaplain to the perpetual vicarage, with the stipulation that he should pay six marks *p.a.* to the abbey and 20s. to the *persona* (fo. 80r of D). George of Vercelli was almost certainly the next rector, to whom the church was probably collated by the legate Guala after Richard's deprivation because of his involvement with the king's enemies. George was probably one of Guala's own nephews, of whom six or seven occur in records relating to England, although this is the only mention of him (Sayers, *Papal Government* 183–5; *Guala's Letters* nos. 7n, 49n). For Exning and other churches of Battle abbey in the diocese, see Harper-Bill, 'Battle Abbey'.

31. Battle Abbey

Notification that when the abbot and convent obtained from the bishop the appropriation of the church of Exning, saving the honourable maintenance of a vicar, he, in order to avoid dissension in the future, caused the vicarage to be taxed by master Richard of Shipton, official of the archdeacon of Sudbury, and master Roger of Raveningham, dean of Fordham, and other trustworthy clergy and laity. The vicar shall have all the altarage and all the tithes of crofts in the parish, which latter are valued at £7 8s. p.a., and in addition the monks shall pay him six marks a year at the two Suffolk synods and shall provide him with an honourable messuage and buildings at their cost, by view of the archdeacon's official and the dean. London, 5 June 1229

> A = PRO E315/53/9. Endorsed: Ordinatio (confirmatio *struck through*) Thome Norwicensis episcopi super taxatione vicarii de Ixning', vii (s. xiii); approx. 160 × 110 mm.; no turn up, single slit, tag and seal missing.
>
> B = Lincoln's Inn ms. Hale 87 (Battle cartulary) fos. 29v–30r. s. xiii med. C = San Marino, Huntington Library, Battle Abbey Papers vol. 29 (Battle cartulary) fos. 81v–82r (70v–71r). s. xiii ex. D = ibid. fo. 82r–v (71r–v) (*inspeximus* by prior William and convent of Norwich. s. xiii ex.

Omnibus Cristi fidelibus ad quos presens scriptum pervenerit Thomas Dei gratia Norwicensis episcopus salutem in Domino. Universitati vestre notum fieri volumus quod cum abbas et conventus de Bello a nobis ecclesiam de Ixning' sibi in proprios usus obtinuissent confirmari, salva honesta sustentatione vicarii pro tempore in dicta ecclesia ministraturi, ne futuris temporibus inter predictos abbatem et conventum de Bello et dictum vicarium pro tempore materia scandali sive discordie possit oriri, ipsam vicariam per dilectos in Cristo filios magistrum Ricardum de Sipton' officialem archidiaconi Subir' et magistrum Rogerum de Raveningham decanum de Fordham et alios fidedignos tam clericos quam laicos taxari fecimus in hunc modum, videlicet quod pro tempore vicarius habebit totum alteragium ipsius ecclesie de Ixning, et omnes decimas omnium croftarum eiusdem parochie, videlicet decimas illarum croftarum que in presentia dictorum magistri Ricardi de Sipton' officialis Subir' et magistri Rogeri de Raveningham decani de Fordham et aliorum fidedignorum taxatione facienda estimate fuerunt ad valentiam septem librarum et octo solidorum; et insuper dictus abbas et conventus de Bello solvent vicario pro tempore annuatim sex marcas ad duas synodos Suffok', et providebunt vicario honestum mesuagium cum domibus honestis ad sumptus suos, per visum dictorum officialis archidiaconi Subir' et decani de Fordham. In cuius rei testimonium presentes litteras fieri fecimus et sigillo nostro muniri. Dat' London' quinto die Iunii pontificatus nostri anno tertio.

> On 9 November 1229 abbot Richard and the convent issued notifications of the appropriation by the bp, to take effect on the death of the rector and vicar, saving a vicarage of twenty-five marks (£16 13s. 4d.), and of the taxation of that vicarage (Bodl. Sussex charters A3/77–78). In 1254 the church was valued at £30 13s. 4d. and the vicarage at £12, in 1291 at £46 13s. 4d. and £16 13s. 4d. respectively (*VN* 431; *Taxatio* 121).

*32. Battle Abbey

Mandate to Gilbert of Yaxley (Iakeslea), *official of the archdeacon of Sudbury, to induct Raymond the monk, proctor of the abbot and convent, into corporal possession of a pension of one hundred shillings a year from the church of Exning.* [Shortly before 7 November 1229]

> Mention in a notification of induction *de speciali mandato domini Thome Norwicensis episcopi*, 7 November 1229 (PRO, E210/1483).

> Gilbert of Yaxley had succeeded Richard of Shipton as archdn's official since 5 June 1229 (no. 31).

33. Battle Abbey

Mandate to the official of the archdeacon of Sudbury to induct Raymond the monk, proctor of the abbot and convent, into corporal possession of the church of Exning and to give him protection therein, saving to Thomas the clerk, son of Lambert, citizen of London, the vicarage consisting of certain portions as taxed. He is to compel objectors by ecclesiastical censure.
[Thorpe, 16 March 1231]

> B = San Marino, Huntington Library, Battle Abbey Papers vol. 29 (Battle cartulary) fos. 81v–82r (70v–71r). s. xiii ex.

Dilecto filio in Cristo officiali archidiaconi Subir' salutem in Domino. Mandamus vobis quatinus Reymundum monachum procuratorem abbatis et conventus de Bello in corporalem possessionem ecclesie de Ixning' cum omnibus ad ipsam pertinentibus, quam dictis abbati et conventui in proprios usus concessimus et carta nostra confirmavimus, solempniter mittatis et missum tueamini, salva in eadem Thome clerico filio Lamberti civis London' vicaria in certis portionibus per nos et officiales nostros taxata, resistentes si quem inveneritis censura ecclesiastica compescendo. Actum apud Torp' .xvii.[a] kalendas Aprilis pontificatus nostri anno quinto.

[a] xviii B. *Such a date would be very eccentric, since* .xviii. kalendas Aprilis *should be the ides of March.*

It is almost certain that this is an *actum* of bp Thomas, who had appropriated the church to Battle (no. 31); the monk Raymond occurs in no. 32.

34. Binham Priory

Inspeximus *and confirmation of the general confirmation of bishop John of Oxford [EEA 6 no. 167]. Grant also to the monks in* proprios usus, *for hospitality, of the church of Little Ryburgh, saving honourable and competent maintenance for a chaplain as vicar.* Thornage, 15 April 1230

B = BL ms. Cotton Claud. D xiii (Binham cartulary) fos. 44v–45v. s. xiv med. C = ibid. fos. 46v–47v (*inspeximus* by prior Simon and convent of Norwich). s. xiv med.

Omnibus Cristi fidelibus ad quos presens scriptum pervenerit Thomas Dei gratia Norwicensis episcopus salutem in Domino. Inspeximus cartam bone memorie Iohannis Norwycensis episcopi predecessoris nostri super beneficiis, elemosinis [et] possessionibus monachis de Binham concessis in hec verba conceptam [*EEA* 6 no. 167]. Nos autem predictam concessionem et confirmationem predecessoris nostri prefatis monachis de Binham factam ratam habentes et acceptam, ipsam quantum in nobis est auctoritate episcopali confirmamus. Gratiam etiam specialem et pleniorem ipsis monachis de Binham religionis favore facere volentes, ecclesiam de Parva Riburg' cum omnibus ad ipsam pertinentibus ad hospitalitatem domus de Binham plenius sustinendam prefatis monachis concedimus et presentium tenore in proprios usus inperpetuum confirmamus, salva honesta et conpetenti sustentatione capellani vicarii[a] in dicta ecclesia pro tempore ministraturi, nobis et successoribus nostris pro tempore presentandi ab ipsis et per nos et successores nostros instituendi, salvis etiam in omnibus reverentia et obedientia nobis et successoribus nostris et sacrosancte Norwycensis ecclesie consuetudinibus debitis vel consuetis. In cuius rei testimonium presentes literas fieri fecimus et sigillo nostro muniri. Dat' apud Thorendis[b] manerium nostrum .xvii. kalendas Maii pontificatus nostri anno iiii[to]. Testibus: magistro R. de Biln' archidiacono Nortfolch, magistro Andrea de Croyenden,[c] magistro Iohanne de Sparham, Wimero[d] senescallo, Iohanne Terri, magistro Iohanne de Huntingdon',[e] Dionisio de Catton',[f] Roberto de Patesle,[g] Roberto de Crowdon',[h] Laurentio de Bononia, Ada[j] de Helmham, Godefrido parcario, Alano de Blunwill', Warino Lehtlage.

ᵃ sic B, C   ᵇ Thornegge C   ᶜ Croinden' B   ᵈ Wymon C   ᵉ Huntendon' C
ᶠ Cotton' C   ᵍ Ponteslee C   ʰ Croudon' C   ʲ Adam B, C

There is no subsequent evidence that a vicarage was established. In 1254 the church was valued at twelve marks, in 1291 at thirteen marks, in neither case with mention of a vicarage (*VN* 421, *Taxatio* 89b).

Thornage, where this *actum* was issued, was an episcopal manor; see, for example, *EEA* 6 no. 269.

35. Blackborough Priory

Inspeximus *and confirmation of the charters of bishops John of Oxford and John [de Gray], whereby they granted to the nuns* in proprios usus *the church of Middleton and a mediety of the church of Wetherden, saving the honourable maintenance of vicars therein* [*EEA* 6 nos. 171–2, 329–30].

[20 December 1226 × 16 August 1236]

B = BL ms. Egerton 3137 (Blackborough cartulary) fo. 61r (29r). s. xiv ex.

Omnibus Cristi fidelibus ad quos presens scriptum pervenerit Thomas Dei gratia Norwicensis episcopus salutem in Domino. Inspeximus cartas bone memorie I. primi et I. secundi episcoporum Norwicensium predecessorum nostrorum in quibus continebatur quod priorisse et monialibus de Blakebergh' ecclesiam de Midelton' et medietatem ecclesie de Wetherden' cum omnibus pertinentiis suis in proprios usus perpetuo possidendas concesserunt et confirmaverunt, salva honesta sustentatione vicariorum qui pro tempore in dictis ecclesiis ministrabunt. Nos autem concessiones predictas gratas habentes et acceptas, eas presentis scripti nostri testimonio et sigilli nostri appositione duximus roborandas. Dat' etc.

At Middleton in 1254 the prioress's portion was assessed at £5 and the vicarage at £2; the prior of Norwich had a portion of 20s and the abbot of Notley had separated tithes worth £1 13s. 4d. (*VN* 383). For the other mediety of Wetherden, of which the abbot of Bury held the advowson, see *EEA* 6 no. 177; there in 1254 the rector's portion was valued at £6, the prioress's portion at £6 13s. 4d.; while the master of the schools of Bury St Edmunds had the portion of £2 granted by abbot Samson and confirmed by bp John of Oxford (*VN* 425).

36. Bury St Edmunds, St Saviour's Hospital

Inspeximus *and confirmation of a charter of bishop John de Gray, by which he granted to the brethren* in proprios usus *two portions of the church of [Long] Melford, the third part being reserved for the maintenance of a vicar* [*EEA* 6 no. 337]. *Confirmation also of all those portions of tithes of the manors of the abbot and convent of Bury, as detailed in another charter of the same bishop [EEA 6 no. 339].*   Redgrave, 17 December 1227

> B = Ipswich, Suffolk R.O., HD 1538/169/19 (St Saviour's cartulary) fo. 21r–v. s. xiv. C = ibid. fo. 22r–v (*inspeximus* by prior Simon and the convent of Norwich). s. xiv. D = Oxford, Bodl. Suffolk roll 2 (*inspeximus* by archbp Boniface of Savoy of C, 18 February 1266). s. xv in.
> Pd from B, C and D in *Bury Hospital Charters* no. 182.

Omnibus Cristi fidelibus has literas inspecturis Thomas Dei gratia Norwycensis episcopus salutem in Domino. Noveritis nos cartam bone memorie Iohannis secundi predecessoris nostri inspexisse conceptam in [hec] verba: [*EEA* 6 no. 337]. Nos autem predictam predecessoris nostri concessionem et confirmationem in hac parte dictis fratribus factam ratam habentes et acceptam, eam presentis scripti testimonio et sigilli nostri appositione duximus corroborandam. Confirmamus etiam omnes eis portiones quas habent de decimis abbatis et conventus sancti Edmundi in maneriis suis sicut contineri perpenditur in carta dicti I. predecessoris nostri. In cuius rei testimonium presentes literas fieri fecimus et sigillo nostro muniri. Dat' apud Redgrave .xvi. kalendas Ianuarii anno pontificatus [nostri] primo.

> In 1254 the portion of the *persona* was assessed at £13 6s. 8d. and that of St Saviour's at £26 13s. 4d.; the monks of Stoke by Clare also received 5s. *p.a.* from the church (*VN* 436). In 1291 the incumbent's benefice was listed as a secular rectory assessed at £20 (*Taxatio* 122).

37. Butley Priory and Leiston Abbey

Notification by the bishop, the dean of Norwich and the prior of Horsham St Faith that, acting on the mandate of Pope Gregory IX, dated at Rieti, 28 July 1234, delegating to them jurisdiction in a case brought by the prior and convent of Butley against the abbot and convent of Leiston and others of Norwich, Lincoln and London dioceses concerning injuries inflicted upon them in relation to lands, tithes, debts and other matters, they called together the parties, whereupon Butley alleged that the church of Knoddishall was in possession of the lesser tithes from the canons' house in that parish called 'le Westhus' and of the oblations and obventions of the lay servants dwelling therein, but Leiston detained and refused to restore them. The judges heard the exceptions advanced by Leiston and the arguments advanced by both parties, and finally the matter was settled in their presence in this manner: Butley renounced to Leiston all parochial rights, in tithes as in other matters, which they had or might have in the said grange or the secular servants dwelling therein, saving the oblations, obventions and all dues of the parishioners of Butley who should remain there for any length of time. If parishioners of any church which pertains neither to Leiston nor to Butley should remain for any time at the grange, each of them should go to their own church, but Leiston should place no impediment in the way of their going to Knoddishall church, and there receiving the rites of the Church, if they so wish. Butley renounced all parochial right which it had or might have in the demesne lands of 'Westhus' and Leiston, cultivated and uncultivated, which Leiston had at the time of the relaxation of the general interdict and from which tithes were not then paid to Knoddishall church, and renounced also the tithes of various properties which Leiston held in demesne, a perambulation having been conducted between the two churches of Leiston and Knoddishall in the time of abbot Philip and Prior William. So that peace might be made between the two houses, Leiston conceded to Butley various tithes. The judges delegate approved this composition and confirmed it by papal authority, ratifying it with their seals. Butley, 18 November 1235

B = BL ms. Cotton Vesp. E xiv (Leiston cartulary) fos. 65v–66v. s. xiii med.
Pd from B in *Leiston Cartulary* no. 90.

Omnibus has litteras inspecturis Thomas Dei gratia Norwicensis episcopus, decanus Norwicensis et prior sancte Fidis de Horsford salutem eternam in Domino. Noverit universitas vestra nos mandatum domini pape suscepisse in hec verba: Gregorius episcopus, servus servorum Dei, venerabili fratri episcopo et dilectis filiis decano Norwicensi et priori sancte Fidis Norwicensis diocesis, salutem et apostolicam benedictionem. Querelam prioris ac conventus de Buttele recepimus, continentem quod abbas et conventus de Leyston', Premonstratensis ordinis, et quidam alii Norwicensis, Lincolnienis et Londoniensis diocesum super terris, decimis, debitis et rebus aliis iniuriantur eisdem. Ideo discretioni vestre per apostolica scripta mandamus quatinus, partibus convocatis, audiatis causam et apellatione remota fine debito decidatis, facientes quod decreveritis per censuram ecclesiasticam firmiter observari. Testes autem qui fuerint nominati si se gratia, odio vel timore subtraxerint, per censuram eandem apellatione cessante cogatis veritati testimonium perhibere. Quod si non omnes hiis exequendis [fo. 66r] potueritis interesse tu, frater episcope, cum eorum altero ea nichilominus exequaris. Datum Reatum quinto kalendas Augusti pontificatus nostri anno octavo. Huius igitur auctoritate mandati priore et conventu de Buttere in contentionem suam contra abbatem et conventum de Leystune sub hac forma proponente, dicunt prior et conventus de B. quod cum ecclesia de Cnoteshale fuisset in possessione minutarum decimarum provenientium de domo eorum que dicitur le Westhus in parochia de Cnoteshale et oblationum et obventionum servientium secularium in dicta domo commorantium, abbas et conventus de Leyston' eas iniuste detinent et reddere contradicunt. Partibus in iure coram nobis constitutis, exceptionibus ex parte dictorum abbatis et conventus propositis et rationibus utriusque partis auditis et intellectis, tandem lis inter partes in presentia nostra hoc fine conquievit, videlicet quod dicti prior et conventus renuntiaverint omni iuri parochiali tam in decimis quam in omnibus aliis rebus quod habuerunt vel habere potuerunt in dicta grangia vel servientibus secularibus ibidem commorantibus, salvis oblationibus et obventionibus et omnibus provenientibus parochianorum dictorum prioris et conventus de quacumque sua parochia provenientibus in dicta grangia pro quocumque tempore commorantium priori et conventui memoratis. Si vero parochiani alicuius ecclesie qui pro aliquo tempore non fuerit dictorum abbatis et conventus vel prioris et conventus in dicta grangia fuerint commorantes, unusquisque eorum libere propriam adeat ecclesiam, abbate et conventu prenominatis nullum impedimentum procurantibus quo minus dictam ecclesiam de Cnoteshale adeat si voluerit et iura ibidem percipiat ecclesiastica. Item renuntiaverunt dicti prior et conventus omni iuri parochiali quod habuerunt vel habere potuerunt in dominicis de Westhus et de Leystun' cultis et incultis que dicti abbas et conventus habuerunt tempore relaxationis generalis interdicti de quibus decime ecclesie prefate de Cnoteshale tunc temporis non fuerant persolute, et decimis [fo. 66v] terre de Keleshalelond iacentis sub bosco de Grendelheg et campi qui vocatur Oldelond et duarum acrarum terre que vocantur Radismere, quas dicti abbas et conventus tenent in dominico, puralea etiam inter dictas ecclesias de Leyston' et de Cnoteshale tempore Philippi abbatis et conventus et Willelmi prioris et conventus dictorum facta et sigillis utriusque domus roborata in suo robore perdurante. Et ut inter dictas domus de Leyston' et de Buttele pax perpetua, firma et inconcussa in posterum permaneat, dicti abbas et conventus decimas terre que vocatur Erburestoft et duarum acrarum terre quas Willelmus Fukeman tenuit, et sex peciarum terre quas Walter Rakebald et Galfridus frater eius tenent, et unius rode terre de feodo Ade de monasterio iacentis versus occidentem de le Stablecroft, pro bono pacis priori et conventui in perpetuum concesserunt memoratis. Nos autem compositionem prenominatam ratam et gratam habentes, eam autoritate domini pape nobis commissa confirmamus et sigillorum nostrorum munimine roboramus. Actum apud Buttele in octabis sancti Martini anno gratie m. cc. tricesimo quinto.

> The location of the perambulation at the time of the relaxation of the interdict is approximate, since prior William of Butley was dead by January 1213 and the interdict was only lifted, after eighteen months negotiation, in July 1214. The record of the perambulation was in fact sealed by the parties much later, on the day of this judicial ruling in November 1235 and as

part of the composition; it is in fact a list of those in the parish of Knodishall who should pay tithes to Leiston (*Leiston Cartulary* no. 89; cf. 20–1, 32).

38. Canterbury, Christ Church Cathedral Priory

Grant to the monks *in proprios usus, in honour of St Thomas and for the use of guests and the poor who flock to the cathedral on his feast-day, of the church of Deopham, saving the honourable maintenance of a perpetual vicar to be presented by them with the advice of the bishop and his successors; the vicarage shall be of the value of ten marks.*   London, 12 February 1227

>   A = Canterbury D. & C. Ch. Ant. D14. Endorsed: Carta Thome de Blumvile episcopi Norwicensis de ecclesia de Depeham in proprios usus concessa (s. xiii med.); Diepeham, registratur (s. xiv in.); approx. 169 × 90 + 20 mm.; parchment tag, seal, red wax, counterseal.
>   B = Canterbury D. & C. Ch. Ant. D12 (*inspeximus* by prior William and convent of Norwich, 19 March 1227 × 18 March 1228). s. xiii med. C = ibid. Reg. B (Christ Church cartulary) fo. 219r. s. xiii ex. D = ibid. Reg. E (Christ Church cartulary) fo. 391r. s. xiii ex. E = Lambeth Palace Library, register of archbp Warham i fo. 92r (as B). s. xvi in.

Omnibus Cristi fidelibus ad quod presens scriptum pervenerit Thomas Dei gratia Norwicensis episcopus salutem in Domino. Ad universorum notitiam volumus pervenire nos causa Dei et religionis favore et in honorem beati Thome martiris concessisse et in proprios usus contulisse priori et monachis ecclesie Cristi Cantuariensi ecclesiam de Depham' cum omnibus ad eam pertinentibus, ad usus hospitum et pauperum die solempnitatis prefati martiris Thome ibidem confluentium, salva honesta sustentatione vicarii perpetui qui in eadem ministrabit ecclesia ad presentationem predictorum monachorum cum consilio nostro et successorum nostrorum pro tempore faciendam, et a nobis et successoribus nostris instituendi et in prefata ecclesia ministraturi. Ordinavimus autem in predicta ecclesia vicariam decem marcarum, salvis etiam in omnibus reverentia et obedientia nobis et successoribus nostris et sacrosancte Norwicensis ecclesie consuetudinibus debitis et consuetis. In cuius rei testimonium presentes literas fieri fecimus et sigillo nostro muniri. Dat' London' pridie idus Februarii pontificatus nostri anno primo.

>   For the grant by bp William Turbe of the church to the monks, after a long dispute between them and Henry de Ria in the time of archbp Theobald, see *EEA* 6 no. 67, and for a confirmation by bp John of Oxford, after a dispute between the monks and Robert the priest, ibid. no. 182. For a quitclaim to the monks by Richard de Blundeville, probably the bp's brother, of all right to the advowson, made while Thomas was bp-elect (27 October × 20 December 1226), and witnessed by the bps of London and Chichester, see Canterbury D. & C. Ch. Ant. D15. The Blundevilles held a third part of the Ria manor in Deopham, to which had been attached a third part of the advowson (Blomefield, *Norfolk* ii 491–2). For the detailed taxation of the vicarage, see below no. 39.

39. Canterbury, Christ Church Cathedral Priory

Grant to the monks in proprios usus, *out of veneration for St Thomas and for the sustenance of guests and pilgrims who flock to the cathedral on his feast day, and having in mind his own death, of the church of Deopham, saving the honourable maintenance of a vicar to be presented by them with the advice of the bishop and his successors. The vicar shall receive all the offerings of the altar and the tithes of the fields called 'Tweyt' and 'Sumercroft', except for the great tithe of seven acres of 'Tweyt' due to the monks of Norwich. The vicar shall have two acres to the east of the churchyard, in which is sited the old messuage of the prior and convent of Canterbury, and three acres of the free land of the church to the south, and also 16s. 4d. from the monks' proctor at Michaelmas. The vicar shall discharge all customary obligations of the church to bishop and archdeacon. Two parts of the cost of repair of ornaments and utensils shall be borne by the monks and the third part by the vicar.* [10 June × 15 October 1227]

> A = Canterbury D. & C. Ch. Ant. D16. Endorsed: Carta Thome de Blumvil' Norwicensis episcopi de ecclesia de Depeh' in proprios usus concessa (s. xiii med.); Diepham, registratur (s. xiv in); approx. 218 × 104 + 20 mm.; parchment tag; fragment of seal, green wax, counterseal.
> B = Canterbury D & C. Ch. Ant. D9 (*inspeximus* by prior and convent of Norwich, 1227). s. xiii med. C = ibid. Reg. B (Christ Church cartulary) fo. 219r. s. xiii ex. D = ibid. Reg. E (Christ Church cartulary) fo. 319r–v. s. xiii ex.

Omnibus has litteras inspecturis Thomas Dei gratia Norwicensis episcopus salutem in Domino. Ad universorum notitiam volumus pervenire nos Dei causa et religionis favore et ob venerationem beati Thome martiris et in memoria obitus nostri concessisse et dedisse priori et monachis ecclesie Cristi Kantuariensis ecclesiam de Dypeham cum omnibus pertinentiis suis ad sustentationem hospitum et peregrinorum in sollempnitatibus dicti martiris ad predictum monasterium confluentium in proprios usus perpetuo possidendam, reservata honesta sustentatione vicarii qui pro tempore in prefata ministrabit ecclesia, nobis et successoribus nostris per consilium nostrum et successorum nostrorum a predictis priore et monachis presentandi et a nobis instituendi. Et ne inposterum a quoquam in dubium devocetur que pro tempore in predicta vicarii ministrantis debeat esse portio, portiones singulas ad vicariam spectantes presentibus litteris duximus inferendas. Habebit siquidem pro tempore vicarius prescripte ecclesie omnes obventiones alteragii ipsius ecclesie cum decimis provenientibus de campis qui vocantur Tweyt et de Sumercroft in parochia de Dypeham, salvis decimis monachorum Norwicensium quas habent in predicto campo, scilicet duabus garbis de septem acris de Tweyt. Item habebit dictus vicarius duas acras terre iuxta cimiterium ecclesie de

Dyeph' ex parte orientali in quibus est situm vetus mesuagium quod predictorum prioris et monachorum Cantuariensium fuit, et tres acras de libera terra ipsius ecclesie que se extendunt ex parte australi ecclesie versus austrum, et sexdecim solidos annuos et quatuor denarios singulis annis a procuratore monachorum percipiendos insuper in eadem villa in festo sancti Michaelis, in quorum solutione si cessaverint, concesserunt dicti monachi quod per nos et successores nostros ad solutionem dicte pecunie appellatione remota canonice compellantur. Sustinebit itaque vicarius qui pro tempore fuerit onera episcopalia et archidiaconalia consueta, et salva in omnibus reverentia et obedientia nobis et successoribus nostris et sacrosancte Norwicensis ecclesie consuetudinibus debitis vel consuetis et decimis quas habent monachi Norwicenses in eadem parochia. De provisione autem nostra et consensu monachorum, ad reparationem et emendationem ornamentorum et utensilium dicte ecclesie volumus quod due partes a monachis inveniantur, et tertia pars a vicario, ita quod competenter et honeste dicta ecclesia deserviatur. Ut hec autem nostra concessio et confirmatio rate et stabiles in perpetuum permaneant, de consensu capituli nostri presens scriptum sigilli nostri munimine roboravimus. Hiis testibus: magistro Alano de Becles archidiacono Suthb' tunc officiali domini Norwicensis, magistro Roberto de Bilneh', magistro Nicholao de Framingeham, Henrico capellano, Iohanne Terry, Dionisio de Cotton', Roberto de Ponte Tegle, Willemo de Fordeham.

> The taxation of the vicarage was made by Richard of Shipton, official of the archdn of Sudbury, on the bp's orders, on 10 June 1227. The document, which lists the names of twelve clerks and twelve laymen by whose oath the inquisition was made, is more detailed than the episcopal ordination above (Canterbury D. & C. Ch. Ant. D18). Mr Alan of Beccles was no longer official by 16 October 1227 (no. 89). In August 1227 the prior and convent of Norwich granted to the monks of Christ Church all the great tithe which they held in Deopham for 24s. *p.a.* (ibid. D11). In 1254 the church was assessed at £10 13s. 4d. and the vicarage at £1 (*VN* 399).

40. Castle Acre Priory

Institution of Edmund of Walpole, clerk, to the church of St Mary, [Great] Dunham, at the presentation of the prior and monks. Wisbech, 23 July 1227

> B = BL ms. Harley 2110 (Castle Acre cartulary) fo. 129v (123v). s. xiii med.

Omnibus Cristi fidelibus ad quos presens scriptum pervenerit Thomas Dei gratia Norwicensis episcopus salutem in Domino. Ad universorum volumus notitiam pervenire nos admisisse Edmundum de Walepol clericum ad ecclesiam beate Marie de Dunham cum omnibus ad eam pertinentibus, ad presentationem prioris et monachorum de Acra, eiusdem ecclesie verorum ut dicitur patronorum, et ipsum in eadem ecclesia personam canonice instituisse, salvis in omnibus reverentia et obedientia nobis et successoribus nostris et sacrosancte Norwicensis ecclesie consuetudinibus debitis vel consuetis. In cuius rei testimonium presentes litteras fieri fecimus et sigillo nostro muniri. Dat' apud Wysebeche .x^{mo}. kalendas Augusti pontificatus nostri anno primo.

For the early history of this church, see *EEA* 6 no. 195 n.

41. Castle Acre Priory

Institution of William de Alençon, clerk, to the church of Kempstone, at the presentation of the prior and monks.   Foulden, 5 December 1227.

B = BL ms. Harley 2110 (Castle Acre cartulary) fo. 130v (124v). s. xiii med.

Omnibus Cristi fidelibus ad quos presens scriptum pervenerit Thomas Dei gratia Norwicensis episcopus salutem. Ad universorum notitiam volumus pervenire nos admississe Willelmum de Alezon clericum ad ecclesiam de Kemestun' cum omnibus pertinentiis suis, ad presentationem prioris et monachorum de Acra eiusdem ecclesie verorum patronorum ut dicitur, et ipsum in eadem personam canonice instituisse, salvis in omnibus nobis et successoribus nostris reverentia et obedientia et sacrosancte Norwicensis ecclesie consuetudinibus debitis vel consuetis. In cuius rei testimonium presentes litteras fieri fecimus et sigillo nostro muniri. Dat' apud Fueldon' nonas Decembris pontificatus nostri anno primo.

The church had been granted to the monks *in proprios usus*, when it should be vacated by the present incumbent, by bp John of Oxford (*EEA* 6 nos. 199–200). It was again appropriated by bp Walter de Suffield in February 1246, and twelve months later he ordained a vicarage therein (fos. 131v–133r of B).

42. Castle Acre Priory

Institution of Robert of Narborough, clerk, to the church of Haverhill, at the presentation of the prior and monks.   Burwell, 28 August 1228.

B = BL ms. Harley 2110 (Castle Acre cartulary) fo. 129v (123v). s. xiii med.

Omnibus Cristi fidelibus ad quos presens scriptum pervenerit Thomas Dei gratia Norwicensis episcopus salutem in Domino. Ad universorum notitiam volumus pervenire nos admisisse dilectum nobis in Cristo Robertum de Nerburg' clericum ad ecclesiam de Haverhill' cum omnibus ad ipsam pertinentibus, ad presentationem prioris et monachorum de Castellacra eiusdem verorum patronorum, ipsumque Robertum clericum personam in eadem canonice instituisse, salvis in omnibus reverentia et obedientia nobis et successoribus nostris et sacrosancte Norwicensis ecclesie consuetudinibus debitis vel consuetis. In cuius rei testimonium presentes litteras fieri fecimus et sigillo nostro muniri. Dat' apud Burewell' .v. kalendas Septembris pontificatus nostri anno .ii°.

> The appropriation of Haverhill at the next vacancy of the church projected by bp John of Oxford (*EEA* 6 nos. 198, 200) was not put into effect, and the church was only finally appropriated to the monks by royal licence of 8 May 1393 (*CPR 1391–96*, 289).
>
> Burwell, where this document was issued, although in Cambridgeshire, was in the diocese of Norwich (*VN* 431).

43. Castle Acre Priory

Institution of Robert of Creake, chaplain, to the perpetual vicarage of the church of [West] Newton, at the presentation of the prior and monks.

[North or South] Elmham, 18 December 1228.

B = BL ms. Harley 2110 (Castle Acre cartulary) fo. 129v (123v). s. xiii med.

Omnibus Cristi fidelibus ad quos presens scriptum pervenerit Thomas Dei gratia Norwicensis episcopus salutem in Domino. Ad universorum notitiam volumus pervenire nos admisisse dilectum nobis in Cristo Robertum de Crec capellanum ad perpetuam vicariam ecclesie de Neuton' cum omnibus ad dictam vicariam pertinentibus, ad presentationem dilectorum filiorum prioris et monachorum de Acra, ipsumque R(obertum) capellanum perpetuum vicarium in eadem instituisse, salvis in omnibus reverentia et obedientia nobis et successoribus nostris et sacrosancte Norwicensis ecclesie consuetudinibus debitis vel consuetis. In cuius rei testimonium presenti scripto sigillum nostrum apposuimus. Dat' apud Elmham manerium nostrum .xv. kalendas Ianuarii pontificatus nostri anno secundo.

> West Newton had originally been appropriated to the monks by bp William Turbe (*EEA* 6 no. 73). In 1254 and 1291 the church was valued at £5 6s. 8d., and in the latter assessment the vicarage was noted as not subject to the tenth (*VN* 389; *Taxatio* 87b).

44. Castle Acre Priory

Grant to the monks in proprios usus *of the church of St Mary Magdalene, Wiggenhall, with all its appurtenances, saving honourable and sufficient maintenance of a vicar who shall minister therein, which vicarage the bishop has caused to be taxed by master Robert of Bilney. The vicar shall have all the altarage with the lesser tithes, the tithe of vegetables and half the tithe of hay; the remaining revenues shall be put to the use of the prior and monks, and the vicar shall discharge all the ordinary burdens on the church which are customary.* [North or South] Elmham, 18 December 1228

B = BL ms. Harley 2110 (Castle Acre cartulary) fo. 129r (123r). s. xiii med. C = ibid. fo. 129r (123r) (*inspeximus* by prior William and the convent of Norwich). s. xiii med. D = ibid. fo. 126r (133r) (*inspeximus* by bp. Walter de Suffield, 13 April 1248). s. xiii med.

Universis presens scriptum inspecturis Thomas Dei gratia Norwicensis episcopus salutem in Domino. Ad universorum notitiam volumus pervenire nos Dei causa ac religionis favore concessisse et dedisse dilectis in Cristo filiis priori et monachis de Acra ecclesiam sancte Marie Magdalene de Wigehale in usus proprios perpetuo possidendam cum omnibus ad ipsam pertinentibus, salva honesta et sufficienti sustentatione vicarii qui pro tempore in prefata ministrabit ecclesia, quam vicariam per dilectum in Cristo filium magistrum Robertum de Bilneya fecimus taxari, videlicet ut pro tempore vicarius habeat totum alteragium cum decimis minutis et decimis leguminum et medietatem decime feni. Cetera omnia cedant in usus predictorum prioris et monachorum. Volumus etiam ut pro tempore vicarius sustineat omnia predicte ecclesie onera ordinaria debita et consueta, salvis etiam in omnibus reverentia et obedientia nobis et successoribus nostris et sacrosancte Norwicensis ecclesie consuetudinibus debitis vel consuetis. In cuius rei testimonium presenti scripto sigillum nostrum apposuimus. Dat' apud Elmham[a] manerium nostrum .xv. kalendas Ianuarii pontificatus nostri anno secundo.

[a] Helmam C

The church had originally been appropriated to the monks by bp John of Oxford (*EEA* 6 nos. 199–200). In 1254 the church was assessed at £10 13s. 4d. and the vicarage at £4 (*VN* 382), but in 1291 the church was valued at £16 and the vicarage was not subject to the tenth (*Taxatio* 80).

45. Castle Acre Priory

Institution of John of Palgrave, clerk, to the vicarage of the church of St Mary Magdalene, Wiggenhall, as taxed by master Robert of Bilney [as in no. 44].
[North or South] Elmham, 18 December 1228

B = BL ms. Harley 2110 (Castle Acre cartulary) fo. 129r (123r). s. xiii med.

Universis presens scriptum inspecturis Thomas Dei gratia Norwicensis episcopus salutem in Domino. Ad universorum notitiam volumus pervenire nos ad presentationem dilectorum in Cristo filiorum prioris et monachorum de Acra Dei causa admisisse Iohannem de Pagrave clericum ad vicariam ecclesie sancte Marie Magdalene de Wigehale et ipsum vicarium in dicta ecclesia instituisse, que quidem vicaria ad mandatum nostrum per dilectum filium magistrum R(obertum) de Biln' taxata est, ita videlicet ut pro tempore vicarius habeat totum alteragium cum omnibus decimis minutis et decimis leguminum et medietatem decime feni. Cetera vero omnia cedant in usus predictorum prioris et monachorum de Acra. Volumus etiam ut pro tempore vicarius sustineat omnia predicte ecclesie onera ordinaria debita et consueta, salva etiam nobis et successoribus nostris reverentia et obedientia et sancte Norwicensis ecclesie consuetudinibus debitis et consuetis. In huius autem rei testimonium presenti scripto sigillum nostrum apposuimus. Dat' apud Elmham .xv. kalendas Ianuarii pontificatus nostri anno secundo.

46. Castle Acre Priory

Inspeximus and confirmation of the charter of bp John I whereby he granted to the monks in proprios usus *the church of Herringby when vacated by Robert Haltein, clerk.* Gaywood, 11 June 1233

B = BL ms Harley 2110 (Castle Acre cartulary) fo. 129r–v (123r–v) (*inspeximus* by prior Simon and the convent of Norwich). s. xiii med.

Omnibus Cristi fidelibus ad quos presens scriptum pervenerit Thomas Dei gratia Norwicensis episcopus salutem in Domino. Inspeximus cartam bone memorie I(ohannis) Norwicensis episcopi predecessoris nostri in hec verba: [*EEA* 6 no. 202]. Nos autem concessionem et confirmationem dicte ecclesie de Haringebi prefatis monachis de Acre a predecessore nostro taliter factam ratam habentes et acceptam, ipsam quantum in nobis est auctoritate episcopali confirmamus. In cuius rei testimonium presentes litteras fieri fecimus et sigillo nostro muniri. Dat' apud Gaywd' manerium nostrum die sancti Barnabe apostoli pontificatus nostri anno .vii^{mo}.

For the final ordination of a vicarage at Herringby by bp William Ralegh, see below no. 128.

47. Castle Acre Priory

Institution of Sebastian of Ferentino, clerk, nephew of James Romanus, dean of Holt, to the church of Westbriggs, at the presentation of the prior and monks, the true patrons. Norwich, 23 November 1233

B = BL ms. Harley 2110 (Castle Acre cartulary) fo. 124v (118v). s. xiii med.

Omnibus Cristi fidelibus ad quos presens scriptum pervenerit Thomas Dei gratia Norwicensis episcopus salutem in Domino. Ad universorum notitiam volumus pervenire nos ad presentationem prioris et monachorum de Castelacra, verorum ut dicitur patronorum ecclesie de Westbrige, admisisse Sebastianum de Ferentino clericum, nepotem domini Iacobi Romani decani de Hout, ad predictam ecclesiam de Westbrige cum omnibus ad ipsam pertinentibus ipsumque S. clericum personam in eadem canonice instituisse, salvis in omnibus reverentia et obedientia nobis et successoribus nostris et sancte Norwicensis ecclesie consuetudinibus debitis vel consuetis. In cuius rei testimonium presentes litteras fieri fecimus et sigillo nostro muniri. Dat' apud Nortwicum die sancti Clementis pontificatus nostri anno .vii°.

> James Romanus is more commonly known as James of Ferentino, a kinsman of John of Ferentino, archdn of Norwich (*Fasti* i 64). He was resident in Norfolk and was active in ecclesiastical administration, especially in the vacancy of the see following bp Blundeville's death (p. xxix–xxx).

48. Castle Acre Priory

Inspeximus *of charters of bishops John of Oxford and John de Gray whereby they granted to the monks* in proprios usus *the church of Methwold after the death or resignation of master Thomas,* persona, *saving an honourable and competent vicarage for the support of a perpetual vicar* [*EEA* 6 nos. 199–200, 343]. *Approving this measure, the bishop now conceded to them the church* in proprios usus *after the death of resignation of J[ohn] of Vercelli, saving the foresaid vicarage.*   Gaywood, 1 August 1235

> B = BL ms. Harley 2110 (Castle Acre cartulary) fo. 129v (123v). s. xiii med. C = ibid. fos. 130v–131r (124v–125r) (*inspeximus* by prior Simon and the convent of Norwich). s. xiii med.

Omnibus Cristi fidelibus ad quos presens scriptum pervenerit Thomas Dei gratia Norwicensis episcopus salutem in Domino. Inspeximus cartas Iohannis primi et Iohannis secundi predecessorum nostrorum continentes ipsos pietatis intuitu et religionis favore canonice concessisse et confirmasse dilectis in Domino filiis priori et monachis de Castelacra ecclesiam de Melewde cum omnibus ad ipsam pertinentibus in usus proprios inperpetuum possidendam post decessum vel recessum magistri Thome¹ persone ecclesie de Melewde, salva honesta et competenti vicaria ad opus vicarii perpetui in eadem ecclesia pro tempore ministraturi. Nos autem factum predecessorum nostrorum in hac parte ratum habentes et acceptum, dictam ecclesiam de Melewde post decessum vel recessum I. Vercellensis persone ecclesie memorate dictis priori et monachis de Castellacra quantum in nobis est auctoritate episcopali concedimus et confirmamus in usus proprios perpetuo possidendam, salva in eadem vicaria memorata, salvis etiam in omnibus reverentia et obedientia nobis et successoribus nostris et sacrosancte Norwicensis ecclesie consuetudinibus debitis vel consuetis. In cuius rei testimonium presenti scripto sigillum nostrum apponi fecimus. Dat' apud Gaywd' die sancti Petri ad Vincula pontificatus nostri anno nono.

[1] This is Thomas Brito (*EEA* 6 no. 199).

John of Vercelli, a nephew of the former legate Guala, in April 1244 received papal licence to retain Methwold and various other benefices (*Reg. Inn. IV* no. 610). For a survey of his English livings, see *Guala's Letters* no. 109n; see also Sayers, *Papal Government* 178–80, 184–5). The appropriation had not yet taken effect in December 1249, when bp Suffield inspected the charters of his predecessors (fo. 133r of B). The monks of Lewes had a portion of £2 in the church. In 1254 the church was assessed at £21 6s. 8d. and in 1291 at £22 13s. 4d., but no vicarage is listed (*VN* 388; *Taxatio* 88).

49. Colchester, St John's Abbey

General confirmation for the monks of their possessions in the diocese of Norwich. Terling, 17 April 1227

B = Colchester, Essex R.O., Acc. 38 pt 1 (Colchester cartulary) pp. 65–6. s. xiii ex.
Pd from B in *Colchester Cartulary* i 115–16.

Omnibus sancte matris ecclesie filiis presentem paginam inspecturis vel audituris Thomas Dei gratia Norwicensis episcopus salutem in Domino sempiternam. Cum ex iniuncto nobis cure pastoralis officio teneamur singulos nostre iurisdictioni subiectos, maximeque viros religiosos, paterna caritate diligere et eorum immunitatibus providere, illos quadam speciali affectione promovere debemus quorum fama clarior et religio circa Dei cultum certis documentis noscitur esse ferventior. Hinc est quod dilectorum filiorum abbatis et monachorum Colecestrie honestatem et religionem attendentes, ecclesias, redditus et possessiones subscriptas, in quarum possessione ab antiquo extitisse predictos abbatem et conventum Colecestrie indubitanter accepimus, ipsis abbati et monachis libere et pacifice in usus proprios in puram et perpetuam elemosinam possidendas episcopali auctoritate concedimus et presenti carta confirmamus, scilicet prioratum de Snapes cum suis pertinentiis, et de eodem prioratu dimidiam marcam annuatim percipiendam, salvis nobis et successoribus nostris prioris pro tempore institutione et destitutione, et obedientia et reverentia Norwicensis ecclesie debita et consueta; item ecclesiam de Aldeburg et ecclesiam de Wicham cum earundem ecclesiarum omnibus pertinentiis, salvis in eisdem ecclesiis honestis sustentationibus vicariorum qui in prefatis ministrabunt ecclesiis; item manerium de Wicham, quod fuit Roberti de Saukevill', cum suis pertinentiis; item duas partes decimarum tam garbarum quam minutarum decimarum de dominico Willelmi de Ambli in Elmesete, et sex acras terre; item duas partes decimarum de garbis de antiquo dominico Thoraldi filii Baldwini in Stokes; item omnes decimas tam maiores quam minores de una carucata terre Richardi de Ikewrde in Maneston [p. 66] et de eadem carucata terre quadraginta solidos annuos; item duas partes decimarum de garbis de dominico Gerardi de Wachesham in Floketun' cum quatuor acris terre et quadam pastura adiacente; item duas partes decimarum de garbis de dominico Ermegoti de Wenham in parochia de Capeles; item sexaginta solidos annuatim percipiendos de firma per manum persone de Ereswelle et eius successorum rectorum ecclesie de Ereswelle secundum continentiam carte cyrographate inter abbatem et conventum Colecestrie ex una parte et P. rectorem ecclesie de Ereswelle ex altera confecte pro duabus partibus decimarum tam maiorum quam minorum provenientium de dominico Radulfi de Rofa in Ereswelle et Cukelesworde et pro duabus acris terre et pro omnibus decimis molendinorum de Ereswell' et de Bertun'; item viginti quatuor solidos annuatim percipiendos per manum prioris de Butele et eius successorum secundum continentiam carte cyrographate inter ecclesiam sancti Iohannis Colecestrie et ecclesiam de Buttele confecte pro decimis de dominicis de Feneberwe et de Glemham quas de eis ad firmam tenent; item quatuor solidos annuatim percipiendos per manum rectoris ecclesie de Intewode de decimis de dominico Henrici de Gessinges in villa de Gondestorp ab antiquo ad monasterium sancti Iohannis Colecestr' pertinentibus; item duodecim solidos de priore et monachis de Stokes annuatim percipiendos de quodam feudo, sicut carta cyrographata inter eos confecta testatur; item advocationem medietatis ecclesie de Emingestun'; item decem solidorum redditum de Iohanne de Geddinges et eius heredibus in villa de Bukesale; item quadraginta solidos annuos de Margeria de Creysi et eius heredibus, sicut carta ipsius testatur. Et in huius rei testimonium hanc cartam fieri fecimus et sigillo nostro muniri. Dat' apud Terlinges quintodecimo kalendas Maii pontificatus nostri anno primo. Hiis testibus: magistro Alano archidiacono Subir', tunc officiali, magistro Roberto de Bilney, Henrico capellano, Radulfo de Blunvill', Dionisio clerico et aliis.

This *actum* was inspected and confirmed by prior William and the convent of Norwich, although the text is not recited in the cartulary copy (*Colchester Cartulary* i 117).

49A. Colchester, St John's Abbey

Confirmation for the monks of a pension of 60s to be received in perpetuity as the farm paid by the rector of Eriswell and his successors for two parts of the great and lesser tithes of the demesne of Ralph of Rochester in Eriswell and Coclesworth, for two acres of land and for the tithe of mills in Eriswell and Barton [Mills], according to the terms of a chirograph made between the abbot and convent and Peter rector of Eriswell. Terling, 17 April 1227

> B = Colchester, Essex R.O., Acc. 38 pt 2 (Colchester leger book) fos. 230v–231r (*inspeximus* by Robert of Tuddenham, patron of Eriswell church). s. xiv in.

Omnibus sancte matris ecclesie filiis presentem paginam inspecturis vel audituris Thomas Dei gratia Norwicensis episcopus salutem in Domino sempiternam. Cum ex iniuncto nobis cure pastoralis officio teneamur singulos nostre iurisdictioni subiectos, maximeque viros religiosos, paterna caritate diligere et eorum immunitatibus providere, illos quadam speciali affectione promovere debemus quorum fama clarior et religio circa Dei cultum certis documentis noscitur esse ferventior. Hinc est quod dilectorum filiorum abbatis et monachorum Colecestrie honestatem et religionem attendentes, pensionem subscriptam, in cuius possessione ab antico extitisse predictos abbatem et conventum Colecestrie indubitanter accepimus, ipsis abbati et monachis libere et pacifice in usus proprios in puram et perpetuam elemosinam possidendam episcopali auctoritate concedimus et presenti carta confirmamus, scilicet sexaginta solidos annuatim percipiendos de firma per manum persone [fo. 231r] de Ereswell et eius successorum rectorum ecclesie de Ereswell, secundum continentiam carte cirograffate inter abbatem et conventum Colecestrie ex una parte et Petrum rectorem ecclesie de Ereswell ex altera confecte, pro duabus partibus decimarum tam maiorum quam minorum provenientium de dominico Radulphi de Rofa[1] in Ereswell et Cukelesworthe et pro duabus acris terre et pro omnibus decimis molendinorum de Ereswell et de Berton'. Et in huius rei testimonium hanc cartam fieri fecimus et sigillo nostro muniri. Dat' apud Terlingg' quintodecimo kalendas Maii pontificatus nostri anno primo. Hiis testibus: magistro Alano archidiacono Subir' tunc officiali, magistro Roberto de Bilney, Henrico capellano, Radulpho de Blumvill', Dionisio clerico et aliis.

> [1] For the identification as Ralph of Rochester, see PRS n.s. xxxii no. 241.

> For the original episcopal confirmation of these tithes by John of Oxford, see *EEA* 6 no. 208. See also no. 49B below. Neither of these *acta* are noticed in J. L. Fisher, 'The Leger Book of St John's Abbey, Colchester', *Trans. Essex Archaeological Society* n.s. 24 (1951), 77–127.

49B. Colchester, St John's Abbey

Notification that, after seemingly interminable litigation between the monks and Peter, rector of Eriswell, over two parts of the great and lesser demesne tithes of Ralph of Rochester in Eriswell and Coclesworth and all the tithes of the mills of Eriswell and Barton [Mills], they at last subscribed to the bishop's ordinance in this matter. He ordered the monks to produce documentation and sworn witnesses in support of their case, and that an inquisition should be held by means of a jury of twelve convened by the [rural] dean, and imposed on the rector and the monks' proctor an oath that his judgement in this matter would be observed. He decreed that the rectors of Eriswell should receive the demesne tithes and the tithes of the mills, notwithstanding the fact that they had pertained by right for sixty years or more to the monks; in recompense the rectors should pay to the monks 60s a year, which sum is stated by the jurors to be the average annual value of these tithes, to be paid in two equal instalments each year at Colchester. If any rector shall default in this payment, then he shall automatically incur sentence of excommunication, and in each case of default shall pay a fine of 40s to the fabric of Norwich cathedral. This verdict is recorded in a chirograph.

Ipswich, 8 May 1228

B = Colchester, Essex R.O., Acc. 38 pt 2 (Colchester leger book) fos. 232r–34r (*inspeximus* by prior William and the convent of Norwich). s. xiv in.

Universis sancte matris ecclesie filiis ad quos presentes littere pervenerint Thomas Dei gratia Norwicensis episcopus salutem in Domino sempiternam. Cum a nobis petitur quod iustum est et honestum tam vigor equitatis quam ordo exigit rationis ut illud per sollicitudinem officii nostri ad debitum perducatur effectum. Hinc est quod, cum nuper inter religiosos viros abbatem et conventum sancti Iohannis Colecestr' Londoniensis diocesis actores ex parte una et dominum Petrum rectorem ecclesie de Ereswell' nostri diocesis reum ex altera super duabus partibus omnium et singularum decimarum tam maiorum quam minorum provenientium de dominicis terris et tenementis quondam Radulphi de Rofa in Ereswell et Cukelesword ac super omnibus decimis molendinorum de Ereswell et de Berton materia questionis et altercationis, antique[a] contentionis et litis, coram[b] nobis loci diocesano per varios strepitus iudiciales et causarum amfractus, non sine magnis laboribus partium et expensis, quasi immortaliter fuisset diuturnis temporibus agitata, ac demum partes predicte, pro iure suo convenientiam [petentes] quam etiam ecclesiarum suarum predictarum, quantum in ipsis fuit, propter bonum pacis et huius litis dispendia evitandum, super possessione vel quasi et etiam iure percipiendi dictas decimas infuturum pure, sponte et absolute, alte et basse, plene se nostre [fo. 232v] submisissent ordinationi,[c] laudo et arbitrio, prout in litteris submissionis dictarum partium plenius continetur, nos dictas submissiones partium predictarum seu compromissum causa dirimendarum et abbreviandarum litium admittentes, ordinaria potestate nobis in hac parte nichilominus reservata, cupientes ad maiorem nostre conscientie serenationem tam super possessione seu quasi et titulo seu iure percipiendi dictas decimas ex parte dictorum religiosorum allegato fieri certiores, munimenta eorundem, quibus loco pro bonis iuris et tituli uti intendebant, nobis fecimus exhiberi ac super eorum possessiones testes in forma iuris admitti et examinari; quibus publicatis, inspectis diligenter et examinatis, licet ex ipsorum tenore ac testium predictorum depositione dictos religiosos iure speciali et ab antiquo, videlicet per tempus sexaginta annorum et amplius, tam super iure quam possessione dictarum decimarum sufficienter fore munitos luculenter declaretur, virtute cuius iuris seu tituli dictas decimas ab antiquo perceperint et adhuc possideant in presenti, prout per inquisitionem duodecim hominum iuratorum per decanum loci eiusdem de mandato nostro super dictarum decimarum estimatione et valore ac ceteris circumstantiis hoc[d] negotium contingentibus rite factam plenius est compertum, ne tamen plus personarum[e] compromittentium quam dictarum ecclesiarum favisse indempnitatibus videamur, prefatos religiosos, in persona sui procuratoris mandatum sufficiens super hoc exhibentis, et dictum rectorem personaliter comparentem [fo. 233r] iuramento corporaliter prestito oneravimus in premissis quod absque omni collusione et fraudis commisso,[f] ac propter utilitatem utriusque ecclesie supradicte, nostrum super iudicium, arbitrium seu decretum valiturum perpetuo instanter requirebunt; compertoque per inquisitionem duodecim hominum fidedignorum ac iuratorum vicinie de mandato nostro speciali, ut premittitur, in hac parte factam super vera rei estimatione qui harum[g] decimarum notitiam habebant de quibus agitur pleniorem, quod super dictis decimis amicabilis compositio esset utrique parti profutura et utilis, prout dicti vicini[h] super hiis iurati firmiter asserebant. Ex quibus omnibus et singulis nos luculentius informati, rimatis et intellectis ipsius negotii circumstantiis ponderatisque prout nobis est possibile ponderandis, pensatisque utriusque ecclesie supradicte et ipsis presidentium utilitatibus et comodis, equo libramine in statera litibus finem imponi cupientes per viam amicabilis compositionis et auctoritate pontificalis officii ordinamus, decernimus et finaliter diffinimus, tam ex arbitraria potestate quam ex ordinaria iurisdictione procedentes, ut ex hac nostra provisione, ordinatione, pronuntiatione, arbitrio seu sententia rectores ecclesie de Ereswell' predicte qui pro tempore fuerint decimas quascumque de dictis terris et tenementis ac molendinis predictis qualitercumque provenientes integre percipiant et quiete, non obstante quod dicte decime speciali iure dictis religiosis sint debite et consuete ac sufficienti, sexaginta annorum, tempore et amplius legittime prescripte. In recompensationem vero huius perceptionis et emolumenti predictam ecclesiam de Eriswell et ipsius rectores quoscumque in sexaginta solidis argenti annuis, pro eo quod he decime[j] iusto pretio pro tanta pecunie summa iuxta[k] [fo. 233v] inquisitionem duodecim hominum fidedignorum et iuratorum vicinie de mandato nostro speciali ut premittitur super hoc factam annis communibus estimantur, ex predictis omnibus et singulis nostram conscientiam informantes, censuales fore sententialiter decernimus et diffinimus, et ad dictam pecunie summam dictis religiosis annuatim in festo purificationis beate Marie et in festo nativitatis beati Iohannis Baptiste pro equali portione in eorum monasterio apud Colecestr' per nuntium rectoris ecclesie de Ereswell' predicte qui pro tempore fuerit persolvendam auctoritate pontificalis officii ac potestate arbitraria finaliter condempnamus. Et si rectores ecclesie memorate qui pro tempore fuerint seu fuerit eorum aliquis huic ordinationi nostre parere contempserint vel contempserit eorum aliquis, vel in solutione pecunie de qua supra tangitur temporibus seu loco vel modo prestititis defecerint seu defecerit eorum aliquis, in eos et in eum sic deficientes ex nunc et ex tunc maioris excommunicationis sententiam proferimus in hiis scriptis. Adicimus etiam huic pene ut quotiens in dicte pecunie prestatione a quovis rectorum dicte ecclesie cessetur, totiens quadraginta solidi fabrice ecclesie cathedralis sancte Trinitatis Norwici applicandi, etiam sine strepitu iudiciali, nostra ordinatione nichilominus in hac parte rata manente, a rectore reluctante sive subterfugiente[l] exsolvantur, premissorum omnium ut in suis iuribus observentur perpetuo nobis et successoribus nostris coherceonem ecclesiasticam[m] reservantes. In quorum omnium et singulorum testimonium premissorum ad perpetuam rei memoriam has litteras nostras in modum cyrograffi confectas sigilli nostri impressione fecimus communiri. Dat' apud Gipeswic' .viii°. idus Maii anno Domini millesimo CC[mo] vicesimo [fo. 234r] octavo, pontificatus nostri anno secundo.

[a] antice B　　[b] quorum B　　[c] ordinatio B　　[d] huius B　　[e] personis B　　[f] commito B　　[g] huius B　　[h] vicinii B　　[j] huius decimo B　　[k] iuxta *repeated* B　　[l] subterfugio B　　[m] coherceoni ecclesiastica B

If this document were not dated, the obvious assumption would be that it preceded no. 49A and recorded the process by which agreement was imposed on the parties before confirmation by the bp. The year of grace and the pontifical year do, however, correspond, and the *inspeximus* by the prior and convent of Norwich is dated 1 July 1228. This suggests that 8 May 1228, rather than 1227, is indeed the correct date, while the correct dating of no. 49A is supported by its having the same date and place of issue as no. 49. It therefore appears that the bp's confirmation of May 1227 and the chirograph made between the parties mentioned therein did not settle the issue, and this may explain the note of exasperation (e.g. 'quasi immortaliter') at the beginning of this *actum*, which is a somewhat singular document. On the one hand, its prolixity is reminiscent of later medieval episcopal *acta*, designed to cover every eventuality and to safeguard against any possible loophole for appeal. On the other, it is repetitious, badly constructed and lacking in stylistic sophistication, and it is riddled with errors of grammar. It may be that the original was difficult to read, but there seems a strong possibility that this *actum* is in fact an abridged record of proceedings before the bp taken down at the time by a clerk (n.b. 'quorum' for 'coram'), which was never revised but nevertheless came to be considered an official episcopal *actum* and thus to be confirmed by the chapter of Norwich.

50. Colchester, St John's Abbey

Grant to the monks of an annual benefice of one mark from a mediety of the church of Hemingstone, to be rendered at the two Suffolk synods for the use of the precentor. Colchester, 15 October 1231

> B = Colchester, Essex R.O., Acc. 38 pt 1 (Colchester cartulary) p. 66. s. xiii ex. C = ibid. (*inspeximus* by prior Simon and convent of Norwich). s. xiii ex.
> Pd from B and C in *Colchester Cartulary* i 118–9.

Omnibus Cristi fidelibus presentes litteras inspecturis vel audituris Thomas Dei gratia Norwicensis episcopus salutem in Domino. Ad universorum notitiam volumus pervenire nos ordinasse quod abbas et conventus monachorum sancti Iohannis Colecestr' habeant et percipiant unam marcam annuam nomine beneficii de medietate ecclesie de Hemmingestun' ad opus precentoris sancti Iohannis Colecestr' ad duas synodos Suffolchie singulis annis inperpetuum, salvis etiam in omnibus reverentia et obedientia nobis et successoribus nostris et sacrosancte Norwicensis ecclesie consuetudinibus debitis vel consuetis. In cuius rei testimonium presentes litteras fieri fecimus et sigillo nostro muniri. Dat' apud Colecestriam in crastino sancti Kalixti pape pontificatus nostri anno quinto.

> On 25 November 1202, after an assize of *darrein presentment*, Robert (of Ashbocking) son of Ernald, the claimant, quitclaimed to Adam, abbot of Colchester, and his successors and to Ernald Ruffus all right in the advowson of Hemingstone, for which they gave him 20s. (*Colchester Cartulary* 516; *Fines* ii no. 386). It was noted that the advowson of one mediety pertained to the abbot, and of the other to Ernald Ruffus and his heirs, and that neither had any claim in the other's mediety. Probably shortly thereafter, Robert of Ashbocking notified bp John of Norwich that he had enquired diligently into the monks' right to the advowson, which had pertained to his ancestors, and because he wished to heed the advice of his friends and not to be in a state of sin, recognising that the monks had a clear right, he wished him to institute the monks' presentee without hindrance by himself or his heirs (*Colchester Cartulary* 260). After the bp's grant above, however, abbot William (either 1238–45 or 1245–72, but presumably before 1254) quitclaimed to the lord William de Ros that part of the advowson pertaining to the abbey, and also granted him and his heirs the tenement of 'Humiliard' previously held by Robert of Ashbocking, for forty marks in cash and the annual rent of a clove (ibid. 662). In 1254 the church was valued at fifteen marks, with no mention of any portion of the monks (*VN* 456).

51. Coxford Priory

Grant to the canons in proprios usus *of a mediety of the church of St Mary, Burnham [Westgate], saving honourable and competent provision for a vicar to minister therein.* Norwich, 27 December 1230

B = Norfolk R. O., ms. SUN/8 (Coxford cartulary) fos. 55v–56r. s. xiii ex. C = ibid. fo. 56r (*inspeximus* by prior William and convent of Norwich). s. xiii ex.

Omnibus Cristi fidelibus ad quos presens scriptum pervenerit Thomas Dei gratia Norwicensis episcopus salutem in Domino. Ad universorum notitiam volumus pervenire nos Dei intuitu et religionis favore concessisse, contulisse et presenti carta confirmasse dilectis [fo. 56v] filiis in Cristo priori et canonicis de Cok' medietatem ecclesie sancte Marie de Burnham, que de eorum existit patronatu, cum omnibus ad dictam medietatem pertinentibus, habendam in proprios usus et perpetuo possidendam, salva honesta et competenti sustentatione vicarii in dicta ecclesia pro tempore ministraturi, salvis etiam in omnibus obedientia et reverentia nobis et successoribus nostris et sacrosancte Norwicensis ecclesie consuetudinibus debitis vel consuetis. In huius rei testimonium presentes litteras fieri fecimus et sigillo nostro muniri. Datum apud Norwicum die sancti Iohannis Evangeliste pontificatus nostri anno quinto.[a]

[a] *dating clause om.* B

A mediety of the church was granted to the canons by Matthew Capelein, son of Richard son of Guy of Burnham (fo. 39v of B). In 1254 both the parson's mediety and the portion of the prior of Coxford were valued at £7 17s., and in 1291 at £8 (*VN* 419; *Taxatio* 89b).

52. Coxford Priory

Grant to the canons in proprios usus *of the church of Houghton, to take effect on the death or resignation of master John of Houghton, archdeacon of Bedford, saving a vicarage of one hundred shillings for a suitable* persona *to be nominated by the bishop and his successors and to be presented to them by the canons.* [Bedingham, 23 March 1227]

B = Norfolk R. O., ms. SUN/8 (Coxford cartulary) fo. 56r. s. xiii ex. C = ibid. (*inspeximus* by prior William and convent of Norwich, 3 July 1230). s. xiii ex.

Omnibus Cristi fidelibus ad quos presens scriptum pervenerit Thomas Dei gratia Norwicensis episcopus salutem in Domino. Ad universorum notitiam volumus pervenire nos causa Dei et religionis favore concessisse ac canonice contulisse et presenti carta nostra confirmasse dilectis in Cristo filiis priori et conventui de Cok' ecclesiam de Houton' cum omnibus pertinentiis suis in proprios usus habendam et perpetuo possidendam post decessum vel recessum magistri Iohannis de Houton' archidiaconi Bedeford', qui eandem ecclesiam optinere dinoscitur, salva vicaria centum solidorum persone ydonee a nobis et successoribus nostris pro tempore nominande et ab eis nobis et successoribus nostris presentande per nos et successores nostros pro tempore conferenda, qui in prefata pro tempore ministrabit ecclesia, salvis etiam in omnibus reverentia et obedientia nobis et successoribus nostris et sacrosancte Norwicensis ecclesie consuetudinibus debitis vel consuetis. In cuius rei testimonium presentes litteras fieri fecimus et sigillo nostro muniri. Dat' apud Bedingham decimo kalendas Aprilis pontificatus nostri anno primo.

> The church is Houghton in Brothercross hundred. In 1254 it was valued at £10, and the vicarage at only £3 6s. 8d. (*VN* 420). In 1291 the church was assessed at £10, excluding the vicarage not subject to the tenth (*Taxatio* 89b). John of Houghton was archdn of Bedford 1218–31, and then of Northampton; he died 1246 × 47 (*Fasti* iii 31–2, 42).

53. Ely Cathedral Priory

Grant to the monks, at the instance of G[eoffrey] bishop of Ely, his kinsman, of a perpetual benefice of twenty shillings in the church of Rushmere [St Andrew], to be rendered to them by the prior and canons of Holy Trinity, Ipswich, when they receive the church in proprios usus.

[20 December 1226 × 17 December 1228]

> B = CUL, EDR ms. G3/28 (Ely cartulary) p. 207. s. xiii ex. C = Bodl. ms. Laud misc. 647 (*Liber Eliensis*) fo. 130r. s. xiv in.

Thomas Dei gratia Norwicensis[a] episcopus viris venerabilibus domino priori et conventui Elyensis ecclesie salutem in Domino sempiternam. Noveritis nos ad instantiam venerabilis fratris et cognati nostri domini G. Elyensis episcopi concessisse vobis mera voluntate et pietatis intuitu ut cum ecclesia de Ressemere[b] dilectis filiis nostris priori et canonicis[c] sancte Trinitatis de Gypewyco[d] in proprios usus cesserit, iidem canonici solvant vobis imperpetuum singulis annis viginti solidos argenti nomine beneficii. Et in huius rei testimonium has litteras vobis mittimus patentes. Valete semper in Domino.

> [a] Norwycensis B   [b] Rissemere C   [c] filiis priori et canonicis nostris C   [d] Gipewico C

> The church is Rushmere St Andrew, in the rural deanery of Carlford, rather than Rushmere in the deanery of Lothingland. In 1291 it is listed as a church of Holy Trinity, Ipswich, valued at £9 6s. 8d., with a vicarage assessed at £4 6s. 8d.; there is no mention of Ely's benefice therein, although the cathedral priory is credited with £1 10s. *de redditibus et perquisitis* (*Taxatio* 116, 128b). The terminal date is the death of Geoffrey de Burgh, bp of Ely.

54. Ely Cathedral Priory

Institution of Alan the chaplain to the church of Bridgham, at the presentation of the prior and monks.   Ipswich, 3 February 1227

B = CUL, EDR ms. G3/28, pp. 206b–7. s. xiii ex. C = Bodl. ms. Laud misc. 647 (*Liber Eliensis*) fo. 130r. s. xiv in.

Omnibus Cristi fidelibus ad quos presens scriptum pervenerit Thomas Dei gratia Norwicensis[a] episcopus salutem in Domino. Ad universorum notitiam volumus pervenire nos ad presentationem dilectorum filiorum prioris et monachorum de Ely admississe[b] Alanum capellanum ad ecclesiam de Bergham,[c] eiusdem ecclesie ut dicitur verorum patronorum, et ipsum in eadem personam canonice instituisse, salvis in omnibus reverentia et obedientia nobis et successoribus nostris et sacrosancte Norwicensis[a] ecclesie consuetudinibus debitis vel consuetis. In cuius rei testimonium presentes litteras fieri fecimus et sigillo nostro muniri. Dat' apud Gypewyc'[d] .iii°. nonas Februarii pontificatus nostri anno primo.

[a] Norwycensis B   [b] admisisse C   [c] Bercham C   [d] Gipeswich' C

54A. Ely Cathedral Priory

Institution of master William of Massingham to the church of Stoke [by Ipswich], both according to the papal mandate addressed to the bishop ordering him to provide him with an ecclesiastical benefice, and at the petition and presentation of the prior and convent, the true patrons.

Norwich, 6 January 1235

B = Bodl. ms. Laud. mis. 647 (*Liber Eliensis*) fo. 149v. s. xiv in.

Omnibus Cristi fidelibus ad quos presens scriptum pervenerit Thomas Dei gratia Norwicensis episcopus salutem in Domino. Ad universorum notitiam volumus pervenire nos, tam de mandato apostolico ad providendum magistro Willelmo de Massingham in ecclesiastico beneficio nobis directo, quam ad presentationem prioris et conventus Elyensis, verorum ut dicitur patronorum ecclesie de Stokes, predictam ecclesiam de Stoke cum omnibus ad ipsam pertinentibus memorato magistro W. contulisse ipsumque in eadem canonice instituisse personam, salvis in omnibus reverentia et obedientia nobis et successoribus nostris et sancte Norwicensis ecclesie consuetudinibus debitis vel consuetis. In cuius rei testimonium presentes litteras fecimus fieri et sigillo nostro muniri. Dat' apud Norwicum die epiphanie Domini pontificatus nostri anno nono.

For the identification of Stoke, see *Liber Eliensis*, Appx D 416–7. The church was valued in 1291 at £10, and Ely's lands there at £26 9s. 6¼d. (*Taxatio* 119b, 125).

55. Eye Priory

Grant to the monks in proprios usus *of the church of All Saints, Dunwich.*
                                        Bury St Edmunds, 28 August 1228

> B = Essex R. O., D/DBy. Q 19 (Eye cartulary) fo. 70v. s. xiii ex.
> Pd from B in *Eye Cartulary* i no. 161.

Omnibus Cristi fidelibus ad quos presens scriptum pervenerit Thomas Dei gratia Norwycensis episcopus salutem in Domino. Ad universorum notitiam volumus pervenire nos causa Dei et religionis favore concessisse et presenti carta nostra confirmasse dilectis filiis in Cristo priori et conventui Eye nostre dyocesis ecclesiam omnium sanctorum de Donewyco cum omnibus ad ipsam pertinentibus, habendam in proprios usus et perpetuo possidendam, salvis etiam in omnibus reverentia et obedientia nobis et successoribus nostris et sacrosancte Norwycensis ecclesie consuetudinibus debitis vel consuetis. In cuius rei testimonium presentes litteras fieri fecimus et sigillo nostro muniri. Dat' apud sanctum Eadmundum quinto kalendas Septembris pontificatus nostri anno secundo.

> The original pension received from this church was 5s. *p.a.*, as confirmed by bp William Turbe (*EEA* 6 no. 92, *Eye Cartulary* i no. 44). For the first recorded institution of a vicar in 1239, see below no. 132. For a brief history of the church, see *Eye Cartulary* ii 45.

56. Eye Priory

Notification that, since a pension of one bezant in the church of St Martin, Dunwich, is vacant, and since Peter of Dunwich, clerk, has long since held the vicarage, recognising that there should be a single rector of a church and wishing therefore to unify this church, he has instituted the said Peter as persona, *at the presentation of the monks.*   Dorchester, 20 January 1231

> B = Essex R. O., D/DBy. Q 19 (Eye cartulary) fo. 71r. s. xiii ex.
> Pd from B in *Eye Cartulary* i no. 164.

Omnibus Cristi fidelibus ad quos presens scriptum pervenerit Thomas Dei gratia Norwycensis episcopus salutem in Domino. Cum pensio unius bisantii vacaret in ecclesia sancti Martini de Donewyco, et Petrus de Donewyco clericus vicariam prefate ecclesie iam dudum optinuisset, attendentes quod unius ecclesie unicus debeat esse rector et ob hoc[a] dictam ecclesiam unire volentes, ad omnium volumus notitiam pervenire nos predictam pensionem prefate ecclesie consolidasse et dictum P. clericum ad presentationem prioris et conventus Eye dicte ecclesie verorum patronorum personam in solidum canonice instituisse, salvis in omnibus reverentia et obedientia nobis et successoribus nostris et sacrosancte Norwycensis ecclesie consuetudinibus debitis et consuetis. In cuius rei testimonium presentes litteras fieri fecimus et sigillo nostro muniri. Dat' apud Dorkecestr' die sanctorum Fabiani et Sebastiani pontificatus nostri anno quinto.

[a] hanc B

A pension to the monks of 30s. *p.a.* is listed in bp William's confirmation charter (*EEA* 6 no. 92; *Eye Cartulary* i no. 44); for the institution of Peter as vicar in 1211, see *EEA* 6 no. 344; *Eye Cartulary* i no. 163; he was to pay a pension to the rector as well as to the monks. For a brief history of the church, see *Eye Cartulary* ii 46. For episcopal efforts to unify divided churches, see Cheney, *From Becket to Langton* 127-9.

57. Eye Priory

Inspeximus *and confirmation of the confirmation for the monks by bishop William Turbe of two parts of the demesne tithe of Hugh of Rickinghall in the parish of Rickinghall [Superior]* [*EEA* 6 no. 89]. *Confirmation of the lease to Sampson the chaplain, the vicar, of these tithes, to be held for an annual rent of 8s. After his death or resignation, they may resume possession of these tithes, as adjudged to them by papal judges-delegate.*   Eye, 27 March 1231

B = Essex R. O., D/DBy. Q 19 (Eye cartulary) fos. 26v-27r. s. xiii ex.
Pd from B in *Eye Cartulary* i no. 39.

Omnibus has litteras inspecturis Thomas Dei gratia Norwicensis episcopus salutem in Domino. Inspeximus cartam Willelmi Turbe episcopi Norwicensis predecessoris nostri continentem duas garbas de dominico Hugonis de Rikinghal' in parrochia de Rikingehal' priori et monachis Eye esse confirmatas et pleno iure ad dictos priorem et monachos pertinere. Nos autem cartam et confirmationem predicti predecessoris nostri dictis monachis Eye super dictis decimis factam ratam habentes et acceptam, ipsam quantum in nobis est episcopali auctoritate confirmamus. Preterea cum predicti prior et monachi Eye prefatas decimas de Rikingehal' dilecto nostro Sampsoni capellano vicario ecclesie de Rikingehal' ad firmam perpetuam suo perpetuo pro octo solidis per annum concesserint et dimi- [fo. 27r] serint, eandem firmam eadem auctoritate episcopali confirmamus, concedentes dictis monachis Eye ut, non obstante predicta firma decimarum, post decessum vel recessum dicti Sampsonis capellani possessionem suam in dictis decimis libere ingredi possint, quas auctoritate eorundem[a] iudicum a domino papa delegatorum inspeximus similiter dictis monachis adiudicatas.[b] In cuius rei testimonium presentes litteras fieri fecimus et sigillo nostro muniri. Dat' apud Eyam .vi°. kalendas Aprilis pontificatus nostri anno quinto.

[a] eorundam B   [b] *the construction here is ungrammatical, due to an obvious lacuna in the transcript.*

Bp William Turbe had confirmed to the monks the tithes of Rickinghall (*EEA* 6 no. 89; *Eye Cartulary* i no. 40). The award of the tithes to them by papal judges-delegate (the abbot and prior of Langley) was made on 21 July 1220; Hugh of Rickinghall and William the vicar were condemned to pay five marks for the tithes they had unjustly taken for the past five years (*Eye Cartulary* i no. 81); shortly before this an agreement had been reached that William the vicar should hold the tithes for 6s. 8d. *p.a.* (ibid. no. 63). For discussion, see ibid. ii 76–7.

58. Eye Priory

Institution of John of Bedfield, clerk, as persona *of the church of Playford, which has been vacant for so long that appointment has devolved upon the bishop by the decree of the [Fourth Lateran] Council, saving the rights of anyone.* Glemham, September 1232

B = Essex R. O., D/DBy. Q 19 (Eye cartulary) fo. 131r. s. xiii ex.
Pd from B in *Eye Cartulary* i no. 350.

Omnibus Cristi fidelibus ad quos presens scriptum pervenerit Thomas Dei gratia Norwicensis episcopus salutem in Domino. Cum ecclesia de Playford per tantum tempus vacaret quod ipsius ordinatio auctoritate concilii ad nos esset devoluta, ad universorum notitiam volumus pervenire nos predictam ecclesiam de Playford auctoritate premissa Iohanni de Bedefeud[a] clerico commississe ipsumque in eadem personam canonice instituisse, salvo iure uniuscuiusque, salvis etiam[b] in omnibus reverentia et obedientia nobis et successoribus nostris et sacrosancte Norwicensis ecclesie consuetudinibus debitis vel consuetis. In cuius rei testimonium presentes literas fieri fecimus et sigillo nostro muniri. Dat' apud Glemham mense Septembris pontificatus nostri anno sexto.

[a] Bredefeud B   [b] et cetera B

In 1227–8 an assize of *darrein presentment* was held when the prior claimed the advowson against the bp of Norwich and Alan of Withersdale. The prior produced a charter of bp John of Oxford by which he instituted William of Bech at the presentation of the monks (*EEA* 6 no. 226), and although Alan of Withersdale alleged that William de Bech had been presented by Peter Walter, who was then in his custody (as ward), the prior recovered seisin (*Eye Cartulary* ii no. 391). The *actum* above suggests that the monks' right to presentation was still contested. Some five years after this *actum*, judges-delegate, acting on a mandate of pope Gregory IX dated 28 February 1237, adjudicated in a case brought by the monks against John clerk of Bedfield and A[lan] of Withersdale], knight; they petitioned that John should be removed from the church, which he had occupied in contravention of their right of patronage, withholding for several years the pension of 5s. *p.a.* due to them from the church. John proved by the production of (this) document that the church had been collated to him by bp Thomas, on whom ordination had devolved following a long vacancy; the monks' right of patronage was upheld, and John was in future to pay the customary pension (ibid. i no. 70).

The advowson was still in contention in 1268, when on 3 February Thomas of Clare recognised the prior's right and quitclaimed, in return for which he received twenty marks (ibid. i no. 392).

58A. Frostenden Church

Notification that master Richard of Wenden has petitioned the bishop to make provision for a rector, with the consent of the patron, whom Richard has informed from the time when he was beneficed elsewhere that he should present a suitable persona. *The bishop, approving the resignation, intention and solicitude of Richard, has on his resignation taken the church into his own hands.* [20 December 1226 × 23 January 1236]

> B = Strood, Rochester, Medway Archives, ms. DRc/L4 (notification of proceedings before papal judges-delegate). s. xiii med.

Omnibus Cristi fidelibus presentes literas inspecturis Thomas Dei gratia Norewicensis episcopus salutem in Domino. Noverit universitas vestra quod magister Ricardus de Wenden' nobis humiliter supplicavit ut provideremus ecclesie de Frostinden nostre diocesis super rectore ydoneo de consensu patroni, quem idem R. monuit a tempore quo alias fuit beneficiatus quod ydoneam personam ad dictam ecclesiam de Frostinden presentaret. Nos autem resignationem, voluntatem et sollicitudinem dicti magistri approbantes, predictam ecclesiam ad eius resignationem in manus nostras recepimus.

> This *actum* was produced in court in the first stage of the prolonged litigation resulting from archbp Edmund's refusal to confirm the election of Wenden to the bpric of Rochester on 26 March 1235, on the main ground that patronage pertained to the archbp of Canterbury. For an account of the ultimately successful case of the monks of Rochester, see *Anglia Sacra* i 348–9; for papal documents, *Reg. Greg. IX* nos. 2731, 3261, 4197; see also Churchill, *Canterbury Administration* i 283–4; Gibbs and Lang, *Bishops and Reform* 75–6; Sayers, *Papal Judges-Delegate* 17, 173, 280, 283. The case was first heard by the abbot of Walden as papal judge-delegate with mr John of Tynemouth and Philip the chaplain, subdelegates respectively of the prior of Merton and the archdn of Northampton, whose report is B; they were appointed some time before 29 July 1236, and their notification records that the hearing began on the morrow of the feast of St Vincent (23 January), which must therefore be 1236. Mr Richard of Wenden (? Wenden Tofts, Essex; *Fasti* ii 77 n. 2) was before his election official of the bp of Rochester and rector of Bromley, Kent, on his institution to which it is probable that he resigned Frostenden. He was also a prebendary of St Paul's, London (B), but should be distinguished from mr Richard of Wendover (*Fasti* i 46, 64, 76).

59. Gloucester Abbey

Notification that he has discovered from the matricula *of the church of Norwich and from other instruments exhibited by the monks that they should*

receive an annual pension of six marks from the church of St Peter Mancroft in Norwich, which he concedes and confirms by episcopal authority.
London, 23 October 1227

    B = PRO C150/1 (now SR3/38, Gloucester cartulary) fo. 140r (123r). s. xiv ex. C = ibid. (*inspeximus* by prior William and convent of Norwich). D = Gloucester Cathedral Library, St Peter's register A fo. 133r (*inspeximus* by prior William and convent of C, 27 May 1339). s. xiv ex.
    Pd from B and C in *Gloucester Cartulary* ii 33, nos. 475–76; calendared from D in D. Walker, 'A Register of the Churches of the Monastery of St Peter's Gloucester' in *An Ecclesiastical Miscellany*, Publs. of Bristol and Gloucestershire Archaeological Society, Records Section, 2 (1976), 3–58, no. 88.

Omnibus Cristi fidelibus ad quos presens scriptum pervenerit Thomas Dei gratia Norwicensis[a] episcopus salutem in Domino. Cum fidem habeamus per matriculam Norwicensis ecclesie et per quedam alia instrumenta[b] nobis a monachis Glouc' in iure exhibita quod dicti monachi Glouc' debeant percipere sex marcas annuas nomine pensionis de ecclesia sancti Petri de Mannecroft[c] in Northwico, dictam pensionem prefatis monachis ob favorem religionis concedimus et eam auctoritate episcopali ipsis[d] confirmamus. In cuius rei testimonium presentes litteras fieri fecimus[e] et sigillo nostro muniri.[f] Dat' London' decimo kalendas Novembris pontificatus nostri anno primo.

    [a] Northwic' D   [b] instrumenta alia D   [c] Manecroft D   [d] ipsis *om.* D   [e] fieri fecimus *om.* D   [f] communiri D

    A notification by archbp Theobald as papal legate (1150 × 1159) to bp William of Norwich records that he had conceded to abbot Hamelin and the monks the right to dispose as seemed best to them of the church of St Peter in the marketplace of Norwich, which they held (*Gloucester Cartulary* ii 34, no. 479, where wrongly ascribed to archbp Becket; also Saltman, *Theobald* 342–3, no. 120). Bp Thomas's confirmation was confirmed by archbp Langton (*Gloucester Cartulary* ii 35, no. 480; *Acta Langton* no. 117). Later in the thirteenth century the official of the archdn of Norwich found by inquisition that the monks had received this pension from before the time of Robert of Gloucester, archdn of Sudbury (d. by 28 October 1222), who had been rector (*Gloucester Cartulary* ii 35, no. 481). There was litigation in the Norwich consistory court in 1347, when the monks recovered the pension with arrears from Michaelmas 1343 (Walker, 'Register' no. 87). In 1254 the monks' portion was valued at five marks and the vicarage at eight marks (*VN* 386); in 1291 the monks' portion was assessed at six marks and the church at £25 (*Taxatio* 78).

60. Great Bricett Priory

Grant to the canons in proprios usus *of the church of Wattisham, saving honourable and competent provision for a vicar.*
Ixworth, 25 November 1230

    B = King's College, Cambridge, GBR 290 (*inspeximus* by prior Henry and the convent of

Christ Church, Canterbury, 9 September 1289). s. xiii ex. C = ibid. GBR 291 (as B). s. xiv in.

Omnibus Cristi fidelibus ad quos presens scriptum pervenerit Thomas divina gratia Norwicensis[a] episcopus salutem in Domino. Ad universorum notitiam volumus pervenire nos causa Dei et religionis favore concessisse et presenti carta confirmasse dilectis filiis in Cristo priori et canonicis de Bresete ecclesiam de Wathisham[b] cum omnibus ad ipsam pertinentibus, habendam et tenendam in proprios usus et perpetuo possidendam, salva honesta et competenti sustentatione vicarii in dicta ecclesia pro tempore ministraturi per nos et successores nostros instituendi, salvis etiam in omnibus reverentia et obedientia nobis et successoribus nostris et sacrosancte Norwicensis[a] ecclesie consuetudinibus debitis vel consuetis. In cuius rei testimonium presentes litteras fieri fecimus et sigillo nostro muniri. Dat' apud Ixewrth die sancte Katerine virginis pontificatus nostri anno quarto.

[a] Norwycensis B   [b] Wachesham C

There is no further mention of a vicarage in the thirteenth century. In 1254 the portion of the *persona* was valued at six marks, and that of Castle Acre priory at two marks (*VN* 436). In 1291 the church, appropriated to the priory, was valued at eight marks (*Taxatio* 122).

61. Haughmond Abbey

Inspeximus *and confirmation of the charters of bishops John I [of Oxford] and John II [de Gray], whereby among other things they granted to the canons* in proprios usus *the church of Hunstanton, saving honest and competent provision for a vicar* [*EEA* 6 nos. 223–4, 347]. *He now ordains that the vicarage shall consist of fifteen marks as taxed by the archdeacon of Norfolk, the bishop's official, to which vicarage, whenever it is vacant, the abbot and convent shall present as* persona *whomsoever the bishop wishes, without difficulty or contradiction; if after warning they fail to present, the bishop shall nevertheless institute to the vicarage.*   Blofield, 26 May 1229

B = Shrewsbury Borough Library, Haughmond Abbey Cartulary, insert between fos. 120–21. s. xv ex.
Pd from B in *Haughmond Cartulary* no. 618.

Omnibus Cristi fidelibus ad quos presens scriptum pervenerit Thomas Dei gratia Norwicensis episcopus salutem in Domino. Inspeximus cartas bone memorie Iohannis primi et Iohannis secundi predecessorum nostrorum abbati et conventui de Haghmon' concessas, inter cetera continentes quod dicti predecessores nostri Deo intuitu et religionis favore concesserunt et confirmaverunt dictis abbati et conventui de Haghmon' ecclesiam de Hunstanton' nostre diocesis in proprios usus perpetuo possidendam, salva honesta et competenti sustentatione vicarii in dicta ecclesia pro tempore ministraturi. Nos autem dictorum predecessorum factum in hac parte gratum habentes et acceptum, prefatam ecclesiam de Hunstanton' dictis abbati et conventui confirmamus, salva honesta et competenti vicaria .xv. marcarum per dilectum et fidelem nostrum officialem, archidiaconum Norfolch', de precepto nostro taxata ad opus vicarii perpetui in dicta vicaria pro tempore ministraturi, ad quam vicariam quotiens vacari contigerit dicti abbas et conventus [*verso*] de Haghmon personam quamcumque voluerimus nobis et successoribus nostris sine difficultate aliqua ac alicuius pravitatis et contradictionis obstaculo presentabunt, quod si post commonitionem eis a nobis faciendam personam a nobis et successoribus nostris nominandam presentare distulerint, nos et successores nostri ipsis irrequisitis quemcumque voluerimus vicarium in eadem instituemus. Predictam autem collationem et ordinationem dicte vicarie de consensu et voluntate dictorum abbatis et conventus de Haghmon' nobis et successoribus nostris reservavimus, salvis etiam in omnibus reverentia et obedientia nobis et successoribus nostris et sacrosancte Norwicensis ecclesie consuetudinibus debitis vel consuetis. In cuius rei testimonium presentes literas fieri fecimus et sigillo nostro muniri. Dat' apud Blafeld manerium nostrum septimo kalendas Iunii pontificatus nostri anno tertio.

The sources of the vicar's revenue are delineated in no. 62 below, which was modified in some particulars by bp Ralegh (no. 135). In 1254 the church was valued at £16, the vicarage at £5 5s. 4d. and the portion of the prior of St Winwaloe (at Wereham) at 10s. (*VN* 406). In 1291 the church was assessed at £18, the vicarage at £6 13s. 4d. and St Winwaloe's portion at 13s. 4d. (*Taxatio* 89).

62. Haughmond Abbey

Notification of the ordination of a vicarage in the church of Hunstanton, taxed at the bishop's command by master Robert, his official and archdeacon of Norfolk, and Walter persona *of Thorpe. The vicar shall have all the altarage of the church with all the lesser tithes and oblations, except for the tithe of the sea, of which he shall receive only a tenth part. He shall have the buildings in the churchyard of Hunstanton and ten acres of free land, with the meadow called 'Redmedewe', and he shall have also the chapel of St Edmund with all its appurtenances and oblations. The vicar shall discharge all the due and accustomed obligations of the church, and to extraordinary obligations the abbot and vicar shall contribute* pro rata.   Bury St Edmunds, 31 May 1229

B = Shrewsbury Borough Library, Haughmond Abbey Cartulary, fo. 120v. s. xv ex.
Pd from B in *Haughmond Cartulary* no. 620.

Omnibus Cristi fidelibus ad quos presens scriptum pervenerit Thomas Dei gratia Norwicensis episcopus salutem in Domino. Universitati vestre notum fieri volumus quod cum abbas et conventus de Haghmon' tam a nobis quam a predecessoribus nostris ecclesiam de Hunstanton' sibi in proprios usus optinuissent confirmari, salva honesta sustentatione vicarii pro tempore in dicta ecclesia ministraturi, ne futuris temporibus inter predictos abbatem et conventum et dictum vicarium materia scandali sive discordie possit oriri, ipsam vicariam per dilectos in Cristo filios magistrum Robertum officialem, archidiaconum Norfolchie, et Walterum personam de Thorp' taxari fecimus in hunc modum, videlicet quod vicarius habebit totum alteragium predicte ecclesie cum omnibus decimis minutis et obventionibus, exceptis decimis maris, de quibus percipiet vicarius decimam decime tantum. Item, predictus vicarius habebit edificia sua in cimiterio de Hunstanstun' et decem acras libere terre cum prato quod vocatur Redmedwe. Item, habebit vicarius capellam sancti Edmundi cum omnibus pertinentiis et obventionibus suis. Sustinebit autem dictus vicarius omnia onera debita et consueta; ad extraordinaria autem onera contribuent dictus abbas et dictus vicarius pro rata. In cuius rei testimonium presentes literas fieri fecimus et sigillo nostro muniri. Dat' apud sanctum Edmundum pridie kalendas Iunii pontificatus nostri anno tertio.

63. Hickling Priory

Inspeximus *and confirmation of the* inspeximus *by bp John II of bp John I's grant to the canons* in proprios usus *of a mediety of the church of Waxham, with provision to be made for a vicar to serve that mediety* (*EEA* 6 nos. 230, 351). [20 December 1226 × 16 August 1236]

B = Bodl. ms. Tanner 425 (Hickling cartulary) fos. 40v–41r (pp. 82–3). s. xiii med.

Omnibus [a-]Cristi fidelibus ad quos presens scriptum pervenerit[-a] Thomas Dei gratia Norwicensis episcopus salutem in Domino. Noverit universitas vestra nos inspexisse cartam bone memorie I. quondam episcopi predecessoris nostri in hac forma: [*EEA* 6 no. 351]. Nos autem predictas confirmationes ratas et gratas habentes, eas presenti scripto nostro[b] et sigilli nostri appositione duximus roborandas. Dat' etc. T(estibus) etc.

[a-a] *om.* B   [b] presentis scripti nostri B

64. Hickling Priory

Grant to the canons in proprios usus *of the* personatus *of the church of Waxham, which is of their advowson.*[20 December 1226 × 16 August 1236]

B = Bodl. ms. Tanner 425 (Hickling cartulary) fo. 41r (p. 83). s. xiii med.

Omnibus [a-] Cristi fidelibus ad quos presens scriptum pervenerit [-a] Thomas Dei gratia Norwicensis episcopus salutem in Domino. Ad universorum volumus pervenire notitiam nos causa Dei et religionis favore concessisse et canonice contulisse et presenti carta nostra confirmasse dilectis in Cristo filiis priori et conventui de Hikeling' personatum ecclesie de Waxtunesham, qui de patronatu predictorum prioris et canonicorum esse dinoscitur, in proprios usus habendum et[b] in perpetuo possidendum, salvis in omnibus obedientia et reverentia nobis et successoribus nostris[c] et sacrosancte Norwicensis ecclesie consuetudinibus debitis vel consuetis.

[a-a] *om* B   [b] et *om.* B   [c] nostris *om.* B

The abbot of St Benet of Holme had a portion of 13s. 4d. in the church, which in 1254 was assessed at £8 and in 1291 at £6 *preter portionem* (*VN* 415; *Taxatio* 86b).

65. Holme, St Benet's Abbey

Notification to the prior and dean of Rochester, papal judges-delegate, that, since he has heard that N[icholas] Pincerna, clerk, to whom he had committed the custody only of the church of Swanton [Abbot], is now bringing an action before them by apostolic mandate as rector, claiming two-thirds of the great tithe, in order that they should not be deceived he informs them that two-thirds of the tithe of the monks' demesne, which are claimed by him, have pertained to the monastery from times long past.

[20 December 1226 × 16 August 1236]

B = BL ms. Cotton Galba E ii (St Benet cartulary) fo. 48v. s. xiii ex. C = Bodl. ms. Norfolk roll 82 (St Benet roll) hh. s. xiv in. D = BL ms. Cotton roll iv 57 (St Benet roll) no. 31. s. xiv. E = Norfolk R.O., DCN 40/8 (St Benet cartulary) fo. 24v (35v). s. xiv ex.

Venerabilibus viris et amicis in Cristo karissimis priori et decano Roffensibus Thomas Dei gratia Norwicensis episcopus salutem in Domino. Audivimus quod N. Pincerna clericus, cui custodiam tantum ecclesie de Swanton'[a] nostre diocesis[b] commisimus, dilectos filios in Cristo abbatem et conventum sancti Benedicti de Hulmo super duabus garbis decimarum de dominico eorum in predicta villa de Swanton'[a] sub appellatione rectoris dicte ecclesie per litteras apostolicas coram vobis nititur fatigare, et ne ad ipsius suggestionem[c] vestra possit discretio in iudicando circumveniri, presentibus vobis duximus significandum quod decime duarum garbarum de eorum dominico petitarum ad eorum monasterium ab antiquo spectaverunt. Valete.

[a] Swaneton' B C   [b] nostre diocesis *om.* C   [c] fatigationem B

An undated notification by Nicholas, rector of Swanton Abbot, records a composition reached in his litigation against the monks before papal judges-delegate at Rochester. After he had made restitution for all the tithes which he had detained from them, he was permitted to hold them in future of the abbot and convent for an annual payment of 3s., as his predecessors had been accustomed to hold them (fos. 24v–25r of E).

66. Holme, St Benet's Abbey

Grant to the monks in proprios usus *of the church of Scottow, to take effect on the death or resignation of master Michael of Ringsfield and R. of Wyverstone, the rectors, saving an honourable and competent vicarage to be taxed by the bishop or his successors, at each vacancy of which the abbot and convent shall present that suitable* persona *whom the bishop and his successors wish, and if they fail to do so, the bishops may nevertheless institute to the vicarage.* Norwich, 29 March 1232

B = BL ms. Cotton Galba E ii (St Benet cartulary) fo. 48r–v. s. xiii ex. C = BL ms. Cotton roll iv 57 (St Benet roll) no. 56. s. xiv.

Omnibus Cristi fidelibus ad quos presens scriptum pervenerit Thomas Dei gratia Norwicensis episcopus salutem in Domino. Ad universorum notitiam volumus pervenire nos Dei causa et religionis favore concessisse et presenti carta nostra confirmasse dilectis nobis in Cristo abbati et conventui sancti Benedicti de Hulmo ecclesiam de Scothowe cum pertinentiis, habendam et tenendam et in proprios usus perpetuo possidendam post decessum vel recessum magistri Michaelis de Ringgesfeld[a] et R. de Wiverdeston' eiusdem rectorum, salva honesta et competenti vicaria in dicta ecclesia per nos vel successores nostros pro tempore taxanda, ad quam vicariam quotiens vacare contigerit dicti abbas et conventus personam idoneam[b] quamcumque nos et successores nostri voluerimus nobis presentabunt et presentatum admittemus. Et si forte omiserint vel necglexerint presentare, nos et successores nostri nichilominus personam idoneam[b] quamcumque voluerimus vicarium in eadem instituemus, salvis etiam nobis in omnibus reverentia et obedientia et successoribus nostris et sacrosancte Norwicensis ecclesie consuetudinibus debitis vel consuetis. In cuius rei testimonium presentes litteras fieri fecimus et sigillo nostro muniri. Dat' apud Norwicum quarto kalendas Aprilis pontificatus nostri anno sexto. Hiis testibus: domino W. priore Norwicensi, magistro R. de Biln(eia) archidiacono Norf(olchie), magistris Andrea de Croydene et R. de London',[c] domino Dionisio clerico nostro, Iohanne Terri et aliis.

[a] Ryngesfeld C   [b] ydoneam C   [c] B *ends here with* etc.

The church had originally been granted to the abbey by king Henry I (*St Benet of Holme* i no. 4; *Regesta* ii no. 1095). There is no evidence that it was divided into medieties in the late twelfth century (*St Benet of Holme* i nos. 251, 289). In 1254 the church was assessed at £25 6s. 8d. and in 1291 at £26 13s. 4d.; the vicarage is not listed (*VN* 366; *Taxatio* 82b). According to an *actum* of bp William Bateman, dated 31 December 1348, the church had been held *in proprios usus* by the monks, but they had lost it some time before 1338 because they could not defend its possession in the royal court. Bateman restored the appropriation (*Reg. Bateman* nos. 12–15). This *actum* provides a good example of the use of *persona* not, as was usual in the twelfth century, meaning 'rector', but here 'vicar'; see subject index, *s.v. persona*.

67. Holme, St Benet's Abbey

Mandate to the official of the archdeacon of Norwich to induct the abbot and convent into corporal possession of the church of Scottow, which he has granted to them in proprios usus, *saving an honourable and competent vicarage to be taxed by the bishop when he comes to that area.*

Gaywood, 6 December 1233

B = BL ms. Cotton Galba E ii (St Benet cartulary) fo. 48v. s. xiii ex.

Thomas Dei gratia Norwicensis episcopus dilecto filio in Cristo officiali archidiaconi Norwicensis salutem in Domino. Mandamus vobis quatinus abbatem et conventum sancti Benedicti de Hulmo in corporalem possessionem totius ecclesie de Scothowe, quam eis in proprios usus concessimus et confirmavimus, sollempniter mittatis et missos tueamini, salva honesta et competenti vicaria in eadem ecclesia per nos cum ad partes illas venerimus secundum facultates ecclesie taxanda. Dat' apud Gaywde die sancti Nicholai pontificatus nostri anno septimo. Valete.

68. Holme, St Benet's Abbey

Confirmation for the monks of all the tithes of their own manors, which they have peacefully possessed, either themselves or through farmers, from time immemorial.

Norwich, 6 January 1234

B = BL ms. Cotton Galba E ii (St Benet cartulary) fo. 48v. s. xiii ex. C = Bodl. ms. Norfolk roll 82 (St Benet roll) y. s. xiv in. D = ibid., Norfolk roll 83 (St Benet roll) b. s. xiv in. E = ibid. c (*inspeximus* by prior Roger and the convent of Norwich). F = BL ms. Cotton roll iv 57 (St Benet roll) no. 22. s. xiv. G = Norwich, Norfolk R.O., DCN register VIII (St Benet cartulary) fo. 19v (27v). s. xiv ex.

Omnibus Cristi fidelibus ad quos presens scriptum pervenerit Thomas Dei gratia Norwicensis[a] episcopus salutem in Domino. Ad universorum notitiam volumus pervenire nos confirmasse dilectis filiis in Cristo abbati et monachis sancti Benedicti de Hulmo omnes decimas in maneriis suis, quas ipsi per se vel per firmarios suos pacifice possederunt et inconcusse a tempore quod excedit memoriam hominum. In cuius rei testimonium presentes litteras fieri fecimus et sigillo nostro muniri. Dat' apud Norwicum[a] die Epiphanie Domini pontificatus nostri anno octavo.

[a] Norwyc' C, F

The *inspeximus* by the prior and convent was issued on the same day as the bp's *actum*.

69. Ipswich, Priory of St Peter and St Paul

Grant to the canons in proprios usus *of the church of Cretingham, made with the assent of Alexander the* persona *and the lady Agnes of Cretingham, and to take effect after Alexander's death. During his lifetime the canons shall receive from him an annual pension of six marks, saving to him the remaining portions of the church, and saving after his death a competent vicarage to be taxed by the bishop or his successors.* Playford, 16 September 1235

A[1] = PRO E42/302. Endorsed: Appropriatio ecclesie de Cretingham priori Gipwici (s. xvi in); approx. 174 × 87 + 15 mm.; parchment tag, seal, green wax, counterseal.
A[2] = PRO E42/460. No medieval endorsement; approx. 151 × 57 + 11 mm.; parchment tag, fragment of seal, green wax, counterseal.

Omnibus Cristi fidelibus ad quos presens scriptum pervenerit Thomas Dei gratia Norwicensis episcopus salutem in Domino. Ad universorum notitiam volumus pervenire nos Dei causa et religionis favore, et de voluntate et consensu Alexandri persone et ad presentationem domine Agnetis de Cretingeham,[a] vere ut dicitur patrone ecclesie de Cretingeham',[a] concessisse et presenti carta confirmasse dilectis nobis in Cristo priori et canonicis sancti Petri de Gypewic'[b] predictam ecclesiam de Cretingeham'[a] cum pertinentiis, habendam et[c] tenendam et in proprios usus perpetuo possidendam post decessum dicti Alexandri persone, percipiendo de dicta ecclesia temporibus predicti Alexandri sex marcas annuas nomine pensionis, salvis dicto Alexandro quoad vixerit residuis portionibus ecclesie memorate, salva etiam post decessum dicti Alexandri vicaria competenti secundum facultates ecclesie taxanda per nos vel successores nostros, salvis etiam in omnibus reverentia et obedientia nobis et successoribus nostris et sancte Norwicensis ecclesie consuetudinibus debitis vel consuetis. In cuius rei testimonium presentes litteras[d] fieri fecimus et sigillo nostro muniri. Dat' apud Pleyford' sexto decimo die Septembris pontificatus nostri anno nono, presentibus priore sancte Trinitatis de Gypewic',[e] magistro Alexandro de Walepol, Iohanne Terry, Adam de Elmham et aliis.

[a] Cretingham' A[2]   [b] Gipwic A[2]   [c] et *om.* A[1]   [d] literas A[2]   [e] Gipewic' A[2]

The monks held a benefice of six marks in the church, conceded by bp John of Oxford at the petition of Ernald de Coleville and Agnes his wife, after a final concord made in the *curia regis* on 18 October 1198 (*EEA* 6 no. 247; PRS os xxiv no. 25). Agnes of Cretingham is almost certainly Ernald's widow. The taxation of the vicarage was effected during the vacancy following bp Thomas's death by Anger, abbot of West Dereham, vicegerent of the archbp of Canterbury and the archdns, on 7 March 1237. Having inspected and confirmed bp Thomas's *actum*, he ordained that the vicar should receive all the altarage of the church and its chapel, and should have two acres of the free land of the church, the tithe of hay and of the mills, and the annual rent pertaining to the church, with the lesser tithes and other obventions; the prior and convent were to have all the rest of the land, one acre of meadow and the great tithe, and they should discharge all the obligations of the church to the bp and provide decently for ornaments and the other ecclesiastical necessities of church and chapel (PRO E40/14021). In 1254 the church was valued at twenty-two marks, and in 1291 at twenty marks (*VN* 466; *Taxatio* 117).

70. Ixworth Priory

Inspeximus *and confirmation of the grant by John of Oxford to the canons* in proprios usus *of the church of Little Melton* (Appx I no. 9). *This is to take effect on the death or resignation of Robert of Massingham, the present rector, and suitable provision is to be made according to the church's resources for a vicar to minister therein.* Bury St Edmunds, 5 June 1230

B = Emmanuel College, Cambridge, muniments box 20, A1 (Ixworth priory roll) no. 4. s. xiv. C = ibid. no. 5 (*inspeximus* by prior William and convent of Norwich).

Omnibus Cristi fidelibus ad quos presens scriptum pervenerit Thomas Dei gratia Norwicensis episcopus salutem in Domino. Inspeximus cartam Iohannis primi predecessoris nostri Norwicensis episcopi continentem ecclesiam de Parva Melton cum omnibus ad ipsam pertinentibus canonicis de Ixewrth in proprios usus ab eodem esse concessam ex donatione Radulfi de Monte Kanesi eiusdem patroni. Nos autem dicti predecessoris nostri concessionem dictis canonicis de Ixewrth de dicta ecclesia factam ratam habentes et acceptantes,[a] prefatam ecclesiam de Parva Melton cum suis pertinentiis Dei intuitu et religionis favore dictis canonicis de Ixewrth post decessum vel recessum Roberti de Massingham eiusdem rectoris in proprios usus concedimus et confirmamus, salva honesta et competenti sustentatione vicarii secundum facultates ecclesie in dicta ecclesia pro tempore ministraturi, salva etiam in omnibus reverentia et obedientia nobis et successoribus nostris et sacrosancte Norwicensis ecclesie consuetudinibus debitis et consuetis. In cuius rei testimonium presentes literas fieri fecimus et sigillo nostro muniri. Dat' apud sanctum Edmundum die sancti Bonifacii martiris pontificatus nostri anno quarto.

[a] habemus et acceptamus B

Despite the grant of the church by Ralph de Montchesney, confirmed by bp John of Oxford, there was a subsequent dispute, and after an assize of *darrein presentment* Warin de Montchesney on 5 June 1228 in the *curia regis* quitclaimed the advowson to prior Gilbert of Ixworth. On 19 May 1220 pope Honorius III had issued letters of protection (*Iustis petentium desideriis*) for the priory, mentioning specifically the churches of Hainford, Hunston and Little Melton, and on 5 February 1245 pope Innocent IV also issued letters of protection (*Sacrosancta Romana ecclesia*), mentioning specifically the churches of Walsham le Willows and Little Melton (nos. 6, 8 of B).

71. Kersey Hospital

Notification that the bishop has taken under his special protection the house which Thomas de Burgh built and committed in perpetuity to the ordinance of the bishop and his successors. [20 December 1226 × 16 August 1236]

B = King's College, Cambridge, KER 638 (Kersey charter roll) m.3r. s. xiv in.

Omnibus Cristi fidelibus presentes literas inspecturis vel audituris Thomas Dei gratia Norwicensis episcopus salutem in Domino sempiternam. Noveritis nos divine pietatis intuitu domum de Kerseye, quam nobilis vir Thomas de Burgo construxit ac nostre ordinationi et successorum nostrorum inperpetuum commisit, sub nostra protectione speciali cum omnibus bonis dicte domui ab ipso T. collatis et conferendis et ab aliis suscepisse. In cuius rei testimonium presentes literas fieri fecimus et sigillo nostro muniri. Dat' etc.

The community of the Blessed Virgin Mary and St Anthony at Kersey was founded *c.* 1218 as a hospital by Thomas de Burgh, husband of Nesta of Cockfield; it was soon converted into a priory (*MRH* 161). The church of Kersey was valued at five marks in 1254 (*VN* 436).

72. Kersey Hospital

Confirmation for the hospital of its rents and possessions and of the mother and parish church of Kersey with its advowson, granted to them by the noble lady Nesta of Cockfield, lady of Lindsay, in her widowhood. The bishop concedes to the canons in proprios usus *the said church, for their maintenance and that of the sick and poor resorting thereto.*   Norwich, 2 May 1228

B = King's College, Cambridge, KER 638 (Kersey charter roll) m.3r. s. xiv in.

Omnibus Cristi fidelibus ad quos presens scriptum pervenerit Thomas Dei gratia Norwicensis episcopus salutem in Domino. Cum nobilis mulier Nesta de Kokefeud[a] domina de Leleseye tempore viduitatis sue terras, redditus, possessiones et ecclesiam matricem et parochialem de Keresey cum advocatione eiusdem divine[b] amoris intuitu hospitali, scilicet de Kerseye, dederit et assignaverit, ad omnium volumus pervenire notitiam nos dictarum terrarum, reddituum, possessionum et ecclesie predicte concessionem, donationem et assignationem ratam habentes et acceptam, ipsam presentis scripti testimonio et sigilli nostri appositione duximus confirmandam et coroborandam, prefatam ecclesiam de Kereseye cum omnibus ad ipsam pertinentibus ad sustentationem canonicorum ibidem Deo servientium et ad sustentationem egrorum et pauperum ibidem confluentium in proprios usus dictis canonicis concedentes et presenti carta nostra confirmantes, salvis in omnibus reverentia et obedientia [nobis] et successoribus nostris et sacrosancte Norwicensis ecclesie consuetudinibus debitis vel consuetis. In cuius rei testimonium presentes literas fieri fecimus et sigillo nostro muniri. Dat' apud Norwycum .xi°. kalendas Iunii pontificatus nostri anno secundo.

[a] Bokefeund B   [b] divinis B

Despite the reading in B, there is no doubt that the widow of Thomas de Burgh was Nesta of Cockfield, in Babergh hundred and not far from Kersey; see, for example, *CRR* x 161–2.

73. Lewes Priory

Notification that, having learned from an authentic instrument of bishop William his predecessor that the medieties of the churches of [West] Walton and Walpole are bound to the payment to the monks of an annual pension of ten marks, lest discord should arise between the rectors of these medieties he has ordained that the rector of the mediety of Walpole should pay six marks a year and the rector of the mediety of [West] Walton four marks a year.

Hoxne [20 December 1230 × 24 March 1231]

A = PRO E40/14117. Endorsed: T. Norwycensis episcopi de ecclesiis de Waltun' et de Walpol', IX (s. xiii med.); approx. 165 × 96 + 21 mm.; single slit, tag and seal missing.

Omnibus Cristi fidelibus ad quos presens scriptum pervenerit Thomas Dei gratia Norwicensis episcopus salutem eternam in Domino. Cum ex autentico instrumento bone memorie Willelmi quondam Norwicensis episcopi pro certo cognovimus medietates ecclesiarum de Waltun' et de Walpol' monachis de Lewes teneri in consueta pensione decem marcarum, ne tractu temporis inter rectores dictarum medietatum occasione solvende pensionis possit materia discordie suboriri, ita duximus ordinandum, ut videlicet rector medietatis de Walpol' sex marcas, rector vero medietatis de Waltun' quatuor marcas annuas memoratis monachis persolvat. Act' apud Hoxne anno gratie millesimo ducentesimo tricesimo, pontificatus nostri anno quinto. Testibus: magistro Roberto archidiacono Northf' et officiali Norwicense, magistro Andrea de Croyndene, magistro Alexandro de Walp', Reginaldo, Dionisio, Roberto clericis et aliis.

The medieties of both churches were confirmed to the monks by bp William Turbe (1161 × 73), who also confirmed the joint pension of ten marks (*EEA* 6 nos. 111, 113). In 1254 the churches were listed as divided into bp's portions (£33· 6s. 8d. in Walpole, £11 6s. 8d. in West Walton) and prior's portions (£40 and £13 6s. 8d. respectively), with in addition the portion of the prior of Lewes assessed at £5 in each church (*VN* 382). In 1291 the valuation was, at Walpole, John's portion £42 13s. 4d. and John of Langton's portion £30 13s. 4d., with the prior's portion of £5; and at West Walton, William's portion £14, Nicholas's portion £12, and the prior's portion £2 13s. 4d. (*Taxatio* 80). No. 74 makes it clear that Lewes held a mediety of both the churches of Walpole, St Andrew and St Peter; the two portions of Walpole ascribed to individuals in the *Taxatio* presumably represent the two churches, both handsomely endowed.

74. Lewes Priory

General confirmation for the monks of their possessions in the diocese of Norwich, granted after inspection of the confirmation by bishop William Turbe [EEA 6 no. 111].   Hoxne, [1 × 24] March 1231

A = PRO E40/13997. Endorsed: Thome Norwicensis generalis (s. xiii); confirmatio omnium possessionum Norwicensis diocesis conventus Lewes (s. xv); pressmark; approx. 157 × 276 + 26 mm.; parchment tag, seal missing.

Omnibus Cristi fidelibus ad quos presens scriptum pervenerit Thomas Dei gratia Norwicensis episcopus salutem eternam in Domino. Noveritis nos inspexisse et manibus nostris contrectasse cartam bone memorie Willelmi quondam Norwicensis episcopi predecessoris nostri, in qua continetur monachos de Lewes canonice adeptos fuisse quecumque bona in diocesi Norwicensi [que] dinoscuntur optinere, ac eundem eisdem monachis predicta bona concessisse et confirmasse. Inde est quod nos prefatos monachos sub episcopali tuitione suscipientes omnia bona que in diocesi Norwicensi habere noscuntur auctoritate Dei et sancte Norwicensis ecclesie et nostra eis concedimus et confirmamus et futuris temporibus canonice possidere decernimus, in quibus hec nominatim duximus exprimenda: in primis monasterium de Acra cum appenditiis suis, in mariscis mediam ecclesiam de Waltona et in Walpol' medietatem duarum ecclesiarum, et in eisdem ecclesiis pensionem decem marcarum, et medietatem capelle de Enemede cum pertinentiis suis,[a] et decimas de dominico suo et hominum suorum, ecclesiam de Gimingham cum terris et decimis et omnibus ad eam pertinentibus et decimam de dominico in omnibus, et in eadem ecclesia nomine pensionis et pro decimis de dominico quinque marcas, ecclesiam sancte Elene de Santona cum ecclesia[b] eiusdem ville et terris et decimis et omnibus ad eas pertinentibus, et in eis nomine pensionis septem solidos et sex d., ecclesiam sancti Bartholomei de Ykeburg cum terris et decimis et omnibus ad eam pertinentibus, et in eadem quadraginta d. nomine pensionis, et in eadem villa unam marcam redditus, ecclesiam sancte Marie de Feltewelle cum terris et decimis et omnibus appenditiis suis, et in eadem centum solidos nomine pensionis, decimam de dominico comitis in Melewde in omnibus rebus, decimam de dominico de Sculetorp in omnibus rebus, decimam de dominico de Herlinge in omnibus rebus, ecclesiam de Wiltona cum omnibus pertinentiis suis, et in eadem quinquaginta solidos nomine pensionis, ecclesiam sancti Petri in Tefford cum appenditiis suis, et in ea .xii. d. nomine pensionis, et in eadem villa ecclesiam sancte Margarete cum appenditiis suis, et in ea duos solidos nomine pensionis, duas ecclesias de Burnehamestorp, scilicet sancte Marie et sancti Petri, cum omnibus pertinentiis suis, et in eisdem quadraginta solidos nomine pensionis, ecclesiam de Harpele cum terris et decimis et omnibus ad eam pertinentibus, et in ea triginta solidos nomine pensionis, et in eadem villa decimam de dominico Walteri de Bech in omnibus rebus, cum duodecim acris terre, ecclesiam de Sireford cum omnibus appenditiis suis, et in eadem duas marcas nomine pensionis, ecclesiam de Toftes cum pertinentiis suis, et in ea duas marcas nomine pensionis, ecclesiam de Ristun et dimidiam ecclesiam de Redlingtuna cum pertinentiis suis, et in eisdem quadraginta solidos nomine pensionis, et decimam de dominico in omnibus rebus et decimam serte et terram Alferi, apud Hapesburg' unum sochmannum et terram Brumanni Tatti et terram vidue et terram quam tenuit Hugo presbiter et decimam Widonis de Skekketun' et decimam Rogeri de Kerdestun' in omnibus rebus, et decimam de dominico de Hadestun' in omnibus rebus, decimam de dominico de Bestede in omnibus rebus, in Hillingtun' decimam de dominico Rogero de Staveli in omnibus rebus, ecclesiam de Fugeldun' cum capella sancti Edmundi cum universis ad easdem pertinentibus in terris liberis, decimis et decimationibus et omnimodis obventionibus, et in eisdem centum solidos nomine pensionis, ecclesiam de Colvestun' cum pertinentiis suis, et in eadem dimidiam marcam nomine pensionis, ecclesiam de Meretun' cum pertinentiis suis quam dedit Galfridus Baynard, et in eadem dimidiam marcam nomine pensionis, decimam quoque de dominico eiusdem ville in omnibus rebus, et sexaginta acras terre et quatuor acras prati et viginti acras terre quas tenebat Ulfketel', que omnia Radulfus frater predicti Galfridi predictis monachis non tanquam ad ecclesiam ipsam pertinentia sed sicut laycum feodum suum contulit possidenda, ecclesiam de Lettona cum appenditiis suis, et in eadem viginti solidos nomine pensionis, ecclesiam de Risinges cum appenditiis suis, et in ea quinque solidos nomine pensionis et de uno sochemanno .xii. d., et in eadem villa terras quas comes War(ennie) ibidem dedit quas tenuit Gillebertus, solvendo singulis annis quadraginta solidos, ecclesiam sancti Petri de Lenn' cum appenditiis suis, et in ea decem solidos nomine pensionis, decimam de dominico de Kenewik in omnibus rebus, ecclesiam de Hagenet cum terris et decimis et omnibus ad eandem pertinentibus ex dono Gilleberti de Gant, et in eadem ecclesia quadraginta solidos nomine pensionis et decimam de dominico in omnibus rebus, terras etiam quas Petrus sacerdos filius Brunsune tenuit per servitium duorum solidorum, et duas summas de brasio quas Adam predicte ecclesie homo reddere solebat pro grava una, ecclesiam de Helcham cum omnibus pertinentiis suis in usus proprios possidendam, salva honesta et competenti sustentatione vicarii in eadem pro tempore ministrantis. Confirmamus etiam predictis monachis plenariam decimam de omnibus dominicis comitis War(ennie), videlicet de blado, de feno, de porcellis, de angnis, de velleribus, de caseis, de molendinis, et plenariam decimam denariorum de omnibus redditibus et aliis undecumque proventibus, sicut karte ipsorum testantur, in parochia Norwicensi constitutis; et sicut dominia et redditus eorum creverint, itaque crescent decime monachorum, et quamvis ex illis denariis in procuratione comitis sive aliorum quorumlibet expendatur, plenaria tamen decima ex illis reddetur predictis monachis secundum kartas ipsorum comitum. Pax benefactoribus, gratia conservantibus. Dat' apud Hoxne anno gratie millesimo ducentesimo tricesimo pontificatus nostri anno quinto mense Martio. Testibus: magistro Roberto archidiacono Northfolchie et officiali Norwicensi, magistro Andrea de Croyndein', magistro Iohanne medico, Iohanne Terri, Reginaldo de Ringstede, Dionisio, Willelmo de Fordham clericis, Henrico capellano, Roberto clerico et aliis.

[a] *probably an ellipsis at this point*   [b] *sic ms., possibly in error for* capella

75. Monks Horton Priory

Confirmation for the monks of an annual pension of three marks which they have long been accustomed to receive from the church of Stanstead.

Glemham, May 1234

B = BL ms. Add. 5516 (fragment of Monks Horton cartulary) fo. 7r (p. 13). s. xiv ex.
Pd in Scott, 'Charters of Monks Horton Priory' 279.

[O][a]mnibus Cristi fidelibus ad quos presens scriptum pervenerit Thomas Dei gratia Norwicensis episcopus salutem in Domino. Ad universorum notitiam volumus pervenire nos Dei causa et religionis favore concessisse et presenti carta nostra et auctoritate episcopali confirmasse dilectis filiis in Cristo priori et monachis de Horton' ordinis Cluniacensis annuatim pensionem trium marcarum quam ab antiquo consueverunt percipere de ecclesia de Stansted' nostre diocesis, salvis in omnibus reverentia et obedientia nobis et successoribus nostris et sancte Norwicensis ecclesie consuetudinibus debitis vel consuetis.

In cuius rei testimonium presentes literas fecimus fieri et sigillo nostro muniri. Dat' apud Glemham mense Maii pontificatus nostri anno octavo.

^a *Space for initial.*

The church had originally been granted to the monks by Robert de Vere and his wife and was confirmed to them by bp William Turbe (*EEA* 6 no. 125) and by Nicholas cardinal-bp of Tusculum, the papal legate, between September 1213 and December 1214 (Scott, 'Charters of Monks Horton' 279). In 1254 the church was valued at ten marks and in 1291 at £10; in neither assessment is this pension mentioned (*VN* 437; *Taxatio* 122b).

76. Norwich Cathedral Priory

Confirmation for the monks of various pensions: from the church of Lynn, twenty marks; from the church of Yarmouth, twenty marks and twenty lasts of herrings; from the church of Aldeby, ten marks; from the church of Martham, 100s.; from the church of Cressingham, four marks; from the church of Blickling, one mark; from the chapel of Langham, 10s.; from the vicarage of Hemsby, 2s.; from the church of Thorpe, 8s.; from the church of Wicklewood, 4s.; from the churches of St Martin and St Olave in Norwich, 6s.; from the church of St George in Norwich, 10s.; from the church of Wiggenhall St German, half a mark; from the church of Henley, 20s.; from the church of Plumstead, half a mark, and from the church of Catton, 7s.

[20 December 1226 × 16 October 1227]

B = Norfolk R.O., DCN 40/5 (cellarer's cartulary) fos. 10v–11r (9v–10r). s. xiii ex. C = ibid., DCN 40/1 (general cartulary) fos. 37v–38r (26v–27r, 23v–24r). s. xiv in. D = ibid. fos. 228v–29r (219v–20r) (*inspeximus* by bp John Salmon, 9 March 1302). E = ibid., DCN 40/2/1 (general cartulary) fo. 25v (16v, 98v). s xiv in. F = ibid., DCN 40/4 (episcopal charters) pp. 81–82. s. xv in. G = ibid. pp. 270–71. H = ibid. pp. 220–22 (as D).
Pd in *Norwich Cathedral Charters* i no. 186; from C in *First Register* 112–14.

Omnibus Cristi fidelibus ad quos presens scriptum pervenerit Thomas Dei gratia Norwicensis episcopus salutem in Domino. Ad universorum volumus pervenire notitiam^a nos concessisse et presenti carta confirmasse dilectis in Cristo filiis priori et monachis Norwicensis ecclesie omnes pensiones suas subscriptas, videlicet de ecclesia de Lenn'^b viginti marcas et de ecclesia de Gernemuta^c viginti marcas et viginti lez^d de allece,^e de ecclesia de Aldeby^f decem marcas, de ecclesia de Martham centum solidos, de ecclesia de Cressingham quatuor marcas, de ecclesia de Blicling'^g unam marcam, de capella de Langham decem solidos, de vicaria de Hemesbi duos solidos, de ecclesia de Thorp octo solidos, de ecclesia de Wiclewode^h quatuor solidos, de ecclesiis sanctorum Martini et Olavi^j in Norwico sex solidos, de ecclesia sancti Georgii in Norwico decem solidos, de ecclesia sancti Germanni de Wigenhale^k dimidiam marcam, de ecclesia de Henleia viginti solidos, de ecclesia de Plumstede dimidiam marcam, de ecclesia de Catton'[l] septem solidos.[m] Et ut hec nostra concessio[n] et confirmatio perpetue firmitatis robur obtineat, eam presenti scripto et sigilli nostri appositione corroboramus. Hiis testibus: magistro Alano de Beccles[o] archidiacono Subir', officiali nostro, magistro Nicholao de Houtun', magistro Michaele de Ryngesfeld,[p] magistro Alexandro de Munci, magistro Roberto de Bilneia, Henrico capellano nostro, Ricardo de Geytun'[q] et Dionisio clericis.

[a] Ad universorum notitiam volumus pervenire C, E [b] Len' C, D, G, H [c] Gernemut B, E, F, H [d] leez C, D, E [e] allec F [f] Audeby B; Aldebi F; Alby G; [g] Bicklingg' B; Bliclyngge C; Bliclinng' D [h] Wiclewde B; Wyclewode D [j] Elene C; Helene E [k] Wigehale B; Wygehal' D; Wygehall' F; Wygehall H [l] Cattun B; Cattone H [m] septem solidos *om.* B [n] concessio nostra B [o] Becles B [p] Ryngefeld B, E; Ryngesfeld D; Rugebi F [q] Geytone B, D; Geiton' F; Geitone H

Mr Alan of Beccles had been succeeded as official by 16 October 1227 (no. 89).

77. Norwich Cathedral Priory

Inspeximus *and confirmation of a charter of bishop John II by which he conceded and confirmed to the monks all their tithes sequestrated from parish churches both on the bishop's demesne manors and other manors, to be disposed for the use of their church; and for greater security they are enumerated thus: the tithes of Langham, [North] Elmham, Thornage, Blofield, Beighton, Thorpe, Marsham, Homersfield, Hoxne, Swanton [Morley], Cockthorpe, Witchingham, Deopham, Buxton, Postwick, Scarning, Hockering, Threxton, [Great] Bircham, Whitlingham, Shotesham, Sparham, Irmingland, Intwood, Wroxham, Barford, Blickling, Filby, Raveningham, Chedgrave, Wangford, North Creake and Sprowston.* [20 December 1226 × 16 October 1227]

B = Norfolk R.O., DCN 40/1 (general cartulary) fo. 37r–v (26r–v, 23r–v). s. xiv in. C = ibid. fo. 228r–v (219r–v) (*inspeximus* by bp John Salmon, 9 March 1302). D = ibid. fo. 235r–v (226r–v) (another *inspeximus* by bp Salmon, same date). E = ibid., DCN 40/2/2 (almoner's cartulary) fo. 91r–v (74r–v, 220r–v). s. xiv in. F = ibid., DCN 40/1 (general cartulary) fo. 25r–v (16r–v, 98r–v). s. xiv in. G = ibid., DCN 40/4 (episcopal charters) pp. 265–66. s. xv in. H = ibid. pp. 265–66. J = ibid. pp. 216–17 (as C). K = ibid. pp. 227–29 (as D). L = ibid. pp. 232–34 (as D).
Pd in *Norwich Cathedral Charters* i no. 180; from B in *First Register* 110–12.

Omnibus Cristi fidelibus ad quos presens scriptum pervenerit Thomas Dei gratia Norwicensis episcopus salutem in Domino. Noverit universitas vestra nos inspexisse cartam bone memorie predecessoris nostri Iohannis quondam Norwicensis episcopi secundi, per quam dilectis filiis priori et monachis Norwicensibus concessit et confirmavit omnes decimas suas ab ecclesiis parrochialibus sequestratas, tam de dominicis maneriis episcopalibus quam de aliis, ad commodum ecclesie sue libere disponendas. Nos autem ipsius vestigiis inherentes dictam concessionem et confirmationem ratam habentes et gratam eam auctoritate nostra confirmamus et corroboramus. Ad maiorem autem securitatem prenominatas decimas duximus exprimendas, videlicet decimas de Langham, de Elmham, de Thornedys,[a] de Blofeld,[b] de Beghetone,[c] de Thorpe',[d] de Marsham, de Humeresfeld, de Hoxne, de Swantone,[e] de Cokethorp',[f] de Wichingham,[g] de Depham, de Buxtone,[h] de Possewic', de Skerninge,[j] de Hokeryngge,[k] de Threkestone,[l] de Brecham,[m] de Wythlyngham,[n] de Shotesham,[o] de Sparham, de Irminglond,[p] de Intewode,[q] de Wroxham,[r] de Bereforde,[s] de Bliclingg',[t] de Filebi, de Raveningham,[u] de Chadegrave,[w] de Wangeford,[x] de Northcrek',[y] de Sproustone.[z] Memoratas igitur decimas dilectis filiis priori et monachis Norwicensibus confirmantes, presens scriptum in testimonium sigillo nostro duximus muniendum. Testibus:[aa] magistro Alano de Beccles officiali nostro, magistro Nicholao de Houtun',[bb] magistro Michaele[cc] de Ryngesfeld,[dd] magistro Alexandro de Muncy,[ee] magistro Roberto de Bilneye,[ff] magistro Willelmo de Randest'.[gg]

[a] Tornedis C, G; Thorned' D, K, L; Thornedes E; Thornedis J   [b] Blafeud B, C, D, F, K, L; Blafeld G; Blafeude J   [c] Begeton' E; Begetun' G, H; Beghtone J; Beghton K   [d] Torp' H; Thorpe K   [e] Swanthun' B; Swanetone E; Suanthun F; Swantetun' G   [f] Kokestorp' F, G, H   [g] Wychingham C, D, L; Wichlingham F   [h] Buxstone B; Bucston' E; Bucstun' F, G, H; Buxton J   [j] Skeringe F; Skernyngg J; Skernynge K, L   [k] Hokerinng' F; Hokering G, K; Hokeringg C, J; Hokerynge L   [l] Thekestone B; Trekestone C; Trecston' E; Thekeston F; Trecstan G   [m] Becham B; Beicham G; Bercham J; Berkham K   [n] Wythlingham C, D, L; Witligham E; Withingham F; Witlingham G   [o] Sotesham B; Schotesham D   [p] Irmiglod E; Irmingfeld G; Irmynglonde J; Irmyngland K; Irmynglond L   [q] Intewod D, L; Intewde G   [r] Wrockesham B; Wrokesham F; Wrogsham G, H   [s] Bereford B; Berford E   [t] Blyclyngge B; Bliclinge G; Bliclyngg' L   [u] Laveningham G; Faveningham H; Ravenyngham J, K   [w] Chategrave B; Chattegrave G, H   [x] Wangeforde D, K; Wangford G   [z] Sprouston B; Sproustun G   [aa] E *ends here with* etc.   [bb] Houthun' B; Houtone C, D, L; Howtone J, K   [cc] Nicholao E, G   [dd] Kingesford' G   [ee] Mouncy B; Munt' E, G, H   [ff] Biln' B; Kiln' G   [gg] Kandelt' B; Randesle J; Randester K

Mr Alan of Beccles had been succeeded as official by 16 October 1227 (no. 89). There is no extant *actum* of bp Gray which enumerates these tithes. The marginal note to E specifies that these are lesser tithes. See also no. 84 below.

78. Norwich Cathedral Priory

Confirmation for the monks, for the use of the cellarer, of the following tithes: two parts of all the tithes of the bishop's demesne at Thornage and half of all the bishop's demesne tithes at Langham and a third of the bishop's demesne tithes at Homersfield; two parts of the demesne tithes of Margaret de Cressy in Postwick and Wroxham; two parts of the demesne tithes of the late Hubert de Ria in Swanton [Morley], Buxton, 'Kinestorp' [in Buxton], Hockering and Deopham; two parts of the demesne tithes of Oliver de Vaux in Shotesham, of Ralph de Tiville in Intwood, of William of Sparham in Sparham, of Roger son of Osbert in Witchingham, of John of Barford in Barford, of Ralph son of Simon in Irmingland, of Simon de Nuiers in [North] Elmham, of Wigan Brito in Threxton, of Roger Gulafre in Scarning, of Geoffrey de Leuns in Witchingham, and of Warin of Thorpe in Cockthorpe; and all the demesne tithes of William of Fring in Fring, of the late Thurstan the deacon in Thornham, and of the fee of the lordship of Cressingham, which is called 'Osegoteshag'. [20 December 1226 × 16 October 1227]

> A = Norwich, Norfolk R.O., DCN 43/40. Endorsed: De decimis minutis (s. xiii); pressmark; Hugh of Mursley's notarial mark; approx. 148 × 115 + 20 mm.; parchment tag, seal missing.
> B = Canterbury, D. & C. Ch. Ant. N1 (*inspeximus* by prior Nicholas and convent of Christ Church Canterbury, 1249, of *inspeximus* by bp Walter Suffield, 29 April 1245). s. xiii med. C = Norfolk R.O., DCN 40/5 (cellarer's cartulary) fo. 11r–v (10r–v). s. xiii ex. D = ibid. fos. 11v–12r (10v–11r) (*inspeximus* by bp Suffield). E = ibid. fo. 12r–v (11r–v) (as B). F = ibid. DCN 40/7 (general cartulary) fos. 32v–33r (as D). s. xiii ex. G = ibid. DCN 40/1 (general cartulary) fo. 37r (26r, 23r). s. xiv in. H = ibid. fo. 228r (219r) (*inspeximus* of D by bp John Salmon, 9 March 1302). J = ibid. DCN 40/2/2 (general cartulary) fo. 16r (98r). s. xiv in. K = ibid. DCN 40/4 (episcopal charters) pp. 88–90. s. xv in. L = ibid. pp. 115–8 (as D). M = ibid. pp. 298–300 (as D). N = ibid. pp. 218–20 (as H).
> Pd from A in *Norwich Cathedral Charters* i no. 193; from C in *First Register* 110.

Omnibus Cristi fidelibus ad quos presens scriptum pervenerit Thomas Dei gratia Norwicensis episcopus salutem in Domino. Noverit universitas vestra nos concessisse et hac carta nostra confirmasse dilectis in Cristo filiis priori et monachis Norwicensibus ad opus cellerarie sue omnes decimas subscriptas, videlicet duas partes decimarum omnium de dominio nostro de Tornedis et dimidiam partem decimarum omnium de dominio nostro de Langham, tertiam etiam partem omnium decimarum de dominico nostro de Humeresfeld, et duas partes decimarum de dominico Margerie de Cressi in villis de Possewic' et de Wrogesham, duas etiam partes decimarum de dominicis Huberti quondam de Ria in villis de Swanetun', Buscton', Kinestorp, Hokering, Depham, et duas partes decimarum de dominico Oliveri de Vallibus in Sotesham, et duas partes decimarum de dominico Radulfi de Tivill' in Intewde, duas etiam partes decimarum omnium de dominico Willelmi de Sparham in eadem villa, et duas partes decimarum de dominico Rogeri filii Osberti in Witlingham, duas etiam partes decimarum de dominico Iohannis de Bereford in eadem villa et de dominico Radulfi filii Simonis in Irminglond', et duas partes decimarum de dominico Simonis de Nuiers in Elmham et de dominico Wigani Britonis in Trecstan, duas etiam partes decimarum de dominico Rogeri Gulafr' in villa de Skerninges et de dominico Gaufridi de Leuns in villa de Wichingham, duas etiam partes decimarum de dominico Warini de Torp' in Kokestorp', omnes etiam decimas provenientes de dominico Willelmi de Frenges in eadem villa et de dominico Turstini quondam diaconi in Tornham et de feodo dominici de Cressingham quod vocatur Osegoteshag' in eadem villa. Memoratas igitur decimas ad opus cellerarie sue dictis monachis confirmantes, presens scriptum in testimonium sigillo nostro duximus muniendum. Testibus: magistro Roberto de Biln' clerico nostro, Henrico capellano nostro, Iohanne Terri et Dionisio et Ricardo de Geiton' clericis nostris, Reimundo de Wimundeh', Iohanne de Hildolvest'.

Mr Robert of Bilney had become official by 16 October 1227 (no. 89).

79. Norwich Cathedral Priory

Confirmation for the monks, for the use of the almonry, of various tithes which they are known to have possessed for many years past; that is: two parts of the demesne tithe of Robert son of Thomas in the vill of Wangford; two parts of the great and lesser demesne tithes of the same Robert in the vills of Raveningham and Chedgrave; two parts of the great and lesser demesne tithes of Philip of Chedgrave in Chedgrave; two parts of the great tithe of the demesne of Hervey of Stanhoe in the vill of North Creake; two parts of the great tithe of the demesne of William de Munteni in the vill of Sprowston; two parts of the demesne tithe of the monks of Norwich in the vill of Catton; and all the tithes of their barns outside Norwich and of the produce of their gardens. [20 December 1226 × 16 August 1236]

B = Norfolk R.O., DCN 40/2/2 (almoner's cartulary) fo. 91r (81r, 220r). s. xiv in.
Pd from B in *Norwich Cathedral Charters* i no. 195.

Omnibus Cristi fidelibus ad quos presens scriptum pervenerit Thomas Dei gratia Norwicensis episcopus salutem in Domino. Noverit universitas vestra nos concessisse et presenti carta confirmasse dilectis filiis priori et monachis Norwicensibus omnes decimas subscriptas ad opus elemosinarie sue, quarum possessione a multis retroactis temporibus gavisi fuisse dinoscuntur, videlicet duas partes decimarum in villa de Wangeford de dominico Roberti filii Thome, duas etiam partes maiorum et minorum[a] decimarum de dominico ipsius Roberti in villa de Ravenigham et in villa de Chategrave, et duas partes maiorum et minutarum decimarum de dominico Philippi de Chategrave in eadem villa; similiter duas partes decime garbarum de dominico Hervei de Stanho in villa Northcreik' et duas partes decime garbarum de dominico Willelmi de Munteni in villa de Sprouston', duas etiam partes decimarum de dominico prioris et conventus Norwicensis in villa de Catton' et omnes decimas de horreis ipsorum extra Norwicum et de exitibus gardini sui provenientes. Memoratas igitur decimas ad opus elemosinarie Norwicensis confirmantes presens scriptum in testimonium sigillo nostro duximus muniendum. Testibus etc.

[a] maiores et minores B

Mr Robert of Bilney had become official by 16 October 1227 (no. 89).

80. Norwich Cathedral Priory

Confirmation for the monks, for the use of the almonry, of two parts of the great tithe from the demesne of William de Munteni in the vills of Catton and Sprowston, as they are known to have received them hitherto, for the use of the poor. [20 December 1226 × 16 October 1227]

> B = Norfolk R.O., DCN 40/1 (general cartulary) fo. 37v (26v, 23v). s. xiv in. C = ibid. fos. 40v–41r (29v–30r, 26v–27r). D = ibid. fo. 228v (219v) (*inspeximus* by bp John Salmon, 9 March 1302). E = ibid., DCN 40/2/2 (almoner's cartulary) fo. 64r (52r, 65r). s. xiv in. F = 40/2/1 (general cartulary) fo. 25v (16v). s. xiv in. G = ibid. fo. 28r (19r). H = ibid., DCN 40/4 (episcopal charters) pp. 87–88. s. xv in. J = ibid. p. 275. K = ibid. pp. 217–18 (as D).
> Pd in *Norwich Cathedral Charters* i no. 192; from B in *First Register* 112; from C in ibid. 124–26.

Omnibus Cristi fidelibus hoc scriptum visuris Thomas Dei gratia Norwicensis episcopus salutem in Domino. Noverit universitas vestra nos pietatis intuitu concessisse et confirmasse dilectis filiis priori et monachis Norwicensibus ad opus elemosinarie sue duas partes decime garbarum de dominico Willelmi de Munteni in villis de Catton[a] et de Sproustone[b] sicut eas hactenus melius possedisse et plenius percepisse dinoscuntur usibus pauperum profuturas; et in huius rei testimonium presens scriptum sigillo nostro duximus muniendum. Testibus:[c] magistro Alano archidiacono Subir', officiali nostro, Nicholao de Houton',[d] magistro Roberto de Bilneia,[e] Henrico capellano nostro, Iohanne Terri et Dionisio clericis nostris, Edmundo clerico prioris Norwicensis et multis aliis.[f]

[a] Cattune C, E, F, G; Cattone D, K   [b] Sproustun' E, F; Sproustune G; Sprouston' H
[c] E *ends here with* etc.   [d] Houtune C, G; Houtone D; Houtun E   [e] Bilneye C; Bilneya D
[f] E *adds note*: Ista carta est in thesaurario.

Mr Robert of Bilney had become official by 16 October 1227 (no. 89).

81. Norwich Cathedral Priory

Inspeximus *and confirmation for the monks of the grant* in proprios usus *by bishop John de Gray of the church of Hindolveston, for the use of the cellarer, to take effect when it falls vacant. They shall cause it to be served by chaplains to be appointed and removed by themselves* [*EEA* 6 no. 397].

[20 December 1226 × 16 October 1227]

> B = Norfolk R.O., DCN 40/7 (general cartulary) fo. 24r (23r). s. xiii ex. C = ibid., DCN 40/1 (general cartulary) fo. 40r–v (29r–v, 26r–v). s. xiv in. D = ibid. fos. 230v–31r (221v–22r) (*inspeximus* by bp John Salmon, 9 March 1302). E = ibid., DCN 40/2/1 (general cartulary) fo. 27v (18v). s. xiv in. F = ibid., DCN 40/4 (episcopal charters) pp. 85–86. s. xv in. G = ibid. pp. 273–74. H = ibid. pp. 185–86 (as D).
> Pd in *Norwich Cathedral Charters* i no. 190; from C in *First Register* 122–24.

Omnibus Cristi fidelibus ad quos presens scriptum pervenerit Thomas Dei gratia Norwicensis episcopus salutem in Domino. Noverit universitas vestra nos inspexisse cartam bone memorie Iohannis Dei gratia Norwicensis episcopi secundi predecessoris nostri[a] in hec verba: [*EEA* 6 no. 397; *Norwich Cathedral Charters* i no. 158]. Nos igitur dictam concessionem ratam habentes et gratam, eam presenti scripto et sigilli nostri appositione corroboravimus. Hiis[b] testibus: magistro Alano de Becles[c] archidiacono Subir', officiali nostro, magistro Nicholao de Houtun',[d] magistro Roberto de Biln', Henrico capellano nostro, Iohanne[e] Terri et Dionisio clericis nostris, Ricardo de Geiton',[f] Henrico de Tunstall'.[g]

> [a] secundi predecessoris nostri *om.* F [b] His D, F [c] Beccl' B, D, G; Bekel' E; Becell' F; Beccle H [d] Hueton' C; Houtone D; Huetone E; Houtun' G; Howton H [e] Henrico F [f] Geytone C; Getton' G; Gaiton H [g] Tunstale C, E

Mr Robert of Bilney was official by 16 October 1227 (no. 89). The church of Hindolveston was assessed at £10 in 1254 and £11 6s. 8d. in 1291 (*VN* 368; *Taxatio* 82).

82. Norwich Cathedral Priory

Inspeximus *and confirmation for the monks of the grant* in proprios usus *by bishop John de Gray of the church of Wighton, for the use of the cellarer, to take effect when it falls vacant. They shall cause it to be served by chaplains to be appointed and removed by themselves* [*EEA* 6 no. 388].

[20 December 1226 × 16 October 1227]

> B = Norfolk R.O., DCN 40/5 (cellarer's cartulary) fo. 26v (25v). s. xiii ex. C = ibid., DCN 40/4 (episcopal charters) pp. 90–91. s. xv in. D = ibid. pp. 277–78.
> Pd in *Norwich Cathedral Charters* i no. 194.

Omnibus Cristi fidelibus ad quos presens scriptum pervenerit Thomas Dei gratia Norwicensis episcopus salutem in Domino.[a] Noverit universitas vestra nos inspexisse cartam bone memorie Iohannis Norwicensis episcopi secundi predecessoris nostri in hec verba: [*EEA* 6 no. 388; *Norwich Cathedral Charters* i no. 153]. Nos igitur dictam concessionem et confirmationem ratam habentes et gratam, eam presenti scripto et sigilli nostri appositione corroboramus. Testibus: magistro Alano de Becles,[b] archidiacono Subir' officiali nostro, magistro Nicholao de Houtun',[c] magistro Roberto de Bilneya,[d] Iohanne de Terri, Dionisio, Ricardo de Geytun[e] clericis nostris.

[a] in Domino *om.* B   [b] Becca C; Beccl' D   [c] Houton' D   [d] Biln'C, D   [e] Gaiton' C; Geiton' D

Mr Robert of Bilney was official by 16 October 1227 (no. 89).

83. Norwich Cathedral Priory

Inspeximus *and confirmation for the monks of the grant* in proprios usus *by bishop John de Gray of the church of St Andrew, Trowse, to take effect when it falls vacant, for the use of the sacrist, saving an annual pension of two* aurei *to be paid by the sacrist to the cellarer* [*EEA* 6 no. 379].

[20 December 1226 × 16 August 1236]

B = Norfolk R.O., DCN 40/7 (general cartulary) fos. 29v–30r. s. xiii ex. C = ibid. DCN 40/1 (general cartulary) fo. 39v (28v, 25v). s. xiv in. D = ibid. fo. 231r (222r) (*inspeximus* by bp John Salmon, 9 March 1302). E = ibid., DCN 40/2/1 (general cartulary) fos. 26v–27r (17v–18r, 99v–100r). s. xiv in. F = ibid., DCN 40/4 (episcopal charters) pp. 82–83. s. xiv in. G = ibid. pp. 271–72. H = ibid. pp. 187–88 (as D).
Pd in *Norwich Cathedral Charters* i no. 187; from C in *First Register* 120.

Omnibus sancte matris ecclesie filiis Thomas Dei gratia Norwicensis episcopus salutem in Domino. Litteras bone memorie Iohannis quondam Norwicensis episcopi inspeximus in hec verba: [*EEA* 6 no. 379; *Norwich Cathedral Charters* i no. 162]. Nos autem istam donationem, concessionem, confirmationem gratam habemus et ratam et inconcussam volumus in eternum permanere eamque presentium tenore duximus roborandam.

Mr Robert of Bilney was official by 16 October 1227 (no. 89). See also no. 91.

84. Norwich Cathedral Priory

Inspeximus *of a charter of bishop John II confirming to the monks all tithes sequestrated from parish churches, both in the demesne manors of the bishop and in others, to be freely disposed for the use of their church. Out of concern for the poor, the bishop now confirms all tithes which pertain to the monks' alms, that is: two parts of the great tithe of the demesne of Robert son of*

Thomas in the vill of Wangford, two parts of the great and lesser demesne tithes of the same Robert in the vills of Raveningham and Chedgrave, two parts of the great and lesser demesne tithes of Philip of Chedgrave in that vill, two parts of the great tithe of the demesne of Hervey of Stanhoe in the vill of North Creake and two parts of the great tithe of the demesne of William de Munteni in the vill of Sprowston. [20 December 1226 × 16 August 1236]

    B = Norfolk R.O., DCN 40/2/2 (almoner's cartulary) fo. 91r (81r, 220r). s. xiv in.
    Pd in *Norwich Cathedral Charters* i no. 196.

Omnibus Cristi fidelibus ad quos presens scriptum pervenerit Thomas Dei gratia Norwicensis episcopus salutem in Domino. Noverit universitas vestra nos inspexisse cartam bone memorie Iohannis quondam Norwicensis episcopi secundi predecessoris nostri, per quam dilectis filiis priori et monachis Norwicensibus concessit et confirmavit omnes decimas suas ab ecclesiis parochialibus sequestratas, tam de dominicis maneriis episcopalibus quam de aliis, ad comodum ecclesie sue libere disponendas. Nos autem, ipsius vestigiis inherentes et necessitatibus pauperum paterno affectu compatientes, omnes decimas ad elemosinam dictorum monachorum pertinentes per Norwicensem dyocesim auctoritate nostra eis confirmamus, quas etiam nominatim exprimere ad maiorem pauperum securitatem dignum duximus, videlicet duas partes decime garbarum in villa de Wangeford de dominico Roberti filii Thomae, duas etiam partes omnium decimarum tam maiorum quam minutarum de dominico memorati Roberti in villa de Ravenigham et in villa de Chategrave, et duas partes tam maiorum quam minutarum decimarum de dominico Philippi de Chategrave in eadem villa, similiter duas partes decime garbarum de dominico Hervei de Stanho in villa de Northcreik' et duas partes decime garbarum de dominico Willelmi de Munteny in villa de Sprouston'. Memoratas igitur decimas dilectis filiis priori et monachis Norwicensibus ad opus elemosinarie sue confirmantes, presens scriptum in testimonio sigillo nostro duximus muniendum. Testibus etc.

    The charter of bp Gray is apparently not extant. See also no. 77 above.

85. Norwich Cathedral Priory

Inspeximus *and confirmation of the grant to the monks by bishop John de Gray,* in proprios usus *for the use of the cellarer, of the church of Wiggenhall St German, to take effect when it falls vacant, saving to the bishop and his successors pontifical and parochial rights, with indult to enter into possession when it fall vacant. They shall cause the church to be served by chaplains whom they may themselves appoint and remove* [*EEA* 6 no. 401].

Homersfield, 24 January 1227

A = Norwich, Norfolk R.O., DCN 43/36. Endorsed: De Vigenhale (s. xiii); de Wigenhal' (s. xiv); pressmark; Hugh of Mursley's notarial mark; approx. 194 × 85 + 24 mm.; damaged seal on parchment tag, green wax, counterseal.
B = Norfolk R.O., DCN 40/5 (cellarer's cartulary) fo. 47v (50v). s. xiii ex. C = ibid. DCN 40/1 (general cartulary) fo. 38v (27v, 24v). s. xiv in. D = ibid. fo. 229v (220v) (*inspeximus* by bp John Salmon, 9 March 1302). s. xiv in. E = ibid. DCN 40/2/2 (general cartulary) fo. 26r (17r, 99r). s. xiv in. F = ibid. DCN 40/4 (episcopal charters) pp. 76–7. s. xv in. G = ibid. pp. 266–7. H = ibid. pp. 177–8 (as D).
Pd from A in *Norwich Cathedral Charters* i no. 181; from C in *First Register* 116.

Omnibus Cristi fidelibus presens scriptum visuris vel audituris Thomas Dei gratia Norwicensis episcopus salutem in Domino. Inspeximus cartam predecessoris nostri I. bone memorie in hac forma conceptam: [*EEA* 6 no. 401; *Norwich Cathedral Charters* i no. 144]. Nos autem premissam concessionem gratam et acceptam habentes, eam presentis scripti munimine duximus roborandam. Dat' apud Humeresfeld' nono kalendas Februarii pontificatus nostri anno primo.

The church was valued at £16 both in 1254 and 1291 (*VN* 382; *Taxatio* 80).

86. Norwich Cathedral Priory

Grant to the monks in proprios usus *of the church of Worstead, to take effect after the deaths of John of Worstead and Adam of Worstead, who now hold the church, saving the maintenance of a perpetual vicar to minister therein.*

Norwich, 22 March 1227

B = Norfolk R.O., DCN 40/5 (cellarer's cartulary) fo. 23r (22r). s. xiii ex. C = ibid., DCN 40/1 (general cartulary) fos. 38v–39r (27v–28r, 24v–25r). s. xiv in. D = ibid. fos. 229v–30r (220v–21r) (*inspeximus* by bp John Salmon, 9 March 1302). E = ibid., DCN 40/2/1 (general cartulary) fo. 26r–v (17r–v, 99r–v). s. xiv in. F = ibid. fo. 28r (19r, 101r). G = ibid., DCN 40/4 (episcopal charters) p. 87. s. xv in. H = ibid. pp. 274–5. J = ibid. pp. 179–80 (as D).
Pd in *Norwich Cathedral Charters* i no. 191; from C in *First Register* 116–18.

Omnibus Cristi fidelibus ad quos presens scriptum pervenerit Thomas Dei gratia Norwicensis episcopus salutem in Domino. Cum quanto[a] possumus vigilantie studio virorum religiosorum profectibus intendere constringimur et eorum desideria que a ratione non discrepant quantum secundum Deum possumus et iustitiam effectu prosequente exaudire et adimplere, eapropter ad universorum notitiam volumus[b] pervenire nos dilectis in Cristo priori et monachis Norwicensibus, qui in religione fervidi et operibus caritatis dinoscuntur esse devoti, ecclesiam de Wrthested'[c] cum omnibus pertinentiis suis, post decessum domini Iohannis de Wrthsted[d] et Ade de Wrthsted'[d] qui nunc prefatam optinent ecclesiam, imperpetuum in proprios usus possidendam concessisse, salva honesta sustentatione vicarii perpetui qui in prefata ecclesia pro tempore ministrabit, salvis in omnibus reverentia et obedientia nobis et successoribus nostris et sacrosancte Norwicensis ecclesie consuetudinibus debitis vel consuetis. In cuius rei testimonium presentes litteras fieri fecimus et sigillo nostro muniri. Dat' apud Norwicum undecimo kalendas Aprilis pontificatus nostri anno primo.

^a quanta *all MSS*.   ^b ad universorum volumus notitiam G   ^c Wrtstede B; Wurthstede C; Wurstede D; Wurthested J   ^d Wrstede B; Wurstede C; Wurthestede D; Wurthested J

For the induction of the monks into corporal possession in 1235, see no. 93. In 1254, however, the church was valued at £10 and the portion of the prior of Norwich at only £2 and 'bona' of 26s. 8d. (*VN* 415). In July 1256 bp Walter Suffield ordained a vicarage (*Norwich Cathedral Charters* i no. 208), and in 1291 the church was assessed at £16 13s. 4d. and the vicarage at £5 (*Taxatio* 87).

87. Norwich Cathedral Priory

Inspeximus *and confirmation of the grant to the monks by bishop John de Gray*, in proprios usus *for the use of the almoner, of the church of [West] Beckham, to take effect when it falls vacant, saving an annual pension of three shillings to be received by the cellarer from the almoner, with indult to enter into possession when it falls vacant. They shall cause the church to be served by chaplains whom they may themselves appoint and remove [EEA 6 no. 395].*   Ipswich [25 March × 15 October] 1227

A = Norwich, Norfolk R.O., DCN 43/39. Endorsed: Becham ii (s. xiv); approx. 170 × 80 + 15 mm.; slit for sealing, tag and seal missing.

B = Norfolk R.O., DCN 40/2/1 (almoner's cartulary) fos. 66v–67r (57v–58r, 264v–65r). s. xiv in.

Pd from A in *Norwich Cathedral Charters* i no. 197.

Omnibus Cristi fidelibus ad quos presens scriptum pervenerit Thomas Dei gratia Norwicensis episcopus salutem in Domino. Noverit universitas vestra nos inspexisse cartam bone memorie Iohannis Norwicensis episcopi secundi predecessoris nostri in hec verba: [*EEA* 6 no. 395; *Norwich Cathedral Charters* i no. 152]. Nos igitur dictam concessionem et confirmationem ratam habentes et gratam, eam presenti [scripto]^a et sigilli nostri appositione corroboramus. Testibus: magistro Alano de Beccles archidiacono Subir', officiali nostro, magistro Roberto de Biln', Henrico capellano nostro, Ricardo de Geiton clerico. Dat' apud Gipewicum anno dominice incarnationis millesimo ducentesimo vicesimo septimo.

^a *om.* A

Mr Alan of Beccles had been succeeded as official by mr Robert of Bilney by 16 October 1227 (no. 89). The church is West Beckham in the deanery of Ingworth and the hundred of South Erpingham; it was valued at £10 in 1254, when the appropriation had probably not taken effect (*VN* 367); in 1291 it was listed as appropriated to the monks of Norwich and assessed at £4 (*Taxatio* 82b); the actual receipts were far greater (*VN* 567). Three-quarters of the church of East Beckham in the deanery of Repps and the hundred of North Erpingham were appropriated to Weybourne priory (*Taxatio* 86).

88. Norwich Cathedral Priory

Inspeximus *and confirmation of the grant to the monks by bishop John de Gray,* in proprios usus *for the use of the precentor, of the church of St Mary, [Great] Plumstead, to take effect when it falls vacant, saving an annual pension of ten shillings to be received by the cellarer from the precentor, with indult to enter into possession when it falls vacant. They shall cause the church to be served by chaplains whom they themselves may appoint and remove* (*EEA* 6 no. 404). Norwich, 6 April 1227

> A = Norwich, Norfolk R.O., DCN 43/38. Endorsed: Plumsted' (s. xiii); pressmark; Hugh of Mursley's notarial mark; approx. 215 × 88 + 13 mm.; damaged seal on parchment tag, green wax, counterseal.
> B = Norfolk R.O., Norwich DCN 40/7 (general cartulary) fo. 31r–v. s. xiii ex. C = ibid. DCN 40/1 (general cartulary) fo. 39r (28r, 25r). s.xiv in. D = ibid. fo. 230r (221r) (*inspeximus* by bp John Salmon, 9 March 1302). s.xiv in. E = ibid. DCN 40/2/2 (general cartulary) fo. 26v (17v, 99v). s. xiv in. F = ibid. DCN 40/4 (episcopal charters) pp. 79–81. s. xv in. G = ibid. pp. 268–9. H = ibid. pp. 166–7 (as D).
> Pd from A in *Norwich Cathedral Charters* i no. 184; from C in *First Register* 118.

Omnibus sancte matris ecclesie filiis ad quos presens scriptum pervenerit Thomas Dei gratia Norwicensis episcopus salutem in Domino. Noverit universitas vestra nos inspexisse cartam[a] bone memorie predecessoris nostri domini I. Norwicensis episcopi in hec verba: [*EEA* 6 no. 404; *Norwich Cathedral Charters* i no. 160]. Hanc igitur dationem, concessionem et confirmationem gratam accipientes et devotam, eam presenti scripto nostro et sigilli nostri munimine confirmavimus et roboravimus. Hiis testibus: magistro Alano de Becles archidiacono Subyr', officiali Norwicensi, magistro Roberto de Tywa archidiacono Suff', Henrico capellano, magistro Roberto de Bilneye. Dat' apud Norwicum .viii. idus Aprilis pontificatus nostri anno primo.

[a] cartas A

> The church was valued at £10 both in 1254 and 1291 (*VN* 366; *Taxatio* 78b), although the actual receipts were very much greater (*VN* 567, 585).

89. Norwich Cathedral Priory

Grant to the monks in proprios usus, *for the use of the almonry, of a mediety of the church of All Saints, Wicklewood, with all its appurtenances, of which they have the right of patronage by the gift of Agnes de Reflei, to take effect after the death or resignation of Robert of Brockdish,* persona, *and William de Reflei, vicar of that mediety.*   London, 16 October 1227

> B = Norfolk R.O., DCN 40/1 (general cartulary) fo. 38r (27r, 24r). s. xiv in. C = ibid. fo. 229v (220v) (*inspeximus* by bp John Salmon, 9 March 1302). D = ibid., DCN 40/2/2 (almoner's cartulary) fo. 43r (31r, 44r). s. xiv in. E = ibid., DCN 40/2/1 (general cartulary) fos. 25v–26r (16v–17r, 98v–99r). s. xiv in. F = ibid., DCN 40/4 (episcopal charters) p. 81. s. xv in. G = ibid. pp. 269–70. H = ibid. p. 176 (as C).
> Pd in *Norwich Cathedral Charters* i no. 185; from B in *First Register* 114.

Omnibus Cristi fidelibus ad quos presens scriptum pervenerit Thomas Dei gratia Norwicensis episcopus salutem in Domino. Ad universorum notitiam volumus pervenire[a] nos Dei causa et religionis favore concessisse et presenti carta nostra confirmasse dilectis filiis in Cristo priori et conventui Norwicensibus[b] ad opus elemosinarie sue medietatem ecclesie Omnium Sanctorum de Wiclewode[c] nostre diocesis cum omnibus ad ipsam pertinentibus, in qua ius patronatus habere dinoscuntur ex donatione Agnetis de Rifle,[d] habendam in proprios usus et perpetuo possidendam post decessum vel recessum Roberti de Brokedyss[e] persone et Willelmi de Riflei vicarii predicte medietatis, salvis in omnibus reverentia et obedientia nobis et successoribus nostris et sacrosancte Norwicensis ecclesie consuetudinibus debitis vel consuetis. In cuius rei testimonium presentes litteras sigillo nostro duximus muniendas. Hiis testibus: magistro Roberto de Biln' officiali nostro, Wimaro persona de Fakenham,[g] Henrico capellano nostro, Dionisio clerico, Alano de Blunvile,[h] Edmundo clerico, Ricardo de Geytone[j] clerico. Dat' London' .xvii. kalendas Novembris pontificatus nostri anno primo.

> [a] volumus pervenire notitiam F   [b] Norwici G   [c] Wyclewode C; Wiclewde F   [d] Rifley C, H; Reflei D   [e] Brokedys C; Brokedis D, F, G, H   [f] F *ends here with* etc.   [g] Fagenham B, E; Fakkeham F; Fakeham H   [h] Blumvill' C, G; Blumvile F, H   [j] Gaiton' D, F, H; Geiton' G   [k] Septembris F

> The appropriation had apparently not taken effect before 1249, when bp Suffield confirmed it, saving a vicarage which should not be burdensome to the monks (*Norwich Cathedral Charters* i no. 207). The church was valued at £5 in 1254 and £5 6s. 8d. in 1291 (*VN* 398; *Taxatio* 85b).

*90. Norwich Cathedral Priory

Mandate to the rural dean of Flegg to induct the monks into corporal possession of the church of Martham, which he has granted them in proprios usus.

[20 December 1226 × 16 August 1236]

> Mentioned by jurors at an inquisition into the patronage of the church, 10 October 1273.
> Pd in *Norwich Cathedral Charters* ii no. 357.

> For the appropriation of the church, see Appx II 22.

91. Norwich Cathedral Priory

Notification that whereas bishop John [II] his predecessor had granted the church of Wighton to the monks in proprios usus, *thereafter Pandulph, in contravention of this concession, caused there to be ordained therein a vicarage which was beyond the church's resources, to the prejudice and injury of the monks* [Appx II 3]. *Since he is obliged to rectify injustices and to provide for the indemnity of his church, the bishop now grants that all vicars instituted at the presentation of the monks shall hold the said vicarage according to the previous assessment, paying annually to the cellarer 100s p.a. at the two Norwich synods, without any subtraction or diminution.*

Norwich, 17 February 1233

> B = Norfolk R.O., DCN 40/5 (cellarer's cartulary) fo. 26r–v (25r–v). s. xiii ex. C = ibid., DCN 40/1 (general cartulary) fos. 39v–40r (28v–29r, 25v–26r). s. xiv in. D = ibid. fo. 230r–v (221r–v) (*inspeximus* by bp John Salmon, 9 March 1302). E = ibid., DCN 40/2/1 (general cartulary) fo. 27r (18r, 100r). s. xiv in. F = ibid., DCN 40/4 (episcopal charters) pp. 83–85. s. xv in. G = ibid. pp. 272–73. H = ibid. pp. 182–83 (as D).
> Pd in *Norwich Cathedral Charters* i no. 188; from C in *First Register* 120–22.

Universis has litteras visuris vel audituris[a] Thomas Dei gratia Norwicensis episcopus salutem in Domino. Licet ex officii nostri debito omnium ecclesiarum nostre diocesis curam gerere teneamur, specialiter tamen ad honorem et profectum Norwicensis ecclesie summo opere nos decet intendere que in agendis suis tanto nos debet invenire favorabiles et benignos[b] quanto speciali privilegio dilectionis gratam illi tenemur pre aliis facere specialem, que nobis pre aliis specialius est commissa. Sane cum bone memorie I. predecessor noster dilectis filiis nostris monachis de Norwico ecclesiam de Wictone[c] sine omni subtractione in proprios usus habendam intuitu caritatis concessisset, nichil sibi nec successoribus suis[d] excepto iure episcopali retinendo et parrochiali, P. bone memorie antecessor noster contra predictam concessionem et confirmationem veniendo ibidem vicariam secundum facultates ipsius ecclesie superfluam taxari fecit, in ipsorum monachorum preiudicium et gravamen.

Unde cum ad nos spectare dinoscatur minus iuste distracta revocare atque indempnitati ecclesie nostre previdere, caritatis intuitu concessimus ac presenti carta nostra confirmavimus[e] predictis monachis nostris de Norwico quod singuli vicarii per dictorum monachorum liberam presentationem ac nostram et successorum nostrorum institutionem in dicta ecclesia pro tempore preficiendi dictam vicariam secundum taxationem prehibitam habeant et possideant, solvendo singulis annis celerario dicte domus, cuius officio dicta ecclesia appropriatur, centum solidos ad duos sinodos Norwicenses[f] et in eisdem synodis sine omni subtractione vel diminutione; et hec omnia concessimus salvis dictis monachis presentatione predicta et nobis et successoribus nostris iure pontificali et parochiali. In cuius rei testimonium has literas fieri fecimus et sigillo nostro muniri. Dat' apud Norwicum in crastino cinerum pontificatus nostri anno septimo.

[a] vel audituris *om.* F [b] et benignos *om.* F [c] Wichton C, E; Wychtone D; Wihktun F; Wichtone H [d] nichil sibi nec successoribus suis *om.* B [e] confirmamus G [f] de Norwyco D; Norwici G [g] et parochiali *om.* F

Both in 1254 and 1291 the church was assessed at £26 13s. 4d., and separated tithes at £5 (*VN* 375; *Taxatio* 81b). Wighton was not, therefore, a poorly endowed church. For bp John de Gray's grant to the monks, see *EEA* 6 nos. 388, 391.

92. Norwich Cathedral Priory

Grant in proprios usus, *for the use of the almonry, of the church of St Andrew, Attlebridge, with all its appurtenances, of which they hold the right of patronage by the gift of Heymer, rector of Felthorpe, and by the subsequent assent and confirmation of William son of Thomas of Swafield, to take effect on the death or resignation of Walter son of Geoffrey, the rector, saving provision for the maintenance, according to the resources of the church, of a competent chaplain who shall minister therein.* Thorpe, 5 June 1234

B = Norfolk R.O., DCN 40/1 (general cartulary) fo. 40r (29r, 26r). s. xiv in. C = ibid. fo. 230v (221v) (*inspeximus* by bp John Salmon, 9 March 1302). D = ibid., DCN 40/2/2 (almoner's cartulary) fo. 30r (18r, 31r). s. xiv in. E = ibid., DCN 40/2/1 (general cartulary) fo. 27r–v (18r–v, 100r–v). s. xiv in. F = ibid., DCN 40/4 (episcopal charters) p. 78. s. xv in. G = ibid. p. 267. H = ibid. pp. 183–4 (as C).
Pd in *Norwich Cathedral Charters* i no. 182; from B in *First Register* 122.

Omnibus Cristi fidelibus ad quos presens scriptum pervenerit Thomas Dei gratia Norwicensis episcopus salutem in Domino. Ad universorum notitiam volumus pervenire nos Dei causa et religionis favore concessisse et presenti carta nostra confirmasse dilectis in Cristo filiis priori et conventui Norwicensibus ad opus elemosinarie sue ecclesiam sancti Andree de Atlebrigg'[a] nostre diocesis cum omnibus ad ipsam pertinentibus, in qua ius patronatus habere dinoscuntur ex donatione Heymeri rectoris ecclesie de Felethorp'[b] et ex subsequenti assensu et confirmatione Willelmi filii Thome de Swathefeld,[c] habendam et tenendam in proprios usus in perpetuo possidendam post decessum vel recessum Walteri filii Galfridi eiusdem ecclesie rectoris, salva secundum facultates ecclesie competenti sustentatione capellani in dicta ecclesia pro tempore ministraturi, salvis etiam in omnibus reverentia et obedientia nobis et successoribus nostris et sacrosancte Norwicensis ecclesie consuetudinibus debitis vel consuetis. In cuius rei testimonium presentes litteras fieri fecimus et sigillo nostro muniri. Dat' apud Thorpe[d] manerium nostrum quinto die Iunii pontificatus nostri anno octavo.[e]

[a] Attlebrigg' C, D; Atlebrig' F; Athebrig' F; Attebrigge H   [b] Felthorpe D, E; Filetorp' F; Feletorp' G   [c] Swathefeud CFGH   [d] Thorp C, H: Torp' G   [e] F *ends, incorrectly, in later hand*: 1238

The church was valued at £3 6s. 8d. in 1254 and £4 in 1291 (*VN* 363; *Taxatio* 78b).

93. Norwich Cathedral Priory

Confirmation to the monks in proprios usus *of the church of Worstead, of which they are known to have the right of patronage. Following the death of John, late rector, and on the resignation of Adam, clerk of Worstead, he has inducted the monks into possession of the church.*

Norwich, [25 March × 19 December 1235]

B = Norfolk R.O., DCN 40/5 (cellarer's cartulary) fo. 21r (20r). s. xiii ex. C = ibid., DCN 40/1 (general cartulary) fo. 40v (29v, 26v). s. xiv in. D = ibid. fo. 230v (221v) (*inspeximus* by bp John Salmon, 9 March 1302). E = ibid., DCN 40/3/1 (general cartulary) fo. 27v (18v, 100v). s. xiv in. F = ibid., DCN 40/4 (episcopal charters) pp. 78–9. s. xiv in. G = ibid. pp. 267–8. H = ibid. pp. 184–5 (as D).
Pd in *Norwich Cathedral Charters* i no. 183; from C in *First Register* 124.

Universis sancte matris ecclesie filiis ad quos presens scriptum pervenerit Thomas Dei gratia Norwicensis episcopus salutem in Domino. Ad universorum volumus pervenire notitiam nos Dei intuitu et favore religionis concessisse, dedisse et hac [presenti] carta nostra confirmasse dilectis in Cristo filiis priori et monachis Norwicensibus ecclesiam de Wrthstede,[a] in qua ius patronatus habere dinoscuntur, cum capella sancti Andree et omnibus ad ipsam spectantibus, in proprios usus perpetuo possidendam. Nos itaque post decessum Iohannis quondam rectoris dicte ecclesie ad resignationem Ade clerici de Wurthstede[b] memoratos priorem et monachos in possessionem eiusdem ecclesie induximus et pacifica fecimus possessione gaudere. Hanc itaque ecclesiam memoratis priori et monachis confirmamus, salvo nobis et successoribus nostris imperpetuum iure pontificali et parrochiali. Testibus: magistris Roberto et Alano archidiaconis, magistro Alexandro de Walepol',[c] Dionisio de Catton'[d] et Iohanne Terri clericis. Dat' apud Norwicum anno Domini millesimo CC° XXXV pontificatus nostri anno nono.[e]

[a] Wrstede B, E; Wrthested F; Worthestede G, H   [b] Wrstede B; Wurthestede D; Wrthestede E; Wrthested F; Wurthested' G   [c] Walpol D, E; Walpole H   [d] Cottone B, D; Cottun' F; Cotton' G; Cattone H   [e] quinto F, H

For reckoning of the beginning of the year as 25 March, see Introduction, p. lxx. For bp Blundeville's appropriation of the church, see no. 86.

94. Norwich Cathedral Priory

Grant to the monks in proprios usus, *for the use of the almonry, of a mediety of the church of All Saints, Wicklewood, of which they hold the right of patronage by the gift of Nigel of Happisburgh, chaplain.*

[Thorpe, 23 September 1235]

B = Norfolk R.O., DCN 40/1 (general cartulary) fo. 38r–v (27r–v, 24r–v). s. xiv in. C = ibid. fo. 229v (220v) (*inspeximus* by bp John Salmon, 9 March 1302). D = ibid., DCN 40/2/2 (almoner's cartulary) fo. 42r (30r, 43r). s. xiv in. E = ibid., DCN 40/2/1 (general cartulary) fo. 27v (18v, 100v). s. xiv in. F = ibid., DCN 40/4 (episcopal charters) p. 85. s. xv in. G = ibid. p. 273. H = ibid. pp. 176–77 (as C).
Pd in *Norwich Cathedral Charters* i no. 189; from B in *First Register* 114–16.

Omnibus Cristi fidelibus ad quos presens scriptum pervenerit Thomas Dei gratia Norwicensis episcopus salutem in Domino. Ad universorum notitiam volumus pervenire nos Dei causa et religionis favore concessisse et presenti carta nostra confirmasse dilectis filiis in Cristo priori et conventui Norwicensi[a] ad opus elemosinarie sue medietatem ecclesie omnium sanctorum de Wiclewode[b] nostre diocesis cum omnibus ad ipsam pertinentibus, in qua ius patronatus habere dinoscuntur ex donatione Nigelli de Hapesburgh[c] capellani,[d] habendam in proprios usus et perpetuo possidendam, salvis in omnibus reverentia et obedientia nobis et successoribus nostris et sacrosancte Norwicensis ecclesie consuetudinibus debitis vel consuetis. In cuius rei testimonium presentes litteras sigillo nostro duximus muniendas. Dat' apud Thorp[e] in crastino sancti Mauritii pontificatus nostri anno nono.

[a] Norwici E, F   [b] Wiclewod D; Wicclewde F   [c] Hapesburg C; Hapesburge D, F; Happesburgh H   [d] capellani om. B, E   [e] Torp' G

For the appropriation of the other mediety by bp Blundeville, see no. 89.

95. Norwich, St Paul's Hospital

Confirmation of the churches and tithes granted to the hospital.

Thorpe, 26 February 1227

> A = Norwich, Norfolk R.O., DCN 43/37. Endorsed: Confirmatio T. episcopi de ecclesiis et minutis decimis; de decimis hospitalis (s. xiii); Thome I episcopi (s. xiv); pressmark; Hugh of Mursley's notarial mark; approx. 158 × 135 + 20 mm.; damaged seal on parchment tag, green wax, counterseal.
> B = Canterbury, D. & C. Ch. Ant. N1 (*inspeximus* by prior Nicholas and convent of Christ Church, Canterbury, 1249). s. xiii med. C = Norfolk R.O., DCN 40/5 (cellarer's cartulary) fo. 12r–v (11r–v) (as B). s. xiii ex. D = BL ms. Cotton roll ii 19 (*inspeximus* of hospital's charters by bp John Salmon, 17 March 1302) no. 13. s. xiv in. E = Norfolk R.O., DCN 40/1 (general cartulary) fo. 240v–41r (*inspeximus* by bp Salmon, 9 March 1302). s. xiv in. F = ibid. DCN 40/4 (episcopal charters) pp. 213v–14r (as E). s. xv in.
> Pd from A in *Norwich Cathedral Charters* i no. 257.

Omnibus Cristi fidelibus ad quos presens scriptum pervenerit Thomas Dei gratia Norwicensis episcopus salutem in Domino. Ea que in pias causas a Dei fidelibus concessa sunt et collata, ut hiis usibus quibus sunt deputata firma et inconcussa permaneant, episcopalis expedit auctoritatis patrocinio communiri. Eapropter ad universorum volumus pervenire notitiam nos Dei causa et pietatis intuitu canonice dedisse et confirmasse Deo et hospitali sancti Pauli in Norwico ecclesias omnes decimasque subscriptas cum omnibus ad ipsam pertinentibus in proprios usus et sustentationem pauperum in eodem hospitali languentium inperpetuum profuturas, videlicet ecclesiam sancti Pauli in Norwico, in villa de Ormesby ecclesias sancti Michaelis et sancti Pauli et sancti Andree et sancte Margarete, decimas quoque omnes aule de Ormesby et [de] omnibus terris ad dominium eiusdem aule pertinentibus et de ovibus eiusdem aule, ex donatione illustrissimorum regum Anglie Henrici primi et Henrici secundi, preterea tertiam partem decime de maneriis nostrorum de Blafeld', de Beketon', de Torp, de Tornedis, de Langham cum suis pertinentiis, et duas partes decime dominii nostri de Marsham, et tertiam partem decime dominii de Blicling', et medietatem omnium decimarum de dominio prioris Norwicensis in Taverham et de dominio monachorum Norwicensium in Neuton', et duas partes decimarum de dominio Roberti de Hulmo in Fileby, salva in omnibus reverentia, honore et debitis consuetudinibus sancte Norwicensis ecclesie. Hanc autem donationem nostram et confirmationem nostram, ut stabilis et illibata perseveret, presenti scripto et sigilli nostri attestatione corroboramus. Hiis testibus: magistro Alano archidiacono Sudbir', magistro Roberto de Bileneie, Iohanne Terri, Henrico capellano, Dionisio clerico, Ricardo de Geiton' clerico, Henrico de Tunstal' clerico, Adam de Birlingham. Dat' apud Torp .iiii^{to}. kalendas Martii pontificatus nostri anno primo.

96. Norwich, Church of St Martin, Coslany

Notification by the bishop, prior W[illiam] and the convent that, when a dispute was heard before the archbishop of Canterbury and his fellow judges-delegate between themselves and Richard of Reedham, clerk, concerning the church of St Martin of Coslany, at last an amicable composition was reached whereby the prior and convent conceded and leased that church to Richard as perpetual farmer for his lifetime, rendering therefrom to the infirmarer as his farm 10s. a year in equal instalments at the Easter and Michaelmas synods. He will discharge all the obligations of the church to the bishop, and they will renounce all hostility against him over the receipts of this church. For greater security, both parties have submitted to the jurisdiction of the same judges in regard to enforcement of the terms of this composition, and to a penalty of ten marks in case of contravention.

[20 December 1226 × 12 April 1235]

A = Norfolk R.O., DCN 45/24/1. Endorsed: Compositio de ecclesia sancti Martini de Koselannie ad firmam dimissa (s. xiii); pressmark; approx. 230 × 90 + 20 mm., indented at upper margin, inscribed: Cyrografum inter priorem et conventum Norwic' et Ricardum de Redh' (inverted); five parchment tags, to the centre of which is attached damaged episcopal seal, green wax, counterseal, and to the second from left another episcopal seal, counterseal showing martyrdom of St Andrew (presumably of bp of Rochester).

Omnibus Cristi fidelibus ad quos presens scriptum pervenerit Thomas Dei gratia episcopus Norwicensis, W. prior Norwicensis et eiusdem loci conventus salutem eternam in Domino. Noveritis quod cum inter nos ex una parte et Ricardum de Redeh' clericum ex altera coram venerabili patre Cantuariensi archiepiscopo et eiusdem coniudicibus super ecclesiam sancti Martini in Coselan' auctoritate apostolica questio verteretur, tandem dicta questio amicabiliter in hunc modum conquievit, videlicet quod nos dicti prior et conventus dimisimus et concessimus dictam ecclesiam nostram cum omnibus ad eam pertinentibus dicto Ricardo tamquam perpetuo firmario omnibus diebus vite sue tenendam et habendam, reddendo inde annuatim infirmario Norwicensi decem solidos nomine firme, videlicet ad sinodum paschalem proximam post tempus compositionis istius quinque solidos et ad synodum sancti Michaelis quinque solidos, et omnia honera pontificalia sustinebit, omni contradictione, malitia, circumventione, impetratione et choactione ordinum ratione dicte ecclesie suscipiendorum facta vel facienda contra dictum Ricardum cessantibus. Ad maiorem itaque securitatem dicte compositionis in perpetuum durature tam nos quam dictus Ricardus subiecimus nos dictorum iudicum iurisdictioni, ut ipsi eam habeant liberam et perpetuam de communi assensu nostro compellendi per censuram ecclesiasticam partem dicte compositioni resistentem totiens ad solutionem decem marcarum nomine pene solvendarum quotiens aliqua partium contra compositionem istam per liquidas probationes in aliquo inveniatur rebellis, ipsa compositione nichilominus auctoritate iudicum predictorum in suo statu et robore remanente, et renunciavimus hinc inde omnibus impetratis et impetrandis et omni auxilio et iuris remedio competenti et competituro. In huius autem rei testimonium nos unacum sigillis iudicum et partis adverse huic scripto signa nostra apposuimus. Valete.

Prior William son of Odo probably died in 1235 and was commemorated on 12 April; his successor first occurs on 4 September 1235 (*Fasti* ii 60). In 1254 the portions of the monks and of the rector were both assessed at 6s. 8d. (*VN* 387), and in 1291 the church, appropriated to the monks, was valued at 12s. (*Taxatio* 78).

96A. Pentney Priory

Grant to the canons in proprios usus *of the church of All Saints, Shotesham, with all its appurtenances, saving honourable maintenance of a vicar who shall minister therein.*　　　　　　　　　　　　　Gaywood, 21 July 1227

B = Norfolk R.O., FEL 31 (transcripts relating to Shotesham). s. xvi in.

Universis presentes litteras inspecturis Thomas Dei gratia Norwicensis episcopus salutem in Domino. Ad universorum notitiam volumus pervenire[a] nos intuitu Dei et religionis favore concessisse et dedisse priori et canonicis de Pentneye, quos sancta erga Dominum devotio et apud homines honeste vite conversatio reddunt multipliciter commendatos, ecclesiam Omnium Sanctorum de Shotesham cum omnibus pertinentiis suis, in proprios usus perpetuo possidendam, salva honesta sustentatione vicarii qui pro tempore in prefata ministrabit ecclesia, salvis etiam[b] nobis et successoribus nostris reverentia et honore et sancte Norwicensis ecclesie consuetudinibus debitis et consuetis. In huius rei testimonium presentes litteras fieri fecimus et sigillo nostro muniri. Dat' apud Geywode duodecimo kalendas[c] Augusti pontificatus nostri anno primo.

[a] pervenire et B　　[b] et B　　[c] calend' B

For the 'foundation' charter of Robert de Vaux and the confirmation by William his son, see *Monasticon* VI (i) 69–70; these include the advowsons of All Saints and St Botulph's, Shotesham. In 1254 the two churches were valued together at seventeen marks, and the vicarage of All Saints at 10s. (*VN* 401). In 1291, the church of All Saints was valued at £8, apart from the vicarage not liable to the tenth, and St Botulph's at £5 6s. 8d. (*Taxatio* 84).

*97. Royal Justices

Letter testifying that the church of Rushmere [St Andrew] is not vacant.

[Trinity term, 1227]

Mention of letter produced in *curia regis*.
Pd in *CRR* xiii no. 296.

Gilbert Marshal claimed the advowson against the prior of Ipswich, almost certainly Holy Trinity, to which the church was appropriated by 1291 (*Taxatio* 117b). The prior pleaded that an assize of *darrein presentment* should not be held, because the church was not vacant, but rather mr Richard of Kirkham was *persona*. Gilbert was unable to contravert this testimony and was in mercy for a false claim.

*98. Royal Justices

Letter testifying to the legitimate birth of Richard de Ros.

[28 May 1228 × 25 July 1229]

Mention of letter produced in *curia regis*.
Pd in *CRR* xiii no. 2133.

A case was brought before the justices in eyre in Norfolk (28 May – 25 July 1228, see Crook, *General Eyre* 83) by Richard de Ros against Constantine the chaplain and Agnes daughter of Richard by assize of *mort d'ancestor* relating to four acres and a messuage in Hopton. Calling various persons to warrant, she alleged that the assize should not be taken because Richard was a bastard. A writ was despatched to the bp ordering him to enquire into the truth of this allegation. At Westminster in Easter term 1229 Richard was adjudged to have recovered seisin, and various exchanges of land between the parties were made.

*99. Royal Justices

Letters patent testifying that Warin son of Hugh, Robert his brother and Walter son of Robert are clerks, and claiming them for episcopal jurisdiction.

[Hilary term, 1231]

Mention of letter produced in the *curia regis*.
Pd in *Bracton's Notebook* ii no. 490.

Alice, widow of William of Waldingfield, appealed these three men of the death of her husband; the bp certified that they were clerks and despatched the subprior of Chipley to claim them, and they were delivered to the bp as clerks.

*100. Royal Justices

Notification that Agnes, widow of Albert¹ de Neville, was legitimately married to him. [Easter term, 1231]

> Mention of letter produced in *curia regis*.
> Pd in *CRR* xiv no. 1502.

> Agnes claimed from various persons land in Hethel, Nf., and Alnesbourne, Sf., as her dower; they alleged that she should not have these, as she had never been legitimately married to him. The bp was ordered to conduct an inquisition, and thereafter she recovered seisin.

> ¹In the record, the late husband is initially called Osbert, but twice thereafter Albert. An Albert de Neville made a grant to Norwich cathedral priory, which has been dated 1219 × 35 (*Norwich Cathedral Charters* ii no. 234); the legend on the seal affixed to this original deed has AUBERTI, on the counterseal ALBERN.

*101. Royal Justices

Letters patent by which the bishop claims for his jurisdiction the prior of Horsham St Faith, indicted on a charge of incitement to assault. [Easter term 1231]

> Mention of letter produced in the *curia regis*.
> Pd in *CRR* xiv no. 1364; *Bracton's Notebook* ii no. 548.

> The prior was claimed by the abbot of St Benet of Holme, acting on the bp's behalf, and was to be produced before the justices on their next eyre.

102. St Neots Priory

Grant to the monks of a perpetual benefice of five marks a year in the church of Heveningham, to be received at the two Suffolk synods after the death or resignation of Nicholas the clerk, now rector. Confirmation also of the grants in proprios usus *by his predecessors of the churches of Cratfield and Ubbeston, saving therein vicarages which he has caused to be taxed by master Robert of Bilney, archdeacon of Norfolk, and to which when they are vacant they should present suitable* personae. [Thorpe, 11 September 1229]

> B = BL ms. Cotton Faust. A iv (St Neots cartulary) fo. 110r. s. xiii med.

Omnibus Cristi fidelibus ad quos presens scriptum pervenerit Thomas Dei gratia Norwicensis episcopus salutem in Domino. Noverit universitas vestra nos divini amoris intuitu et religionis favore concessisse et presentis scripti testimonio confirmasse dilectis nobis in Cristo priori et conventui sancti Neoti quinque marcas annuas nomine perpetui beneficii de ecclesia de Heveningham nostre diocesis post decessum vel recessum Nicholai clerici rectoris eiusdem singulis annis ad duas sinodos Suffolk' percipiendas. Ecclesias de Crattefeld et de Obeston' sibi a predecessoribus nostris in proprios usus concessas eis auctoritate eadem confirmamus, salvis vicariis in predictis ecclesiis quas per dilectum nostrum in Cristo magistrum Robertum de Biln(eia) archidiaconum Norfolk' taxari fecimus, ad quas cum vacare contigerint nobis idoneas personas presentabunt, salvis etiam in omnibus nobis et successoribus nostris obedientia et reverentia et sacrosancte Norwicensis ecclesie consuetudinibus debitis et consuetis. In cuius rei testimonium presentes litteras fieri fecimus et sigillo nostro muniri. Dat' apud Torp .iii°. idus Septembris pontificatus nostri anno iii°.

For the pension of 20s. *p.a.* previously received from Heveningham, see *EEA* 6 no. 280. In 1254 and 1291 the monks still received only a portion of 20s. *p.a.* from the church (*VN* 445; *Taxatio* 118b). The appropriation of Cratfield church had been effected by 26 March 1233 (no. 104), and in 1254 there was a vicarage valued at 30s. *p.a.* established in the church of Ubbeston (*VN* 445).

103. St Neots Priory

Grant to the monks in proprios usus *of the church of Barton Bendish, to take effect on the death or resignation of Roger of Elmham, chaplain, the rector, who while he lives shall pay them ten marks a year according to the bishop's ordinance, saving an honourable and competent vicarage to be taxed by the bishop or his successors according to the resources of the church, to be conferred by the bishop on whomsoever he may wish.*

[North or South] Elmham, 24 June 1242

B = BL ms. Cotton Faust. A iv (St Neots cartulary) fo. 110r. s. xiii med.

Omnibus Cristi fidelibus ad quos presens scriptum pervenerit Thomas Dei gratia Norwicensis episcopus salutem in Domino. Ad universorum notitiam volumus pervenire nos Dei causa et religionis favore concessisse et presenti carta confirmasse dilectis nobis in Cristo priori et monachis sancti Neoti ecclesiam de Bertunebinnedich cum omnibus ad ipsam pertinentibus habendam, tenendam et perpetuo possidendam in proprios usus post decessum vel recessum Rogeri de Elmham capellani, eiusdem rectoris. Concessimus etiam et confirmavimus dictis priori et monachis sancti Neoti ut de predicta ecclesia de Berton' quamdiu dictus Rogerus capellanus vixerit .x. marcas annuas percipiant ex ordinatione nostra, salva honesta et competenti vicaria per nos vel successores nostros in dicta ecclesia pro tempore taxanda secundum facultates ecclesie per nos vel successores nostros cuicumque voluerimus inperpetuum conferenda, salva etiam possessione et iure dicto R. capellano quod in eadem habere dinoscitur quoad vixerit, salvis etiam in omnibus reverentia et obedientia nobis et successoribus nostris et sacrosancte Norwicensis ecclesie consuetudinibus debitis et consuetis. In cuius rei testimonium presentes litteras fieri fecimus et sigillo nostro muniri. Dat' apud Elmham manerium nostrum die sancti Iohannis Baptiste pontificatus nostri anno sexto.

> For an earlier grant of the church *in proprios usus*, which was obviously ineffective when the *personatus* was vacated, see *EEA* 6 no. 277. For the claim of the priory of Stoke by Clare to the church, see *Stoke by Clare Cartulary* iii 19. In 1254 the monks of St Neots' revenues therein were valued at £13 6s. 8d., the portion of Stoke by Clare at £2 and the rector's portion at £3 6s. 8d., and separately listed is a pension of 50s. paid by the current rector (*VN* 407, 485). In 1291 the rectory was assessed at only £4 6s. 8d. (*Taxatio* 88).

104. St Neots Priory

Institution of Thomas the clerk to the perpetual vicarage of the church of Cratfield, at the presentation of the prior and monks, saving to them their portion therein. Lest dissension should arise in the future, he has caused the vicar's portion to be taxed by master R[obert] of Bilney, archdeacon of Norfolk. The vicar shall have all the altarage, half of the free lands pertaining to the church, all the great tithe of the demesne and half the tithe of hay of the vill, and the tithe of mills. The remainder of the revenues shall be received by the prior and convent. [11 September 1229 × 27 March 1233]

B = BL ms. Cotton Faust. A iv (St Neots cartulary) fo. 140v. s. xiii med.

Omnibus Cristi fidelibus presentes literas inspecturis Thomas Dei gratia Norwicensis episcopus salutem in Domino. Ad universorum[a] notitiam volumus pervenire nos admisisse dilectum nobis in Cristo Thomam clericum ad perpetuam vicariam ecclesie de Crattefeld cum omnibus ad ipsam pertinentibus, ad presentationem prioris et conventus sancti Neoti, ipsumque Thomam clericum vicarium perpetuum in eadem instituisse, salva dictis priori et conventui sancti Neoti portione quam in eadem habere noscuntur. Et ne futuris temporibus inter dictos priorem et conventum sancti Neoti et dictum Thomam vicarium super portionibus suis oriatur[b] dissentio, portionem dicti vicarii per dilectum filium magistrum R. de Billn(eia) archidiaconum Norfolch' in hunc modum taxari fecimus, videlicet quod dictus vicarius habebit totum altaragium et medietatem liberarum terrarum ad dictam ecclesiam pertinentium et totam decimam bladi de dominico domini ville et medietatem fenorum ville et decimam molendinorum. Totum autem residuum cedet in usus dictorum prioris et conventus sancti Neoti, salvis etiam in omnibus reverentia et obedientia nobis et successoribus nostris et sancte Norwicensis ecclesie consuetudinibus debitis vel consuetis. In cuius rei testimonium etc.

ᵃ universe B   ᵇ orriatur B

After no. 102. Mr Robert of Bilney was probably no longer archdn by 27 March 1233 (*Fasti* ii 66). In 1254 the church was valued at £12 and the vicarage at £2 6s. 8d. (*VN* 445).

105. Sibton Abbey

Inspeximus and confirmation of a charter of bishop John [of Oxford] by which he granted to the monks, for the maintenance of hospitality and for the sustenance of Christ's poor, the tithes and all oblations pertaining to the church of St Peter, Sibton, to take effect when it should be vacated by Thomas, then persona, *with provision to be made for a rector [EEA 6 no. 282]. He has ordained that the vicar shall have all the tithes and oblations of the church, with the exception of the great tithe and the tithes of vegetables and wood, which he has confirmed to the monks.*   Redlingfield, 14 April 1227

B = Ipswich, Suffolk R.O., HD 1538/345; no. 12 of original documents in bound volume (*inspeximus* by the official of the bp of Norwich, 3 November 1434, of *inspeximus* by prior Simon of Elmham and convent of Norwich). s. xv med.
Pd from B in *Sibton Cartulary* iv no. 1005 (vii).

Omnibus Cristi fidelibus ad quos presens scriptum pervenerit Thomas Dei gratia Norwicensis episcopus salutem in Domino. Inspeximus cartam bone memorie I. predecessoris nostri in hac forma conceptam: [*EEA* 6 no. 282; *Sibton Charters* iv no. 1005 (iii)]. Nos autem predictas concessionem et confirmationem ratam habentes et acceptam, eam presentis scripti munimine duximus roborandam, estimationem autem vicarie predicte ecclesie et eiusdem taxationem presentibus literis duximus inserendam, videlicet ut pro tempore vicarius predicte ecclesie percipiat omnes decimas et obventiones sepedicte ecclesie preter decimas garbarum legiminumque,ᵃ quas ut predictum est religionis favore dictis monachis confirmavimus. Datum apud Redelingefeld' .xviii. kalendas Maii pontificatus nostri anno primo.

ᵃ garbarumque leguminum B; *thereafter* ac silvarum, *in slightly later hand and interlined, but this interlineation is not noted in the notary's eschatochol.*

In 1254 the church was valued at £2 13s. 4d. and in 1291 at £4, and the priors of Horsham St Faith and Rumburgh held portions (*VN* 445–46; *Taxatio* 118b).

106. Sibton Abbey

Institution of Ralph of Ubbeston, chaplain, to the perpetual vicarage of St Peter, Sibton, with the chapel of Peasenhall, at the presentation of the monks.

Ralph shall receive as a vicarage all the tithes and oblations of the church, except the great tithe and the tithe of vegetables, which the bishop confirms to the monks in proprios usus. Sibton, May 1234

> B = Ipswich, Suffolk R.O., HD 1538/345; no. 12 of original documents in bound volume (*inspeximus* by the official of the bp of Norwich, 3 November 1434). s. xv med.
> Pd from B in *Sibton Cartulary* iv no. 1005 (iv).

Omnibus Cristi fidelibus ad quos presens scriptum pervenerit Thomas [Dei] gratia Norwicensis episcopus salutem in Domino. Ad universorum notitiam volumus pervenire nos intuitu Dei ad presentationem abbatis et conventus de Sibeton admisisse Radulfum de Hubbeston' capellanum[a] ad vicariam perpetuam ecclesie sancti Petri de Sibeton cum capella de Pesenhal' et omnibus ad eam pertinentibus, et ipsum Radulfum capellanum vicarium in eadem canonice instituisse. Taxationem autem predicte vicarie presentibus literis duximus inferendam, scilicet quod predictus Radulfus capellanus omnes decimas et obventiones dicte ecclesie nomine vicarie percipiet, preter decimas garbarum et leguminum,[b] quas dictis monachis de Sibet' in proprios usus confirmamus. In cuius rei testimonium presentes literas fieri fecimus et sigillo nostro muniri. Dat' apud Sibeton mense Maii pontificatus nostri anno octavo.

[a] capellanum *interlined* B   [b] ac silvarum *interlined* B, *but not noted by the notary in his eschatocol.*

107. Spinney Priory

Notification that he has taken under his protection and that of the church of Norwich the religious community of Spinney in the vill of Wicken, founded by Hugh Malebiche and Beatrix his wife for three canons regular, dedicated to the Blessed Virgin Mary and the Holy Cross, and endowed with fifty-five acres of arable to the north and marshland to the south, as is demonstrated by their charters. He has confirmed to master Hervey the canon, presented to him by Hugh and Beatrix, and to the canons there serving God their site with its appurtenances and possessions. Thornage, 1 May 1228

> B = Canterbury D. & C. Ch. Ant. N 24 (notarial transcript by John Alani of Beccles, 23 April 1281) no. 4. s. xiii ex.

Omnibus Cristi fidelibus ad quos presens scriptum pervenerit Thomas Dei gratia Norwicensis episcopus salutem in Domino. Cum nobilis vir Hugo Malebyse et Beatrix uxor eius pro salute animarum suarum et predecessorum suorum et successorum quendam locum qui dicitur Spinetum in villa de Wykes aptum religioni cum quinquaginta quinque acris terre arabilis versus aquilonem et cum marisco versus austrum usque ad filum cum omnibus suis pertinentiis Deo et beate Marie et in honore sancte crucis ad sustentationem trium canonicorum regularium concesserint et dederint et cartis suis confirmaverint, nos laudabile eorum propositum in hac parte attendentes predictum locum cum omnibus pertinentiis suis auctoritate episcopali confirmamus et sub protectione nostra et sacrosancte Norwycensis ecclesie suscipimus, magistro Herveo canonico a predictis H. Malebyse et B. uxore sua nobis presentato et canonicis ibidem Deo pro tempore famulantibus dictum locum cum pertinentiis suis et possessionibus assignatis confirmantes, salvis in omnibus reverentia et obedientia nobis et successoribus nostris et sacrosancte Norwycensis ecclesie consuetudinibus debitis vel consuetis. In cuius rei testimonium presentes litteras fieri fecimus et sigillo nostro muniri. Dat' apud Thornh' manerium kalendas Maii pontificatus nostri anno secundo.

> For the endowment of the community, see *VCH Cambridgeshire* ii 249. The notarial transcription of twelve charters was made at Burwell during archbp Pecham's metropolitical visitation of the diocese (C. R. Cheney, *Notaries Public in England in the Thirteenth and Fourteenth Centuries* (Oxford 1972), 34–5).
>
> For other *acta* dated at Thornage, see nos. 34, 129. It was an episcopal manor (*EEA* 6 no. 269), and in the Valuation of 1254 is listed as Thornage Episcopi (*VN* 373).

108. Spinney Priory

Inspeximus and confirmation of the charter of Hugh of Kniveton, rector of Wicken, recording that when Hugh Malebiche and Beatrix his wife, his patrons, founded in the parish of Wicken a monastery for canons regular serving God under the Rule of St Augustine and gave them lands and possessions, wishing to safeguard their liberty and the indemnity of the mother church, they conferred on the church of Wicken two tenants, Richard de Cruce and John Clewe, with their sequela, *in order that the canons should in perpetuity be exempt from the payment of obventions and great and lesser tithes from all their possessions in the parish; to this the rector has consented.*

[1 May 1228 × 17 January 1230]

> B = Canterbury D. & C. Ch. Ant. N 24 (notarial transcript by John Alani of Beccles, 23 April 1281) no. 7. s. xiii ex.

Omnibus Cristi fidelibus presens scriptum visuris vel audituris Thomas Dei gratia Norwycensis episcopus salutem in Domino. Noveritis nos inspexisse cartam Hugonis de Knivetone rectoris ecclesie de Wykes in hec verba: Omnibus Cristi fidelibus has literas inspecturis et audituris Hugo de Knyveton' persona ecclesie de Wykes salutem in Domino. Cum Hugo Malebyse et Beatrix uxor eius patroni mei monasterium in parochia de Wikes construxerint, in quo canonici regulares sub regula beati Augustini Deo deserviunt, et eisdem canonicis terras et alias possessiones de dominico suo contulerint, sicuti carte eorum evidenter testantur, volentes dicti patroni mei eorum libertati prospicere et salvare indempnitatem matricis ecclesie, contulerunt duos tenentes de Wykes, scilicet Ricardum de Cruce et Iohannem Clewe, cum tota sequela sua ecclesie de Wykes, ita quod predicti canonici sint immunes in perpetuum a prestatione obventionum, decimarum tam garbarum quam aliarum omnium minutarum seu provenientium de omnibus rebus et possessionibus in parochia de Wykes proveniendorum. Ego vero, attendens dictorum patronorum meorum laudabile propositum, maxime cum ecclesia mea conservatur illesa, de consilio prudentium virorum pro me et successoribus meis predictis canonicis predictam immunitatem benigne concessi. Nos autem dictam compositionem ratam et gratam habentes, eam auctoritate nostra duximus confirmandam. Hiis testibus: magistro (Roberto) de Bylneya[a] officiali Norwycensi et multis aliis.

[a] Byneya B

Almost certainly before no. 109, in which the church of Wicken is granted *in proprios usus*; probably after no. 107.

109. Spinney Priory

Grant to the canons in proprios usus *of the parish church of St Mary of Wicken, which is of their advowson by the gift of Hugh Malebiche and Beatrix his wife, to take effect on the death of Hugh of Kniveton, the present rector. In the meantime, with the rector's consent, they are to receive an annual pension of one mark at the Easter synod of Suffolk. The grant is made saving honourable maintenance for a vicar, to be assessed by the bishop or his successors according to the resources of the church. The canons shall present a suitable* persona *of their choice to the bishop at each vacancy, but if they fail so to do, he may nevertheless institute a vicar of his own choice.*

Colchester, 17 January 1230

B = Canterbury D. & C. Ch. Ant. N 24 (notarial transcript by John Alani of Beccles, 23 April 1281) no. 6. s. xiii ex.

Omnibus Cristi fidelibus presens scriptum visuris et audituris Thomas Dei gratia Norwycensis episcopus salutem in Domino. Ad omnium volumus pervenire notitiam nos Dei causa et religionis favore concessisse, dedisse et presenti carta nostra confirmasse dilectis in Cristo filiis priori et canonicis de Spineto ecclesiam eiusdem ville, videlicet ecclesiam parochiale sancte Marie de Wykes cum omnibus ad ipsam pertinentibus, que de ipsorum canonicorum patronatu ratione collationis eis a nobili viro Hugone Malebyse et Beatrice uxore sua facte esse dinoscitur, in proprios usus suos perpetuo habendam et possidendam post decessum dilecti filii in Cristo Hugonis de Knyvetone nunc eiusdem ecclesie rectoris. Interim autem volumus et concedimus ut dicti prior et canonici omnino unius marce pensione[m] de predicta ecclesia de voluntate predicti H. rectoris percipiant, eis singulis annis in synodo Suffolch' paschali solvendam, salva honesta sustentatione vicarii in dicta ecclesia pro tempore ministraturi a nobis vel successoribus nostris secundum facultates eiusdem ecclesie providenda et taxanda, ad quam vicariam quotiens vacare contigerit dicti prior et canonici personam ydoneam quemcumque voluerint nobis et successoribus nostris presentabunt, et nos eundem sine difficultate instituemus. Si autem dicti prior et canonici presentare omiserint vel neglexerint, nos et successores nostri quemcumque voluerimus ipsis irrequisitis nichilominus instituemus vicarium in eadem ecclesia, salvis etiam in omnibus reverentia et obedientia nobis et successoribus nostris et sacrosancte Norwycensis ecclesie consuetudinibus debitis vel consuetis. In cuius rei testimonium presentes literas fieri fecimus et sigillo nostro muniri. Dat' apud Colecestr' sextodecimo kalendas Februarii pontificatus nostri anno quarto.

> On 15 March 1261 the canons received an indult from Pope Alexander IV that since the church of Wicken was by common estimation valued at no more than twelve marks, they might in future have it served by one of their own number, as in fact it long had been (no. 12 of B). In 1254 the church had been assessed at thirteen marks (*VN* 431), and in 1291 it was valued at £12, and the portion of Rumburgh priory at 15s. (*Taxatio* 121).

*110. Thornham Church

Institution of Ralph de Blundeville as persona *of the church, from which he is to receive an annual pension of one mark.*

[*c.* August 1233 × 16 August 1236]

> Mention and recitation of charter in *CRR* xvi no. 78.

Profert cartam Thome quondam Norwicensis episcopi que testatur quod de voluntate et assensu Roberti Budement rectoris ecclesie de Torenham, que extitit de patronatu suo, contulit dilecto filio in Cristo Radulpho de Blumvill' archidiacono Suff''[1] marcam nomine pensionis de dicta ecclesia annuatim percipiendam et ipsum personam instituit, salva vicaria predicti Roberti.

[1]*Sic*; there is no evidence that Ralph was ever archdn of Suffolk, and elsewhere in this record he is correctly described as archdn of Norfolk.

Ralph de Blundeville, archdn of Norfolk, was summoned in Trinity term 1237 to answer by whose presentation he held the church of Thornham, the advowson of which pertained to the king by reason of the vacancy of the bishopric. Ralph stated that he held the church by the gift and advowson of bp Thomas, who gave him 2s. (*sic*) therefrom as a pension, saving to the vicar his vicarage for his lifetime; this was three years before the bp's death. When the vicar died, Ralph entered into the church by reason of the vacancy of the vicarage. He was ordered to appear at Michaelmas and to produce documentation, and this he would do saving the liberty of the church, as it seemed to him that he should not have been called to answer in this case. He eventually appeared by attorney on 18 November 1237 and produced the charter above, and also a letter of the abbot of West Dereham, vicegerent of the archbp of Canterbury and the archdns during the vacancy of the see, stating that by the examination of witnesses and documents he had established that Ralph had received an annual pension of a mark from the church, to which bp Thomas had admitted him and instituted him as *persona*, and the abbot by his own authority consolidated the vicarage to the *personatus*. For the complex history of the church of Thornham, see no. 143; for the litigation at the papal *curia* by which Ralph was deprived of his archdeaconry of Norfolk because of his subsequent assumption of a benefice with cure of souls at Thornham, see *Reg. Greg. IX* no. 4738, and above pp. xlviii–ix.

111. Tonbridge Priory

Confirmation for the canons of the grant by Richard of Clare, late earl of Hertford, of the advowson of the church of Stradishall.

London, 3 November 1227

B = PRO E135/15/17 (notarial record, in form of roll, of evidences produced before bp of Norwich, 4 February 1297). s. xiii ex.

Omnibus Cristi fidelibus ad quos presens scriptum pervenerit Thomas Dei gratia Norwycensis episcopus salutem in Domino. Ad universorum notitiam volumus pervenire quod cum clare memorie Ricardus de Clare quondam comes Hertford' causa Dei et religionis favore ius patronatus ecclesie de Stradeshulle Deo et ecclesie sancte (Marie) Magdalene de Tonebrigge et canonicis ibidem Deo servientibus concesserit et carta sua confirmaverit, nos ipsius comitis concessionem et confirmationem dictis canonicis in hac parte factam ratam habentes et acceptam, ipsam presentis scripti testimonio et sigilli nostri appositione duximus roborandam. In cuius rei testimonium presentes litteras fieri fecimus et sigillo nostro muniri. Dat' London' .iii. nonas Novembris pontificatus nostri anno primo.

The charter of Richard of Clare, also transcribed on the roll, was attested by Gilbert de Glanville, bp of Rochester (1185–1214); the earl is therefore Richard I (1173–1217), the founder of the priory. In 1254 the church was valued at £10 and the canons' portion at 6s. 8d. (*VN* 439). For discussion of the archives of Tonbridge priory, including nos. 111–12, see C. R. Cheney, 'A Papal Privilege for Tonbridge Priory', *BIHR* 38 (1965), 192–200, repr. in *Medieval Texts and Studies* (Oxford 1973) 66–77.

112. Tonbridge Priory

Notification that when Gilbert earl of Gloucester granted to the canons the advowson of the church of Stradishall with the chapel of Denston and begged the bishop to concede them in proprios usus, *he consented and conceded to them various portions as a benefice; that is, the chapel of Denston with its parish, with both great and lesser tithes and its demesne lands, which comprise twenty-three and a half acres of land, half an acre of meadow, the tithe of two mills and all other offerings from the vill which pertain to the chapel, and also various properties, rents and tithes pertaining to the church of Stradishall (listed). All other portions shall be held by the rector of Stradishall, to whom is committed the cure of souls, and he shall discharge the customary burdens on the church, except that the prior and canons shall in perpetuity provide, at their own cost, a suitable chaplain to serve the chapel, to whose maintenance the rector of Stradishall shall contribute half a mark annually at the two Suffolk synods.* [4 November 1227 × 25 October 1230]

   B = PRO E135/15/17 (notarial record, in form of roll, of evidences produced before bp of Norwich, 4 February 1297). s. xiii ex.

Omnibus Cristi fidelibus ad quos presens scriptum pervenerit Thomas Dei gratia Norwycensis episcopus salutem in Domino. Ad universorum notitiam volumus pervenire quod cum nobilis vir Gilebertus comes Gloucestr' dilectis in Cristo priori et canonicis de Tonebrige ius patronatus ecclesie de Stradeshulle cum capella de Denardeston' contulisset et nobis humiliter supplicasset ut ecclesiam illam in proprios usus predictis canonicis concederemus, nos precibus dicti comitis condescendentes Dei causa et religionis favore predictis priori et canonicis portiones predicte ecclesie subscriptas nomine beneficii imperpetuum duximus concedendas, videlicet capellam de Denardeston cum tota parochia, tam in decimis maioribus et minoribus quam in terris dominicis, silicet viginti et tribus acris et dimidia terre et dimidia acra prati, et decimis duorum molendinorum que sunt in villa illa, et omnibus aliis[a] huiusmodi obventionibus de villa illa ad ipsam capellam provenientibus, et duodecim acras de dominica terra ecclesie de Stradeshulle, silicet quinque acras terre intra terram Hugonis filii Petri versus gravam ecclesie de Stradeshulle et medietatem ipsius grave et redditum decem denariorum quos Avelina vidua consuevit reddere ipsi ecclesie, et decimas garbarum omnimodorum bladorum tantummodo que provenient de terris subscriptis, silicet de sex viginti acris terre quas Iohannes de la Londe tenet in villa de Stradeshulle, et de tribus acris terre et dimidia Ade molendinarii in eadem villa, et de quatuor acris terre Willelmi sutoris, et de tribus acris terre Ricardi Putehak, et de quindecim acris terre Willelmi sub bosco, et de quadraginta acris terre Rogeri filii Odonis, et de septem acris terre Walteri capellani, et de novemdecim acris terre Willelmi Lemmer, et de tresdecim acris terre Willelmi de Hamel, et de tresdecim acris terre Thome filii Galfridi,[b] et de decem[c] acris terre Rogeri carpentarii, et de tribus acris terre et dimidia Alani clerici, et de duabus acris terre Aveline vidue, et dimidia acra terre Willelmi Prest, et de septem acris terre et dimidia Gileberti ad pontem, et de duodecim acris terre Thome Trone in predicta villa de Stradeshull'. Residuas autem portiones omnes habebit rector ecclesie de Stradeshulle quicumque fuerit pro tempore, et omnes minutas decimas et obventiones de predictis parochianis provenientes, cui rectori curam animarum nos vel successores nostri committimus,[d] et idem[e] sustinebit onera predicte ecclesie ordinaria debita et consueta, eo excepto quod predicti prior et canonici capellanum ydoneum in predicta ecclesia[f] ministrantem imperpetuum sumptibus suis invenient, ad cuius sustentationem rector ecclesie de Stradeshull' dimidiam marcam annuam fideliter contribuet in duabus synodis Suffolchie. In cuius rei testimonium etc. Dat' etc.

[a] alter B   [b] Galfride B   [c] decim B   [d] commitimus B   [e] et idem *over erasure*
[f] *sic* B, *rectius* capella

After no. 111, and before the death of Gilbert, earl of Hertford and Gloucester, on 25 October 1230. Denston was subsequently valued separately from Stradishall, at fourteen marks both in 1254 and 1291 (*VN* 439; *Taxatio* 121b).

113. Walsingham Priory

Grant to the canons in proprios usus *of the church of Bedingham, to take effect on the death or resignation of Peter Romanus,* persona, *and master Vincent of Beck, vicar.*   [20 December 1226 × 29 October 1233]

Mention and recitation of charter in a case in the *curia regis, a die sancti Michaelis in j. mensem*, 1233.

Et prior venit et dicit quod ecclesia illa non est vacans, quia ipse habet ecclesiam in proprios usus de concessione et confirmatione domini Thome de Blunvill' Norwicensis episcopi per cartam ipsius episcopi quam profert et que testatur quod Dei causa et favore religionis et ad venerationem beate Virginis dedit et concessit priori et canonicis de Walsingeham ecclesiam sancti Andree de Bedingeham cum omnibus pertinentiis suis in proprios usus habendam et perpetuo possidendam post decessum vel recessum Petri Romani tunc persone et magistri Vincentii de Beck' tunc vicarii etc.

Pd in *CRR* xv no. 603.

The prior of Walsingham was summoned to answer why he had impeded royal presentation to Bedingham, claimed because the lands of Hubert de Burgh were in the king's hands (from November 1232 to 28 May 1234). The prior claimed that the church was not vacant, because the canons had received it *in proprios usus* by the concession of the bp, whose charter he produced. He stated further that Nicholas de Stuteville had granted the advowson to Hubert who, in the time of bp Pandulph, had in the king's presence and at the king's request granted it to the canons by charter. This charter was now lost, by fire or otherwise, although the prior had himself made use of it. In 1254 the prior's portion was assessed at £16 13s. 4d., Reyner's portion at £13 6s. 8d. and the vicarage at £2 13s. 4d. (*VN* 405); in 1291 both the prior's and Reyner's portions were valued at £13 6s. 8d. and the vicarage at £5 (*Taxatio* 84).

Beck is probably the place of that name within the parish of Bylaugh (Nf.); see *Norwich Cathedral Charters* i 246 (index).

114. Walsingham Priory

Grant to the prior and canons in proprios usus *of the church of Oulton, saving a vicarage of ten marks, that is, the vicarage should each year be leased at farm for ten marks. The canons shall, at each vacancy, present for institution a suitable man whom the bishop wishes, and if they fail so to do, he may nevertheless institute without consultation with them.*

Norwich, 12 March 1230

B = BL ms. Cotton Nero E vii (Walsingham cartulary) fo. 91r (86r). s. xiii ex. C = ibid. fo. 30v (25v, 28v) (*inspeximus* by prior Simon and convent of Norwich, 12 March 1250). s. xiii ex.

Omnibus Cristi fidelibus ad quos presens scriptum pervenerit Thomas Dei gratia Norwicensis episcopus salutem in Domino. Ad omnium volumus pervenire notitiam nos Dei intuitu et religionis favore concessisse et presenti carta nostra confirmasse dilectis filiis in Cristo priori et canonicis de Wausingham[a] ecclesiam de Oulton'[b] cum omnibus ad ipsam pertinentibus, habendam et tenendam in proprios usus et perpetuo possidendam, salva vicaria decem marcarum ad opus vicarii in eadem pro tempore ministraturi, ita scilicet quod dicta vicaria possit singulis annis dari ad firmam pro decem marcis, ad quam vicariam quotiens vacare contigerit dicti canonici virum ydoneum quemcumque voluerimus nobis et successoribus nostris presentabunt, et nos eundem in eadem instituemus. Et si forte dicti canonici omiserint vel neglexerint presentare secundum formam prescriptam, nos nichilominus ipsis inconsultis et irrequisitis quemcumque voluerimus vicarium in eadem instituemus, salvis etiam in omnibus reverentia et obedientia nobis et successoribus nostris et sacrosancte Norwicensis ecclesie consuetudinibus debitis vel consuetis. In huius rei testimonium presentes litteras fieri fecimus et sigillo nostro muniri. Dat' apud Norwicum die sancti Gregorii pontificatus nostri anno quarto. Test(ibus) etc.

[a] Wals' B   [b] Oweltone B

In 1225 the canons of Missenden had attempted unsuccessfully in the *curia regis* to claim the advowson against Hubert de Burgh, claiming that it had been given to them by Walter son of William of Penn (*CRR* xii no. 372; for background, see *EEA* 6 no. 433n.). The church was granted by Hubert to Walsingham, where his mother was buried, *in proprios usus*, after his creation as earl of Kent on 14 February 1227 (fo. 91r of B). In 1254 the portion of the canons was valued at £6 13s. 4d., the vicarage at £1 (*VN* 367; cf. ibid. 115 n. 2); in 1291 the whole church, appropriated to the canons, with the vicarage, was assessed at £6 13s. 4d. (*Taxatio* 81b).

115. Walsingham Priory

Grant to the canons in proprios usus *of the church of Oulton, saving a vicarage for the use of a perpetual vicar, as taxed by the archdeacon of Norfolk, the bishop's official. The vicar shall have all the altarage, with all the lesser tithes and oblations, free lands, homages, rents and other appurtenances of the church. He shall have the great tithe of certain listed lands within a delineated circuit, but from all lands beyond this circuit the canons shall have the great tithe and the tithe of vegetables. Whenever the vicarage falls vacant, the canons shall present to the bishop that suitable* persona *whom he wishes, and if they fail so to do, the bishop may nevertheless institute the vicar whom he wishes.* [Probably 12 March 1230 × October 1232]

B = BL ms. Cotton Nero E vii (Walsingham cartulary) fo. 91r–v (86r–v). s. xiii ex.

Omnibus Cristi fidelibus ad quos presens scriptum pervenerit Thomas Dei gratia Norwicensis episcopus salutem in Domino. Ad universorum notitiam volumus pervenire nos Dei causa et religionis favore concessisse et presenti carta confirmasse dilectis filiis in Cristo priori et canonicis de Wals' ecclesiam de Oulton' cum omnibus ad ipsam pertinentibus, habendam et tenendam in proprios usus et perpetuo possidendam, salva vicaria ad opus vicarii perpetui in dicta ecclesia pro tempore ministraturi in certis portionibus per archidiaconum Norf(ol)c(hie) officialem nostrum in forma subscripta taxata, videlicet quod pro tempore vicarius habeat totum alteragium predicte ecclesie cum omnibus decimis minutis et obventionibus, liberis terris, [fo. 91v] homagiis, redditibus et aliis contingentibus ad dictam ecclesiam spectantibus. Item vicarius habebit decimas garbarum provenientes de omnibus terris que consistunt in ambitu a semita que se extendit a porta Hugonis filii Iohannis persone inter domus Matildis filie Basilie et Silverun filii Goddardi versus orientem, et a fine illius semite per divisam que est inter terras Willelmi filii Blacson' et Godefridi ad monasterium similiter quousque perveniatur ad viam regiam versus orientem, et per illam viam regiam versus aquilonem se extendentem usque ad domum Hugonis le King, et a domo predicti Hugonis le King per viam ducentem ad domum Hugonis filii Alexandri, et a domo predicti Hugonis filii Alexandri per rivulum dividentem parochias de Irminglond et de Owelton' usque ad Blakebrigg' per moram quousque perveniatur ad domum predicti Hugonis filii Iohannis persone. De omnibus autem terris que extra ambitum predictum consistunt, prior et canonici de Wals' percipient decimas garbarum et leguminum. Quotienscunque autem dictam vicariam vacare contigerit, dicti prior et canonici de Wals' personam ydoneam quemcumque voluerimus nobis et successoribus nostris ad eandem presentabunt, et nos et successores nostri ipsum vicarium instituemus. Et si forte dicti prior et canonici omiserint vel neglexerint presentare, nos et successores nostri quemcumque voluerimus nichilominus ibidem vicarium instituemus, salvis etiam in omnibus reverentia et obedientia nobis et successoribus nostris et sacrosancte Norwicensis ecclesie consuetudinibus debitis vel consuetis. In cuius rei testimonium presentes litteras fieri fecimus et sigillo nostro muniri. Dat' etc. Test(ibus) etc.

> After no. 114; master Robert of Bilney, who was both archdn of Norfolk and bp's official, had probably ceased to act as official by October 1232, when master Richard of Shipton occurs in that capacity. On 27 March 1233 a certain R. occurs as both archdn and official (no. 117), but it is possible that this refers back to Bilney. If so, the same might be the case with this *actum*, and the *terminus ad quem* would then be 16 August 1236.

116. Waltham Abbey

Grant to the canons in proprios usus, *with the assent of his cathedral chapter, of the church of St Peter, Guestwick, to take effect after the death of Ralph son of Peter, the rector, saving a competent vicarage to be taxed when the church should fall vacant; to which the canons shall at each vacancy present a suitable* persona *whom the bishop wishes, and if they fail so to do, the bishop may nevertheless institute without consultation with them. The vicar shall discharge all the canonical obligations of the church, that is, archidiaconal and decanal procurations. The abbot and convent shall bear two parts of the costs of defects in books and ecclesiastical ornaments, and the vicar the third part.* London, 16 October 1227

> B = BL ms. Cotton Tib. C ix (Waltham cartulary) fo. 150v. s. xiii med.
> Pd in *Waltham Charters* no. 579

Omnibus Cristi fidelibus ad quos presens scriptum pervenerit Thomas Dei gratia Norwicensis episcopus salutem in Domino. Ad universorum notitiam volumus pervenire nos causa Dei et religionis favore et assensu capituli nostri Norwicensis concessisse et presenti carta nostra confirmasse dilectis in Cristo filiis abbati et conventui ecclesie sancte Crucis de Waltham ecclesiam sancti Petri de Geistweit nostre diocesis cum omnibus ad ipsam pertinentibus, habendam in proprios usus et perpetuo possidendam post decessum Radulfi filii

Petri eiusdem ecclesie rectoris, salva vicaria competenti rationabiliter taxanda cum ecclesiam predictam vacare contigerit, ad quam vicariam quosciens vacare contigerit nobis et successoribus nostris predicti abbas et conventus de Waltham personam ydoneam quamcumque voluerimus sine difficultate ac alicuius pravitatis et contradictionis obstaculo presentabunt, et nos et successores nostri libere et absolute autoritate diocesana in vicaria predicta eundem instituemus. Et si forte dicti abbas et conventus omiserint vel neglexerint tempore oportuno presentare, nos et successores nostri ipsis irrequisitis vicarium instituemus ibidem, salvis etiam in omnibus reverentia et obedientia nobis et successoribus nostris et sacrosancte Norwicensis ecclesie consuetudinibus debitis vel consuetis. Dictus autem vicarius pro tempore omnia onera canonica prefate ecclesie sustinebit, videlicet in procurationibus archidiaconorum et decanorum. Dicti autem abbas et conventu omnes defectus ecclesie tam in libris quam in ornamentis ecclesiasticis quoad duas partes, et vicarius quoad tertiam partem, sustinebunt. Dat' Lond' septimo decimo kalendas Novembris pontificatus nostri anno primo. Hiis testibus etc.

> For the initial episcopal confirmation by bp John de Gray of the gift of the church by Everard son of Ralph of Guist, see *EEA* 6 no. 423. For papal confirmation of the appropriation by Gregory IX, 7 May 1237, see fo. 151r of B. See also no. 153 and note.

117. West Dereham Abbey

Grant to the canons in proprios usus *of the church of St Andrew, [West] Dereham, which is of their patronage and in which he has instituted them as* personae, *saving the honourable maintenance of a perpetual vicar, which the bishop has caused to be taxed by R., archdeacon of Norfolk, his Official. The vicarage shall consist of the altarage, and also three marks from the farm of the free land of the church or of the tithes, or from both.*

Thorpe, 27 March 1233

> B = BL ms. Add. 46353 (West Dereham cartulary) fos. 12v–13r (5v–6r). s. xiv in. C = ibid. fo. 13r (6r) (*inspeximus* by prior Simon and convent of Norwich, 6 January 1236). s. xiv in.

Omnibus Cristi fidelibus presens scriptum inspecturis Thomas Dei gratia Norwycensis episcopus salutem in Domino. Ad universorum volumus notitiam pervenire nos divine pietatis intuitu et favore religionis concessisse, dedisse et hac presenti carta nostra confirmasse dilectis in Cristo filiis abbati et canonicis de Derham ecclesiam sancti Andree de^a Derham cum omnibus ad eam pertinentibus, que de ipsorum advocatione esse dinoscitur, in proprios et perpetuos usus convertendam et habendam, ipsosque^b personas canonice instituisse in eadem, salva honesta sustentatione perpetui vicarii nobis et successoribus nostris pro tempore ab ipsis presentandi qui in eadem ecclesia ministrabit, quam per[c] dilectum nostrum R. archydiaconum Norfolch' officialem nostrum sic fecimus taxari, videlicet ut vicarius totum habeat alteragium, et insuper de libera terra vel de decimis eiusdem ecclesie sive de utrisque ad valentiam trium marcarum, ita scilicet quod singulis annis pro tribus marcis possit dari ad firmam, salvis etiam nobis et successoribus nostris debita obedientia et reverentia [et] sancte Norwycensis[d] ecclesie consuetudinibus debitis vel consuetis. In cuius rei testimonium presentem cartam fieri fecimus et sigillo nostro muniri. Dat' apud Thorp dominica Palmarum pontificatus nostri anno septimo.

[a] ecclesiam sancti Andree de *interlined* B   [b] -que *interlined* B   [c] per *interlined* B
[d] sancte Norwycensis *repeated* C

There were two churches in West Dereham at the time of the abbey's foundation in 1188, and both came into the canons' possession with the vill. St Peter's was appropriated to them by bp John of Oxford (*EEA* 6 no. 312). The two churches stood in the same churchyard, and eventually in 1401 the canons obtained a papal indult permitting the unification of the parishes and releasing the parishioners from the obligation to maintain St Peter's in repair (*CPL* 1396–1404 415–16). An *actum* of bp Suffield refers to the abbey having been founded in the parish church of St Andrew, which probably means that this church was used for conventual purposes while the abbey church was being built (fo. 13r of B; see Colvin, *White Canons* 133–34). In a final concord of 2 July 1218 William of Timworth, the claimant, had remitted to abbot Ralph and his successors the advowson, and in return was received into all the benefits and prayers of the abbey (fo. 12v of B). Bp Suffield subsequently allowed the canons to have the church served by suitable chaplains removable at their will (ibid. fo. 12v). In 1254 the churches of St Andrew and St Peter were assessed together at £13 6s. 8d., and in 1291 at £14 (*VN* 408; *Taxatio* 88b).

118. West Dereham Abbey

Grant to the canons in proprios usus *of the church of Stradsett, which is of their patronage by the gift of Osbert of Stradsett, knight, to take effect on the death or resignation of master Ralph of Syderstone the rector, saving a vicarage of five marks, to be raised by granting certain portions at farm, to which the canons shall at each vacancy present to the bishop a suitable* persona.

Snettisham, 30 July 1231

B = BL ms. Add. 46353 (West Dereham cartulary) fo. 72r (65r). s. xiv in.

Omnibus Cristi fidelibus presens scriptum inspecturis Thomas Dei gratia Norwicensis episcopus salutem in Domino. Ad universorum volumus notitiam pervenire nos Dei causa et religionis favore concessisse et presenti carta nostra confirmasse dilectis in Cristo filiis[a] abbati et conventui de D. ecclesiam de

Strates(ete) cum omnibus ad ipsam pertinentibus, que de eorum patronatu esse dinoscitur ex donatione Osberti de Strattes(ete) militis, habendam et tenendam et in proprios usus perpetuo possidendam post decessum vel recessum magistri Radulfi de Sidestern' eiusdem rectoris, salva vicaria quinque marcarum, scilicet que possit pro quinque marcis dari ad firmam, per nos vel successores nostros in certis portionibus in eadem ecclesia taxanda, ad quam cum vacare contigerit predicti abbas et conventus personam ydoneam nobis vel successoribus nostris presentabunt, salvis etiam nobis et successoribus nostris in omnibus reverentia et obedientia et sancte Norwicensis ecclesie consuetudinibus debitis vel consuetis. In cuius rei testimonium presentes litteras fieri fecimus et sigillo nostro muniri. Dat' apud Snetesh(am) tertio kalendas Augusti nostri anno quinto.

[a] filiis in Cristo filiis B

For the charter of Osbert of Stradsett, see fo. 72r of B; the church was granted for the sustenance of the poor and needy who might come to the abbey gate. In 1254 the church was assessed at £5 6s. 8d., with no mention of a vicarage (*VN* 410); in 1291 the appropriated church was listed at £6 (*Taxatio* 88b).

119. West Dereham Abbey

Grant to the canons in proprios usus *of the church of Ringland, to take effect on the death or resignation of Stephen son of Thomas of Walton, the vicar, saving a vicarage of six marks for the maintenance of a perpetual vicar to be chosen by the bishop and his successors and to be presented by the canons for institution. The canons and the vicar shall discharge the customary obligations of the church in respect of their portions therein.*

Norwich, 5 April 1227

B = BL ms. Add. 46353 (West Dereham cartulary) fo. 271r (264r). s. xiv in. C = ibid. fo. 271v (264v) (*inspeximus* by prior William and convent of Norwich, 12 February 1228). s. xiv in.

Omnibus Cristi fidelibus ad quos presens scriptum pervenerit Thomas Dei gratia Norwicensis episcopus salutem in Domino. Noverit universitas vestra nos divine pietatis intuitu et ob favorem religionis concessisse et hac carta nostra confirmasse abbati et canonicis de D. ecclesiam de Ringelande cum omnibus ad eam pertinentibus post decessum vel recessum Stephani filii Thome de Waltona[a] eiusdem ecclesie vicarii in proprios usus habendam et possidendam in perpetuum, salva vicaria sex marcarum ad sustentationem perpetui vicarii qui[b] a nobis et successoribus nostris electus a predictis abbate et canonicis presentatus in eadem vicaria instituetur; ita tamen quod tam[c] idem abbas et canonici quam vicarius pro tempore honera predicte ecclesie debita et consueta pro portionibus suis sustinebunt, salvis nobis et successoribus nostris iure parochiali et pontificali. Datum apud Norwicum[d] nonas Aprilis pontificatus nostri anno primo.

    [a] Waltone C   [b] qui *om.* B   [c] quod tam *om.* C   [d] Northwic' C

    A previous grant *in proprios usus*, to take effect on the death of the same vicar, had been made by bp Gray (*EEA* 6 no. 430). Stephen son of Thomas of Walton, although styled vicar, probably took the bulk of the revenues of the church, which was poorly endowed, being valued at £5 in 1254 and £6 in 1291 (*VN* 369; *Taxatio* 82).

120. Wix Priory

Inspeximus *and confirmation of a charter of bishop John [of Oxford]* [*EEA* 6 no. 314] *by which, with the consent of the patrons and rector, he has granted to the nuns an annual benefice of five marks in the church of Bildeston.*

                                                          Ixworth, 23 November 1231

    A = PRO E42/459. Endorsed with sign similar to greek δ; approx. 144 × 55 + 15 mm.; damaged seal on parchment tag, green wax, counterseal, in seal bag of white linen with green and brown thread decoration.
    B – Longleat, North Muniment Room 1163 (charter roll of Wix priory, 4th entry). s. xiv ex.

Omnibus Cristi fidelibus ad quos presens scriptum pervenerit Thomas Dei gratia Norwicensis episcopus salutem in Domino. Inspeximus cartam bone memorie Iohannis primi predecessoris nostri inter cetera continentem quinque marcas annuas nomine annui beneficii de ecclesia de Bildeston' de consensu et voluntate patronorum et rectoris dicte ecclesie tunc temporis monialibus de Wikes caritatis intuitu esse concessas et confirmatas. Nos autem factum predecessoris nostri in hac parte gratum habentes et acceptum, dictas quinque marcas annuas de prefata ecclesia de Bildeston' in perpetuum percipiendas memoratis monialibus de Wik' auctoritate episcopali confirmamus. In cuius rei testimonium presentes literas fieri fecimus et sigillo nostro muniri. Dat' apud Ixewurd' die sancti Clementis pontificatus nostri anno quinto.

    In 1254 and 1291 the prioress's portion was listed as only two marks (£1 6s. 8d.) (*VN* 436; *Taxatio* 122b).

121. Wymondham Priory

General confirmation for the monks of their possessions in the diocese of Norwich.   [20 December 1226 × 16 August 1236]

B = BL ms. Cotton Titus C viii (Wymondham cartulary) fos. 22r–23v (34r–36v). s. xiii med.

Omnibus sancte matris ecclesie filiis Thomas permissione divina Norwycensis ecclesie minister humilis salutem in Domino. Cum [ex] episcopalis officii debito universis subiectis nostris paternam sollicitudinem exhibere debeamus, ne in hiis que ad nos spectant iuris sui lesionem sustineant, specialius tamen viros religionem et artioris vite regulam professos confovere et propensius episcopali auctoritate protegere tenemur, ut pacis et unitatis iocunditatem habentes omnipotenti Domino sub tranquillitate liberius famulentur. Sunt autem apud Wymundham in ecclesia beate Marie viri honesti, monachi Deo devoti, sub regula beati Benedicti Domino servientes assidue, quibus ex pia fidelium voluntate ecclesie, redditus, elemosine et plura collata sunt beneficia, et ne in hiis que canonice et iustis modis adquisita possident perturbationem sentiant vel detrimentum, ea iam dictis monachis in prefata ecclesia Deo servientibus et inperpetuum servituris confirmamus. Hec autem propriis duximus exprimenda vocabulis: ecclesiam de Wymundham cum omnibus pertinentiis suis, universas videlicet decimationes de dominio Willelmi pincerne regis Henrici primi in bladis, pratis, parcis, haraciis, molendinis, vivariis et omnibus aliis rebus unde decimationes provenire solent, cum reliqua tota decimatione totius ville, et in eadem villa curiam propriam cum pomeriis, alnetis, vivariis ipsam curiam cingentibus, et molendinum de curia, et molendinum de Westwade cum .xxx. acris de terra arabili et pastura eidem molendino adiacentibus, et nemus de Biskelund, et nemus parvum de Suthwude, vivarium de Typford, Wycham et assarta et homines quos habent in Sudwude, et totam terram quam habent in dominio in Northfeld, Silesfeld et in Estfeld cum omnibus lancettis suis et tenementis eorum et cum omnibus liberis hominibus suis et eorum tenementis tam de feodo comitis Warenn' quam de alio, et in Theldesbothesmede terram ad unam vaccariam faciendam cum communitate pasture; in Bukeh' decimam haracii sui, et in nemoribus suis habere porcos suos sine pasnagio; in Nelande et in Molesfen et in Brakene .xl. solidatas terre; in Wrampligham terras Grim, Eylsi et Ribaldi; in Coletune terram que fuit Ulf presbiteri cum suis pertinentiis et ecclesiam eiusdem ville cum suis pertinentiis, et in eadem villa terram Adelstani et terram Colemanni le King; in Karletune et in Newehage et Kinburle totam terram quam habent ex dono memorati pincerne; in Karletun' terram que fuit Thurkilli presbiteri cum ecclesia in eadem terra fundata; in Kerebroc tenementum quod Iohannes et Lucas filius eius de illis tenuerunt; totum manerium de Hapesburg, excepta terra Ansgoti camerarii, et ecclesiam et forum cum omnibus pertinentiis suis, videlicet wrek, [fo. 22v] tol et theam et omnibus aliis libertatibus et consuetudinibus; in Burnham duas carucatas terre et unum faldagium et unum molendinum et homines quos habent in eadem villa; duas partes decimarum totius dominii predicti pincerne in eadem villa; ecclesiam de Snetesham cum pertinentiis suis; unam carucatam terre cum falda propria in eadem villa; in Grimeston', in Flicham [et] in Pykeham duas partes omnium decimarum ipsius pincerne; in Redham unum mariscum; in Helingeya terras et piscarias unde annuatim .iii. millenaria et dimidiam anguillarum percipiunt; ex dono Willelmi comitis filii predicti pincerne ecclesiam de Bestorp cum omnibus pertinentiis suis et facultatem piscandi in vivariis eius, sicut carta eius testatur; capellam sancti Thome de Wymundham et pratum de Typford cum turbaria de Oxeker et et maius nemus de Suthwude, ex dono Willelmi comitis filii predicti Willelmi, et .vi. homines cum tenementis suis, .v. in villa de Wymundham et unum in Kyneburle, et unum mariscum in Snetesham quod dicitur le Fresmers, et ecclesiam de Kangham in usus proprios cum pertinentiis suis; ex dono Ade filii Aluredi .xv. acras in Bestorp' et totam terram quam habent ex dono Roberti de Bavent et antecessorum eius in eadem villa; in Bukeham redditum .vi. denariorum ex dono Alexandri coci; in Wymundham et in Hapesburc totam terram quam habent ex dono Rogeri filii Ansgoti; in Wymundham tres acras de feodo Alexandri forestarii, et Godesacr' ex dono Nigelli Rusteng; in Pykeham ex dono Rogeri de Verli mansiunculam unam cum quadam acra terre arabilis; in Burnham terram habent ex dono Willelmi le Veltre; ex dono Ricardi de Curcun .xxvi. acras in Stanfeld; ex dono Willelmi le Curcun .xxxiii. acras de terra arabili cum mansiuncula quadam, et quicquid habent in Wymundham ex dono Anketilli de Stanfeld; ex dono Iohannis de Uvedale Rogerum Palmarium cum toto tenemento suo et servitio; ex dono Radulfi de Rosei in Elingham redditum dimidie marce; ex dono Radulfi Baynard terram quandam unde duos solidos percipiunt annuatim; ex dono patris Matthei Peverel tenementum Iohannis Dod et totum eius servitium in Melton'; in eadem villa dimidiam acram ex dono G. filii Walteri; in Wyklewude ex dono Willelmi filii Odardi terram quandam unde annuatim octo denarios habent; ex dono Eustachii de Riflei redditum .ii. solidorum; ex dono Eudonis de Wyklewude terram unde annuatim .iii. solidos habent; ex dono Hugonis filii Ailwardi unam acram; ex dono Hugonis filii Ulf dimidiam acram; ex dono Ricardi de Dunham terram unde annuatim .vi. denarios habent; terram de feodo Asketilli unde annuatim .vi. denarios habent; in Keteringham terram quam habent ex dono Symonis militis; ex dono Reginaldi de Muncorbin .ii. acras et dimidiam in Wyklewude; in Fritheton' hominem quendam Willelmum nomine ex dono Roberti Fulcher; ex dono Baldewyni filii Eudonis terram quandam [fo. 23r] que iacet sub parco de Torp; in Brakene mansionem quandam ex dono matris Mathei Peverel; in Wutton' hominem unum Rogerum nomine ex dono Hodierne, et Ricardum Noth cum toto servitio et tenemento suo;[1] ex dono Eudonis de Melles .x. acras in Suthwude; in

Wymundham, terram Radulfi Belami cum pertinentiis suis; et in Bestorp et in Atleburg homagium et terras et turbarias cum pertinentiis suis que habent ex dono Yseude filie Ailuredi; et duos homines in Bestorp de dono Willelmi de Arderne; in Wymundham ex dono Matildis de Milliers redditum .ii. solidorum; ex dono Willelmi de Miliers totam decimam de venditione de boscis suis, et decimam molendini sui et parcorum suorum; et in Swangegeya unam acram turbarie ex dono Rogeri Rusteng; ex dono Ricardi de Rode redditum .xiiii. denariorum; et in Wymundham ex dono Nigelli de Burefeld duas acras terre arabilis; et in Karletune et in Wiklewude .xx. acras terre arabilis et unum mesuagium et Alwardum Goboy cum tota secta sua ex dono Roberti de Rifley; et ex dono Nigelli de Riffley duos homines cum tota secta eorum; et ex dono Agnetis de Riffley unum hominem cum tota secta sua in eadem villa; et in Karletun' servitium Eustacii Blac cum tota sequela sua ex dono Walteri filii Iohannis et Ricardi filii Willelmi de Hengham; et in Wymundham ex dono Basilie Noth terram quamdam que vocatur Hungrilond; et in Northwuuttun' et Suthwuttun' et in Geywude totam donationem quam habent de Ricardo Noth, et in Wygenhale quamdam terram que iacet in Gildenegore ex dono eiusdem Ricardi Noth; et in Hakeford ex dono Willelmi de Nuers redditum .v. solidorum; et in Thaverham redditum .xii. d. ex dono Bauday Popi; et in Ydekestorp ex dono Gileberti de Mauquinci redditum .iiii. solidorum; et in Snetesham et in Sarneburne donum Rogeri Rusteng; et donum Radulfi de Verli in Netesham, et unam acram terre ex dono Galfridi filii Walteri, et totam donationem quam habent de dono Ricardi Hakun in Netesham; et .lx. solidos annuos quos percipiunt de vicaria de Netesham ad vestimenta conventus de Wymundham; et de dono[a] Gileberti de Bleudene redditum trium solidorum, et quicquid habent ex dono Ade filii Aluredi; ex dono Willelmi Bluet .x. solidatas terre in villa de Hormesbi, et quicquid habent de Thoma de Arderne vel antecessoribus suis; et in Ludinglond quicquid habent de dono vel testamento Willelmi de Alneto. Hos itaque et omnes alios redditus, elemosinas, beneficia que predicti monachi canonice et rationalibiter adquisita possident, sicut carte donatorum testantur [fo. 23v] vel que iustis modis, Domino largiente, futuris temporibus adquirere poterunt eis confirmamus. Ut hec nostra confirmatio perpetuam habeat firmitatem, eam presenti scripto et sigilli nostri autoritate corroboramus, districtius inhibentes ne quis temeritate vel malitia contra eam venire vel eam aliquatenus infringere presumat.

[a] donum B

[1] To this point this *actum* follows almost verbatim that of bp John of Oxford (*EEA* 6 no. 316).

122. Wymondham Priory

Inspeximus and confirmation of the composition reached between the monks and John of Morley, rector of Flitcham, concerning the great and lesser tithes of the demesne of the earl of Arundel at Flitcham.

North Elmham, 26 April 1230

B = BL ms. Cotton Titus C viii (Wymondham cartulary) fo. 12r (24r). s. xiii med.

Omnibus Cristi fidelibus presentes literas inspecturis Thomas Dei gratia Norwicensis episcopus salutem in Domino. Compositionem quandam inter priorem et monachos de Wimundham ex una parte et Iohannem de Merlay rectorem ecclesie de Flicham ex altera super decimis minutis et grossis de dominico comitis de Arundel provenientibus apud Flicham initam inspeximus, et ipsam rationabiliter factam ratam habentes et acceptam auctoritate episcopali confirmavimus. In cuius rei testimonium presentibus literis sigillum nostrum apponi fecimus. Dat' apud Northelmham .vi. kalendas Maii pontificatus nostri anno quarto.

> There had been an earler dispute over these tithes between Daniel of Morley, *persona*, and the monks, 1178 × 1189 (*EEA* 6 no. 315). Regarding this later conflict, a memorandum of mr Alan of Beccles, the bp's official, details the course of litigation. The case had first been heard before mr Maurice, *vices gerens* for the official, and then before papal judges-delegate (the priors of Spalding and Swineshead and the dean of Hoyland), but eventually, after various other disputes as to whether the case had been withdrawn by papal letters from the jurisdiction of the ordinary, the parties submitted themselves to the decision of the official, and the case was heard by mr Alan in the cathedral church. John of Morley admitted that the great tithe pertained to the monks, who alleged that he had usurped them, but he claimed that he had received the lesser tithes by right of his church, and these he had never usurped. Mr Alan, having examined both witnesses and documents, found that the monks had received the tithes as farmers (*firmarius*) for fifty years or more, from a time before that of John's predecessor Daniel of Morley, and that they had been despoiled thereof by John; but as to true ownership he could not judge, because of John's continual non-appearance (fos. 55v–56r of B). Finally a composition was reached, whereby the monks were to have free disposition of the tithes in autumn 1229, but thereafter John was to hold them for his lifetime for two and a half marks *p.a.*, and should receive two-thirds of any increase in tithe (fo. 55r of B). A memorandum issued by John of Morley states that in 1229 he purchased from the monks two parts of all the tithes, both great and lesser, of the demesne of the earl of Sussex in Flitcham, for two and a half marks *p.a.* (fo. 54v of B). In 1254 the monks had a portion of this sum in the church (*VN* 383).

123. Wymondham Priory

Grant to the monks in proprios usus *of the church of North Wootton, to take effect on the death or resignation of master Vincent of Beck, saving an honourable and competent vicarage to be taxed by the bishop or his successors for the use of a perpetual vicar to be presented by the monks for institution.*

North Elmham, 26 April 1230

B = BL ms. Cotton Titus C viii (Wymondham cartulary) fo. 11v (23r). s. xiii med. C = ibid. fo. 11r (*inspeximus* by prior William and the convent of Norwich). s. xiii med.

Omnibus Cristi fidelibus ad quos presens scriptum pervenerit Thomas Dei gratia Norwicensis episcopus salutem in Domino. Ad universorum notitiam volumus pervenire nos Dei causa et religionis favore concessisse et presenti carta nostra confirmasse dilectis filiis in Cristo priori et monachis de Wimundham ecclesiam de Northwttune cum omnibus ad ipsam pertinentibus, habendam et tenendam in proprios usus et perpetuo possidendam post decessum vel recessum magistri Vincentii de Becco, salva honesta et competenti vicaria per nos vel successores nostros pro tempore taxanda ad opus vicarii perpetui in dicta ecclesia ministraturi, nobis et successoribus nostris ab ipsis priore et monachis de Wimundham presentandi et per nos et successores nostros instituendi, salvis etiam in omnibus reverentia et obedientia nobis et successoribus nostris et sacrosancte Norwicensis ecclesie consuetudinibus debitis vel consuetis. In cuius rei testimonium presentes litteras fieri fecimus et sigillo nostro muniri. Dat' apud Northelmham manerium nostrum .vi. kalendas Maii pontificatus nostri anno quarto.

The church had been granted to the monks by William, second earl of Sussex; for an earlier institution thereto, see *EEA* 6 no. 317. In 1254 the church was assessed at £7 6s. 8d. and the vicarage at £1 6s. 8d. (*VN* 385); in 1291 the church was valued at £6 and the vicarage was not liable to the tenth (*Taxatio* 80b).

For the identification of Beck, see no. 113.

WILLIAM RALEIGH

124. Profession

Profession of obedience made to Edmund [of Abingdon], archbishop of Canterbury. 25 September 1239

> B = Canterbury D. & C. register A (prior's register) fo. 230r. s. xiv med.
> Partly printed in *Canterbury Professions* no. 176; see also no. 122.

+ Ego Willelmus Norwicensis ecclesie electus et a te, reverende pater Edmunde sancte Cantuariensis ecclesie archiepiscope et totius Anglie primas, consecrandus antistes, tibi et sancte Cantuariensi ecclesie et successoribus tuis canonice substituendis debitam et canonicam obedientiam et subiectionem me per omnia exhibiturum profiteor et promitto, et propria manu subscribendo confirmo.+

124A. Bath and Wells

Inspeximus, with Jocelin, bishop of Bath and Wells, and William [Brewer], bishop of Exeter, of various documents concerning the relationship of the two churches and their rights in the election of a bishop.

i. *Pope Alexander [III] to the dean, archdeacon and chapter of Wells, confirming the election of R[eginald de Bohun], archdeacon of Salisbury, to the see of Wells. Anagni, 18 April [1174] (PUE ii no. 133).*

ii. *Pope Alexander [III] to the dean, precentor and chapter of Wells, confirming the canonical rights of election shared with the monks of Bath and the procedure for the conduct of elections. Anagni, 8 January [1174 × 1178] (PUE ii no. 167).*

iii. *Agreement between the churches of Bath and Wells for the joint election of bishops. Sealed by the prior and convent of Bath and dean Alexander and the chapter of Wells.*

iv. *Letter from prior Robert and the convent of Bath to pope Innocent [III] announcing the death of bishop Savaric and the joint election of master Jocelin [of Wells], clerk of their church and canon of Wells.*

v. *Similar letter from dean Alexander and the chapter of Wells.*

vi. *Letters testimonial from the bishops of London, Rochester, Exeter,*

Salisbury, Ely, Coventry, Worcester, Norwich, Lincoln, Chichester and Winchester to pope Innocent [III], recording the election of bishop Jocelin and the assent thereto of king John (*EEA* 4 no. 221; 9 no. 86; 17 no. 72).

vii. *Letter of king John to J[ohn], cardinal deacon of Santa Maria in Latere, coming as papal legate to England, signifying his assent to the said election. Dogmersfield, 23 April [1206].*July 1242

    A = Wells cathedral, D. & C. ch. 40.
    Pd in C. M. Church, 'Roger of Salisbury, First Bishop of Bath and Wells, 1244–1247', *Archaeologia* 52 (1890) 89–112, at 103–7; id., *Chapters in the Early History of the Church of Wells* (1894), Appx S, 397–407; (cal.), *HMCR* Wells ii 554–5.

For the context of this document, see *EEA* 10 pp. xxxi–xxxvi; for the immediate aftermath, Church, 'Roger of Salisbury'.

125. Abbey of Le Bec-Hellouin

Confirmation for the monks of their long-established pensions and tithes in the diocese of Norwich.   London, 17 January 1241

    A = Windsor, St George's Chapel Mun. X G 23. Endorsed: Confirmatio episcopi Norwicensis de portionibus et pensionibus (s. xiii med.); approx. 186 × 75 + 20 mm.; fragment of seal, green wax, counterseal, attached on red cord.
    B = Windsor, St George's Chapel Mun. IV B 1 (*Liber Albus*) p. 221 (fo. 121v). s. xv in.

Omnibus Cristi fidelibus ad quos presens scriptum pervenerit Willelmus de Ralegh Dei gratia episcopus Norwicensis salutem in Domino. Grata Deo et hominibus accepta religio exigit et requirit ut que religiosorum usibus conceduntur, cum huiusmodi concessionibus pietas suffragatur, pontificalis auctoritatis munimine roborentur. Ad universorum igitur notitiam volumus pervenire nos divine pietatis optentu et sancte zelo religionis presenti carta nostra confirmasse religiosis viris abbati et conventui de Becco antiquas pensiones et debitas et etiam decimas omnes quas ex pia predecessorum nostrorum largitione et caritativa fidelium collatione iuste et canonice hactenus in nostra diocesi possederunt, salva in omnibus sancte Norwicensis ecclesie reverentia et dignitate. Quod ut perpetuam optineat firmitatem, presenti scripto sigillum nostrum duximus apponendum. Dat' London' per manum Philippi de Sideham capellani nostri .xvi. kalendas Februarii pontificatus nostri anno secundo.

    Various tithes in Suffolk parishes were granted to Bec by Richard I of Clare before 1086 (*Bec Documents* 21–2 no. 40). No other confirmations by bps of Norwich are apparently extant. There was a prolonged case before papal judges-delegate, beginning in 1235, between the monks and the rectors of Dalham and Withersfield concerning the demesne tithes of John de Valle at Withersfield (Windsor, St George's Chapel Mun. XI G 14–16, 22, 37; cf. Sayers,

Papal Judges-Delegate 82, 94n, 104, 315, 319–21, 324–5). While the records of the case against the rector of Dalham peter out, a few months after this *actum* an amicable composition was reached before Richard prior of Dunstable as papal judge sub-delegate between master Gilbert, rector of Withersfield, and the monks, by which it was agreed that the rectors should in future pay 50s. *p.a.* for these tithes; both parties were to endeavour to obtain a charter of confirmation from the bp (pp. 231–2 of B). A case between the monks and the rector of Great Wratting continued intermittently from 1245 to 1259 (Windsor, St George's Chapel Mun. X G 27; pp. 229–30 of B; Sayers, *Papal Judges-Delegate* 318–9). In 1254 possessions of Bec are listed at East Wretham and Lessingham (*VN* 394, 415); these were specifically confirmed by archbp Pecham on 2 May 1281 (pp. 221–2 of B).

*126. Butley Priory

Taxation of a vicarage in the church of Upton, including the provision that of the eighteen acres held in that vill by master Hugh of Upton by the special concession of the prior and canons, after his death half should be added to the vicar's portion. [25 September 1239 × November 1243]

Mention of charter in Bodl. ms. Suffolk ch. 190 (*inspeximus* by prior Simon and convent of Norwich of a charter of bp Walter Suffield, 11 September 1248).
Pd in *Leiston Cartulary* 156–57 no. 154.

For the terminal date, see p. lxx.
Bp Raleigh's ordinance was reversed by bp Suffield, who assigned all this land to the canons. In both 1254 and 1291 the church was assessed at £16 13s. 4d., but the valuation of the vicarage increased from 13s. 4d. to £6 13s. 4d., presumably because of reassessment by a later bp (*VN* 366; *Taxatio* 78b).

127. Castle Acre Priory

Institution, at the presentation of the monks, of John of Walton, chaplain, to the perpetual vicarage of the parish church of Castle Acre, with the obligation to minister in person therein. The vicarage shall consist of all the altarage of the church, except the tithes of wool, flax, hemp, lambs and mills, which the monks shall receive. The vicar shall also render to the monks annually within the octaves of the feast of the Purification ten pounds of wax, and he shall discharge all the customary obligations of the church.
South Elmham, 10 November [1239 × 1243]

B = BL ms. Harley 2110 (Castle Acre cartulary) fo. 124v (118v). s. xiii med.

Omnibus Cristi fidelibus ad quos presens scriptum pervenerit Willelmus[a] Dei gratia Northwicensis episcopus salutem in Domino. Noverit universitas vestra nos ad presentationem dilectorum filiorum prioris et conventus de Castelacra Iohannem de Wautun' capellanum ad perpetuam vicariam parochialis ecclesie de Castelacra admisisse ipsumque in ea vicarium perpetuum canonice instituisse cum onere ministrandi personaliter in eadem, salvis in omnibus episcopalibus consuetudinibus et Nortwicensis ecclesie dignitate. Consistit autem dicta vicaria in toto alteragio ipsius ecclesie, exceptis decimis lane, lini, canabi, agnorum et molendinorum, que ipsis monachis remanebunt. Vicarius autem solvet singulis annis eidem priori et monachis .x. libras cere de ea que venerit ad altare infra octavas Purificationis, et omnia onera eiusdem ecclesie ordinaria, consueta et debita sustinebit. In cuius rei testimonium presenti scripto sigillum nostrum duximus apponendum. Dat' apud Suthelmam .iiii^{or}. idus Novembris.

[a] de Ralle *interlined* B

In January 1238 Henry of Holkham, official of the archdn of Norwich, issued notification that during the vacancy of the see and by the archdn's authority he had admitted John, chaplain of Walton, to the perpetual vicarage, which consisted of a daily prebend to be received from the monks' cellarer and cook, just as his predecessors received it; John was also to receive from the sacrist 10s. 6d. *p.a.*, and also 4s. 4d. *p.a.* from the Sunday pennies, a penny from each mass for which an oblation was given, legacies and oblations made to him personally, the proceeds of confessions in Lent and half of the payments for trentals (fos. 129v–130r of B). In 1254 the church was valued at £16 and the vicarage at £3 6s. 8d., in 1291 the church at £17 6s. 8d. and the vicarage at £4 13s. 4d. (*VN* 383; *Taxatio* 80b).

128. Castle Acre Priory

Notification that, since he has inspected the charters of bishops John [I] and Thomas his predecessors [EEA 6 no. 202; above, no. 46], by which they granted to the monks in proprios usus *the church of Herringby, and since the monks have long received twenty shillings as an annual pension from Robert Haltein, sometime vicar, and now that he is dead they have demonstrated their possession, and since when he proceeded by inquisition to tax the vicarage he found that because of the poverty of the church little could accrue to them beyond the maintenance of a vicar, with the consent of the prior and convent of Norwich he has ordained that they should receive annually from the vicar three marks, payable at the two Norwich synods, and that they should in perpetuity be content with this portion. At each vacancy they shall present to the bishop a suitable* persona, *who shall in perpetuity have as his vicarage the church with all its appurtenances, with no diminution, paying to the monks the said three marks and discharging the obligations of the church to bishop and archdeacon.* Norwich, 1 December 1240

B = BL ms. Harley 2110 (Castle Acre cartulary) fo. 130r (124r). s. xiii med.

Omnibus Cristi fidelibus ad quos presens scriptum pervenerit Willelmus[a] Dei gratia episcopus Norwicensis salutem in Domino. Noverit universitas vestra quod cum inspexissemus cartas pie memorie I. et Th. episcoporum predecessorum nostrorum, per quas dilectis in Cristo filiis priori et conventui de Castellacra ecclesiam de Haringeby, in qua ius optinent patronatus, in proprios usus habendam perpetuo contulerunt, et hiidem monachi .xx. solidos annuos nomine pensionis de eadem per manus Roberti Hauteyn quondam ipsius ecclesie vicarii diutius percepissent, tandem eodem Roberto rebus humanis exempto et ipsis monachis coram nobis de sua possessione docentibus, cum ad eiusdem vicarie taxationem pro officii debito procedere curaremus et per inquisitionem super ecclesie predicte facultatibus diligentius factam inveniremus quod parum plus ultra vicarii sustentationem, propter eiusdem ecclesie tenuitatem, accrescere posset monachis antedictis, nos de dilectorum in Cristo filiorum Simonis prioris et conventus nostri Norwicensis assensu ita duximus providendum, quod predicti monachi tres marcas annuas per manus vicarii qui pro tempore fuerit percipiant de eadem ecclesia in duabus sinodis Norwicensibus inperpetuum nomine portionis, et hac perpetuo portione contenti [sint]. Personam idoneam ad vicariam ipsam nobis et successoribus nostris quotiens eam vacare contigerit presentabunt per nos et et successores nostros canonice instituendam, qui nomine vicarie habebit inperpetuum ecclesiam ipsam cum omnibus ad eam pertinentibus sine qualibet diminutione, solvendo monachis supradictis annuatim tres marcas prenominatas, et omnia onera ipsius ecclesie tam episcopalia quam archidiaconalia perpetuo sustinebit. Quod ut perpetuam optineat firmitatem, presens scriptum tam sigilli nostri quam capituli nostri Norwicensis munimine duximus roborandum. Hiis testibus: magistris Willelmo de Clara, Rogero Pincerna et Waltero Exon', Iohanne de Chelebauton', Iohanne de Leoministter, Ricardo de Freton, Thoma de B(r)ecles et Willelmo de Duneswell' clericis et aliis. Dat' per manum Philippi de Sydeham capellani nostri apud Norwicum kalendas Decembris pontificatus nostri anno secundo.

[a] Willelmus de Rale *interlined* B

The appropriation was originally conceded by bp John of Oxford *c.* 1196, to take effect on the death of Robert Haltein, who was not then described as vicar; it was confirmed by bp Blundeville (*EEA* 6 no. 202; *EEA* 3 no. 406; above, no. 46). In 1256, however, bp Suffield instituted a clerk to the church, rather than to the vicarage (fo. 133v of B). In 1254 the church was valued at £5 and the prior's portion at £2 (*VN* 376).

129. Colchester, St John's Abbey

Institution, at the presentation of the monks, of Adam of Westley, chaplain, to the perpetual vicarage of Aldeburgh, with the obligation to minister person-

ally therein. The vicarage shall consist of the whole church and chapel with its appurtenances, except for the great tithe, which the monks of Snape shall receive in whole, and they shall be quit of payment of great or lesser tithe from their demesne in Aldeburgh. The vicar shall render to the monks of Snape three marks p.a. *at the two Norwich synods, and shall discharge all the customary episcopal and archidiaconal obligations on the church.*

Thornage, 3 December 1242

B = Colchester, Essex R.O., Acc. 38 pt 1 (Colchester cartulary) p. 66. s. xiii ex.
Pd from B in *Colchester Cartulary* i 117–18.

Omnibus Cristi fidelibus ad quos presens scriptum pervenerit Willelmus Dei gratia episcopus Norwycensis salutem in Domino. Noverit universitas vestra nos ad presentationem abbatis et conventus sancti Iohannis Colecestr' patronorum et personarum ecclesie de Aldeburgh dilectum in Cristo filium Adam de Westle capellanum ad vicariam ipsius ecclesie admisisse [et] ipsum in ea canonice vicarium perpetuum instituisse, cum onere ministrandi personaliter in eadem, salvis in omnibus episcopalibus consuetudinibus et Norwycensis ecclesie dignitate. Consistit autem ipsa vicaria in tota dicta ecclesia et capella cum omnibus ad easdem pertinentibus, excepta tamen [decima] garbarum, quam monachi de Snapes integre possidebunt, et quieti remanebunt a prestatione decimarum maiorum et minorum de dominico suo in Aldeburgh. Vicarius etiam solvet dictis monachis tres marcas annuas in duabus synodis Norwycensibus, et sustinebit omnia onera episcopalia et archidiaconalia debita et consueta. Quod ut perpetuam optineat firmitatem, presenti scripto sigillum nostrum duximus apponendum. Hiis testibus: magistro Rogero Pincerna Suffolch', Willelmo de Clare Subyr' archidiaconis, Willelmo de Exon', Philippo de Godalminges et Iohanne de Chelebautona capellanis, Iohanne de Leoministre, Waltero de Briche et Willelmo de Donckeswelle clericis et aliis. Dat' per manum predicti archidiaconi Suffolch' apud Thornedische .iii. nonas Decembris pontificatus nostri anno quarto.

For the original appropriation of the church by bp John of Oxford, see *EEA* 6 no. 208. It was granted to the dependant priory of Snape by abbot Adam, *c.* 1194 × 1238, for an annual rent of ten marks, presentation to the vicarage being reserved to the mother house, although in 1300 Snape resigned the church, because it was burdensome and unprofitable (*Colchester Cartulary* ii 558–60). In 1254 the church, with the chapel of Hazlewood, was valued at £6 13s. 4d. and the vicarage at £4 13s. 4d. (*VN* 443); in 1291 the church was assessed at £8 and the vicarage at £6 13s. 4d. (*Taxatio* 119b).

130. Creake Abbey

Grant, with the consent of prior Simon and the convent of Norwich, to the canons in proprios usus, *on account of their notable hospitality and the pov-*

erty of their foundation, of the church of All Saints, Wreningham, of which they hold the advowsons and the possession of which they acquired from the archdeacon during the vacancy of the see; they shall cause them to be served by suitable ministers and shall discharge all the ordinary and extraordinary obligations. [25 September 1239 × 7 January 1241]

B = Christ's College Cambridge, Creake Abbey muniments 7 (*inspeximus* by prior and convent of Norwich, 14 February 1267). s. xiii ex.

Omnibus Cristi fidelibus ad quos presens scriptum pervenerit Willelmus Dei gratia Norwycensis episcopus salutem in Domino. Etsi viros religiosos lege nobis diocesana subiectos pro sue religionis reverentia specialiter protectionis gratia propensius prosequi teneamur, illos tamen nos convenit favore precipuo et speciali gratie munere confovere qui, licet minima sint egestate constricti, pro sue tamen possibilitatis modulo caritatis operibus insistere non desistunt, exiguum quod habent libenter inpertiendo. Cum igitur dilecti filii abbas et canonici de Crek, hospitum susceptione et elemosinarum largitione precipui, in tanta fuerint paupertate fundati quod nisi pia mater ecclesia Norwycensis de sue benignitatis clementia pulsantibus ipsis gratie ianuam aperiret, cogerentur in sui ordinis ignominia puplice mendicare, nos de dilectorum filiorum Simonis prioris et conventus nostri Norwycensis assensu divine pietatis optentu dedimus, concessimus et hac carta nostra confirmavimus prefatis abbati et canonicis ecclesiam beate Margarete et Habeton et medietatem ecclesie Omnium Sanctorum de Wrenigham, in quibus ius optinent patronatus, quarum etiam possessionem vacante sede Norwycensi per loci archidiaconum adepti fuerunt, in proprios usus suos inperpetuum possidendas, salvis in omnibus episcopalibus consuetudinibus et Norwycensis ecclesie dignitate. Predicti vero abbas et canonici facient ipsis ecclesiis per ministros ydoneos deserviri, et omnia onera earundem tam ordinaria quam extraordinaria perpetuo sustinebunt. Quod ut perpetuam optineat firmitatem presens scriptum tam sigilli nostri quam capituli nostri Norwycensis munimine duximus roborandum. Hiis testibus: magistro Galfrido de Ferring' tunc officiali nostro etc.

Mr William of Clare was official by 8 January 1241 (140). Both church and mediety were granted by Robert of Narford, kt, who had acquired the advowson of Hapton from William le Puleys (or Pailleys) in the *curia regis* in 1224 (*Creake Cartulary* no. 6; Rye, *Norfolk Fines* 38 no. 158). The mediety of Wreningham was confirmed by Alice, his widow, daughter of John Punchard (*Creake Cartulary* no. 4). A charter of Ralph of Blundeville, archdn of Norfolk, records his appropriation of that mediety of Wreningham freely resigned into his hands by Clement of Stalham, clerk, 25 September 1237 (Christ's College, Cambridge, Muniments ms. At 32). These appropriations were confirmed by bp Roger Scarning in 1267 (ibid., At 31).

131. Exeter Cathedral

Indulgence of thirty-five days granted to those of his diocese, and of other dioceses whose diocesans ratify this grant, who, penitent and confessed, visit the cathedral to pray or who grant it alms; this grant is to be valid forever.

Exeter, 20 June 1242

> A = Exeter, Cathedral Archives, D. & C. 2089. No medieval endorsement; approx. 155 × 85 + 14 mm.; parchment tag, damaged seal, wax, counterseal.
> Calendared in *HMCR Various Collections* iv 67, no. 2089.

Omnibus Cristi fidelibus ad quos presens scriptum pervenerit Willelmus de Raleg' Dei gratia Norwycensis episcopus salutem eternam in Domino. Cum inter cetera caritatis opera sacra sanctorum limina visitare in conspectu altissimi non immerito sit acceptum, nos de Dei misericordia, gloriose virginis genetricis eius, beati Petri apostoli omniumque sanctorum meritis confidentes, omnibus parochianis nostris et aliis quorum diocesani hanc nostram indulgentiam ratam habuerint, qui ecclesiam cathedralem Exoniensem in honore gloriose virginis Marie et beati Petri apostolorum principis consecratam orandi gratia visitaverint, si de peccatis suis vere contriti fuerint et confessi, triginta et quinque dies de iniuncta sibi penitentia misericorditer relaxamus, concedentes hanc nostre relaxationis gratiam perpetuo duraturam. Dat' Exon' .xii. kalendas Iulii pontificatus nostri anno tertio.

132. Eye Priory

Institution of John de Sunburne, chaplain, nominated by the bishop to the prior and convent and presented by them, to the perpetual vicarage of All Saints, Dunwich, in which he is to minister in person. He and his successors shall hold in perpetuity as their vicarage the church with all its appurtenances, rendering to the monks annually in the name of their personatus *twenty-one marks, that is, five marks at Christmas, Easter and the Nativity of St John the Baptist and six marks at Michaelmas, on pain of forty shillings payable to the bishop and his successors if he should default at any term. The vicar shall discharge the obligations of the church to bishop and archdeacon; saving to the bishop and his successors the right, whenever the vicarage is vacant, of nominating to the monks the* persona *to be presented by them.*

Blofield, 30 December 1239

> B = Essex R. O., D/DBy. Q 19 (Eye cartulary) fo. 29r–v. s. xiii ex.
> Pd from B in *Eye Cartulary* i no. 45.

Omnibus Cristi fidelibus ad quos presens scriptum pervenerit Willelmus Dei gratia episcopus Norwicensis salutem in Domino. Noverit universitas vestra nos ad presentationem dilectorum filiorum prioris et conventus de Eya patronorum[a] et personarum ecclesie Omnium Sanctorum de Donewico dilectum in Cristo filium Iohannem de Sunburne capellanum, prius eis nominatum a nobis, ad perpetuam ipsius ecclesie vicariam per nos sub forma subscripta taxatam admisisse, [fo. 29v] ipsumque in ea canonice vicarium perpetuum instituisse cum onere ministrandi personaliter in eadem. Idem vero Iohannes et successores sui eiusdem ecclesie vicarii habebunt et tenebunt inperpetuum nomine vicarie a predictis monachis ecclesiam ipsam cum omnibus ad eam pertinentibus sine qualibet diminutione, solvendo monachis ipsis singulis annis nomine personatus viginti et unam marcas argenti ad quatuor terminos subscriptos, videlicet ad natale Domini quinque marcas, ad Pascha quinque marcas, ad festum nativitatis sancti Iohannis Baptiste quinque et ad festum sancti Michaelis sex marcas, sub pena quatraginta solidorum totiens nobis vel successoribus nostris solvendorum quotiens in aliquo terminorum ipsorum cessatum fuerit in solutione predicta. Et vicarius honera ipsius ecclesie tam episcopalia quam archidiaconalia perpetuo sustinebit, salvo nobis et successoribus nostris quotiens vicariam ipsam vacare contigerit iure nominandi personam presentandam ad eandem et ipsis monachis presentandi nominatam, salvis etiam in omnibus episcopalibus consuetudinibus et Norwicensis ecclesie dignitate. Quod ut perpetuam optineat firmitatem presenti scripto sigillum nostrum duximus apponendum. Hiis testibus: magistris Galfrido de Fering' tunc officiali nostro, Waltero de Sufeud et Waltero de Exon', Iohanne de Chelebauton', Iohanne de Leoministr', Thoma de Breccles et Willelmo de Dunkeswell' clericis et aliis. Dat' per manum Philippi de Sydesham capellani nostri aput Blafeud .iii. kalendas Ianuarii pontificatus nostri anno primo.

[a] patronarum B

> In 1254 the church was assessed at £10 and in 1291 at £10 13s. 4d. (*VN* 444; *Taxatio* 118). That the patronage was disputed is indicated by a quitclaim before the justices in eyre in 1268 by the five sons of John of Dunwich to the monks of all right in the advowson (*Eye Cartulary* ii no. 389). For a brief history of the church, see ibid. ii 45. 'Sunburne' is unidentified; one of the Sombornes in Hampshire is most likely.

133. Eye Priory

Confirmation for the monks, having inspected grants, concessions and confirmations of his predecessors, of the parish church of Eye and the churches of St Leonard and All Saints, Dunwich, of various pensions and of tithes which they receive; and of other possessions justly acquired now or in the future.   Cherbourg, 21 April 1242

B = Essex R. O., D/Dby. Q 19 (Eye cartulary) fo. 28r–v. s. xiii ex.
Pd from B in *Eye Cartulary* i no. 41.

Omnibus Cristi fidelibus ad quos presens scriptum pervenerit Willelmus Dei gratia episcopus Norwicensis salutem in Domino. Cura nos admonet suscepti regiminis et ratio postulat equitatis preces et petitiones religiosarum personarum que rationi concordant et ab ecclesiastica honestate non dissonant clementer admittere et utiliter effectu prosequente complere. Cum igitur dilecti in Cristo prior et conventus de Eya nobis supplicaverint ut donationes et concessiones et cartas predecessorum nostrorum inspectas super piis collationibus eis factis confirmaremus, nos eorum precibus inclinati ecclesiam parrochialem de Eya, ecclesias sancti Leonardi et Omnium Sanctorum de Donewico, duas marcas quas percipiunt de ecclesia sancti Petri, decem marcas de ecclesia sancti Iohannis cum candela, triginta solidos de ecclesia sancti Martini, unam marcam de ecclesia sancti Nicholai, quinque solidos de ecclesia sancti Bartholomei de Donewico, unam marcam de ecclesia de Badingeham, viginti solidos de ecclesia de Bedefeud', quinque solidos de ecclesia de Pleiford', unam marcam de ecclesia de Laxfeud, unam marcam de ecclesia de Thorendon', quatuor solidos de ecclesia de Stok', quatuor solidos de ecclesia de Pelecoc, quinque solidos de ecclesia de Parva Thornham, quatuor solidos de ecclesia de Melles, unam marcam de ecclesia de Iakel', duas marcas de ecclesia de Beuseya cum candela, et oblationem candele quam percipiunt de ecclesia de Satesham; necnon et separatas decimas quas iidem percipiunt, videlicet in Eya, in Flemewrd',[1] in Thorend', in Rikingehal', in Reidon', in Giselingham,[a] in Selfhangr', in Brom, in Neylond,[2] in Parva Thornham,[b] in Stradebroc,[c] in Bradel',[3] in [fo. 28v] Fresingefeud, in Witingeham, in Laxfeud, in Huntingefeud, in Linestede, in Ystede,[4] in Benges, in Pesehal', in Buckeslawe, in Holesle, in Hasketun', in Badingeham, in Dinnevetun', in Hukehell', in Thatingetun', in Burendis, in Omundeswude,[5] in Leystun', in Creting', in Redelingefeud, in Gosewolde,[6] in Briseworde, in Bedingefeud, in Wiverdestun', in Benehal', in Keletun', in Snape,[7] in Stok', in Acolt, in Bedefeud, que omnia predicta ante tempora nostra auctoritate predecessorum nostrorum pacifice possiderunt. Possessiones etiam et decimas, quascumque homines et redditus suos et quecumque bona largitione pontificum, regum, comitum, baronum vel quorumcumque aliorum fidelium seu aliis quibuscumque iustis modis adepti fuerint, et omnia que possident et in posterum iustis modis[d] dante Domino poterunt adipisci, dum tamen de feodo nostro nichil recipiant sine nostra aut successorum nostrorum licentia speciali, ut de cetero inperpetuum firma eis et eorum posteris illibata permaneant eisdem concedimus et auctoritate pontificali confirmamus. In cuius rei robur et testimonium huic scripto sigillum nostrum duximus apponendum. Dat' apud Cherbug' per manum magistri Rogeri archidiaconi Subir' .xi. kalendas Maii pontificatus nostri anno. iii.

    ^a in Giselingham *interlined* B   ^b *followed by* in Scb, *not expunged* B   ^c *first* r *interlined* B   ^d dnodis B
    ¹ Flimworth in Eye   ² Naylondi in Wreningham   ³ Bradley in Stradbroke   ⁴ Instead in Weybread   ⁵ In Tannington and Brundish   ⁶ In Thrandeston   ⁷ In Fressingfield

134. Eye Priory

Inspeximus *and confirmation of a grant and confirmation, made in the form of a chirograph, by abbot Henry of Bury St Edmunds to prior William and the monks and their successors of the place called 'Atburctre' in the parish of Thornham Magna* [Pelecoch]*, with its chapel and all appurtenances acquired or to be acquired, for the use of the sick and the poor. The prior shall render to the abbot and church of Bury each year at the feast of the translation of St Edmund two candles, as sign and witness of the abbot's barony, and the abbot is not to be vouched to warranty.* Hoxne, 2 May 1243

    B = Essex R. O., D/DBy. Q 19 (Eye cartulary) fo. 30r. s. xiii ex.
    Pd from B in *Eye Cartulary* i no. 48.

Omnibus Cristi fidelibus ad quos presens scriptum pervenerit Willelmus Dei gratia episcopus Norwicensis salutem in Domino. Noverit universitas vestra nos cyrographum inter venerabilem virum H. Dei gratia abbatem sancti Eadmundi ex una parte et dilectos filios Willelmum priorem de Eya et conventum eiusdem loci ex altera confectum inspexisse in hec verba: Omnibus sancte matris ecclesie filiis et cetera. Nos vero dictum cyrographum et in eo rite contenta approbantes, eadem episcopali auctoritate ad dictorum prioris et conventus instantiam pie duximus confirmanda. Dat' aput Hoxn' .vi. nonas Maii pontificatus nostri anno quarto.

    The chirograph itself (*Eye Cartulary* i no. 47) is dated at Elmswell, 9 March 1243. The place-name is derived from the chapel of St Edburga, which in the 1220s and 1230s was served by Vitalis, an anchorite; for full discussion, see ibid. ii 50–2.

*134A. Haughmond Abbey

Mandate to the rural dean of Heacham to induct the abbot and convent, in the person of prior Alexander of Ercall, their proctor, into corporal possession of the church of Hunstanton, according to the tenor of their documents read in the rural chapter of Heacham, saving a suitable vicarage to be taxed by the bishop and to be conferred on a vicar to be nominated by him.

                                          [Shortly before 4 October 1240]

Mention in a notification by the rural dean, who had received similar mandates from mr William of Clare, bp's official, and mr Robert de Carleville, official of the archdn of Norfolk; dated 4 October 1240.

Pd in *Haughmond Cartulary* no. 625.

135. Haughmond Abbey

Notification that, having inspected the charters of bishop Thomas [nos. 61–2] and the prior and convent of Norwich, by which they granted the church of Hunstanton in proprios usus *to the monks, he has confirmed them, saving a perpetual vicarage to be held by a vicar nominated by the bishop and his successors and to be presented by the abbot and convent, who shall have all the altarage of the church and of the chapel of St Edmund, the tithe of mills and all the lesser tithes, except the tithes of the sea, and eighteen acres of arable, with the meadow called 'Redemedewe' and the manse. The vicar shall discharge all obligations to the bishop and the archdeacon.*

Fakenham, 30 October 1240

B = Shrewsbury Borough Library, Haughmond Abbey Cartulary, fos. 120v–21r. s. xv ex.
Pd (calendar) from B in *Haughmond Cartulary* no. 622.

Omnibus Cristi fidelibus ad quos presens scriptum pervenerit Willelmus Dei gratia episcopus Norwicensis salutem in Domino. Noverit universitas vestra quod inspectis cartis bone memorie Thome episcopi predecessoris nostri et capituli nostri Norwicensis per quas dilectis in Cristo abbati et conventui de Haghmon' ecclesiam de Hunstanton' in proprios usus concesserunt et confirmaverunt, concessionem et confirmationem predictam ratam habemus et eam quantum in nobis est confirmamus, [fo. 121r] salva imperpetuum ipsius ecclesie vicaria per nos taxata sub hac forma, videlicet quod vicarius qui pro tempore fuerit ad nostram et successorum nostrorum nominationem a predictis abbate et conventu presentandus habebit nomine vicarie totum altaragium, tam ipsius ecclesie quam capelle sancti Edmundi, et decimas molendinorum et omnes minutas decimas, excepta decima maris, et decem et octo acras terre arabilis cum prato quod vocatur Redmedewe et mansum vicarie prius assignatum; et omnia onera eiusdem ecclesie episcopalia et archidiaconalia perpetuo sustinebit. Quod ut perpetuam optineat firmitatem, presenti scripto sigillum nostrum duximus apponendum. Hiis testibus: magistris Willelmo de Clara, Rogero Pincerna et Waltero de Exon' etc. Dat' per manum Philippi de Sydeham capellani nostri apud Fakenham .iii°. kalendas Novembris anno Domini millesimo ducentesimo quadragesimo.

For the confirmation of no. 61 by prior William and the convent of Norwich, see *Haughmond Cartulary* no. 619. The differences between bp William's ordination and no. 62 are that here the vicar is assigned the tithe of mills and eighteen rather than ten acres, but not a tenth of the tithe of the sea. For the assessment by the dean of Heacham of six acres each of good, mediocre and poor land, see ibid. no. 624. For the induction of the abbot and convent into corporal possession, on 4 October 1240, see no. 134A. In 1286 the vicar complained of the low assessment of his vicarage, but bp Middleton confirmed Raleigh's ordination (*Haughmond Cartulary* no. 623).

136. Holme, St Benet's Abbey

Inspeximus *and confirmation of a charter of bp William Turbe by which he granted to the monks* in proprios usus *the churches of Neatishead, Irstead and Woodbastwick, for the service of the altar and the repair of the buildings* [*EEA* 6 no. 99]. [25 September 1239 × November 1243]

B = BL ms. Cotton Galba E ii (St Benet cartulary) fo. 48v. s. xiii ex. C = Bodl. ms. Norfolk roll 82 (St Benet roll) o. s. xiv in.

Omnibus Cristi fidelibus ad quos presens scriptum pervenerit Willelmus Dei gratia Norwicensis episcopus salutem in Domino. Cartam bone memorie Willelmi quondam predecessoris nostri inspeximus in hec verba: [*EEA* 6 no. 99; *St Benet of Holme* i no. 91]. Nos autem dictam cartam et in ea rite contenta rata habentes, eadem auctoritate pontificali quantum ad nos pertinet confirmamus. In cuius rei testimonium presenti scripto signum nostrum duximus apponendum.

For the terminal date, see p. lxx.
In 1254 Neatishead was assessed at £13 6s. 8d. or £16 13s. 4d., in different mss, with no note of a vicarage (*VN* 414); in 1291 it was valued at £18 13s. 4d., apart from a vicarage not subject to the tenth (*Taxatio* 86b). Woodbastwick was valued at £6 13s. 4d. in 1254, and in 1291 as appropriated to the abbey and including its vicarage, at £8 (*VN* 365; *Taxatio* 78b). The appropriation of Irstead had apparently not taken place by 1291; the church was valued at £5 in 1254 and £8 in 1291, and in both assessments the portion of the abbot of Holme was listed as 13s. 4d. (*VN* 414; *Taxatio* 87).

137. Holme, St Benet's Abbey

Inspeximus *and confirmation of the chirograph, dated 23 May 1243, made between abbot Robert and the convent on the one part and Isabelle, daughter of Robert of Caister, on the other, concerning two-thirds of the great tithe of her demesne in Caister [-by-Yarmouth], which the monks allege pertain by law to them but which she asserts to be of her advowson, saving ten shillings rendered therefrom to the monks. Eventually an amicable composition was reached whereby the monks quitclaimed all right to the tithes and Isabelle in return granted them in perpetuity 20s. a year, to be paid at the feast of the Annunciation. Both parties have submitted themselves in this matter to the jurisdiction of the bishop or his official.* Hoxne, 5 September 1243

> B = BL ms. Cotton Galba E ii (St Benet cartulary) fo. 48v. s. xiii ex. C = Bodl. ms. Norfolk roll 82 (St Benet roll) tt. s. xiv in. D = ibid. Norfolk roll 83 (St Benet roll) f. s. xiv in. E = Norfolk R.O., DCN 40/8 (St Benet cartulary) fo. 26r. s. xiv ex.

Omnibus Cristi fidelibus ad quos presens scriptum pervenerit Willelmus Dei gratia episcopus[a] Norwicensis[b] salutem in Domino. Cyrographum inter dilectos in Cristo Robertum abbatem sancti Benedicti de Hulmo et eiusdem loci conventum ex una parte et Isabellam[c] filiam Roberti de Castre[d] ex altera super duabus partibus decimarum garbarum de dominico predicte Isabelle proventium confectum inspexisse in hec verba: Notum sit omnibus tam presentibus quam futuris quod cum inter dominum Robertum abbatem sancti Benedicti de Hulmo et eiusdem loci conventum ex una parte et Isabellam filiam Roberti de Castre[d] ex altera questio[e] verteretur super duabus partibus decimarum garbarum de dominico predicte Isabelle in Castre,[d] quas iidem abbas et conventus ad se de iure spectare dicebant; dicta vero Isabella ad ipsam et ad heredes suos decimarum earundem advocationem in contrarium asseruit pertinere, salvis tantummodo predictis abbati et conventui decem[f] solidis annuis de eisdem. Tandem inter partes ipsas amicabiliter convenit in hunc modum, videlicet quod predicti abbas et conventus remiserunt inperpetuum predicte Isabelle et heredibus suis totum ius et clamium quod habuerunt vel habere potuerunt in decimis antedictis; dicta vero Isabella pro prefata remissione et quieta clamantia[g] concessit sepedictis abbati et conventui pro se et heredibus suis viginti[h] solidos sterlingorum solvendos eis annuatim inperpetuum in festo annuntiationis beate Marie apud sanctum Benedictum de Hulmo. Et pro hiis bona fide servandis et fideliter adimplendis, utraque pars se submisit iurisdictioni venerabilis patris episcopi Norwicensis qui pro tempore fuerit vel eius officialis, ut liceat ei partem contra premissa venientem ad predicta plenarie servanda modis quibus melius viderit expedire coherere,[j] nulla sibi appellatione, impetratione, exceptione seu cavillatione aliquatenus incontrarium valitura. Et ne partes contra formam istam venire possint inposterum,[k] factum est inter eos hoc scriptum in modum cyrographi, ita quod utraque pars alterius parti sigillum suum apposuit. Hiis testibus:[l] Henrico filio Katerine de Cattefeud, Iohanne de Ludham, Hermero de Cattefud etc. Act'[m] apud sanctum Benedictum de Hulmo decimo[n] kalendas Iunii anno domini millesimo ducentesimo quadragesimo tertio.[o] Nos igitur dictum cyrographum approbantes et eidem nostrum prebentes assensum, illud cum omnibus in eo rite contentis auctoritate pontificali ad dictorum abbatis et conventus instantiam pie duximus confirmandum. In cuius rei testimonium huic scripto apponi fecimus signum nostrum. Dat' apud Hoxne nonas Septembris pontificatus nostri anno quarto.

^a Norwicensis episcopus B   ^b Norwyc' C   ^c Ysabellam E   ^d Castra B; Castr' F
^e controversia E   ^f .x. E   ^g quieta clamatione E   ^h .xx. E   ^j choercere
^k imposterum C   ^l Testibus etc. C D E   ^m Data E   ⁿ .x. C D E   ^o m cc^o xliiii^o C D E

Abbot Thomas (1175–86) had granted to Robert the clerk, son of Alexander of Caister, for his lifetime, all the abbey's tithes in Caister, for 10s. p.a. (*St Benet of Holme* i no. 254). Robert later, before 1220, granted to the abbey eighty acres of land there (ibid. no. 274). A notification of 1220 records an agreement between the chapter of the collegiate church of St Hildevert of Gournay, to whom had been appropriated in 1198 the five churches of Caister (*EEA* 6 no. 219), and master Walter Rufus, rural dean of Flegg, whereby two-thirds of the demesne tithes of Robert of Caister were to be held by him for his lifetime (fo. 69r–v of B).

137A. Ilketshall St John

Admission, at the presentation of Gilbert son of Thomas, knight, and with the consent of John, rector of the mother church, of Ralph of 'Bulgeben', chaplain, to the chapel of Thomas established in Gilbert's house, and confirmation of the chaplain and the perpetual chantry to be established therein, with all its possessions. Future chaplains shall be presented by Gilbert and his heirs to the bishop and his successors. The rights of the parish church, the bishops and the church of Norwich are to be safeguarded.

South Elmham, 16 November 1243

A = Ipswich, Suffolk R.O., HD1538/259/3 (damaged). Endorsed: De capella et cantaria in (Redenhal *deleted*) (s. xiv) Ilketsale sancti Iohannis (s. xv); approx. 142 × 105 + 8 mm; slit for sealing, tag and seal missing.

Omnibus Cristi fidelibus ad quos presens scriptum pervenerit Willelmus Dei gratia episcopus Norwicensis salutem in Domino. Noverit universitas vestra nos ad presentationem dilecti filii Gileberti filii Thome militis, assensu Iohannis rectoris matricis ecclesie sancti Iohannis de Ilketeleshal' mediante, Radulfum de Bulgeben capellanum ad capellam ipsius Thome in curia sua de Ilketeleshal' sitam, cum omnibus ad ipsam pertinentibus, pietatis intuitu admisisse, ipsamque capellam et perpetuam cantariam habendam in eadem, simul cum omnibus terris, redditibus, possessionibus, libertatibus ac aliis eidem a dicto G. per cartam suam, [cuius] tenorem et formam approbavimus, easdem inspicientes, pure et [. . .] assignatis, cum omnibus [pertin]entiis suis, eisdem G. et heredibus suis et capellanis in eadem perpetuo servientibus, n[obis] et successoribus nostris episcopis Norwicensibus prius ab ipso G. et suis posteris presentan[di]s, auctoritate pontificali confirmasse quantum ad nos pertinet, matricis ecclesie indempnitate in omnibus semper salva, salvis etiam episcopalibus consuetudinibus et Norwicensis ecclesie dignitate. Quod ut perpetuam optineat firmitatem, presenti scripto sigillum nostrum duximus apponendum. Hiis testibus: magistris Rogero Suff' et Willelmo Sub' archidiaconis, Philippo et Iohanne capellanis, Waltero de Brech' et Willelmo de Dunkeswell' clericis nostris et aliis. Dat' apud Suthelmeham' .xvi°. kalendas Decembris pontificatus nostri anno quinto.

> For Gilbert son of Thomas of Ilketshall, see *Sibton Charters* i 65. His father, Thomas son of Gilbert, was still alive in 1230, and Gilbert himself was granted free warren in his demesne lands at Ilketshall and elsewhere in 1248 (*Cal. Ch. R.* i 329). He was a benefactor of Bromholm and Walsingham priories.

138. Longueville Priory

Confirmation for the monks of the pensions from the churches of Witchingham St Mary, Witchingham St Faith, Weston [Longville], [Long] Stratton and Stokesby, which he has found from reliable testimony that they have received for forty years or more. London, 26 June 1240

> A = New College, Oxford, archives no. 12046. Endorsed: Wychyngham, Weston', Stratton', Stoqueby (s. xiii); Pensiones .iiii. ecclesiarum (s. xv); approx. 160 × 85 + 18 mm.; parchment tag; fragment of seal, natural wax varnished light brown.
> Pd from A in *Newington Longeville Charters* no. 103.

Omnibus Cristi fidelibus ad quos presens scriptum pervenerit Willelmus de Ralegh' Dei gratia episcopus Norwicensis salutem in Domino. Noverit universitas vestra quod cum dilecti in Cristo prior et monachi de Longavilla per testes fidedignos iuratos et examinatos nobis constare facerent quod de ecclesia sancte Marie de Wichingeham quindecim marcas, de ecclesia sancte Fidis de Wichingeham tres marcas, de ecclesia de Weston' sex marcas, de ecclesia de Stratton' unam marcam et de ecclesia de Stokeby quinque marcas annuatim, beneficii nomine, quadraginta annis elapsis et amplius pacifice percepissent, nos possessionem ipsorum in hac parte perturbare nolentes, portiones prenotatas eis in pace dimisimus, ipsas episcopali auctoritate confirmantes eisdem, Norwicensis ecclesie per omnia iure salvo. Quod ut perpetuam optineat firmitatem, presenti scripto sigillum nostrum duximus apponendum. Dat' London' per manum Philippi de Sydeham capellani nostri .vi^{to}. kalendas Iulii anno Domini millesimo ducentesimo quadragesimo.

> For earlier episcopal grants of pensions, see *EEA* 6 nos. 116A, 258, 369.

139. Norwich Cathedral Priory

Agreement between the bishop on one hand and the prior and convent on the other concerning a covert of oaks, a holly-wood and heathland adjoining Thorpe, which the bishop and monks used to hold in common. The covert of oaks shall be divided into two parts of equal acreage, the bishop holding the half nearer to Thorpe and the monks the half nearer to the bishop's bridge, both in perpetuity and with the other enjoying no common rights therein, saving to the bishop his land by the bridge beyond the covert to the south. The holly-wood and the heath shall be divided into three parts of equal acreage, of which the two parts nearest to the manor of Thorpe shall be held by the bishop and his successors in perpetuity, without any common right of the monks unless the bishop should, after the partition, by his grace allow them any right therein; the third, more distant, part shall be held by the monks, without any common right of the bishop and his successors. Also by this concord the bishop has remitted and quitclaimed to the monks all right and claim in half the wood of Plumstead, over which there had been discord between them. He also conceded that in their part of the covert, holly-wood and heath the monks might have warren, as the bishop and his predecessors had, if they so wished, but otherwise they should remain without warren. If they should wish to enclose or cultivate their part, the bishop will aid them against all men who have rights of common occupation therein, insofar as according to the law of the land he may. This agreement has been drawn up in the form of a chirograph. Gaywood, 25 October 1239

B = Norfolk R.O., DCN 40/1 (general cartulary) fo. 47v (36v, 33v). s. xiv in.
Pd from B in *Norwich Cathedral Charters* i no. 204.

Sciant omnes Cristi fideles presentes et futuri quod ita[a] convenit inter Willelmum Norwicensem episcopum ex una parte et Simonem priorem Norwicensis ecclesie et eiusdem ecclesie conventum ex altera parte de toto bosco cooperto quercibus et de toto husseto et de tota brueria, quem boscum, quod hussetum et quam brueriam predecessores predicti episcopi et predictus conventus prius tenuerant in communi iuxta Thorp', videlicet quod predictus boscus coopertus quercibus dividatur in duas partes equales numero acrarum, ita quod illa medietas propinquior manerio de Thorp' remanebit episcopo et successoribus suis quieta inperpetuum sine aliqua communa quam predicti prior et conventus in ea habere possint; et alia medietas propinquior ponti episcopi remanebit ipso priori et conventui quieta inperpetuum sine aliqua communa quam predictus episcopus et successores sui in ea habere possint, salva eidem episcopo terra sua iuxta pontem quam habet extra coopertum versus austrum. Predictum vero hussetum et predicta brueria dividantur in tres partes numero acrarum equales sicut prius, quarum due partes propinquiores manerio de Thorp' remanebunt predicto episcopo et successoribus suis quiete inperpetuum sine aliqua communa quam predictus prior et conventus in eis habere possint, nisi forte predictus episcopus post partitionem factam gratiam aliquam eis inde facere voluerit; et tertia pars husseti et bruerie remotior[b] remanebit predicto priori et conventui quiete inperpetuum sine aliqua communa quam predictus episcopus vel successores sui in ea habere possint. Per hanc autem concordiam remisit idem episcopus eidem priori et conventui ius et totum clamium quod habuit in medietate bosci[c] de Plumstede, unde contentio [erat] inter eos, et preterea concessit eis quod in parte predictorum bosci, husseti et bruerie que eis remanebit, habeant ipsi warennam suam sicut ipse episcopus et predecessores sui prius habuerunt si voluerint, sin autem remaneat sine warena. Et quod ad eandem partem claudendam vel excolendam si voluerint, iuvabit eos contra omnes homines qui per occupationem communem in ea habere consueverunt secundum quod per legem terre iuvare poterit. Et ne quis eorum contra hoc vertere possit in posterum, factum est hoc scriptum inter eos in modum cirographi, ita quod parti predicti episcopi apposita sunt sigilla predictorum prioris et conventus et parti predictorum prioris et conventus appositum sigillum predicti episcopi. Hiis testibus: Petro de Ralegh' etc. Data apud Geywode octavo kalendas Novembris pontificatus predicti episcopi anno primo, anno Domini millesimo CC^{mo} XXXIX.

[a] ista B   [b] remotioni B   [c] bossi B

For earlier agreements between bp John de Gray and the monks about Thorpe wood, see *EEA* 6 nos. 408, 410.

140. Norwich Cathedral Priory

Grant to the monks of the church of Bawburgh, of which they have the right of patronage, to be held in perpetuity in proprios usus *after the death or resignation of master William le Poynnur, the rector, saving to the bishop or his successors the taxation of a suitable vicarage, to which the prior and convent shall always hereafter present, and saving all episcopal customs and the dignity of the church of Norwich.*   Newark, 8 January 1241

    A = Norwich, Norfolk R.O., DCN 43/41. Endorsed: Ecclesia de Bauburc (s. xiii); pressmark; Hugh of Mursley's notarial mark; approx. 135 × 132 + 11 mm.; parchment tag, seal missing.

    B = BL ms. Cotton ch. ii 21 (*inspeximus* by archbp Pecham, 15 May 1281). s. xiii ex. C = Norfolk R.O., DCN 40/7 (general cartulary) fos. 28v–29r. s. xiii ex. D = ibid. DCN 40/11 (sacrist's cartulary) fos. 13v–14r. s. xiii ex. E = Canterbury, D. & C. Ch. Ant. N26 (*inspeximus* of B by prior Henry of Eastry of Christ Church Canterbury, 2 April 1302). s. xiv in. F = Norfolk R.O., DCN 42/1/4 (as E). s. xiv in. G = Cambridge UL, ms. Ee v 31 (register of Christ Church Canterbury) fo. 90r (as E). s. xiv in. H = Norfolk R.O., DCN 40/1 (general cartulary) fo. 41r–v (30r–v, 27r–v). s. xiv in. J = ibid. fo. 231r (222r) (*inspeximus* by bp John Salmon, 9 March 1302). s. xiv in. K = ibid. DCN 40/2/1 (general cartulary) fo. 28r–v (19r–v, 101r–v). s. xiv in. L = ibid. DCN 40/4 (episcopal charters) pp. 91–2. s. xv in. M = ibid. pp. 278–79. N = ibid. pp. 188–89 (as J).

Pd from A in Norwich Cathedral Charters i no. 198; from H in *First Register* 126–28.

Omnibus Cristi fidelibus ad quos presens scriptum pervenerit Willelmus de Ralegh' Dei gratia episcopus Norwicensis salutem in Domino. Pontificalis gratie ianuam, quam sepius aperimus remotis pariter et ignotis, dilectis et devotis in Cristo filiis priori et conventui Norwicensibus, quos pro sue sancte conversationis merito et specialis devotionis sinceritate habemus inter ceteros cariores, claudere non debemus. Ad universorum igitur notitiam volumus pervenire nos divine zelo caritatis et honeste reverentia religionis dedisse, concessisse et presenti carta nostra confirmasse predictis priori et conventui ecclesiam de Bauburg', in qua ius optinent patronatus, in proprios usus suos post decessum vel cessionem magistri Willelmi le Poynnur rectoris eiusdem in perpetuum possidendam, salva nobis et successoribus nostris congrua ipsius ecclesie vicarie taxatione, et ipsis priori et conventui libera semper in posterum vicarii presentatione, salvis etiam in omnibus episcopalibus consuetudinibus et Norwicensis ecclesie dignitate. Quod ut perpetuam optineat firmitatem, presenti scripto sigillum nostrum duximus apponendum. Hiis testibus: magistro Rogero le Butiller archidiacono Subyr', Willelmo de Clara tunc officiali nostro et Waltero de Exon', Iohanne de Chelebauton', Iohanne de Leominstr', Ricardo de Freton', Thoma de Breccles et Willelmo de Dunkeswell' clericis et aliis. Dat' per manum Philippi de Sydeham capellani nostri apud Novum Locum .vi^{to}. idus Ianuarii pontificatus nostri anno secundo.

> Since Raleigh had recently been postulated to the see of Winchester, Newark in Surrey is the most likely place-date.
>
> On 12 March 1235 the king wrote to bp Blundeville that if he wished to benefit the abbot and monks of Bon Repos (Côtes du Nord, France) by granting them the church of Bawburgh *in proprios usus*, it would please him well, notwithstanding his recent presentation to the church of John Mansel, his clerk (*Close Rolls 1234–47* 58); some six weeks later Mansel was presented by the abbot and convent (*CPR 1232–47* 101). On 1 July 1235 a plea of warranty of charter was brought in the *curia regis* by prior Simon of Norwich against Eudo abbot of Bon Repos, and by a final concord the abbot recognised the advowsons of Bawburgh and of a mediety of Barford, which the prior and church of Norwich had by his gift, to be the right of the monks, to have and hold in perpetuity in free alms, and he granted warranty (*Norwich Cathedral Charters* i no. 331).
>
> The rubric in D notes that the church was appropriated to the use of the sacrist.

141. Norwich Cathedral Priory

Notification that, when the prior and convent claimed that exemption from episcopal jurisdiction in their manors to which they had been accustomed under his predecessors, the bishop, unwilling to extend his jurisdiction to their detriment, granted of his special grace that they might present to him some suitable man, beneficed and resident in the diocese, as dean, to hold custody of the spirituality of the manors in which, in times past, the bishops did not exercise jurisdiction, as neither has he in his time. Having received an oath of canonical obedience, the bishop will without any difficulty admit this man to custody, reserving to himself jurisdiction in cases of matrimony, crime and testaments. With the monks' consent, he has reserved the right of visitation, correction of sin and the exercise of episcopal jurisdiction to himself and his officials, whenever they may wish to exercise it. The dean presented by the monks shall have the same rights as other deans in the bishopric. If cases initiated in these manors before the bishop or his officials cannot conveniently be concluded therein, he reserves the right to bring them to a conclusion elsewhere and to summon litigants outside the manors. If any men of these manors should elect to be examined by the bishop or his officials in any manner of case, then the bishop and his officials may hear such cases, notwithstanding any objection by the dean. No increase of jurisdiction is to accrue to archdeacons or deans in the said manors because of this concession. Newark, 9 January 1241

B = Norfolk R.O., DCN 40/7 (general cartulary) fos. 24v–25r. s. xiii ex.
Pd from B in *Norwich Cathedral Charters* i no. 202.

Omnibus Cristi fidelibus ad quos presens scriptum pervenerit Willelmus Dei gratia episcopus Norwicensis salutem in Domino. Noverit universitas vestra quod cum dilecti in Cristo filii prior et conventus sacrosancte Norwicensis ecclesie nostris temporibus in suis maneriis episcopalis iurisdictionis exemptionem vendicassent, quam ut dicebant predecessorum nostrorum habere temporibus consueverant, nos in eorundem iniuriam nostram iurisdictionem dilatare nolentes, eisdem de gratia concessimus speciali quod ad custodiam spiritualitatis maneriorum in quibus retro temporibus episcopi iurisdictionis ius et exercitium iurisdictionis non habebant, nec nos tempore nostro iurisdictionem habuimus, aliquem virum idoneum in episcopatu Norwicensi beneficiatum et residentem tanquam decanum nobis possint presentare, et nos ab eodem presentato obedientia recepta canonica, ipsum ad memoratam custodiam sine omni difficultate admittemus, matrimonialium et criminalium necnon testamentariarum causarum cognitionibus in eisdem maneriis nobis specialiter reservatis. De eorundem etiam assensu et voluntate, visitandi et corrigendi peccamen[a] et exercendi iurisdictionem nostram pleno iure in prefatis maneriis cum nos vel officiales nostri ad eadem personaliter voluerimus declinare nobis et officialibus nostris expresse reservavimus, concedentes eisdem quod presentatum ab ipsis in iure quod alii decani [fo. 25r] in nostro episcopatu optinent plenarie conservabimus. Si vero in prefatis maneriis coram nobis vel officialibus nostris incepte cause commode in eisdem nequiverint terminari, extra dicta maneria ipsas causas evocandi et litigantibus diem prefigendi nobis et officialibus nostris potestatem pariter reservavimus. Volumus etiam quod si dictorum maneriorum homines in aliquibus causis movendis nostrum examen vel officialis nostri duxerint eligendum, ut tunc nobis vel eodem officiali easdem causas libere audire liceat, dicti decani contradictione non obstante. Nolumus siquidem quod per hanc concessionem nostram archidiaconis seu decanis in prefatis maneriis ullum iurisdictionis tribuatur incrementum. In huius rei testimonium presenti scripto sigillum nostrum duximus apponendum. Dat' per manum Philippi de Sydeham capellani nostri apud Novum Locum .v^{to}. idus Ianuarii pontificatus nostri anno secundo.

[a] peccatem B; *alternative reading* peccatum

This concession was repeated almost verbatim by bp Suffield in 1246 (*Norwich Cathedral Charters* i no. 210).

142. Norwich Cathedral Priory

Declaration, with the consent of prior Simon and the convent, who hold the personatus, *and of Hugh the vicar, of the revenues of* persona *and vicar of the church of [North] Elmham. The vicarage shall consist of a manse with buildings near to the church to the west and ten acres of free arable land, and all the oblations, obventions and lesser tithes, with the tithe of peas and beans of all the parish, and also the great and lesser tithes from five hundred acres of arable and of all the free land which the monks retained in demesne at the time of the taxation of the vicarage, and from various other named parcels of land, with all the tithes of hay, turbary and mills. No vicar may in the future demand more. All the residue pertains to the* personatus, *that is, the tithe of grain of the whole parish, both from lands long cultivated and from new lands and assarts brought or to be brought under cultivation.*

Norwich, 20 November 1241

A = Norwich, Norfolk R.O., DCN 84/3. Endorsed: De vicaria de Elmham (s. xiii); pressmark; Hugh of Mursley's notarial mark; chirograph indented at upper margin, approx. 140 × 165 + 20 mm.; two parchment tags, seals missing.

B = Norfolk R.O., DCN 40/7 (general cartulary) fo. 29r. s. xiii ex. C = ibid. DCN 40/1 (general cartulary) fos. 41v–42r (30v–31r, 27v–28r). s. xiv in. D = ibid. DCN 40/2/1 (general cartulary) fo. 28v (19v, 101v). s. xiv in. E = ibid. DCN 40/4 (episcopal charters) pp. 94–6. s. xv in. F = ibid. pp. 281–2. G = ibid. pp. 282–5 (*inspeximus* by prior and convent of Norwich and Robert de Winetr', vicar of North Elmham, 21 October 1277). Pd from A in *Norwich Cathedral Charters* i no. 201; from C in *First Register* 128–30.

Omnibus Cristi fidelibus ad quos presens scriptum pervenerit Willelmus Dei gratia episcopus Norwicensis salutem in Domino. Cum ecclesia de Elmeham divisa sit in personatum et vicariam ac de quibusdam proventibus ipsius ecclesie minus certum esset utrum ad personatum vel ad vicariam pertinerent, cum super taxatione vicarii instrumentum auctenticum non appareret, nos volentes omnem dubitationem tollere in hac parte, tam de consensu Simonis prioris et conventus Norwicensium, qui personatum optinent in eadem ecclesia, quam Hugonis vicarii, quid ad personatum et quid ad vicariam de universis proventibus dicte ecclesie debeat pertinere declaravimus in hunc modum, videlicet quod in parte vicarie cedere debeant unus mansus cum edificiis prope ecclesiam ex parte occidentali et decem acre libere terre arabilis, et omnes oblationes, obventiones et minute decime, cum decimis pisorum et fabarum totius parrochie de Elmeham, et etiam omnes decime tam maiores quam minores provenientes ex quingentis acris terre arabilis et ex tota libera terra quam prior et conventus Norwicenses retinuerunt in dominico suo tempore taxationis eiusdem vicarie, que quidem terre in prima dicte vicarie taxatione eidem assignabantur pleno iure decimabiles, et similiter omnes decime tam maiores quam minores provenienties ex novem acris terre arabilis, quarum tres acre et dimidia iacent super Stonhull' de terra quondam camerarii in duabus peciis, et una acra iacet apud Botme(re) de terra Elye le Kedere, et due acre iacent iuxta terram eiusdem Elye de terra Simonis Ymein, et tres dimidie acre in eadem cultura de terra Ricardi Sparuwe, et una acra de terra Henrici Ringe in eadem cultura, cum omnibus decimis feni, turbarie et molendinorum; ita quidem quod nullus vicarius aliquo tempore amplius de proventibus dicte parrochie sibi possit vendicare. Totum autem residuum ad personatum debet pertinere, videlicet omnes decime cuiusque bladi totius dicte parrochie de Elmeham, tam de terris ab antiquo excultis quam de novalibus pasturis et assartis ad culturam redactis et quocumque tempore redigendis in perpetuum. Hanc autem declarationem in perpetuum ratam et firmam haberi volentes, eam pontificali auctoritate confirmavimus, et ut perpetue firmitatis robur optineat, huic scripto in modum cyrographi confecto sigilla dictorum prioris et conventus ac vicarii alternatim unacum sigillo nostro apponi fecimus. Dat' per manum magistri Rogeri Pincerne archidiaconi Subir' apud Norwicum .xii°. kalendas Decembris pontificatus nostri anno tertio.

On 21 September 1278 bp William Middleton and his official, by the agreement of the parties, delivered an extra-judicial decision to resolve the dispute between the prior and convent of

Norwich as rectors and Robert de Winetr' vicar, of North Elmham, regarding responsibility for the maintenance of the chancel, which the monks alleged to have fallen into disrepair because of the vicar's failure to repair the roof. It was decreed that, because of the vicar's ample portion from the church, full responsibility for the repair of the church should fall upon him, with no resort to help from the monastic rector (*Norwich Cathedral Charters* i no. 231). This is an interesting abdication of the normal rectorial responsibility for the chancel.

*143. Norwich Cathedral Priory

Episcopal ordinance recording the restoration of concord between the monks and Roger Hautesce, rector of Thornham. [Shortly before 6 March 1242]

Mention of *actum* in a notification by Roger Hautesce, rector of Thornham, 6 March 1242. Pd in *Norwich Cathedral Charters* ii no. 70.

This ordinance presumably sets out the terms which were later agreed by final concord in the *curia regis* on 3 November 1242 in a case brought by the monks against the rector concerning twelve acres of land and a messuage with appurtenances in Thornham. The prior eventually recognised these to be the right of the rector and his church, and quitclaimed them in perpetuity, and also quitclaimed all right to thirty-six quarters of grain which he and his predecessors used to receive from the rector's predecessors. In return, the rector conceded to the prior a messuage in the churchyard with its buildings and appurtenances, and surrendered all claim to any lands, rents and tenements held by the prior in the vill; this concord was made with the consent of the bp of Norwich, who had notified the king's justices by his letters patent (*Norwich Cathedral Charters* i no. 354).

The dispute was longstanding, and the allegations are recorded in *CRR* xvi no. 1659, a record of proceedings in Hilary term 1241 between the prior and the previous rector of Thornham, mr John de Dya, which records the history of Thornham church back to the time of bp Herbert, when the church and an estate were held by Thurstan the deacon. Bp Herbert granted the church and the service from the land to the monks. After Thurstan's death, the church and land were held in succession by his son and grandson, in return for an increased render to the monks. After the grandson's death, bp John of Oxford granted the church to Roger Merdenpaske, who continued to render forty measures of grain to the monks; but subsequently, at the bp's request, Roger granted most of the revenues of the church to mr Simon of Huntingdon, a member of the bp's *familia*, retaining only £5 *p.a.* for himself as the portion of the *persona*. Meanwhile, bp John de Gray in his general settlement with the monks in 1205 included Thornham among those churches whose advowson was reserved to the bp without need for consultation with the cathedral chapter (*EEA* 6 no. 391)—to state that the bp took the advowson by intimidation, as the prior alleged in 1241, was a distortion of the truth. In 1205 bp Gray also defined the amount of grain due to the monks: thirty-six measures were due from the church and four from the socage tenure (*EEA* 6 no. 407). Simon of Thornham, the vicar (probably Simon of Huntingdon, as stated in 1241), claimed that the land pertained to Thornham church as free alms, rather than being the lay fee of the church of Norwich which had merely been leased to previous incumbents; in January 1209 he agreed to a final concord made before the king's justices whereby he and Gregory his brother should hold the land of the monks for their lifetimes for four measures of grain and 4s. *p.a.*, with reversion to the monks after their deaths (*Fines* ii no. 145). When Roger Merdenpaske resumed receipt of the entire revenue of the church, he allegedly made no claim to this land.

Another conflict arose in 1220 between the monks and the new rector, Robert Buttamund, and after the monks' appeal to Rome the case was heard before papal judges-delegate. The monks alleged that the rector had not for the past eight years paid the render of thirty-six measures of grain due from the church, and he counter-pleaded that this was an unjust demand, because the church had been despoiled of various lands by Gregory, the monks' clerk. The monks won their case and expenses were awarded against the rector (*Norwich Cathedral Charters* ii no. 75).

Probably in 1233, bishop Blundeville persuaded Robert Buttamund, the *persona*, to accept the status of vicar, and instituted to the *personatus*, in this case a small pension in money, his kinsman Ralph de Blundeville. After the vicar's death, Ralph entered into the benefice which constituted the major part of Thornham's revenues, and the incompatibility of this benefice with his archdeaconry of Norfolk resulted in a complex legal process before the legate Otto and ultimately, in March 1239, at the papal *curia* (see no. 110, and *Reg. Greg. IX* no. 4738). By now mr John de Dya had been presented by the crown *sede vacante*, on 10 May 1237 (*CPR 1232–47* 179); and between Hilary term 1241 and March 1242 he had in turn been succeeded by Roger Hautesce, who served as the bp's attorney at the *curia regis* (Appx II 51).

In 1241 the affairs of Thornham church were once again ventilated in the king's court, the monks alleging that a messuage and 230 acres were their lay fee, against the rector's assertion that they were free alms of the church. The prior's attorney stated his case much as summarised above; the rector's case was that the land had been the free alms of the church of Thornham since before the Norman Conquest and had been so until Roger Merdenpaske, after resuming the whole of the church, did not dare to reclaim land which his vicar, because he had enemies at court, had recognised to be the monks' lay fee; none of the previous rectors, John de Dya claimed, had been mere farmers of the monks' lands, and Simon of Huntingdon's agreement as vicar could not harm his case, since it had been made without the assent of bp or rector. After the death of Gregory, the vicar's brother, the prior's servants had, he alleged, occupied the land, but bp Pandulph's seneschal attempted to eject the monks; but the prior made fine with him to stay any action until the bp returned from Rome—which he never did, so that the monks had remained in possession until the present. The royal justices were unable to determine the status of the disputed land and the jurors, when recalled, stated that they believed the land to be the free alms of Thornham church, from which it had never been separated. The bp's ordinance of early 1242, and the subsequent final concord in the *curia regis*, thus ended a dispute which had dragged on for at least thirty-six years.

144. Norwich Cathedral Priory

Settlement between the bishop on the one hand and prior Simon and the convent on the other, whereby the bishop has conceded to the monks in perpetuity, in free, pure and perpetual alms, nine and a quarter perches of land in a croft called 'Struernecroft' and a small parcel of land called 'Chemingrode', both in Thornham, and the monks have granted to him and his successors in exchange two and a half acres and half a perch of land called 'Thornwong'. Norwich, 27 December 1242

 A = Norwich, Norfolk R.O., DCN 43/42. Endorsed: Thornham (s. xiii); pressmark; approx. 183 × 125 + 12 mm., chirograph indented along upper margin; slit for sealing, tag and seal missing.
 B = Norfolk R.O., DCN 40/4 (episcopal charters) pp. 102–4. s. xv in. C = ibid. pp. 288–9.
 Pd from A in *Norwich Cathedral Charters* i no. 203.

Sciant presentes et futuri quod ita convenit inter venerabilem patrem dominum Willelmum de Raleg' Dei gratia episcopum Norwycensem ex una parte et dominum Symonem priorem Norwycensem et eiusdem loci conventum ex altera, sexto kalendas Ianuarii anno Domini M° CC° xlii° apud Norwycum, videlicet quod idem dominus episcopus concessit pro se et successoribus suis in liberam, puram et perpetuam elemosinam dictis priori et conventui et eorum successoribus inperpetuum novem perticatas et quartam partem unius perticate terre in una crufta que vocatur Struernecroft', iacentes in villa de Thornham inter cruftam Willelmi Bursemarc' et cruftam Gileberti filii Roberti, et abuttat super Bradegate versus occidentem, et unam parvam peciam terre que vocatur Chemingrode, et iacet apud Sloches iuxta terram Reginaldi filii Roberti versus aquilonem, et abuttat super terram Thome filii Duce versus orientem, ad faciendum unum mesuagium, habendam et tenendam dictis priori et conventui et eorum successoribus dictam terram, liberam et quietam de eodem episcopo et successoribus suis inperpetuum. Predicti vero prior et conventus concesserunt pro se et pro successoribus suis prefato domino episcopo et successoribus suis in escambium dicte terre duas acras et dimidiam et dimidiam perticatam terre que vocantur Thornwong, et iacent inter terram ecclesie et terram Thome filii Emme, et abuttant super terram dicti domini episcopi versus austrum, habendam et tenendam eidem domino episcopo et successoribus suis predictam terram, liberam et quietam de predictis priore et conventu et eorum successoribus inperpetuum. Et ut predicta perpetuam optineant firmitatem, apposuerunt partes presenti scripto in modum cyrographi confecto altrinsecus signa sua, et remansit pars signo dicti domini episcopi signata penes dictos priorem et conventum et altera pars signo dictorum prioris et conventus signata penes dominum episcopum memoratum. Hiis testibus: magistris Rogero Pincerna Suthff' et Willelmo de Clar' Subyr' archidiaconis, Galfrido de Loden' tunc senescallo dicti domini prioris et Willelmo clerico suo et multis aliis.

145. Norwich Cathedral Priory

Confirmation for the monks of the church of Catton with all its appurtenances, which his predecessor bishop Thomas had granted to them in proprios usus in perpetuity, *saving to the bishop and his successors pontifical and parochial rights.* [April 1242 × November 1243]

A = Norwich, Norfolk R.O., DCN 43/43. Endorsed: Ecclesia de Cattune; in decanatu de Taverham (s. xiii); pressmark; Hugh of Mursley's notarial mark; approx. 153 × 79 + 18 mm.; slit for sealing, tag and seal missing.

B = Norfolk R.O., DCN 40/7 (general cartulary) fo. 30v. s. xiii ex. C = ibid. DCN 40/1 (general cartulary) fo. 41r (30r, 27r). s. xiv in. D = ibid. fo. 231r–v (222r–v) (*inspeximus*

by bp John Salmon, 9 March 1302). E = ibid. DCN 40/2/1 (general cartulary) fo. 28r (19r, 101r). s. xiv in. F = ibid. DCN 40/4 (episcopal charters) p. 92. s. xv in. G = ibid. p. 279. H = ibid. pp. 189–90 (as D).
Pd from A in *Norwich Cathedral Charters* i no. 199; from C in *First Register* 126.

Omnibus Cristi fidelibus presens scriptum visuris vel audituris Willelmus de Raleg' Dei gratia Norwycensis episcopus salutem in Domino. Ad universorum notitiam volumus pervenire nos divine pietatis intuitu et favore religionis concessisse et presenti carta confirmasse dilectis filiis nostris monachis Norwycensibus ecclesiam de Cattune cum omnibus ad eam pertinentibus, quam bone memorie Thomas episcopus predecessor noster concessit et contulit eisdem in proprios usus perpetuo possidendam, salvo nobis et successoribus nostris inperpetuum iure pontificali et parochiali. In cuius rei testimonium presens scriptum sigilli nostri roboravimus munimine. Hiis testibus: magistro Rogero Pincerna Suffolchie, magistro Willelmo de Clare Subir' archidiaconis, Waltero de Exon', Philippo de Godalming' et Iohanne de Chelebaut' capellanis, Rogero Hautesce, Iohanne de Leoministr', Waltero de Briche et Willelmo de Dunkeswell' clericis et aliis.

Mr Roger Pincerna last occurs as archdn of Sudbury in April 1242 and mr William of Clare first on 3 December 1242 (no. 144); for the *terminus ad quem*, see above p. lxx.
Bp Thomas's *actum* is apparently not extant.

145A. Pontigny Abbey

Inspeximus, *with bishops [William Brewer] of Exeter and [Walter Cantilupe] of Worcester, of the confirmation by the late archbishop Edmund of Canterbury in 1238 of archbishop Stephen Langton's grant to the abbey of fifty marks annually from the church of New Romney, to which archbishop Edmund had added ten marks in gratitude for the abbey's services to archbishops Thomas Becket and Langton in their exiles.*

Pontigny, [February × 24 March] 1241

A = Auxerre, Archives départementales de la Yonne H 1406, unnumbered piece. Approx. 295 × 210 mm. Sealing lost.
Pd from A in *EEA* 12 no. 286A.

For discussion, see *EEA* 12 no. 286A. Raleigh was in London on 17 January 1241 (125). It is likely that he, like Brewer, left England with the legate Otto. It is possible that Raleigh set out to answer Gregory IX's summons of August 1240 to a general council next year, but Matthew Paris does not record him as attending (*Chron. Maj.* iv 98). His friendship with St Edmund might provide sufficient reason for the journey, but he is not recorded as being in England again until 14 November 1241 (no. 146).

145B. Pontigny Abbey

Inspeximus, *with bishops [William Brewer] of Exeter and [Walter Cantilupe] of Worcester, of letters of protection granted by archbishop Edmund of Canterbury on 13 November 1240 at Soisy-en-Brie to his chaplain Eustace [of Faversham].* Pontigny, [February × 24 March] 1241

> A = Sens cathedral treasury, Pontigny archive, H 3. Approx. 165 × 125 + 20 mm.; parchment tags, fragments of three seals.
> Pd from A in Lawrence, *St Edmund of Abingdon*, 319; *EEA* 12 no. 286B.

> See no. 145A. St Edmund's last letter had been a request for support for another member of his household, Robert of Essex, directed to bp Raleigh. (Lawrence, *St Edmund of Abingdon*, 267–8).

146. Préaux, Abbey of St Pierre

Confirmation for the monks of various tithes which they have long held in the vills of Aldeby, Haddiscoe and Costessy. North Elmham, 14 November 1241.

> B = Evreux, Archives Départementales, Eure, H711 (s. xiii ex.), fo. 89r no. 226.

Omnibus Cristi fidelibus ad quos presens scriptum pervenerit Willelmus Dei gratia Norwicensis episcopus salutem in Domino. Cum cunctis divino obsequio deputatis, ut eorundem devotio pastoris benignitate pistoris recipiat incrementum, episcopalis auctoritas manus porrigere debeat pietatis hiis qui religionis habitum deferentes contemplationibus insistunt, ne sucgillationibus[a] fraudulentis ipsorum tranquillitas perturbetur, impendetur gratia merito dilatata. Hinc est quod dilectorum nobis in Cristo filiorum abbatis et conventus de Pratell' precibus inclinati, super iure et possessione ipsorum in decimis et obventionibus quas retro temporibus habuerunt in villa de Audeby et de Hadesco et de Costes' diligenter fecimus fieri inquisitionem, et cum per eandem nobis constabat evidenter quia in prefatis villis a tempore cuius non extabat memoria sine interruptione temporis pacifice decimas et obventiones quasdam perceperunt, nos ius et possessionem eorundem approbantes, decimas et obventiones quas hactenus ita percipere consueverunt pontificali auctoritate eisdem confirmamus. In cuius rei testimonium presenti scripto sigillum nostrum duximus apponendum. Datum apud Northelmeham .xviii. kalendas Decembris pontificatus nostri anno tertio.

> [a] succillationibus B.

> Préaux's property in East Anglia was administered from the priory-cell of Toft Monks, where the church and manor had been granted during the reign of William Rufus by Robert de Beaumont, count of Meulan (*MRH* 93; D. Matthew, *The Norman Monasteries and their English Possessions* (Oxford 1962), 53).

140   ACTA OF WILLIAM RALEIGH

*147. Royal Justices

Letter testifying that Richard son of Robert and Roger son of Benedict are excommunicate.   [Shortly before 11 May 1242]

Mention of letter produced in *curia regis*.
Pd in *CRR* xvi no. 2088.

Both men had impleaded the prior of Wymondham as to why he had heard pleas relating to chattels, etc., not relating to testament or matrimony and contrary to a writ of prohibition. Richard son of Robert complained to the justices that a certain Henry the merchant had impleaded him before the prior with regard to six acres of land; Roger son of Benedict complained that John Turf and others had brought him to court and had sought 15s. from him. The prior, it was alleged, ignored the writ of prohibition and heard these pleas, and thereby they had suffered damages. The prior claimed that he should not answer them, because they were excommunicate, and produced the bp's letter. The prior was dismissed *sine die* until they might receive absolution, when it would be decided if those who had brought the pleas before the prior had legitimately so done.

148. Rumburgh Priory

Confirmation for the monks of two-thirds of the great tithe of the demesne in Costessy, Bawburgh, [Honingham] Thorpe, Swaffham, Kettleburgh and Sibton, granted to them by the earls of Richmond and confirmed by earlier bishops, and of the tithes which they canonically hold in Banham, Wilby (Nf.), [North] Tuddenham, 'Faldyates', Taverham, Ilketshall [St Andrew], Chediston, and 'Rothinges' and 'Kyndele' in South Elmham, and of all other tithes of which they are in peaceful possession. South Elmham, 13 November 1243

B = Bodl. ms. Top. Suff. d. 15 (South Elmham cartulary) fos. 38v–39r (35v–36r). s. xvi in.

Omnibus Cristi fidelibus ad quos presens scriptum pervenerit Willelmus Dei gratia Norwicensis episcopus salutem in Domino. Cum dilectorum filiorum prioris et monachorum de Romb' honesta conversatio eos, ut creditur, Deo dignos et hominibus ac gratos efficiat, volentes eis ad eorundem piam instantiam gratiam facere specialem, duas partes decimarum garbarum dominici de Costhes', de Bauburgh', de Thorp', de Swaffham, de Ketilbergh', de Sybeton' sibi a nobilibus viris comitibus Richmund' concessas et a predecessoribus nostris episcopis Norwicensibus confirmatas, et etiam decimas quas canonice optinent in Banham et [fo. 39r] Wilby, Tudneham, Faldyates, Taverham, Ilketshall, Chedstane, Rothinges et Kyndele in Southelmham, et alias omnes in quarum possessione pacifica hactenus extiterunt, ipsis priori et monachis et ecclesie sue de Romeb' imperpetuum auctoritate pontificali pie duximus confirmandas. In cuius rei testimonium presenti scripto apponi fecimus sigillum nostrum. Dat' apud Southelmham idus Novembris pontificatus nostri anno quinto.

> For notification of the grant of the first group of tithes (except Sibton) to bp Everard by Stephen count of Brittany, see *EYC* iv 12–13 (no. 10). In the early thirteenth century Hamo of Sibton and Margaret his wife, tenants of a knight's fee of the honour of Brittany in Sibton, granted two-thirds of their tithe there (PRO ms. E40/3335; cf. *Sibton Cartulary* i 98). For the identification of Wilby, North Tuddenham and Ilketshall St Andrew, see *VN* 395, 400, 459.

149. St Neot's Priory

Charter in favour of the monks.   28 October 1241

> B = BL ms. Cotton Faust. A iv (St Neot's cartulary) fo. 122r (almost half at top cut out, next few lines faded and illegible). s. xiii med.

... eam sigilli [nostri corroborari] fecimus. Hiis testibus: magistris Waltero Norff' et Rogero Subyr' archidiaconis, Philippo de Godelming et Iohanne de Chelebaut' capellanis, Iohanne de Leomenstr' et Willelmo de Donekeswell clericis nostris et aliis. Dat' apud [*illeg.*] .v. kalendas Novembris pontificatus nostri anno tertio.

> It is impossible to determine the content of this *actum*. In the cartulary it follows a grant by Geoffrey Crane of Upwell of marshland for a rent of £2 *p.a.*, 1242, and precedes a grant of marshland and turbary by Hugh bp of Ely. The date and the archdn of Sudbury (1241–2, *Fasti* ii 70) demonstrate that is an *actum* of bp Raleigh.

150. Stoke by Clare Priory

Confirmation for the monks, who have presented to him the charters of his predecessors, of the church of Crimplesham with its tithes and all other appurtenances, which they have peacefully possessed before his time; confirmation also of all other possessions which they rightfully hold or may in the future justly acquire.

    [25 September 1239 × 9 October 1242, possibly before January 1241]

> B = BL ms. Cotton Appx. xxi (Stoke by Clare cartulary) fo. 44r. s. xiii ex. C = ibid. fo. 44r–v (*inspeximus* by prior Simon and the convent of Norwich, 9 October 1242). s. xiii ex. Pd from B and C in *Stoke by Clare Cartulary* i no. 89.

Omnibus Cristi fidelibus ad quos presens scriptum pervenerit Willelmus Dei gratia episcopus Norwicensis salutem in Domino. Cura nos admonet suscepti regiminis et ratio postulat equitatis preces et petitiones religiosarum personarum que rationi concordant clementer admittere et utiliter effectu prosequente complere. Cum igitur dilecti in Cristo filii[a] prior et conventus monachorum de Stok' nobis humiliter supplicaverint ut donationes, concessiones et cartas predecessorum nostrorum inspectas super piis collationibus eis factis confirmaremus, nos eorum precibus inclinati ecclesiam de Cremplesham cum decimis et omnibus aliis ad eam pertinentibus, que ante tempora nostra pacifice possidebant, possessiones quoque, decimas quascumque, homines et redditus suos et quecumque bona largitione pontificum, regum, comitum, baronum seu quorumcumque aliorum[b] fidelium, vel que aliis iustis modis quibuscumque adepti fuerint, et omnia que rite possident et inposterum iuste adipiscent, ut de cetero imperpetuum firma eis et eorum posteris illibata permaneant auctoritate pontificali confirmamus. In cuius rei robur et testimonium huic scripto sigillum nostrum duximus apponendum. Hiis testibus: magistris Rogero Pincerna, Willelmo de Clar' et aliis.

[a] filii et B   [b] clericorum B; aliorum *om.* B

Mr Roger Pincerna first occurs as archdn of Sudbury in January 1241. For a brief history of the church of Crimplesham, see *Stoke by Clare Cartulary* iii 19. The first mention of a vicarage is in 1229, when a case concerning land in the vill was prosecuted by the prior as rector and mr Thomas of Huntingdon as vicar (*CPR 1225-32* 290). In a general confirmation of 1234, pope Gregory IX also specifically mentioned Crimplesham church, recently granted by the bp of Norwich (*Stoke by Clare Cartulary* i no. 138). In 1253 bp Suffield found that the vicarage had not hitherto been taxed (ibid. no. 91).

151. Stoke by Clare Priory

Grant to the monks in proprios usus, *at their petition, of the chapel of St Mary at Bures, with twenty acres of land granted by William de Blaveni, another ten acres with a rent of twenty shillings, all other goods charitably given to the chapel and canonically obtained, and all else which they may by just means acquire for the increase of divine service and the cult of the Glorious Virgin.*   Hoxne, 21 October 1243

B = BL ms. Cotton Appx. xxi (Stoke by Clare cartulary) fos. 41v–42r. s. xiii ex.
Pd from B in *Stoke by Clare Cartulary* i no. 80.

Omnibus Cristi fidelibus ad quos presens scriptum pervenerit Willemus Dei gratia episcopus Norwicensis salutem in Domino. Cura pastoralis nos admonet et ratio postulat equitatis religiosarum personarum petitiones que rationi non dissonant propitius exaudire. Cum igitur dilecti filii prior et monachi de Stok' nobis humiliter supplicaverint et devote quatinus capellam beate Marie de Buris cum quibusdam terris, redditibus ac bonis aliis ipsi capelle assignatis sibi in [fo. 42r] proprios usus confirmare caritatis intuitu dignaremur, nos eorum piis precibus inclinati ipsam capellam de Buris cum viginti[a] acris terre de dono Willelmi de Blawen' et aliis decem acris terre cum redditu[b] decem solidorum, simul cum omnibus bonis eidem capelle caritative collatis sicut ea canonice sunt adepti, necnon et cetera bona que in posterum iustis modis dante Domino poterint adipisci ad divini cultus ampliationem et obsequii ipsius gloriose Virginis sustentationem perpetuam in eadem, ipsis priori et monachis et ecclesie sue auctoritate pontificali duximus confirmanda. In cuius rei testimonium presenti scripto sigillum nostrum duximus apponendum. Datum per manum magistri Rogeri Pincerne archidiaconi Suffolch' apud Hoxn' .xii. kalendas Novembris pontificatus nostri anno quinto.

^a vigintis B   ^b redditum B

The papal confirmation of bp Raleigh's translation to Winchester had been issued on 17 September 1243, but even if news had reached England, the king appealed against this (*Fasti* ii 86). In the mid-thirteenth century a monk acted as warden of the chapel (*Stoke by Clare Cartulary* ii no. 427), which possessed burial rights (ibid. no. 426), had more than one altar (ibid. no. 396) and attracted many gifts from local inhabitants (ibid. nos. 391–2, 410, 413–28 *passim*). For the grant by William de Blaveni, see ibid. nos. 397, 404.

152. Threxton Church

Notification that when a dispute between the prior and convent of Norwich and Paulinus, rector of Threxton, over two-thirds of the great tithe of the demesne of the late Wigan Brito in the vill of Threxton, of which both parties claimed rightful possession, was heard before the bishop, after much altercation they submitted entirely to his ordinance. Having taken the advice of prudent men, and with the consent of the prior and convent of Castle Acre, patrons of the church, he has ordained that these tithes should remain to the church of Threxton and its rectors in perpetuity, with no impediment or reclamation by the prior and convent of Norwich, who each year at the feast of the Annunciation shall receive at Norwich ten shillings for these tithes from the rector, who if he fails in such payment shall be compelled by the bishop and his successors to make due satisfaction. The prior and convent of Norwich have resigned in perpetuity any right to these tithes and any others in the said parish at the time of the making of this ordinance. Drawn up as a chirograph and sealed by the parties and the patrons.   Norwich, 13 April 1243

A = Bodl. ms. Norfolk ch. 505. Endorsed: E xviii, de separatis decimis in Threkest' (s. xiv); approx. 175 × 110 + 15 mm., chirograph indented at top edge; three slits, in centre of which the stub of parchment tag; detached fragment of monastic seal.

B = BL ms. Harley 2110 (Castle Acre cartulary) fo. 131r (125r) (*inspeximus* by prior Simon and convent of Norwich). s. xiii med. C = Norwich, Norfolk R.O., DCN 40/5 (Norwich cellarer's cartulary) fo. 15r (14r). s. xiii ex. D = ibid., DCN 40/1 (Norwich general cartulary) pp. 92–4. s. xv in. E = ibid. pp. 279–81.

Pd from A in *Norwich Cathedral Charters* i no. 200.

Omnibus Cristi fidelibus ad quos presens scriptum pervenerit Willelmus Dei gratia Norwicensis episcopus salutem in Domino. Noverit universitas vestra quod cum inter dilectos in Cristo filios priorem et conventum Norwicenses ex una parte et Paulinum rectorem ecclesie de Threxton' ex altera super decimis duarum garbarum de dominico quondam Wigani Britonis in villa de Threxton', in quarum possessione utraque pars se asseruit extitisse, coram nobis controversia mota fuisset, tandem partibus ipsis post multas altercationes hinc inde habitas se super hiis ordinationi nostre simpliciter et absolute supponentibus, communicato virorum prudentium consilio et dilectorum filiorum prioris et conventus de Castelacra patronorum ecclesie supradicte consensu interveniente, ita duximus providendum, videlicet quod eedem decime cum pertinentiis pacifice remaneant prefate ecclesie de Threxton' et eius rectoribus inperpetuum absque omni reclamatione et impedimento predictorum prioris et conventus Norwicensium, qui singulis annis inperpetuum in festo Annunciationis Dominice percipient a rectore predicte ecclesie qui pro tempore fuerit .x. solidos apud Norwicum pro decimis antedictis, qui si in huiusmodi solutione cessaverit per nos et successores nostros ad satisfactionem debitam compelletur. Et predicti prior et conventus Norwicenses omni iuri quod in predictis decimis et aliis quibuscumque in parrochia dicte ecclesie de Threxton' sitis tempore huius nostre ordinationis habuerunt vel qualitercumque potuerunt habere pro se et ecclesia Norwicensi inperpetuum renuntiarunt, predicta decem solidorum perceptione contenti. Ut igitur ea que coram nobis acta sunt in hac parte perpetue robur optineant firmitatis, presenti scripto in modum cyrographi confecto sigillum nostrum unacum sigillis partium et patronorum predictorum duximus apponendum. Dat' per manum Rogeri archidiaconi Suffolch' apud Norwicum idibus Aprilis pontificatus nostri anno quarto.

> The *inspeximus* by prior Simon (of Elmham, d. 1257) indicates certainly that this is an *actum* of bp Raleigh rather than of bp William Middleton (1278–88). The letter of the prior and convent of Norwich, transcribed in B, notes that they have handed over to the monks of Castle Acre, as patrons of the church, a transcript of the bp's ordinance sealed with their chapter seal.

153. Waltham Abbey

Confirmation for the canons of the grant to them in proprios usos *by bp Thomas de Blundeville of the church of Guestwick, and also of the churches of Guist and Upper Guist and a portion in the church of Scarning which they had previously obtained, and also a portion of the church of St Peter, Wood Norton. He has also confirmed the taxation of the vicarages of the churches of Guestwick, Guist and Scarning made during the vacancy of the see by James of Elmham.*

[North or South] Elmham, 17 November 1241

B = BL ms. Harley 391 (Waltham cartulary) fo. 115v. s. xiii med.

Omnibus Cristi fidelibus presentes litteras inspecturis Willelmus Dei gratia episcopus Norwycensis salutem in Domino. Noverit universitas vestra nos dilectis nobis in Cristo abbati et conventui de Waltham ecclesiam de Geistweyt', quam Thomas de Blumvil bone memorie quondam Norwycensis episcopus de assensu sui conventus in usus proprios eisdem concedebat, auctoritate nostra confirmasse, insuper etiam ecclesias de Geyste et Geystorp et portionem quam in ecclesia de Skerning' retro temporibus optinebant, una cum portione quam optinent in ecclesia sancti Petri de Northun. Taxationes vicariarum de Geystweyt, de Geyst et de Skerningg' factas per dominum Iacobum de Elmham, sede Norwycensi vacante, de speciali gratia comprobantes eisdem pariter confirmavimus. In huius autem rei testimonium sigillum nostrum presentibus duximus apponendum. Dat' apud Elmham quintodecimo kalendas Decembris pontificatus nostri anno tertio.

> For earlier episcopal *acta* concerning these churches, see *EEA* 6 nos. 307–10, 423–5, and no. 116 above. There is a marginal note relating to this *actum* in BL ms. Cotton Tib. C ix fo. 151r, as an annotation to no. 116 above. For the history of these churches, see *Waltham Charters* xli–xliii. James of Elmham was more commonly known, and referred to himself, as James of Ferentino, rural dean of Holt and kinsman of master John of Ferentino, archdn of Norwich, by whom he was commissioned, presumably when it was realised that the vacancy following bp Blundeville's death would be a long one, to conduct institutions *sede vacante* in that archdeaconry. In an undated document, probably of October 1238, he taxed the vicarage of Guestwick as all the altarage and twelve specified pieces of free land; the abbot and convent were also to give the vicar a mark *p.a.* The canons were to retain all tithes of grain, hay and vegetables and the homage of those enfeoffed on the demesne of the church, and if any land should be bequeathed to the church, they might retain it in their own hands for as long as they might wish. The vicar should keep residence and discharge all obligations of the church to bp and archdn (fo. 114v of B). On 24 October 1238, he decreed that the canons should give to the vicar of Guist two marks *p.a.*, and that he should also have the altarage of the church and the proceeds of the chapel of Upper Guist; he should discharge all obligations to bp and archdn, should keep residence and should always have a fellow-chaplain to serve the chapel. A note after this document states that the tithes of a third part of the church of Wood Norton, assessed at five marks, had been conceded by the abbot to the vicar in lieu of the two marks in cash which he used to have. Also in October 1238, James of Ferentino ordered that the vicar of Scarning was to have all the altarage, to keep residence and to discharge all obligations to bp and archdn (fo. 115r of B).

154. West Dereham Abbey

Inspeximus *and confirmation for the canons of the charters of the bishop's predecessors by which they granted* in proprios usus *the churches of St Peter and St Andrew, West Dereham, and St Peter, Ringland, and medieties of the churches of Gayton Thorpe and Holkham.*

[20 December 1226 × 16 August 1236]

B = BL ms. Add. 46353 (West Dereham cartulary) fo. 121r–v (114r–v) (*inspeximus* by prior Simon and convent of Norwich). s. xiii ex.

Omnibus Cristi fidelibus presens scriptum visuris vel audituris Willelmus Dei gratia Norwicensis episcopus salutem in Domino. Ad universorum volumus notitiam pervenire nos inspexisse cartas et confirmationes predecessorum nostrorum episcoporum Norwicensium bone memorie Iohannis primi, Iohannis secundi et Thome de Blunvile, in quibus concesserunt et confirmaverunt abbati et conventui de Derham ecclesias sancti Petri et Andree de Derham et sancti Petri de Riglonde et medietatem ecclesie de Holcam et de Thorpe et ecclesiam de Riglonde[1] cum omnibus pertinentiis suis in usus proprios ad sustentationem fratrum, pauperum et hospitum perpetuo possidendas. Nos igitur, predictas cartas et confirmationes approbantes, intuitu Dei et religionis favore concessimus et presenti pagina confirmavimus predictis dilectis nostris abbati et conventui ecclesias supradictas, videlicet ecclesiam sancti Petri de Derham et medietatem ecclesie de Thorpe integre cum omnibus suis pertinentiis, et ecclesias sancti Andree de Derham et sancti Petri de Riglonde et medietatem ecclesie de Holcam per predecessores nostros taxatas sicut carte ipsorum testantur, salva etiam [*fo. 121v*] dignitate, reverentia et obedientia nobis et successoribus nostris et sancte Norwicensi ecclesie debita et consueta. In cuius rei testimonium fecimus presens scriptum sigillo nostro muniri. Hiis testibus.

[1] This repetition is probably in error for Stradsett.

For the *acta* inspected, see *EEA* 6 no. 312 (St Peter, West Dereham); nos. 427–9 (mediety of Holkham); no. 430 (Ringland); no. 431 (mediety of Gayton Thorpe); above, no. 117 (St Andrew, West Dereham); no. 119 (Ringland). The repetition of Ringland is probably in error for Stradsett, granted *in proprios usus* by bp Blundeville (no. 118). For discussion, see Colvin, *White Canons* 133–4.

APPENDIX I

ADDITIONAL ACTA OF THE BISHOPS OF NORWICH, 1070–1214

EVERARD

1. Wymondham Priory

Confirmation, at the request of Matthew Peverel, of his grant to the monks of the land of John de Bosco and also of an acre of his own demesne.

[12 June 1121 × 1145]

> B = BL ms. Cotton Titus C viii (Wymondham cartulary) fos. 89v–91r (fo. 90 is an original sewn in). s. xiii med.

Ebrardus Dei gratia Norwicensis episcopus omnibus sancte Dei ecclesie fidelibus salutem et benedictionem. Sciatis quod Mattheus Piperellus coram me confessus est ecclesie de Wimundham et monachis ibidem Deo servientibus se terram Iohannis de Bosco et unam acram de dominio suo libere et quiete in omnibus dedisse, sicut in carta propria confirmante declaratur, que in subscripto habetur. Petitione autem eiusdem Mathei [fo. 91r] prefate donationis me esse testem et confirmatorem coram Deo et omni populo insinuo. Valete.

> The charter of Matthew Peverel (thus called in the rubric to both charters) and Adeliza his wife which follows (fo. 91r of B) records their grant to the monks of land in Little Melton held by John de Bosco and Ediva his wife, given for the soul of Geoffrey Picot, Adeliza's brother, for whose salvation Matthew had pledged to the monks five marks of silver. They also granted an acre of their demesne for their own souls and those of their parents and successors, all to be held as freely as the Church should hold alms. Their charter was attested by Matthew and Matthias, their sons. A Matthew Peverel held four fees of the honour of Geoffrey de Mandeville in 1141 (*Regesta* iii no. 276), and a grant of rent in Melton to the cathedral priory was confirmed by pope Alexander III in 1176 (*Norwich Cathedral Charters* i no. 281).

WILLIAM TURBE

2. Crowland Abbey

Notification that, from the testimony of archdeacon Roger, Walter the dean and all the chapter of Diss, he knows with certainty that Ulfketell the priest acknowledged in full chapter that two parts of the tithe of the whole demesne

148   APPENDIX I

of Thelveton pertain, as they have long past, to the monks, from whom he has received them for his lifetime, rendering to them five shillings a year within the octaves of Michaelmas. The bishop confirms these two parts of the tithe to the monks.   [1146 × c. 1173]

   B = Spalding Gentlemen's Society, Crowland cartulary, fo. 199r. s. xiv med.

Universis sancte matris ecclesie filiis Willelmus Dei gratia Norwicensis episcopus salutem. Ex testimonio dilecti filii nostri Rogeri archidiaconi nostri et Walteri decani nostri et totius capituli de Discia plenam fidem firmamque certitudinem tenemus quod Ulfketell' presbiter in pleno capitulo recognovit duas partes decimarum totius dominii de Theveton ad ius monasterii de Croiland et monachorum eiusdem loci pertinere et a multis retro temporibus pertinuisse, et quod idem Ulfketell' presbiter easdem decimas suscepit de predictis monachis tenendas tota vita sua, reddendo eis pro predictis decimis annuatim .v. solidos infra octavas sancti Michaelis, fide ipsius interposita. Hanc igitur iuris sui recognitionem futuris temporibus insinuantes, easdem decimas, duas scilicet partes decimarum totius dominii de Thelveton, memoratis monachis de Croiland confirmamus et episcopalis auctoritatis testimonio corroboramus, et Rogero archidiacono, Waltero decano, magistro Stangrimo, magistro Nicholao, Rogero clerico, Ricardo de Rising' decano, Unsy clerico, Willelmo de Discia, Daniele de Sympling', Gaufrido de Burston', Ricardo de Ridon', Willelmo de Criuland' filio Goscelini et aliis pluribus huius rei testibus.

   For Ulfketell *persona* of Diss, whose son William succeeded him but was deprived by bp John of Oxford, acting on a mandate of pope Alexander III, see C. Duggan, *Twelfth-Century Decretal Collections* (London 1963) 11. This *actum*, relating to a church in the archdeaconry of Norfolk, confirms that Roger was archdn of Norfolk; he had been succeeded in that office before the death of bp William on 17 January 1174 (*Fasti* ii 64–5).

2A. Ely Cathedral Priory

Grant to William son of Theodoric of the church of Sudbourne, at the petition and presentation of prior A[lexander] and the convent.   [1146 × 1163]

   B = Bodl. ms. Laud misc. 647 (*Liber Eliensis*) fo. 104v. s. xiv in.

Universis sancte matris ecclesie filiis Willelmus Dei gratia Norwicensis episcopus salutem. Universitati vestre notum facimus nos concessisse et dedisse in perpetuam elemosinam huic Willelmo filio Theodorici ecclesiam de Suthburne cum omnibus pertinentiis suis, petitione et presentatione A. Elyensis prioris et totius conventus eiusdem ecclesie. Et ne hec nostra donatio futuris temporibus alicuius turbaretur iniuria, eam episcopalis auctoritatis privilegio communimus. Hiis testibus: Walcelino[a] archidiacono, Iohanne monacho et aliis.

[a] Waltero B; see *EEA* 6 no. 93 n. 1.

Prior Alexander first occurs February 1151 × June 1152, and had been succeeded by 1163. For a grant to William son of Theodoric of the church of Melton, see *EEA* 6 no. 86.

3. Nun Cotham priory

Notification by the bishop and Hugh abbot of Bury St Edmunds, acting as judges-delegate on the mandate of pope Alexander III, that the dispute between the nuns and Ralph, clerk of Ailby, concerning the church of Cuxwold, has been terminated thus: Ralph has abandoned his suit against the nuns concerning the church of Keelby and the money that he had demanded from them, and both parties have abandoned all former actions between them; the nuns have granted to Ralph the church of Cuxwold with its appurtenances, to be held for his lifetime, and therefrom he shall render to them each year a pension of one mark, payable in two instalments, and also two candles worth twelve pence. He shall remain always faithful and loyal to them, and shall commit his church to nobody to their detriment nor do any harm to them. Both Ralph and also Philip and Walter, canons, on the nuns' behalf, swore on the Gospels to observe this agreement. [July 1160 × 17 January 1174]

B = Bodl. ms. Top. Lincs. d 1 (Nun Cotham cartulary) fo. 14r–v. s. xiii in.

[U]niversis sancte matris ecclesie filiis Willelmus Dei gratia Norwycensis episcopus et Hugo eadem gratia abbas sancti Edmundi salutem. Controversia inter moniales de Cotun et Radulfum clericum de Alesby ex mandato domini pape Alexandri III coram nobis actitata super ecclesia de Cuchewald hac transactione auctoritate nobis commissa [fo. 14v] interveniente decisa penitus est et determinata. In primis idem Radulfus renuntiavit querele quam movit adversus easdem moniales de Cottun super ecclesia de Keleby et super pecunia quam ab eis exigebat, sicque ab utraque parte remisse sunt omnes querele et offense retroacte inter eos. Moniales vero iamdicte concesserunt predicto Radulfo ecclesiam de Cuchewald tenendam in vita sua cum pertinentiis suis, reddendo singulis annis eisdem monialibus unam marcam argenti nomine annue pensionis et duos cereos, pretii .xii. denariorum, in purificatione beate Marie. Ipsam vero marcam duobus terminis eis solvet, videlicet medietatem in festo sancti Martini, medietatem in nativitate sancti Iohannis, et ad Cotum deferri faciet. Idem quoque Radulfus eisdem monialibus fidelis semper et devotus existet, et ecclesiam illam nulli unquam ad dampnum vel lesionem iuris earundem monialium committet neque conditionem earum faciet deteriorem. Hanc itaque transactionem firmiter et fideliter observandam Radulfus fide et iuramento tactis sacrosanctis ewangeliis presito firmavit. Philippus quoque et Walterus canonici ex parte memoratarum monialium propositis eisdem sacrosanctis ewangeliis[a] iuraverunt quod hanc transactionem in nullo unquam violarent, set firmiter et fideliter observarent. Hiis testibus.

[a] ewangelii B.

Alexander III was elected pope on 7 September 1159, when bp and abbot were both already in office; but presumably the pope did not appoint judges delegate before his formal recognition in July 1160 (*C. & S.* I ii 837); before the bp's death in January 1174. Nun Cotham was founded 1147 × 53. For bp Robert Chesney of Lincoln's confirmation of the grant of Cuxwold church by Alan de Muncells, and his confirmation of Keelby church *in proprios usus*, both 1148 × 66, see *EEA* 1 nos. 203–4. For the grant of Cuxwold church *in proprios usus* by bp Hugh of Avalon, see *EEA* 4 no. 138.

JOHN OF OXFORD

4. Caen, St Stephen's Abbey

Institution of master Ranulf de Bisacia to the personatus *of the church of St Nicholas, Gayton, at the presentation of abbot Samson and the convent, to whom he shall render the due and customary pension of sixty shillings at the two Norwich synods.* [November 1188 × 2 June 1200]

B = Caen, Bibliothèque Municipale ms. 323 (Memorials of St Stephen's, Caen, by dom Jean Baillehache, c. 1600) fos. 64v–65r. s. xvii in. C = Caen, Archives Départementales, Calvados, H 1825 (from B, transcripts from St Stephen's) pp. 28–9. s. xviii.

Omnibus Cristi fidelibus ad quos presens scriptum pervenerit Iohannes Dei gratia Norwicensis episcopus salutem in Domino. Universis notum esse volumus nos concessisse et dedisse magistro Ranulpho de Bisacia ecclesiam sancti Nicollai de Gaithone[a] et ipsum in eadem ecclesia ad presentationem venerabilis viri Sansonis abbatis et conventus monachorum sancti Stephani de Cadomo, ad quos eadem spectat ecclesia, personam canonice instituisse. Hanc itaque ecclesiam cum omnibus ad ipsam pertinentibus memorato magistro Ranulpho confirmamus, reddendo inde annuatim predicto conventui debitam et consuetam pensionem sexaginta solidorum, scilicet ad duas synodos Norwicenses. Et ut hec concessio nostra et institutio firmitatem perpetuam obtineat, eam presenti scripto et sigilli nostri testimonio corroboramus. Testibus: Gaufrido archidiacono, magistro Lamberto, magistro Rogero de Len, Eustachio capellano, magistro Gervasio, Vincentio clerico.

[a] Grenthone B, C

Geoffrey became archdn of Suffolk after 13 November 1188 (*EEA* 6 p. lxxxvii). On the resignation of mr Ranulf, the church was granted by the same bp to the monks *in proprios usus* (*EEA* 6 nos. 180–81; cf. *EEA* 3 no. 365).

5. Coxford Priory

Remission of twenty days' penance to those of his diocese who contribute to the building of the new church of St Mary, in the construction of which the canons are hampered by their poverty. This grant is valid from 30 November 1188 to 29 September 1189.
                                                                30 November 1188

> A = BL ms. Add. Ch. 75321. No medieval endorsement; approx. 130 × 130 mm., tongue cut away from right; tie; fragment of seal, natural wax varnished brown.

Iohannes Dei gratia Norwicensis episcopus universis dilectis filiis per episcopatum Norwicensem constitutis salutem et benedictionem. Cum universos nobis subiectos episcopalis officii auctoritate fovere teneamur et in eis que ad nos pertinent ipsis sollicite providere, specialius tamen et propensius relligiosas domos nobis subiectas in quibus regularis vite et honestatis normam vigere cognoscimus in hiis que secundum Deum sunt promovere debemus. Sunt autem apud Rudham canonici virique relligiosi et honesti Deo famulantes assidue, quibus ad nove fabricam ecclesie erigendam in honore beate virginis Marie fundatam sumptus desunt necessarii; et quod propriis non possunt expensis, pium est et necessarium ut aliorum perficiatur auxiliis. Eapropter universitatem vestram rogamus attentius et exhortamur in Domino et in salutem animarum vobis consulimus ut karitatis manus aperientes predictis canonicis, de bonis vestris aliquas conferatis elemosinas, quatinus bonorum vestrorum pia largitione memorate ecclesie inceptum desiderate forme complementum assequatur, et vos de peccatis indulgentiam a Domino percipere mereamini largiorem. Omnibus itaque memoratis viris ad tam necessarium opus aliqua bona conferentibus peccataque sua confessis et vere penitentibus de misericordia Dei nos confidentes uberius .xx.^{ti} dies de iniuncta sibi penitentia relaxamus. Dat' anno ab Incarnatione Domini M° C° LXXXVIII° a festo sancti Andree usque ad festum sancti Michaelis proximo sequens valiturum.

> Rudham, subsequently known as Coxford, was originally founded by William de Chesney *c.* 1140.

6. Hertford Priory

Confirmation for the monks of the advowsons of the churches of Cavendish and Shipden, the gift of John de Limesy, as testified by his charters.
                                                      [14 December 1175 × 1193]

B = BL ms. Cotton Tib. E vi (register of St Albans abbey, badly damaged by fire) fo. 136r. s. xiv ex.

Omnibus ad quos presens scriptum pervenerit Iohannes Dei gratia [Norwicensis episcopus] salutem. Ad universorum volumus pervenire notitiam nos [concessisse et confirmasse] monachis sancte Marie de Hertford advocationem [ecclesiarum de] Cavenedis et de Sipeden', ex donatione Iohannis de Lymeysi [sicut carte sue] testantur. Et ut nostra concessio et confirmatio perpetuam [habeat firmitatem], eam presenti scripto et sigilli nostri appositione[a] communimus. [Testibus: *illeg.*], archidiacono, magistro Iordano de Ros, Thoma Britone, [*illeg.*] de Wretham, magistro Lamberto, magistro Waltero de [Calna], Rogero.

[a] appone B

For John de Limesy, lord of the barony of Cavendish, d.s.p. 1193, see *English Baronies* 30. His charter is on fos. 136v–37r of B; see also *Monasticon* iii 299–300. The witnesses demonstrate this to be an *actum* of bp John I.

7. Hertford Priory

Grant to the monks in proprios usus *of the church of Cavendish, the gift of John de Limesy, to take effect on the death of Hugh Leidet, the rector, saving provision for a vicar to minister therein.* [13 November 1188 × 1193]

B = BL ms. Cotton Tib. E vi (register of St Albans abbey, badly damaged by fire) fo. 136v. s. xiv ex.

Omnibus Cristi fidelibus ad quos presens scriptum pervenerit Iohannes [Dei gratia] Norwicensis episcopus salutem in Domino. Ad universorum volumus pervenire notitiam [nos] divine caritatis intuitu et religionis [favore][a] concessisse et canonice confirmasse monachis ecclesie sancte Marie de Hertford ecclesiam de Cavenedis in usus suos proprios cum integritate omnium ad ipsam pertinentium post decessum Hugonis Leidet eiusdem ecclesie rectoris perpetuo possidendam ex donatione Iohannis de Lim[esi] illius ecclesie patroni, sicut in ipsius carta continetur, salvis dignitate et debitis consuetudinibus sancte Norwicensis ecclesie et honesta et sufficienti vicarii sustentatione qui in predicta ecclesia ministrabit. Et ut hec concessio et confirmatio nostra perpetua et stabilis perseveret, [eam] presenti scripto et sigilli patrocinio communimus. Testibus: Gaufrido archidiacono, Thoma [Britone], Eustachio [capellano], magistro Iordano de Ros, magistro Gervasio.

[a] favore *om.* B

Geoffrey the chaplain became archdn of Suffolk after 13 November 1188 (*EEA* 6 p. lxxxvi).

John de Limesy died in 1193 (*English Baronies* 30). This charter is noted, from citation in the *curia regis* in a case between the prior and Hugh de Odingselles, husband of Basilia, sister and co-heir of John de Limesy, concerning the church, in 1221 (*EEA* 6 no. 225). In 1291 there was still a secular rectory, valued at £28, while the portions of the priors of Hertford and Stoke by Clare were assessed respectively at £5 and £2 (*Taxatio* 122b).

8. Hertford Priory

Grant to the monks in proprios usus, *by the gift of John de Limesy, of the church of Shipden, to take effect on the death of Walter de Bidun, the rector, saving provision for a vicar to minister therein.* [13 November 1188 × 1193]

B = BL ms. Cotton Tib. E vi (register of St Alban's abbey, badly damaged by fire) fo. 136r. s. xiv ex.

Universis sancte matris ecclesie filiis ad quos presens scriptum pervenerit [Iohanne]s Dei gratia Norwicensis episcopus salutem in Domino. Universitati vestre notum esse volumus nos divine pietatis intuitu et religionis favore concessisse [monachis ecclesie] sancte Marie de Hertford ecclesiam de [Sipendena] in usus suos proprios cum omnibus ad ipsam pertinentibus post decessum Walteri de Bidun eiusdem ecclesie rectoris perpetuo possidendam ex donatione Iohannis de Lymeisy illius ecclesie patroni, sicut in eius carta continetur, salvis dignitate et debitis consuetudinibus sancte Norwicensis ecclesie et honesta et sufficienti vicarii sustentatione qui in eadem ecclesia ministrabit. Et ut hec nostra concessio et confirmatio [perpetua] stabilitate subnixa perseveret, presenti scripto et sigilli nostri appositione communimus. Testibus: Galfrido [archidiacono], Thoma Britone, Eustachio capellano, magistro Iordano de Ros, Vincentio clerico.

Land in Shipden was held in 1240 by Hugh de Odingselles, husband of Basilia, sister and co-heir of John de Limesy. This appropriation apparently never took effect; the advowson was held by the heirs of Hugh and Basilia until the early fourteenth century, and in 1317–8 was granted by John de Odingselles to John Brown of Tottington. In 1336, in response to the rector's petition because of the regular flooding of the churchyard, the crown granted licence for the acquisition of an acre of land to be the site of a new church. In 1355 royal licence was granted for the appropriation of the church by Hickling priory, and then and in 1364 and 1375 the canons presented to the vicarage. On 18 August 1381, however, licence to appropriate was granted to the London Charterhouse, and in 1384 the Carthusians presented to the newly re-ordained vicarage. In the early fifteenth century the vill was abandoned and a new church built at nearby Cromer (Blomefield, *Norfolk* viii 102, 105–6).

9. Ixworth Priory

Confirmation for the canons in proprios usus *of the church of Little Melton, the gift of Ralph de Montchesney, saving the rights for his lifetime of master*

William of Calne, persona, *and saving also the maintenance of a vicar to minister therein.* [*c*. 1182 × 2 June 1200]

> B = Emmanuel College Cambridge, muniments box 20 A1 (roll of priory charters, badly damaged) no. 3. s. xiv.

Omnibus Cristi fidelibus ad quos presens scriptum pervenerit Iohannes Dei gratia Norwicensis episcopus salutem in Domino. Ad universorum volumus pervenire notitiam nos canonice concessisse et confirmasse dilectis filiis canonicis de Ixewrth' ecclesiam de Parva Melton' in usus proprios cum omnibus ad ipsam pertinentibus imperpetuum possidendam, ex [donatione] Radulfi de M[onte Canisio domini] fundi, salva possessione magistri Willelmi de Calna persone eiusdem ecclesie quamdiu vixerit ... suam ..., salva quoque reverentia, obedientia et debitis consuetudinibus sancte Norwicensis ecclesie et honesta sustentatione vicarii qui in ea[dem ecclesia] ministrabit. Et hanc confirmationem nostram, ut stabilis perseveret et illibata, presenti scripto et sigilli nostri appositione communimus. [Testibus]: magistro Lamberto, magistro Gervasio, Vincentio clerico, Vidone clerico.

> The charter of Ralph de Montchesney is no. 1 of B; it is almost totally disintegrated and is copied on the schedule of the roll. Ralph attests *Colne Cartulary* nos. 68–69, dated *c*. 1155, but also occurs 1175 × 1189 (*EEA* 6 no. 270). Mr Gervase occurs after 1182 (ibid. p. lxxxvii). For the later history of the church, see no. 70 and n.

10. Kenilworth and Lewes Priories

Notification by the bishop, W. prior of Westacre and R. dean of Lynn, acting as papal judges-delegate, that when a case between H[ugh], prior of Lewes, and R[obert], prior of Kenilworth, and their communities, concerning a third of the great tithe of the demesne formerly of Roger de Mowbray in Hampton in Arden, was heard before them, eventually an amicable composition was reached whereby the canons of Kenilworth should render annually to the church of Melton [Mowbray], which pertains to the monks of Lewes, two shillings at the feast of St Lawrence for the said tithes.

[14 December 1175 × 1186]

> B = BL ms. Add. 47677 (Kenilworth cartulary) fo. 35v (30v). s. xvi in.

Omnibus etc. Iohannes Dei gratia Norwicensis episcopus et W. prior de Westacre et magister R. decanus de Linna [salutem. Sciatis] quod cum causa verteretur inter H. priorem et monachos de Lewes et R. priorem et canonicos de Kenell' super tertia parte decimarum de garbis dominici quod fuit Rogeri de Moubray in Hampton in Ardena, quam causam summus pontifex [nobis] terminandam commisit, tandem amicabili compositione interveniente sub hac pacis forma sopita est, videlicet quod canonici de Kenell' annuatim reddent ecclesie de Meltun, que ad ius monachorum de Lewes pertinere dinoscitur, duos solidos pro decimis predictis in festo sancti Laurentii apud Kenell' etc.

> Robert, prior of Kenilworth, occurs from the late 1150s to 1188, and his successor occurs *c.* 1188. The predecessor of Hugh, prior of Lewes occurs 1174 × 78, and he himself resigned in 1186 to become abbot of Reading (*HRH* 119, 167). Roger de Mowbray took the cross for the third time in 1185 and died in the Holy Land in 1188 (*Charters of the Honour of Mowbray, 1107–1191*, ed. D. E. Greenway (London 1972), p. xxxii); before 1179 the lordship of his land in Hampton in Arden had passed to his son Nigel (ibid. p. xxxviii and no. 334). W., prior of Westacre, is probably that William who occurs in 1198 and 1200 (*HRH* 189).

JOHN DE GRAY

10A. Flitcham Church

Inspeximus *and confirmation of the charter of Morellus of Morley testifying that a small parcel of land next to the gate of the parsonage house of Flitcham, from the head of the stream as the causeway runs to the mill pond of Anselm of Hillington, pertains to the church. There had been litigation before the bishop concerning this parcel between G. of Norfolk and master D[aniel] of Morley, persona. The bishop confirms that the parcel of land and the causeway shall pertain to the church and its rectors in perpetuity.*

Thorpe, 2 September 1205

> A = Norfolk R.O., ms. Flitcham 703; no endorsement; approx. 158 × 74 + 16 mm.; parchment tag; seal and counterseal, brown wax.

Omnibus ad quos presens scriptum pervenerit Iohannes Dei gratia Norwicensis episcopus salutem in Domino. Inspeximus cartam Morelli de Merleia in qua continetur quedam portiuncula terre que est iuxta portam mansionis ecclesie de Flicham a capite vadi sicut calcea vadit usque ad stagnum molendini Anselmi de Hillingeton, quam ipse Morellus testatur in predicta carta ad ecclesiam de Flicham pertinere; de qua portiuncula coram nobis contentio [erat] inter G. de Norf' et magistrum D. de Merleia personam eiusdem ecclesie. Hanc igitur concessionem predicte portiuncule terre cum calcea ecclesie de Flicham factam eidem ecclesie et eiusdem rectoribus in perpetuum confirmamus, et ad huius rei testimonium huic instrumento sigillum nostrum apposuimus. Hiis testibus: magistro Roberto de Glouc', magistro Rannulfo de Harpel', magistro Roberto de Tywa, Hunfrido, Iordano capellanis, David de Rudebi, Alano de sancto Eadmundo. Dat' apud Torp' per manum magistri G. de Dierham, secundo die Septembris pontificatus nostri anno quinto.

> The rector is Daniel of Morley, the translator of scientific works; for references, see *EEA* 6

no. 315n. G. of Norfolk is probably Gilbert, who occurs as defendant in a case in the *curia regis* concerning half a knight's fee in Creake and Burnham (*Fines* ii no. 58).

11. Henry son of Gerold

Notification that with the consent of master Hugh, persona *of the mother church of Mundford, he has conceded to Henry son of Gerold that he may have a chapel within his residence at Mundford and a chaplain whom he shall maintain at his own expense, who before he ministers there shall take an oath to render immediately to the mother church all obventions received there.*   Norwich, 6 March 1206

> A = Gloucester R.O., ms. D225/T10. Endorsed: Carta Iohannis Dei gratia Norwyc' episcopi (s. xiii), fo. vi ii ˢge (s. xv); approx. 170 × 105 + 12 mm; parchment tag, seal missing.

Omnibus sancte matris ecclesie filiis ad quos presens scriptum pervenerit Iohannes Dei gratia Norwicensis episcopus salutem in Domino. Noverit universitas vestra nos ob favorem divini obsequii concessisse et hac presenti carta nostra confirmasse dilecto filio Henrico filio Geroldi, de assensu magistri Hugonis persone matricis ecclesie de Mundeford, videlicet ut idem Henricus habeat capellam suam infra septa curie sue de Mundeford, et capellanum suum in ea divina ministrantem, quem idem Henricus suis sumptibus honorifice exhibebit, ita quod capellanus qui in ea ministrabit prestabit iuratoriam cautionem antequam ministret in eadem quod sine delatione persolvet matrici ecclesie omnes obventiones quas in predicta capella recipiat, nec aliquid inde in usus proprios retinebit. Hiis t(estibus): magistro Alexandro de sancto Albano, magistro Roberto de Tywa, Iohanne de Uffingtun, Rogero de Norwic', Germano clerico, Alano de sancto Eadmundo, David de Ruddebi et aliis. Dat' apud Norwicum per manum Roberti de Dunelm' pridie nonas Martii pontificatus nostri anno sexto.

> Henry son of Gerold held half a knight's fee in Mundford and half a knight's fee in Cerney, Gloucestershire (*Fines* ii no. 250).

12. Hertford Priory

Inspeximus *and confirmation of the grant to the monks* in proprios usus *by bishop John of Oxford of the church of Cavendish* (Appx I no. 7).
                                                                      '*Crekel*', 27 June 1205

> B = BL ms. Cotton Tib. E vi (register of St Alban's abbey, badly damaged by fire) fo. 136v. s. xiv ex.

Omnibus sancte matris ecclesie filiis [I.] Dei gratia Norwicensis episcopus salutem in Domino. [Noveritis nos inspexisse] cartam bone memorie I. Norwicensis episcopi predecessoris nostri in hec verba conceptam: [Appx. I no. 7].[a] Nos [igitur hanc] concessionem sicut rationabiliter facta est auctoritate nostra con[firmamus et sigilli] nostri appositione corroboramus. Hiis testibus: Humfrido capellano, [Roberto] de Tywa, Iohanne de Offinton, Alano de sancto Edmundo, Iohanne clerico. [Dat' apud] Crekel' per manum magistri G. de Derham .v. kalendas Iulii [pontificatus nostri] anno quinto.

[a] *witnesses omitted*

John de Gray's itinerary is unknown between 12 June and 12 July 1205 (*EEA* 6 p. 379). Cricklade (Wlt.) and Crichel (Do.) seem equally possible.

APPENDIX II

REFERENCES TO ACTS OF THE BISHOPS, 1215–1243

PANDULF VERRACCLO

1. Institution of John of Ferentino (*de Florentin'*, but cf. *CRR* xiv no. 463) to the church of Sproughton [25 July 1215 × Michaelmas 1219, probably Summer 1218 × Michaelmas 1219]. Mention of institution *ex dono domini Pandulfi Norwicensis episcopi* in a case in the *curia regis* in Michaelmas term 1219 between Basilia de Furnival, claimant, and the prior of Holy Trinity, Ipswich, defendant, concerning the advowson. The prior called the bp to warrant, alleging that the church was not vacant, because John of Ferentino was *persona* by the bp's grant; Basilia claimed that the bp had done this unjustly, after she had obtained a writ, and the prior acknowledged this to be true (*CRR* viii 43). There was further litigation at Michaelmas 1220, and Basilia eventually recovered seisin (*CRR* ix 361).

2. Grant to the prior and convent of Prittlewell *in proprios usus* of the church of Stoke, with the dependant chapel of Nayland, saving a vicarage of twenty marks as taxed by mr Alan of Beccles, bp's official, Alexander of Bassingbourn, the rural dean and chaplains and other worthy men of the locality. The prior and convent are to present to the bp a suitable clerk, but if they fail to do so, he may nevertheless institute. The vicar shall have the altarage of the church and all the revenue of the chapel of Nayland, and also a messuage adjoining the churchyard of Stoke with two adjacent crofts. He shall take an oath that the church and chapel shall be faithfully served and that he will alienate nothing pertaining to either, and that he will not defraud the churches of Norwich or Prittlewell of their rights, but will enhance these as far as he is able. If delinquent, he shall submit to the bp's correction, and he may be removed should his excesses so dictate [25 July 1215 × 29 May 1222, probably Summer 1218 × 29 May 1222]. Detailed in a notification by Prior R. and the convent of Prittlewell, 29 May 1222 (Bodl. ms. Essex ch. 220).

3. Ordination of a vicarage in the church of Wighton [25 July 1215 × 16

September 1226, probably Summer 1218 × 16 September 1226]. The monks of Norwich subsequently complained that although bp Gray, granting this church to them *in proprios usus*, had conceded that they might have it served by a removable chaplain, Pandulph had subsequently ordained a vicarage, which they alleged to be beyond the resources of the church (mention in no. 91).

4. Institution to the church of Barningham of William Gernun, probably at the presentation of Eustace of Barningham [25 July 1215 × 16 September 1216]. Mention in a case brought by Robert FitzWalter against bp Thomas in Michaelmas term 1229 as to why he would not institute at his presentation (*Bracton's Notebook* ii no. 355).

5. Advice given to Peter des Roches, bp of Winchester, that prior John and the convent of Newark should pay annually to the prior and convent of Stoke by Clare £6 14s. from the church of Woking, as Stoke has conceded its rights therein to Newark; as legate [Summer 1218 × February 1221]. Mention in *actum* of Peter, bp of Winchester (*Stoke by Clare Cartulary* ii nos. 456–7).

6. Ratification of statutes made by the abbot of Bury St Edmunds for his house, certainly by legatine rather than diocesan authority [Summer 1218 × July 1221]. Mention in a confirmation by pope Innocent IV, 1254 (*Reg. Inn. IV* no. 7220; *CPL* i 294).

7. Appointment of Nicholas Rueland as his attorney in the *curia regis*, Michaelmas term 1219 and again Hilary term 1220 (*CRR* viii 94, 191).

8. Enquiry of pope Honorius III (it is not clear whether in legatine or diocesan capacity) whether an archdn may, without dispensation, also hold a benefice with cure of souls. The pope replied that such a benefice requires personal service, while the archdn's business is to act as *oculus episcopi*, and from this Pandulph would himself know how to deal with such cases [probably early 1220]. Mention in papal decretal, 11 May 1220 (*Reg. Hon. III* no. 2427; *CPL* i 71).

9. Indulgence of forty days granted at the translation of St Thomas Becket, Canterbury 7 July 1220 (*Walter of Coventry* ii 246).

10. Payment of 40s. to William son of Deodatus of Lynn for his quitclaim of land and rent of 9s. *p.a.* in Lynn [29 May 1222 × 16 September 1226] (*King's Lynn* no. 11).

11. Confirmation, as bp, of the grant to Kersey by Nesta of Cockfield of two marks *p.a.* from the church of Lindsay (*Leleseya*), now confirmed to the hospital by Thomas de Burgh, her husband [29 May 1222 × 16 September 1226]. King's College Cambridge KER 638 m. 3r).

12. Refusal to admit Geoffrey, clerk of G. [probably William] de

Montchesney, to church of Catfield [summer 1223 × November 1224]. Mention in papal mandate to the archbp of Canterbury, dated 4 May 1227, to assign the church to Berard de Sezze (Bernardinus de Setia), papal scribe. The church was of the patronage of the abbot and convent of St Benet of Holme and Montchesney, and was given by Montchesney to Geoffrey his clerk, to whom the official of Norwich, not having the authority to institute, gave simple custody. When the bp returned, he refused to institute Geoffrey, and the abbot and convent then granted the church to Berard (*Reg. Greg. IX* no. 81; *CPL* i 117–8).

13. Appointment of William de Chevereville as his attorney in the *curia regis* to represent him against William de Stuteville and Margery de Cressi, Michaelmas term 1223 (*CRR* xi no. 1397).

14. Grant to the abbey of Monte Cassino of two newly built houses in San Germano, February 1224 (Vincent, 'Election' 154).

15. Appointment of mr Alan of Beccles, Bartholomew of Brancaster, Simon of Scarning and mr Lando, any two of whom are to hear the testimony of four knights at Westminster a month after Hilary 1224, by whom it should be known whether the earl of Arundel had accepted the provisions made by Martin of Pattishall at Norwich concerning the making of peace between bp and earl concerning the liberties of Lynn (*CRR* xi no. 2709; cf. no. 2147).

16. Final concord made before the king's justices at Westminster, 23 June 1224, between William de Stuteville, claimant, represented by William of Harleston, and the bp, defendant, represented by William de Chevreville, concerning the advowson of Brisley church. An assize of *darrein presentment* was summoned. The bp recognised the advowson to be the right of William, and he remitted and quitclaimed it, on behalf of himself, his successors and the church of Norwich, to William and his heirs in perpetuity. William granted to the bp the advowson of that mediety of the church of Bilney, with appurtenances, which he and his predecessors had previously held (*Norwich Cathedral Charters* i no. 345). (For earlier stages in this litigation, which had been initiated in the time of bp Gray but adjourned because he was in the king's service overseas, see *CRR* vii 82 (1219), 240; ix, 30, 92, 250, 382 (1220); xi no. 1255 (1223).)

17. Final concord made before the king's justices at Westminster, 23 June 1224, between Margery de Cressi, claimant, and the bp, defendant, called to warrant by William prior of Norwich and represented by William de Chevreville, concerning the advowson of Blickling church. Margery recognised the advowson to be the right of the bp and remitted and quitclaimed it, on behalf of herself and her heirs, to the bp, his successors

and the church of Norwich in perpetuity. The bp recognised the manor of Blickling, with all its appurtenances apart from the advowson, to be right of Margery, to be held of him, his successors and the church of Norwich by the service of one knight, and he took Margery's homage and fealty (*Norwich Cathedral Charters* i no. 352). (For earlier stages in this litigation, see *CRR* viii 15, 82, 190–1 (1219), 240; ix, 30, 250, 353, 382 (1220); xi no. 1255 (1223).)

18. Last will and testament, in which for the most part he left his goods to the Holy Land subsidy and to his successor and the church of Norwich; reference in a papal letter, in which pope Honorius III asked the king to allow Lando, the late bp's proctor, administration of his goods in his dominions (*Reg. Hon. III* no. 6032).

THOMAS BLUNDEVILLE

19. Institution of a clerk to the church of Shipmeadow, at the presentation of Walter son of Bartholomew of Shipmeadow [20 December 1226 × 16 June 1230]. Mention in a case between Walter and Gilbert son of Thomas concerning the advowson, Trinity term 1230 (*CRR* xiv no. 421).

20. Hears appeal of Gerard Brockdish (*Brokedisse*) against sentence passed on him by Richard, dean of Coddenham; the sentence was upheld by the bp, and the dean then compelled him to submit to the sentence [20 December 1226 × Trinity term 1230]. Mention in a case brought in the *curia regis* by Gerard against the dean as to why he had heard a plea concerning two woods and other things not pertaining to testamentary or matrimonial jurisdiction. The dean appeared and stated that he had done nothing in contravention of a writ of prohibition, and both his sentence and the bp's verdict had been passed before any such writ was received (*CRR* xiv no. 392).

21. Grant of the canonical habit to mr William of Guist (*Geyste*), master of the hospital of Creake, with the consent of Alice of Narford, the founder [20 December 1226 × 26 October 1231]. On the latter date king Henry III assumed the patronage of the house (*Creake Cartulary* no. 1).

21A. Grant *in proprios usus* to the monks of Norwich of the church of Catton [20 December 1226 × 16 August 1236]. Mention in confirmation by bp Raleigh (no. 145).

22. Grant to the monks of Norwich cathedral priory *in proprios usus* of the church of Martham, and mandate to the rural dean of Flegg for their corporal induction [1227 × 16 August 1236]. Mention in an inquisition into the patronage of the church shortly after 23 September 1273 (*Norwich Cathedral Charters* ii no. 357). The church had been granted *in proprios usus* by bp John de Gray (*EEA* 6 no. 400), but an earlier *actum* of bp Thomas records only a pension of 100s. *p.a.* (no. 76). The inquisition records that appropriation was conceded by bp Thomas after the death of Adam of Walsingham, the vicar (see *EEA* 6, Appx I no. 74). The church is recorded as appropriated in an *actum* of bp Walter Suffield, 21 February 1246 (*Norwich Cathedral Charters* i no. 205).

23. By the grant of bp Eustace de Fauconberg of London receives *in proprios usus* the church of Terling, Essex, saving a suitable vicarage to be taxed by bp Thomas or his successors, and saving the rights of the church of London. When the church of Terling falls vacant by the death of a bp of Norwich, it shall be taken into the hands of the bp of London until the new elect of Norwich is confirmed. 1 July 1227 (*EEA London* ii no. 235: cf. NRO, DCN 44/154/1, the *inspeximus* by the dean and chapter of St Paul's). There is no record of a vicarage in 1254 (*VN* 345), but in 1291 the vicarage was valued at £2 (*Taxatio* 24).

24. Grant to E[ustorgius] the prior and the convent of Horsham St Faith *in proprios usus* of the church of Hellington (*Helgeton'*) with all its appurtenances, on which occasion the prior and convent conceded to the bp a vicarage of 100s. *p.a.* for a suitable *persona* to be nominated by the bp and his successors and to be presented to them by the monks. 27 November 1227. Mention in a notification by the prior and convent (Bodl. ms. Norfolk ch. 195).

25. Concession by the bp that crown pleas concerning land and fees, which he asserts should be conducted in his court, should on this occasion be heard by Martin of Pattishall and his fellow royal justices, saving the liberties of the church of Norwich. Mention in a writ to the justices in eyre in Norfolk that the king has conceded to the bp that assizes of *novel disseisin*, *mort d'ancestor* and other assizes over which there was dispute should be heard on this occasion by the royal justices in the bp's court in the presence of the bp's bailiffs, saving the rights of the crown. Those to be amerced shall be so amerced in the bp's court according to the custom of the realm by view of the bp's bailiffs, and these amercements are to be held in suspense until Michaelmas next, and not collected by royal or episcopal bailiffs until then; this writ is dated 18 June 1228 (*Close Rolls 1227–31* 56). On 21 July 1228 a further writ ordered the justices to send one of the rolls of their proceedings, sealed with the bp's seal, to the Exchequer before Michaelmas, when it would be discussed in

the king's presence whether amercements were due to king or bp (ibid. 65).

26. Final concord made before Martin of Pattishall, dean of St Paul's, and his fellow royal justices at Ipswich, 6 October 1228, between Robert son of William, claimant, and bp Thomas, tenant, concerning four acres of land and half an acre of meadow at Playford. An assize of *mort d'ancestor* was summoned. Robert remitted and quitclaimed to bp Thomas and his heirs all right and claim, for which quitclaim bp Thomas gave him 20s. (PRO, CP25/1/213/7/90).

27. Agreement made before papal judges-delegates (Martin of Pattishall, dean of St Paul's, Reginald, archdn of Middlesex and mr Robert de Arches, subdelegate of the bp of Rochester) at St Paul's, London, on 4 November 1228, between bp Thomas on the one part and the priors of Binham and Wymondham on the other, with the consent of the prior and convent of Norwich, the abbot and convent of St Albans and the convents of Binham and Wymondham, in order that perpetual peace might be made between them in the controversy over the obedience and reverence owed to the bp and, in respect of their parish churches in the diocese, visitation, procurations and the ordination of vicarages. The priors of Binham and Wymondham should be presented to the bp and should render to him canonical obedience; they should attend the synod, or should send their proctor or their excuse in writing, and they should sit among the other priors, but they need not change from their travelling clothes, that is cloaks and spurs, unless they so wish. It was agreed also that vicars should be instituted by the bp at the presentation of the priors in each of their parish churches in the diocese, that is, Wymondham, Binham, Snettisham, Dersingham and Happisburgh, and that the bp should admit the vicars presented without any difficulty. The taxation of the vicarages of Happisburgh and Snettisham already made shall stand, and the vicarage of Dersingham should consist of seven marks from the obventions of the altar, according to the just estimate of good men of the ruridecanal chapter under oath. In the churches of Binham and Wymondham the vicarages shall be assessed either at a sixth of the valuation made at the time of the twentieth [1215] from the obventions of the altar, to be assigned by the bp to the perpetual vicars when he institutes them; or else an eighth part, in specified portions, of a new valuation to be made by the trustworthy men of the chapter; the bp shall have the option which to impose. It was agreed that for the annual visitation of these parish churches by the bp or his commissary, the bp should have 20s. *p.a.* from Binham and 40s. *p.a.*

from Wymondham, to be paid at the Easter synod at Norwich. This composition was reached in such wise that there should be no diminution of the privileges of the monks of St Albans in other matters, and saving the rights of any other person. Reserved to the abbot of St Albans is the power of correcting the excesses of the monks and of removing and appointing priors, as seems best according to the Rule of St Benedict and the institutes of their order. Sealed with the seals of the bp and of the prior and convent of Norwich, the abbot and convent of St Albans and the priors and convents of Binham and Wymondham, 4 November 1228 (BL ms. Cotton Claudius D xiii fos. 47v–48r; BL ms. Cotton Titus C viii fo. 70r–v; mentioned *Gesta Abbatum* i 278–9).

28. Present at Bury for the feast of St Edmund in the third year after his election (20 November 1228); on the vigil abbot Richard gave benediction, the bp being present and wearing secular headgear (*Memorials of St Edmunds* iii 26).

29. Plea between Hugh Dod, complainant, and the bp's bailiffs at Lynn is adjourned *sine die* at Hugh's request, because the bp has said that he will make satisfaction to him; Hilary term 1229 (*CRR* xiii no. 1416).

30. Appointment of Reginald of Ringstead as his attorney in the *curia regis* to represent him in a case brought by Robert FitzWalter, Easter term 1229 (*CRR* xiii no. 2549).

31. Undertaking given to Hamo Ruffus, in a case brought by him in the *curia regis* against the bp's official for hearing and against Jocelin the chaplain for bringing a case relating to Hamo's lay fee in Westleton in the court Christian, that the bp will not permit Jocelin to implead him in contravention of a royal writ of prohibition; 20 January 1230 (*CRR* xiii no. 2349). (For earlier proceedings in this matter, see *CRR* xiii nos. 2137, 2245; Hamo Ruffus was a ward in the bp's custody, see *CRR* xiv no. 1661).

32. Bp Thomas sought, by reason of his liberty, all the amercements of tenants of his fee, levied both in the shire court and by the justices in eyre. The crown demanded by what warrant, and he replied by reason of the charters of the king's predecessors, specifically of king John, which he produced. He was asked if he wished to have judgement given on his charters, so that if he lost this case he would lose those amercements in perpetuity, but if he won he should have them in perpetuity. The bp agreed to this, but afterwards he said that his predecessors bps Gray and Pandulph were seised of these amercements and that he had found his church so seised, and he could not submit to judgement without the counsel of the archbp and his fellow bps. The crown sought judgement, because the bp had asked for judgement on his charters; Hilary term 1230 (*CRR* xiii no. 2612; *Bracton's Notebook* ii no. 391).

33. Appointment of John Terry as his attorney in the *curia regis* to represent him against the citizens of Norwich in a plea of service, Hilary term 1230 (*CRR* xiii no. 2361); again to represent him against Robert FitzWalter and against the citizens of Norwich, Trinity term 1230 (*CRR* xiv no. 116).

34. Assists at dedication of altar of St Mary at Dunstable priory by Hugh, bp of Ely, 1231 (*Ann. mon.* iii 126).

35. Raises loans for the king; a royal writ, dated 16 July 1231, instructs that those who gave him 200 marks are to receive satisfaction at the Exchequer at Michaelmas if they present the bp's letters testifying to the payments made to him (*Patent Rolls 1225–32* 440).

36. Composition made in the bp's presence between the prior and convent of Westacre on the one part and the lord John of Worstead (*Wrthstede*) and the prior and convent of Shouldham on the other, that the customs long observed to this day concerning lands granted in fee, leased (*locatis*), let at farm (*conductis*), sold, given in dower or in any other way pledged (*obligatis*) or alienated should remain in force; so that if any lands of the parish of St Mary the Virgin, Wiggenhall, which pertains to Westacre priory, or of the church of St German there, which pertains to the lord John of Worstead, or of the church of St Peter, which pertains to Shouldham priory and to the said lord John, should henceforth be alienated in any of the foresaid ways, the customs should cease on the lands thus newly alienated, so that the customary rights of each church with regard to the receipt of tithes from such lands should be unimpaired, and so too that if any land in any of these parishes has before the present time been alienated for a certain term, at the end of such term the receipt of the tithes should revert to the church from whose parish the land had been alienated; but if any land should be given in dower or *maritagium* and should thereafter revert to its former lord, the same right should be observed regarding the receipt of tithes.

Of the tithes of twenty-four acres of the land of John son of Richard in 'Nothesdale', of the two and an half acres of land of Susanna in 'Sadelbowe', of the acre of land of 'Blakenberg' and the half acre at 'Maluchil', the prior and convent of Westacre shall receive half in perpetuity, while of the said twenty-four acres and of Susanna's land the lord John of Worstead and the prior and convent of Shouldham shall in the name of St Peter's church have the other half, while John of Worstead, in the name of St German's church, shall receive half the tithes of 'Blakenberg'. The prior and convent of Westacre shall receive half the tithes of eighteen acres in 'Gernemuedale' between the two ditches of 'Gildenegare', be there more or less, for the lifetime of Amabel wife of Guy Wake, and St

Peter's church shall have the other half; but after Amabel's death St Peter's church shall receive the tithe of these eighteen acres in their entirety. From the ten acres of 'Chevervilledole' by the drove-road of St Peter's and from an acre which was held by Lawrence the shepherd, the prior and convent of Westacre shall receive all the tithes in perpetuity.

It was decreed by *dominus* R[obert] of Bilney, archdn of Norfolk and bp's official, and by others deputed with him by the bp, in the presence of and with the consent of the parties, that the tithes from the six acres of 'Hildebrand' should pertain to St Mary's church in perpetuity, but of the tithes of the two acres and three roods of John Selede in 'Burewenes-neweland', St Mary's shall have one half and St German's the other. The tithes of the two and a half acres of Adam son of Richard, the seven acres of Osbert the priest and the three acres of Seman Huvewine should pertain to St German's.

This was transacted in the church of Wiggenhall St German, with the consent of the parties, in witness whereof both they and the bp affixed their seals. 15 September 1231 (Norfolk R.O., DCN 43/36).

37. Notification to the king's justices at Michaelmas term 1231 that Joan, widow of Henry le Claver, had been solemnly married to a certain Ralph de Sundenlande, but that she was now excommunicate. Mention in a case brought by Joan against William le Claver for her dower, which William denied that she should have, because three years before Henry's death she had married Ralph de Sundenlande at Bramfield (*Braundfeuldiam*). She denied that she had married Ralph, nor in Henry's lifetime had she any husband but him, and Henry died seised of her as his wife, and also of the land which she now claimed as her dower. William repeated his allegation. Afterwards Ralph appeared before the justices at Westminster and stated that eight years before he had married Joan publicly *in facie ecclesie* at Bramfield and that she might not plead without him, and he stated further that Henry had once impleaded him and Joan and had claimed her as his wife, but Henry had died before judgement was given, in the course of the proceedings, and afterwards sentence was given in his, Ralph's, favour by the bp of Norwich, and Joan was adjudged to be his wife. The bp appeared and notified the justices as above, and William le Claver was dismissed *sine die* until Joan should be absolved. (*Bracton's Notebook* ii no. 642).

38. By the grant of abbot John and the convent of Hambye [Manche, Normandy] receives the church of Great Massingham. The church is of their patronage, and they have placed it at the disposal (*ordinationi*) of bp Thomas and his successors, to whom they have conceded the patronage,

so that they may confer it on whomsoever they wish and may dispose of it freely [25 March 1232 × 24 March 1233] (Bodl. ms. Norfolk ch. 249).

38A. Assent given and seal affixed by the bp to an agreement made before papal judges-delegates between the priors and convents of Holy Trinity, Ipswich, and Dodnash concerning rents and tithes in the parish of Bentley. Ipswich, 16 May 1232 (*Dodnash Priory Charters* no. 19).

39. On the day after the Michaelmas synod at Ipswich, 1232, following judgement previously given by the bp's official against Richard [of Hempnall], *persona* of Bacton (Suffolk), in a case brought by the prior and convent of Binham concerning an annual benefice of five marks in that church, Richard sought from the bp absolution from the sentence of excommunication, which the bp conceded. The bp restored to Richard possession of the church, which had been in the hands of the monks because of the judgement of debt against him, and also ordered him to render the annual benefice of five marks to the monks henceforth at the two Norwich synods. The bp also ordered mr Richard of Shipton and the rural dean of Stowe to go in person to the church and to hear the account of the fruits of that church received by the monks' servants, deducting therefrom the autumnal expenses, and to confer upon the monks such receipts as would cover their arrears of the annual benefice from the time that Richard received the church, reserving the residue to the bp's ordinance, but allowing for a petition for reasonable expenses which might be brought before any competent judge (BL ms. Cotton Claudius D xiii fo. 184r; see C. Harper-Bill, 'The Early History of Bacton Church', *PSIA* 37 (1990) 95–101).

40. Refusal by the bp to allow William of Felmingham to present to the church of East Beckham, alleged in a case brought by William against the bp in the *curia regis*, Michaelmas term 1232 (*CRR* xiv no. 2369).

41. In 1233 bp conducts visitation of his diocese, following the papal letter of 1232 to English archbps and bps ordering them to visit all non-exempt monks and canons (*Cotton* 117).

41A. Final concord made before Robert of Lexington and his fellow royal justices at Westminster, 2 July 1234, between the mayor and burgesses of Lynn, petitioners, and Thomas bp of Norwich, defendant, represented by master Thomas of Huntingdon. The mayor and burgesses complained that they had been prosecuted in the court Christian and the bp had excommunicated them because they had made a mayor without his consent. The bp conceded for himself, his successors and the church of Norwich that the burgesses and their heirs might henceforth elect and appoint as mayor whomsoever they wished from among their number, and as soon as he was elected, he should come to the bp wheresoever he might be in the diocese of Norwich, and at the presentation of the worthy (*proborum*) men of Lynn he should be admitted by the bp and his successors without contradiction. In return the burgesses conceded for themselves and their heirs that whosoever might be elected mayor should pledge good faith to the bp in all that pertained to the mayoral office, and should swear to maintain intact insofar as he might the rights of the church of Norwich. Made in the presence of the king, who gave his consent. (Pd in A. Ballard and J. Tait, eds, *British Borough Charters* ii (Cambridge, 1923) 362).

42. Complaint by the bp to the king that the sheriff of Norfolk and Suffolk has released excommunicates captured and detained in the king's prison by royal writ before they have made satisfaction to the church for their injury or contempt. Mention in a royal writ to the sheriff that such excommunicates should not be released before they have made satisfaction, 19 November 1234 (*Close Rolls 1234–37* 13).

43. Grant to the abbot and convent of Langley *in proprios usus* and in perpetuity of the church of Kirby Bedon (*Kirkeby*), saving a vicarage of eight marks comprising all the altarage, to the value of five and a half marks, and also two and a half marks to be paid from the canons' *camera* at the two Norwich synods, saving in all things the reverence and obedience due to the bp and his successors and the customs of the church of Norwich. Detailed in a notification by the abbot of Langley, sealed with the chapter seal, 26 June 1235 (Bodl. ms. Norfolk ch. 228).

44. Annulment of the marriage between Roger of Dauntsey and Matilda, countess of Essex, promulgated by bp Thomas and his fellow papal judges-delegate. This judgement was subsequently reversed by R[alph] bp of Hereford and his fellow judges-delegate, who signified to the king that they were legitimately married. Mention in a royal writ to the sheriff of Bedfordshire and Buckinghamshire ordering him to deliver her lands, etc., to Roger, 3 July 1236 (*Close Rolls 1234–37* 283).

45. Fine made between bp Thomas on the one hand and Roger de Scales and Reginald of Melton (*Meauton*) on the other, whereby the latter should pay the former sixty marks for the custody and marriage of the heirs of the constable of Melton Constable. Mention in a subsequent fine made by them with the king on 2 October 1236, whereby it was agreed that if it could be established that the bp was of sound mind when he made this sale and that he could speak, then it should remain to them quit, but if he was not of sound mind and could not speak they should be in the king's mercy for their bodies and chattels and should render up custody. The

fine with the bp must have been very shortly before his death on 16 August 1236 (*CRR* xv no. 1929).

46. Mention of a grant by the bp to master Gregory, chancellor of the legate Otto, of seventeen marks *p.a.* from the issues of the bpric. Mention in a royal writ to the custodian of the bpric *sede vacante* to make this payment, 8 May 1238 (*CPR 1232–37* 219). If bp Thomas did make such a grant, it was before cardinal Otto was appointed as legate on 12 February 1237, six months after the bp's death.

WILLIAM RALEIGH

46A. Synodal statutes for the diocese of Norwich, probably issued by bp William Raleigh [25 September 1239 × late 1243]. For text and discussion, see *C & S* II i 342–57.

47. Grant to the hospital of St Paul, Norwich, of a third part of the tithes of the bp's assarts at Thorpe [25 September 1239 × late 1243]. Mention in *actum* of bp Suffield, 24 February 1247 (*Norwich Cathedral Charters* i no. 259 (17)).

48. Grant to the monks of Longueville priory *in proprios usus* of the church of Witchingham St Mary [25 September 1239 × late 1243]. Mention in *actum* of bp Suffield, 2 April 1251 (*Newington Longeville Charters* no. 118).

49. Prohibition of a common market customarily held on Saturdays in the churchyard of Reepham (*Refham*). Mention in royal writ to the sheriff to cause another site to be provided, 27 May 1240 (*Close Rolls 1234–37* 193).

50. In the presence of the bp and of bp Walter of Worcester, an agreement was reached between Robert [Grosseteste], bp of Lincoln, and Oliver de Aencurt, kt., that the warren and fishery throughout the manor of Wooburn (Bucks.) shall be common to both of them, except that the fishery of Oliver's weir in the Thames shall remain to him and his heirs. Anything which may need amendment in this agreement shall be amended by the two bps, and they have both appended their seals to this chirograph. Westminster, 29 May 1240 (*Registrum Antiquissimum* iii 37–8, no. 672).

50A. On 18 January 1241 in the cathedral church of Norwich there was heard by mr Hervey of Fakenham, official of the Norwich consistory, a case brought by mr Vincent of Scarning, then master (*rector*) of the schools of Norwich, who claimed that the schools of Rudham by Coxford should be tributary to the schools of Norwich, and that no master should rule those schools except by licence of the master of the schools of Norwich. Eventually, by special mandate of bp William and with the consent of the parties, that is mr Vincent and the prior and convent of Coxford, patrons of the schools of Rudham, an inquisition under oath was taken from trustworthy men, that is masters who had ruled and scholars who had attended the schools of Rudham over a long period, and thereby it became obvious that the schools of Rudham were free from all subjection, oath and tribute to the schools of Norwich and should pertain freely to the collation of the prior and convent of Coxford. The official issued a decree to this effect, sealed with the seal of the consistory (NRO, ms. SUN/8 fos. 59v–60r; cf. Saunders, 'Coxford Priory' 311).

51. Appointment of Ralph of Gayton (*Geyton*) and Roger Hautesce as his attornies in the *curia regis* in a case concerning customs and tolls, Hilary term 1241 (*CRR* xvi no. 1392). They act again as the bp's attornies in 1242 (*CRR* xvii no. 2445).

52. Sequestration of the fruits of the church of Cawston, held by R. Brito. Mention in a writ to the bp ordering that, since Brito is indebted to the king, the sequestration is to be relaxed so that the debt may be more readily paid, 3 May 1242 (*Close Rolls 1234–37* 422).

53. Excommunication of Hugh Jernegan following the verdict against him by the official of Norwich in a case brought by Robert de Wynderville and Olivia his wife, Hugh's sister, concerning his detention of twenty-two marks left to her in the last testament of Hubert, their father, as her *maritagium*. Mention in a case in the *curia regis*, Michaelmas term 1242, where Robert and Olivia were cited by Hugh for prosecuting him in the court Christian contrary to a writ of prohibition (*CRR* xvii no. 838).

53A. Dedication of the church of Waltham abbey, 30 September 1242 (*Chron Maj.* iv 227).

54. Notification that an agreement was made between bp William and the lords William le Blunt and Robert of Pirho (*Pyrrehoe*) kts, to whom the lord Bartholomew of Creake has committed custody of the manor of Flixton, with certain other lands, for the acquittance of his debts to the Jews, concerning disputes which had arisen between them over view of frankpledge of the men of that manor, breaches of the assize of ale, the regulation of gallon-measures, all the articles relating to view of frankpledge, the delivery of judgements thereto pertaining and the receipt of amercements stemming therefrom, with the exception of articles pertaining to the crown, all of which the bp claimed to pertain to him and his court of South Elmham, but which the said knights claimed to pertain to them by right of the liberty of the manor of Flixton. The bp conceded to the knights a term of three years during which the bp's bailiff of South Elmham should once a year, at the summons of the knights' bailiff, come to their court at Flixton to hear by view of the knights' bailiff the frankpledge of their men and to hear pleas of breach of the assizes of ale, of false measures and of gallons, and otherwise as aforesaid. If legitimate gallons are found, in accordance with the gallon which the bp's bailiff shall have brought there, then they shall remain as hitherto, but if not, the false gallons shall be broken, and a true gallon according to the bp's gallon shall be found from gallons nearby, and if they are new gallons, then they shall affix to them the seals of the knights or their bailiff and of the bp's bailiff. On the same day, all amercements relating to the articles of that day shall go to the knights, but if from that day onwards in that same year the knights' men transgress in relation to false measures or similar offences through default of correction by the knights or their bailiff, so long as the complaints have come to them, then until the day of frankpledge the next year the amercement shall be the bp's. For this concession the knights have granted to the bp 5s. for each year of the said term, to be paid in equal instalments at Easter and Michaelmas, unless before the end of the term it can be clarified according to the laws and constitutions of England whether the foresaid liberties pertain by law and custom to the bp or to the manor of Flixton. This was done in the absence of Bartholomew of Creake, who was abroad, and saving to the bp suit of court by the said knights as before at his court of South Elmham, and saving to him also all other pleas of the crown, such as bloodshed and the like, with attachments before the beginning of the term of three years on Ash Wednesday [25 February] 1243. South Elmham, 18 February 1243. (Ipswich, Suffolk R.O., HD 1538/222/3). For Bartholomew of Creake, see Farrer, *Honors and Knights Fees* iii 428–9; his widow, Margery, foundress of Flixton priory, gave the manor to the nuns.

55. Agreement made between the bp and Hugh d'Aubigny, earl of Arundel, concerning their respective rights in Lynn. Prises should henceforth be taken for the bp and his successors and for the earl and his heirs either on board ship, on the quay or in the warehouse (*salario*) as the merchant chooses, so that wine merchants shall, after the prises have been taken, have leave to sell their wine immediately after their arrival. Empty winecasks in the town up to St Margaret's bridge and beyond shall be divided between the bp and the earl. With regard to the pleas of strangers, if they come by water and offend on the water, they shall be attached and fined by the bailiffs of the Tolbooth, common to bp and earl; if they come by water or land and offend in the town up to St Margaret's bridge, they

shall be attached by the bp's bailiffs alone to come before all the justices of the Tolbooth to be judged, and any proceeds shall be divided between bp and earl, unless these are pleas of the crown which the justices may not try in the Tolbooth. Those are termed 'strangers' who stay only a short time in transit in the town, or who have moved here but have been here for less than a year and a day. After they have been here for a year and a day, thereafter any plea arising shall pertain to the bp or his successors in a separate court. If anyone comes here and takes a wife and takes up land, he shall not henceforth be termed a 'stranger'.

The bp's men of the Tolbooth shall each receive 9d. of the bp's portion of the custom of the Tolbooth at Michaelmas, and the bp's bailiffs at their first appointment (*adventum*) shall swear that they will pay this render of 9d. to the earl and his heirs. The earl's bailiffs shall on their first appointment swear an oath of fealty to the bp and his successors, and the bp's bailiffs shall swear that in their office they will act faithfully and courteously to the earl and his successors, and that they will not subtract any right from bp or earl nor cause any diminution of their rights.

The earl concedes, for himself and his heirs, that his bailiffs shall allow the bp's bailiffs return of royal writs, and in this matter shall save the earl's bailiffs harmless.

The measuring of grain on the water, the custom called 'lopcop', tronage, and the measuring of gallons of beer, mead and other brews of merchants coming by water, and the toll of boats, shall pertain in perpetuity, as it has hitherto, to the earl and his heirs, so long as the earl shall instruct his bailiffs that they shall render justice in full to every man and shall deny justice to none. Similarly, the earl shall have as hithero the measurement of salt and coal.

The profits of the Tuesday market shall be rendered as hitherto.

The earl and his heirs shall render fealty to the bp and his successors for any tenement held by them in Lynn, so that there may be greater concord between them, and so that all those in the town, of whosoever they hold, may do the same. The bp and his successors shall swear on oath to pay the annual render of 9d.

The bp's bailiffs shall not on their own intervene on the water, which is common to bp and earl, nor shall the common bailiff of the Tolbooth intervene in the town of Lynn, except as foresaid concerning prises of fish coming by water, conceded to him as aforesaid.

The common bailiffs of the Tolbooth are enjoined, under oath, to show moderation towards merchants, and shall not bring actions against them because of which they might leave the town and go elsewhere.

All profits and revenues from the fair on the vigil, day and morrow of the feast of St Margaret shall remain to the bp and his successors, saving to the earl and his heirs what was previously due to them.

Merchants called 'strangers', who formerly in the said bp's time rendered full toll, and others who may come to the town, in whosesoever's third they dwell, shall in future pay full toll, unless this is relaxed by the special grace of the bp and his successors and the earl and his heirs, except for five merchants whom the earl concedes to the bp to pay half toll, but those who do not pay it are held to sell at will until they are quit of the half toll, and shall so remaining for the future [the meaning of this provision is very obscure].

The bp conceded that his own bailiffs should at their first appointment take a corporal oath that they shall do their best to maintain the concord established between bp and earl and that they shall surrender to the earl's bailiffs jurisdiction in the earl's land, as is stated in the writing delivered to the earl. Drawn up in the form of a chirograph sealed alternately by the earl and John [Maggs] on the one part and the bp and the prior and convent of Norwich on the other. Eccles, Wednesday 15 April 1243 (*King's Lynn* 96–9 no. 75). In the rubric to this agreement, among other matters in dispute to which reference is made in the text is also '*de domo Iohannis Magis in mercato amota*'.

56. Notification that, taking regard of the ancient custom of the diocese, the bp has, with the assent of his chapter, decreed that if rectors of churches survive until dawn of Easter day, they shall have the freedom to dispose of the autumn harvest, contrary custom notwithstanding. This is done of special grace, with reservation of episcopal rights in all other matters. London, 16 September 1243 (i.e. fourth year of pontificate). Pd in *C & S* II i 342, where the editors conjecturally ascribe this statute to Raleigh on the grounds of style of title and dating clause. One reservation must be that Raleigh is not otherwise recorded as being in London in 1243 (see itinerary) and it is perhaps unlikely that he would have come there late in the year, as his conflict with the king over his translation to Winchester came to a head. The ruling on this matter frequently cited in late medieval clerical wills was that of bp Walter Suffield, 4 October 1255 (*C & S* II i 498–501), which states that while it was commonly held that any rector or vicar alive on Easter day might dispose by testament of all fruits to be received by right of his benefice until the next Michaelmas synod, on the other hand there was a longstanding custom that the fruits of churches vacant from Easter day to the Easter (*sic*) synod should be at the disposal of the diocesan. Suffield decreed that all rectors and vicars should be free to dispose by testament of the autumnal fruits of their benefices, saving to the bp the disposal of all churches vacant at Easter and not yet filled, and he admonished his successors not because of this to delay institution to benefices until after Easter.

APPENDIX III

ITINERARIES

PANDULPH VERRACCLO (1215, consecrated 1222, – 1226)

1215

July 25	election as bp	Vincent, 'Election' 161
September 4–5	Dover	*Rot. Litt. Pat.* 182; *EEA* ix, no. 100, Appx II 6–7
shortly after September 13	sets out for Rome	*Rot. Litt. Pat.* 182b
November	Rome, Fourth Lateran Council thereafter remains at *curia*	*C. & S.* II i 48

1218

'midsummer'	arrives in England	*Chron. Maj.* iii 43
June 7	Worcester, translation of St St Wulfstan	*Ann. mon.* iv 409
September 1	appointed legate	*Reg. Hon. III* nos. 1609, 1621
October 18	London	*actum* no. 17
December 3	London, St Paul's, received as legate	*Coggeshall* 186

1219

April 8–9	Caversham	*Hist. Maréchal* ll. 17943–8
April 11–12	Reading	*actum* no. 23; *Rot. Litt. Claus.* i 390
April 17	Oxford, council	Carpenter, *Minority* 128 and refs at n. 1
April 30, May 10, 12, 13, 16	Cirencester	PRO SC1/630–3; *RL* nos. 93–4, 100; *DD* no. 32; *Cirencester Cartulary* 370, no. 410/442
May 16, 18	Lanthony by Gloucester	PRO SC1/6/34–5; *RL* nos. 101–2
May 19	Worcester	PRO SC1/1/41; *RL* no. 22
May 28	Lanthony by Gloucester	PRO SC1/6/36; *RL* no. 103
June 9	Gloucester, council	Carpenter, *Minority* 131 and refs at n. 12
June 11	Lanthony by Gloucester	PRO SC1/6/37

APPENDIX III

June 28–July 3	Hereford, council	Carpenter, *Minority* 149 citing PRO C60/11 m. 4d
July 4	Leominster	PRO SC1/1/42; *RL* no. 27
July 7	Much Wenlock	PRO SC1/1/43, 46; *RL* no. 28; *DD* no. 41
July 10, 11, 12	Shrewsbury	PRO SC1/1/47, 180; *RL* no. 117; *CACW* 7
July 15	Haywood, Lichfield	PRO SC1/1/38, 48; *RL* no. 118
July 17	Darley	PRO SC1/1/49; *RL* no. 119
c. August 2	Norham, meets Alexander king of Scots	*Foedera* I i 157; *Cal. Docs. Scotland* no. 732
August 8	Fenham	PRO SC1/1/50; *Foedera* I i 157
(?) August 28	Cawood	PRO SC1/62/3; Sayers, *Papal Judges-Delegate* 313
August 29	Doncaster	PRO SC1/1/39
September 21	London, New Temple, submission of king of Isles to pope	*CPL* i 69–70
September 24, 27	London	PRO SC1/1/183; *acta* nos. 18, 19
December 14 × 31	Salisbury	PRO SC1/1/167; *RL* no. 48; *CACW* 5–6
December 20	Downton	*actum* no. 5
(?) December 23	Wilton	PRO SC1/1/185
(?) December 29	Downton	PRO SC1/1/184
1220		
January 3	Stanley	PRO SC1/1/166
January 10	Bath	PRO SC1/1/44, 168; *Foedera* I i 157; *RL no.* 62; *DD* nos. 59, 61; *CACW* 6
January 16–17	Wells	PRO SC1/1/45, 169; *RL* no. 64; *DD* no. 62
January 20	Bristol	PRO SC1/1/170; *RL* no. 65; *CACW* 6
January 24–25	Malmesbury	PRO SC1/1/171–3; *Foedera* I i 158; *RL* nos. 67–8; *DD* nos. 63, 65; *CACW* 6–7
January 30	Cirencester	PRO SC1/1/174; *Foedera* I i 158; *CACW* 7
January 31	'Heynes', probably Eynsham	PRO SC1/1/175; *RL* no. 70; *CACW* 7
(?) February 1	Botley	*actum* no. 13
February 8	London	*actum* no. 15
March 8	London, council	*Chron. Maj.* iii 58; *Walter of Coventry* ii 243

April 3	Merton	PRO SC1/1/176; *RL* no. 85
April 26	Dunstable	PRO SC1/1/177; *RL* no. 92
May 5	Shrewsbury, meeting with Llewellyn	*Foedera* I i 159
May 17	Westminster, coronation	*Walter of Coventry* ii 244
June 5	Lincoln	PRO SC1/1/178; *RL* no. 111
June 15	York, Anglo-Scots negotiations	PRO SC1/1/38; *Foedera* I i 160–1; *Patent Rolls 1216–25* 235
June 28	Selborne	PRO SC1/1/38
July 7	Canterbury, translation of St Thomas	*Walter of Coventry* ii 245
July, after 7	London, negotiations for queen Berengaria's settlement	*Patent Rolls 1216–25* 243–5
August 9–11	Oxford, council	Carpenter, *Minority* 205; *Rot. Litt. Claus.* i 437; *Patent Rolls 1216–25* 263
August 25	Cerne Abbas	PRO SC1/1/181
August 26	Sherborne	PRO SC1/1/182
September 1	Exeter	Carpenter, *Minority* 214–5
September 16	Winchester	*Patent Rolls 1216–25* 252
October 8	Stamford	PRO SC1/1/40
October 13, 19	York	Carpenter, *Minority* 220; *Furness Coucher Bk* II ii 316–7
late October, after 24	London, New Temple	*Thorne* col. 1873
November 23–4	Canterbury, St Augustine's abbey	*Thorne* col. 1874
December 9	London	*St Frideswide's Cartulary* ii no. 820

1221

c. January 14	London, council	*Walter of Coventry* ii 247–8
January 25	London, St Paul's	*Walter of Coventry* ii 248
February 3 × 8	Bytham, excommunication of garrison	*Walter of Coventry* ii 249
February 5	London	*Walter of Coventry* ii 249
April 5, 17, 20	Gaywood	BL Add. ch. 36449; *acta* nos. 7–9
April 28	Salisbury, lays first stone of cathedral	*Ann. mon.* i 66
June 27–July 3	Shrewsbury, council	Carpenter, *Minority* 253–4 and refs.
July 19	Westminster, resigns legation	*Fasti* ii 56; *Flores. Hist.* ii 172–3
July 20	Westminster	*Patent Rolls 1216–25* 310–11

early October	departs for Poitou	*Ann. mon.* iii 75; *Patent Rolls 1216–25* 303

1222

May 29	Rome, consecrated as bp	*Ann. mon.* ii 296

1223

June 4	Gaywood	*actum* no. 24

1224

March 9	Stratford [? Langthorne]	*actum* no. 16
May 1	Westminster	*Patent Rolls 1216–25* 437
September 18, 19	Thetford	*acta* nos. 1, 27
November 6, 10, 14, 20	London	*actum* no. 25; *Rot. Litt. Claus.* ii 4b, 7–8b
before December 1	has set out for Rome	*Bracton's Notebook* no. 942

1225

February 25	Rome	*DD* no. 192
May 29, 31	Tivoli	*acta* nos. 2–3
December 27	Rieti	*actum* no. 4

1226

(?) March 17	Rome, S. Maria de Palladio	*actum* no. 14
September 16	dies at Rome	*Fasti* ii 56; *Cotton* 394 (*Bury Chron.* gives August 16)

THOMAS BLUNDEVILLE (1226–1236)

1226

December 20	Westminster, St Katherine's chapel, consecrated as bp	*Fasti* ii 56 (cf. *Bury Chron.* 6, December 21)

1227

January 24	Homersfield	*actum* no. 85
February 3	Ipswich	*actum* no. 54
February 12, 16	London	*actum* no. 39; *Cal. Ch. R.* i 6
February 26	Thorpe	*actum* no. 95
March 22	Norwich	*actum* no. 86
March 23	Bedingham	*actum* no. 52
April 5–6	Norwich	*acta* nos. 88, 119
April 14	Redlingfield	*actum* no. 105
April 17	Terling	*actum* no. 49
July 21	Gaywood	*actum* no. 96A
July 23	Wisbech	*actum* no. 40
early September	Antwerp, meets imperial ambassadors	*Patent Rolls 1225–32* 161–2

ITINERARIES

October 9, 16, 23, 30	London	*acta* nos. 30, 59, 89, 111, 116
December 5	Foulden	*actum* no. 41
December 17	Redgrave	*actum* no. 36

1228

May 1	Thornage	*actum* no. 107
May 8	Ipswich	*actum* no. 49B
May 22	Norwich	*actum* no. 72
August 28	Burwell, Bury St Edmunds	*acta* nos. 42, 55
November 4	London, St Paul's	Appx II 27
November 20	Bury St Edmunds	Appx II 28
December 18	[North or South] Elmham	*acta* nos. 43–5

1229

March 8	(?) [East] Bergholt	*actum* no. 29
(?) April 29	Westminster, council attended by bps	C. & S. II i 168
May 26	Blofield	*actum* no. 61
May 31	Bury St Edmunds	*actum* no. 62
June 5	London	*actum* no. 31
September 11	Thorpe	*actum* no. 102

1230

January 17	Colchester	*actum* no. 108
March 12	Norwich	*actum* no. 114
April 15	Thornage	*actum* no. 34
April 26	North Elmham	*actum* no. 123
June 5	Bury St Edmunds	*actum* no. 70
November 25	Ixworth	*actum* no. 60
December 20 × 27 March 1231	Hoxne	*actum* no. 73
December 27	Norwich	*actum* no. 51

1231

January 20	Dorchester	*actum* no. 56
March 1 × 24	Hoxne	*actum* no. 74
March 16	Thorpe	*actum* no. 33
March 27	Eye	*actum* no. 57
July 30	Snettisham	*actum* no. 118
September (?)	Glemham	*actum* no. 58
September 15	Wiggenhall St German	Appx II 36
October 15	Colchester	*actum* no. 50
November 23	Ixworth	*actum* no. 120
no month given	Dunstable	Appx II 34

1232

March 29	Norwich	*actum* no. 66
May 16	Ipswich	Appx II 38A

June 24	[North or South] Elmham	*actum* no. 103
September (?30)	Ipswich	Appx II 39

1233
February 17	Norwich	*actum* no. 91
March 27	Thorpe	*actum* no. 117
June 11	Gaywood	*actum* no. 67
November 23	Norwich	*actum* no. 47
December 6	Gaywood	*actum* no. 67

1234
January 6	Norwich	*actum* no. 68
May (?)	Glemham	*actum* no. 75
May (?)	Sibton	*actum* no. 106
June 5	Thorpe	*actum* no. 92
October 12	royal council	*C. & S.* II i 200

1235
January 6	Norwich	*actum* no. 54A
March 25 × December 19	Norwich	*actum* no. 93
August 1	Gaywood	*actum* no. 48
September 16	Playford	*actum* no. 69
September 23	Thorpe	*actum* no. 94
November 18	Butley	*actum* no. 37

1236
August 16	dies	*Fasti* ii 57

WILLIAM RALEIGH (1239–43)

1239
July 18	Westminster, baptism of prince Edward	*Chron. Maj.* iii 540
September 25	London, St Paul's, consecrated as bp	*Fasti* ii 57
October 25	Gaywood	*actum* no. 139
December 30	Blofield	*actum* no. 132

1240
(?) January 13	London, council attended by bps	*C. & S.* II i 284
May 15	Gloucester, negotiations with David son of Llewellyn	*Close Rolls 1237–42* 241
May 29	Westminster	Appx II 50
June 26	London	*actum* no. 138
October 30	Fakenham	*actum* no. 135

December 1	Norwich	*actum* no. 128
1241		
January 8–9	Newark (Sy.)	*acta* nos. 140–1
January 17	London	*actum* no. 125
February × March 24	Pontigny	*acta* nos. 145A–B
June 9, July 8	abroad	*CRR* xvi nos. 1664, 1862
November 14	North Elmham	*actum* no. 146
November 17	[North or South] Elmham	*actum* no. 153
November 20	Norwich	*actum* no. 142
November 30	Oxford, council of clergy, letter to Frederick II	*C. & S.* II i 338
1242		
April 21	Cherbourg	*actum* no. 133
June 20	Exeter	*actum* no. 131
July (?)	Wells	*actum* no. 124A
September 30	Waltham, dedication of new church	Appx II 53A; *Chron. Maj.* iv 227; BL ms. Harley 3776 fo. 38v
December 3	Thornage	*actum* no. 129
December 27	Norwich	*actum* no. 144
1243		
February 18	South Elmham	Appx II 54
April 13	Norwich	*actum* no. 152
April 15	Eccles	Appx II 55
May 2, 5	Hoxne	*acta* nos. 134, 137
(?) September 16	London	Appx II 56
September 17	papal confirmation of translation to Winchester	*Fasti* ii 57, 86
October 21	Hoxne	*actum* no. 151
November 6	Ipswich	*Dodnash Charters* no. 23
November 13, 16	South Elmham	*acta* nos. 137A, 148

APPENDIX IV

CORRIGENDA TO *FASTI* ii: *MONASTIC CATHEDRALS, 1066–1300*

ROGER, presumably archdn of Norfolk (pp. 64–5) is certainly so, since he reported to the bp on the church of Diss, within that archdeaconry (Appx I no. 2).

MASTER ROGER PINCERNA (p. 68) first occurs as archdn of Suffolk on 3 December 1242 (no. 129), as no. 144 (old reference, cited in *Fasti*, Norwich ch. 1718) is in fact dated 27 December 1242 rather than 27 May 1242 (*sexto kalendas Ianuarii*).

MASTER ALAN OF BECCLES (p. 70) first occurs as archdn of Sudbury on 19 September 1224 (no. 1).

MASTER WILLIAM OF CLARE (p. 70) first occurs as archdn of Sudbury on 3 December 1242 (no. 129, as above for Pincerna).

INDEX OF PERSONS AND PLACES

Arabic numerals refer to the numbers of the *acta* in this edition. These are followed, where appropriate, by references to the first two appendices (Appx I or II, followed by the arabic number of the entry therein), then to the third appendix (Appx III, followed by the page reference therein), and finally to the Introduction, indicated by the page number in Roman numerals. The bishops whose *acta* are edited in this volume are indexed only when referred to outside the section devoted to their *acta*.

The following abbreviations for counties and religious orders have been used:

Bd.	Bedfordshire	Np.	Northamptonshire
Bk.	Buckinghamshire	Ox.	Oxfordshire
Brk.	Berkshire	Sa.	Shropshire
Ca.	Cambridgeshire	Sf.	Suffolk
Db.	Derbyshire	So.	Somerset
De.	Devon	St.	Staffordshire
Do.	Dorset	Sx.	Sussex
Du.	Durham	Sy.	Surrey
Ess.	Essex	Wa.	Warwickshire
Gl.	Gloucestershire	Wlt.	Wiltshire
Glam.	Glamorgan	Wo.	Worcestershire
Ha.	Hampshire	Yk. (ER)	Yorkshire (East Riding)
He.	Herefordshire	Yk.. (NR)	Yorkshire (North Riding)
Hrt.	Hertfordshire	Yk. (WR)	Yorkshire (West Riding)
Hu	Huntingdonshire	Aug.	Augustinian canons
Li.	Lincolnshire	Ben.	Benedictine
Mx.	Middlesex	Cist.	Cistercian
Nb.	Northumberland	Clun.	Cluniac
Nf.	Norfolk	Gilb.	Gilbertine
		Prem.	Premonstatensian

Acold, *see* Occold
Acra, *see* Castle Acre
Acre, West (Nf.), *See* Westacre
Adam, abbot of St John's, Colchester, 50n, 129n
– man of Haughley church, 74
– the miller, 112
– prior of Butley, 1W
– son of Alfred, 121
– son of Richard, Appx II 36
Aencurt, *see* Aincourt
Agnes, daughter of Richard, 98n
– widow of Albert de Neville, 100
– wife of brother of Hugh son of Ralph, 29
Ailby, Alesby (Li), clerk of, *see* Ralph
Ailured, *see* Alfred
Ailward, son of, *see* Hugh
Aincourt, Aencurt, Oliver de, Appx II 50
Alan, bp's servant, xxxvin
– chaplain, *persona* of Bridgham, 54
– clerk of Stradishall, 112

Albini, *see* Aubigny
Alby, *see* Aldeby
Aldeburgh, Aldeburg (Sf.), chapel (of Hazelwood), 129
– church, 49
— perpetual vicarage in, 49, 129
— vicar of, *see* Westley, Adam of
– demesne of Snape priory at, 129
– tithes from, 129
Aldeby, Alby, Aldebi, Audeby (Nf.), church, 76
– tithes from, 146
Alderford (Nf.), church, xlin
Alençon, Alezon, William de, *persona* of Kempstone, 41
Alesby, *see* Ailby
Alexander II, king of Scots, Appx. II, 176
Alexander III, pope, 124a; Appx I 1n, 2n, 3
– IV, pope, 23n, 109n
– the cook, 121

INDEX OF PERSONS AND PLACES

– dean of Wells, 124A
– the forester, 121
– *persona* of Cretingham, 69
– prior of Ely, Appx I 2A
Alezon, *see* Alençon
Alfer, land of at Ridlington, 74
Alfred, Ailured, Alured, daughter of, *see* Yseult
– son of, *see* Adam
Alice, daughter of John Punchard, widow of William de Puleys, 130n
– widow of William of Waldingfield, 99n
Alnesbourne (Sf.), land at, 100
Alneto, William de, 121
Alto Bosco, Peter de, xliii
Alured, *see* Alfred
Alvechurch, John of, bp's official, xlvi
Ambli, William de, 49
Anabel, wife of Guy Wake, Appx II 36
Anes, *see* Candos
Anger, abbot of West Dereham, vicegerent of archbp of Canterbury and archdns *sede vacante*, 69n, 110n, xxix, xlix
Ansgot the chamberlain, 121
– son of, *see* Roger
Antwerp (Netherlands), Appx III (178); xxv
Apulia, Simon of, bp of Exeter, xx
Arches, mr Robert de, Appx II 27
Arderne, Thomas de, 121
– William de, 121
Ardfert, bp of, *see* John
Arundel, earl of, *see* Aubigny
— bailiffs of, Appx II 55
Ashbocking (Sf.), Robert son of Ernald of, 50n
Asketil, fee of, 121
Attebridge (*ad pontem*), Gilbert, 112
Attleborough, Atleburg (Nf.), homage, land and turbary at, 121
Attlebridge, Atlebrig', Atlebrigg, Attlebrigg' (Nf.), church of St Andrew, 92
— rector of, *see* Walter son of Geoffrey
Aubigny, Albini, Hugh d', earl of Arundel, Appx II 55; xxxviii–xxxix, lviii
– William I d', *pincerna* of King Henry I, 121
– William II d', first earl of Arundel or Sussex, 121
– William III d', second earl, 121, 123n
– William V, fourth earl, Appx II 15; xxix, liv
Audeby, *see* Aldeby
Avalon, Hugh of, bp of Lincoln, Appx I 3n
Avelina the widow, 112
Avenel, Oliver, xxviii
Aylsham, Eilesham, Elesham, Eylesham, Eylisham, Helisham (Nf.), church, 1–5
— vicar of, *see* Roffridus
— vicarage of, 2–5; xxiii, lviii
– manor, 2n

Bacton (Nf.), xxviii
Bacton (Sf.), church, Appx II 39; lx
– *persona of, see* Richard
Bacun, John, bp's clerk, lii
Badingham, Badingeham (Sf.), church, 133
– Okenhill, Hukehell in, separated tithes from, 133
Bainyad, *see* Baynard
Baldwin, son of Eudo, 121
– son of, *see* Thorald
Banham (Nf.), tithes from, 148
Bardolf, William, xxviiin, xliii
Barford, Bereforde, Berford (Nf.), mediety of church, 140n
– tithes from, 77
Barford, Bereford, John of, tithes of, 78
Barking, Berking (Ess. *or* Sf.), mr Richard of, *persona* of Melton, 13
Barlings, Barl' (Li), Prem. abbey, 29
Barnham Broome, Burnham (Nf.), foldage, land and mill at, men of, 121
Barningham (Sf.), church, xli
Barningham, Eustace of, Appx II 4
Barsham, West, Westbarsh' (Nf.), vicarage, 7
Barton Bendish, Berton', Bertunebinnedich (Nf.), church, 103; lvii
— rector of, *see* Elmham, Roger of
Barton Mills, Berton (Sf.), mills at, 49A–B
– tithes from, 49
Basilia, daughter of, *see* Matilda
Bassingbourn, Basingeburn, Bassingburne, Besingburn (Ca.), Alexander of, bp's seneschal, 5, 15, Appx II 2; liv
– constable of Marlborough castle, liv
Bastwick, *see* Woodbastwick
Bataille, William, widow of, see Constantia
Bateman, William, bp of Norwich, 23n
Bath (Som.), Appx 3 (176)
– Ben. cathedral priory, 124A
– prior of, *see* Robert
Bath and Wells, bp, of, *see* FitzGeldewin, Savaric; Wells, Jocelin of
Battle, de Bello (Sx.), Ben. abbey, 1–4, 5n, 30–33; xlii, lix, lxi, lxxi
– abbot of, *see* Reginald; Richard
– monk of, *see* Raymond
Bauburg, Bauburgh', *see* Bawburgh
Bavent, Robert de, 121
Bawburgh, Bauburg, Bauburgh' (Nf.), church, 140; xxixn, xlii, lxii
— rector of, *see* Mansel, John; Poynnur, William le
— vicarage of, 140
– demesne tithes of, 148
Bawsey, Beuseya (Nf.), church, 133
Baynard, Bainyad, Fulk, 19W
– Geoffrey, 74
– Ralph, 74, 121

INDEX OF PERSONS AND PLACES

Beaumont, Robert de, count of Meulan, 146n
Bec, Bec Hellouin (Eure), Ben. abbey, 125; lv, lxxii
Beccles, Becca, Beccl', Beccll', Beceles, Becles, Bekel, mr Alan of, archdn of Sudbury, 39W, 49W, 93W, 95W; Appx IV (182); xliv–xlv, l, lii; *and* bp's official, 1W, 3–4, 49AW, 76W, 80–2W, 87–8W; bp's official, 6, 15, 77W, 122n; Appx II 2, 15; xl, xliv–xlv, xlvii, l; guardian of spiritualities, xxix; rector of Bunwell and Haughley, xliv; rector of Shelland, xlivn
Becham, *see* Bircham, Great
Beck, Bech, mr Vincent de, *persona* of North Wootton, 123
— vicar of Bedingham, 113
– Walter de, demesne tithe of in Harpley, 74
– William de, *persona* of Playford, 58
Becket, St Thomas, archbp of Canterbury, 12, 38–9, 59n, 145A; xxvii, xxxvii
– translation of, Appx II 9; Appx II (177)
Beckham, East (Nf.), church, Appx II 40; xlin–xlii
Beckham, West (Nf.), church, 87
Becles, *see* Beccles
Bedefeud', *see* Bedfield; Bedingfield
Bedeh', *see* Bedingham
Bedfield, Bedefeud (Sf.), separated tithes from, 133
Bedfield, Bedefeud, John of, *persona* of Playford, 58
Bedford, Bedeford (Bd.), archdn of, xl; *see also* Houghton, John of
Bedfordshire and Buckinghamshire, sheriff of, Appx II 44; xli
Bedingfield, Bedefeud', Bedingefeud (Sf.), church, 133
– separated tithes from, 133
Bedingham, Bedingeham (Nf.), Appx III (178)
– church of St Andrew, 113
— *persona* of, *see* Romanus, Peter
— vicar of, *see* Bech, Vincent de
– document dated at, 52
Bedingham, Bedeh', Richard of, clerk, farmer of church of St Martin Coslany, Norwich, 96
Beeston (Nf.), Aug. priory, xixn
Begeton, Begetun, Begheton, *see* Beighton
Beicham, *see* Bircham, Great
Beighton, Begeton, Begetun, Begheton, Beketon (Nf.), tithes from, 77
— of bp's manor, 95
Bekel, *see* Beccles
Beketon, *see* Beighton
Belami, Ralph, 121
Bello, *see* Battle
Benedict, St, Rule of, Appx II 27
Benedict, son of, *see* Robert
Benehal', *see* Benhall

Benges, *see* Byng
Benhall, Benehal' (Sf.), Kelton in, separated tithes from, 133
Bentley (Sf.), land at and tithes from, Appx II 38A
Berch', *see* Bergholt, East
Bereford, Berford, *see* Barford
Berengaria, Queen, Appx III (177)
Bergham, *see* Bridgham
Bergholt, East, Berch' (Sf.), document dated at, 29; Appx III (179)
Berking, *see* Barking
Berkshire, archdn of, *see* Raleigh, William
Berton, Bertun', *see* Barton Bendish; Barton Mills
Bertunebinnedich, *see* Barton Bendish
Bested, Bestede, *see* Heacham
Besthorpe, Bestorp (Nf.), church, fishponds, men and turbary at, 121
Beuseya, *see* Bawsey
Beverley (Yk. ER), minster church, prebendary of, *see* Ferring, Geoffrey of
Beyford, *see* Boxted
Bicchieri, Guala, cardinal priest of S. Martino in Montibus, papal legate; 26n, 30n; xxii, xxv, xliv
Bicklinng', *see* Blickling
Bidun, Walter de, rector of Shipden, Appx I 8
Bigod, Roger, earl of Norfolk, xxxix
– Hugh, earl of Norfolk, Appx II 55; xlin
Bildeston (Sf.), church of, 120
– benefice of nuns of Wix in, 120
Billingford (Nf.), Beck hospital at, xixn
Bilney (Nf.), church, Appx II 16
Bilney, Bilenia, Bileneie, Biln', Bilneh', Bilneya, Bilneye, Bylneya, Byneya (*in error* Hibernia, Kiln'), mr Robert of, 39W, 44–5, 49–AW, 76–7W, 80–2W, 87–8W, 95W; bp's clerk, 78W; lii; clerk, *persona* of Haverhill, 11; xlv; official, 32n, 89W, 108W; archdn of Norfolk and official, 61–2, 73–4W, 115; Appx II 36; xlv, xlvii–xlviii; archdn of Norfolk, 34W, 66W, 102, 104
Binham (Nf.), Ben. priory, 26n, 34; Appx II 27, 39; lx–lxi
– parish churhc, Appx II 27
Bircham, Great, Becham, Beicham (Nf.), tithes, 77
Birlingham, *see* Burlingham
Bisacia, mr Ranulf de, *persona* of St Nicholas, Gayton, Appx I 4
Biskelund, *see* Wymondham
Blac, Eustace, 121
Blacson', son of, *see* William
Blackborough, Blakebergh' (Nf.), Ben. priory (nuns), 35; xlvn
Blafeld, Blafeud, *see* Blofield
Blakenberg, *see* Wiggenhall

INDEX OF PERSONS AND PLACES

Blakenham (Sf.), church, xlii
— *persona* of, *see* Rybo, Richard de
Blatherwycke (Np.), rector of, *see* Raleigh, William
Blaveni, Blavigny, Blawen', Simon de, xxxixn
— his wife, *see* Muriel
– William de, 151
Blickling, Bicklinng', Blicling, Bliclinge, Bliclynge, Blyclynnge (Nf.), church, 76; Appx II 17
– tithes from, 77
— of bp's demesne, 95
Blofield, Blafeld, Blafeud, Blofeld (Nf.), Appx III (179–80)
– bp's manor at, 61, 95
– documents dated at, 61, 132
– tithes from, 77
— of bp's manor, 95
Blois, William of, bp of Lincoln, 124A
Bluet, William, 121
Blundeville, Blumvile, Blumvill', Blunvill', Alan de, 34W, 89W
– Ralph de, 49–AW; archdn of Norfolk (*incorrectly* Suffolk), 110, 130n; xxviiin, xxix, xlviii–xlix; and *persona* of Thornham, 143n; xlviii
– Richard de, 38n
– Robert de, xxiv
– Thomas de, xxiv–xxv; bp of Norwich, 19–20n, 128, 135, 153–4; Appx II 19–46; Appx III (178–80); xx, xxv–xxviii, xxxvii–xxxviii, xl–xlii, ln, liii–lxxii; clerk of Exchequer, xxv; constable of Colchester castle, xxv; constable of Tower of London, xxv; custodian of vacant sees, xxv; dean of Tettenhall, xxv; rector of Ryston, xxv; as papal judge–delegate, 37; Appx II (43); lxi
— kinsman of, *see* Boyton, Robert of
— official of, *see* Beccles, Alan of; Bilney, Robert of; Shipton, Richard of
— seneschal of, *see* Wimer
– William de, constable of Corfe castle, xxv
Blunt, William le, kt, Appx II 54
Blyclynge, *see* Blickling
Bochland, *see* Buckland
Bodham (Nf.), church, xlin
Bohun, Reginald de, bp of Wells, 124A
Bologna, Bononia, Lawrence of, 34W
Bon Repos (Côtes-du-Nord), Cist. abbey, 140n; xxixn, xlii–xliii, lxii
— abbot of, *see* Eudo
Bosco, John de, Appx I 1
Botley, Botel' (Ox.), document dated at, 13; Appx. III (176)
Boxford (Sf.), mediety of church, xlin
Boyland, Roger of, bp's attorney, liii
Boyton (Sf.), Robert of, kinsman of bp Blundeville, xxxiiin, xlviiin

Bracon Ash, Brakene (Nf.), house at, 121
Bradel', *see* Stradbroke
Braiseworth, Briseword (Sf.), seprated tithes from, 133
Brakene, *see* Bracon Ash; Nayland
Bramfield, Braundfeuldia (Sf.), Appx II 37
Brancaster (Nf.), Bartholomew of, Appx II 15; liv
Bratton (De.), Odo of, vicar of Bratton Fleming, xxx
Bratton Fleming (De.), rector of, *see* Raleigh, William
– vicar of, *see* Bratton, Odo of
Braundfeuldia, *see* Bramfield
Brech', Briche, Walter de, clerk, 129W, 145W; bp's clerk, 137AW
Breckles, Becles, Breccles (Nf.), Thomas of, clerk, 128W, 132W, 140W; liii
Brentwood (Ess.), arrest of Hubert de Burgh at, xxviin
Bresete, *see* Bricett
Brewer, William, bp of Exeter, 124A, 145A–B; xxxvn
Bricett, Great, Bresete (Sf.), Ben. priory, 60
— prior of, xl
Briche, *see* Brech'
Bridgham, Bergham (Nf.), church, 54
— *persona* of, *see* Alan the chaplain
Briseword, *see* Braiseworth
Brisley (Nf.), church, Appx II 16
Bristol (Gl.), Appx III (176)
– castle, custodian of, *see* Ferentino, John of Harpley, Ranulf of
Brito, R., *persona* of Cawston, Appx II 52
– Thomas, Appx I 6–8W; *persona* of Methwold, 48
– Wigan, tithes of, 78, 152
Brittany, count of, *see* Stephen
– honour of, 148n; xli
Brockdish, Brokedis, Brokedyss (Nf.), Gerard, Appx II 20
– Robert of, rector of All Saints Wicklewood, 20n, 89
Brome, Brom (Sf.), separated tithes from, 133
Bromley (Kent), rector of, *see* Wenden, Richard of
Brown, John, Appx I 8n
Brundish, Burendis (Sf.), separated tithes from, 133
– Omundeswude, separated tithes from, 133
Buckenham, Bukeh', Bukeham (Nf.), rent in and tithes from, 121
Buckeslawe, *see* Buxlow
Buckland, Bochland, Geoffrey of, archdn of Norfolk, xlviii; royal justice, xlviii
Bucston', Bucstun, *see* Buxton
Budement, *see* Buttamund

INDEX OF PERSONS AND PLACES

Bugbrooke (Np.), rector of, *see* Sydenham, Philip of
Bukeh', Bukeham, *see* Buckenham
Bukesale, *see* Buxhall
Bulgeben, Ralph of, chaplain of chantry at Ilketshall St John, 137A
Bungay, Bungeia (Sf.), xxxix
– church of Holy Trinity, 29
— vicar of, *see* Ranulf the chaplain
– inhabitants of, *see* Hugh son of Ralph; Turkil, William; William son of Reginald
– priory, liin
Bunwell, Bunewell' (Nf.), demesne tithe of Hadeston in, 74
– rector of, *see* Beccles, Alan of
– tithes from, 10
Burefeld (*unid.*), Nigel of, 121
Burendis, *see* Brundish
Bures, Buris (Ess. and Sf.), chapel of St Mary, 151
Burewell', *see* Burwell
Burewenesneweland, *see* Wiggenhall
Burgh, Geoffrey de, Exchequer clerk, xxv, xlvii; archdn of Norwich, xxv, xlvn, xlvii; bp of Ely, 53; xxv, xlvn, xlvii
– Hubert de, earl of Kent, 113n, 114n; xxii, xxv–xxvi, xxxviii
– Thomas de, 71; Appx II 11
Burlingham, Birlingham (Nf.), Adam of, 95W
Burnehamestorp, *see* Burnham Thorpe
Burnham (Nf.), rural dean of, *see* Henry
Burnham, Richard son of Guy of, his son, *see* Capelein, Matthew
Burnham, *see also* Barnham Broome; Burnham Westgate
Burnham Thorpe, Burnehamestorp (Nf.), church of St Mary, 74
– church of St Peter, 74
Burnham Westgate, Burnham (Nf.), church of St Mary, 51
Bursemarc', William, 144
Burston (Nf.), Geoffrey of, Appx I 11W
Burwell, Burewell' (Ca.), document dated at, 42; Appx III (179)
Bury St Edmunds, sancti Eadmundi (Sf.), abbey, 2n, 6, 35n; Appx II 28; xlin, lvi, lxi, lxv
— abbot of, Appx II 6; *see also* Henry; Hugh; Richard; Samson
— barony of, 134
— sacristan of, papal judge-delegate, 10
— sacristy of, 8
— tithes of, 36
– documents dated at, 55, 62, 70; Appx III (179)
– hospital of St Saviour, 36
– scholars of, 35n
Butiller, le, *see* Pincerna

Butley, Butele, Buttele (Sf.), document dated at, 37; Appx III (180)
– Aug. priory, 37, 126
— prior of, 49; *see also* Adam; William
Buttamund, Budement, Robert, rector, subsequently vicar, of Thornham, 110, 143n
Buxhall, Bukesale (Sf.), rent in, 49
Buxlow, *see* Knodishall
Buxton, Bucston', Bucstun' (Nf.), tithes from, 77–8
– Kinestorp in, tithes from, 78
Bylneya, Byneya, *see* Bilney
Byng, Benges, *see* Pettistree
Bytham (Li.), Appx III (177)

Caen, Cadonum (Calvados), Ben. abbey of St Stephen, Appx I 4
– abbot of, *see* Samson
Caen, Walter de, xlin
Caister on Sea, Castr' (Nf.), tithes from, 137
Caister, Castr', Robert of, his daughter, *see* Isabelle
Calne, Calna, mr Walter of, Appx I 6W
– William of, mr, Official, xliv; *persona* of Little Melton, Appx I 9
Calthorpe (Nf.), church, xlin
Cambridge (Ca.), university, chancellor of, xl
Camera, Richard de, *persona* of Exning, 30n; rector of Haughley, xliv
Candos, Sara de, xlin
Canterbury, Cantuariensis, Kantuariensis (Kent), Appx III (177)
– archbp, as papal judge-delegate, 96; *see also* Becket, Thomas; Grant, Richard le; Langton, Stephen; Morton, John; Pecham, John; Rich, Edmund; Walter, Hubert; Winchelsey, Robert
— Official of, in Norwich diocese *sede vacante*, see Beccles, Alan of; Suffield, Walter
— vicar of, in Norwich diocese, *see* John, bp of Ardfert
— vicegerent of, in Norwich diocese *siede vacante*, *see* Anger
– archbpric *sede vacante*, 124A
– cathedral priory of Christ Church, 19n, 38–9; Appx II 9; lxxi
– Ben. abbey of St Augustine, Appx III (177)
Cantilupe, Walter de, bp of Worcester, 145A–B; Appx II 50; xxxvn
Capel St Mary, Capeles (Sf.), tithes from, 49
Capelein, Matthew, 51n
Carbrooke, Kerebroc (Nf.), tenement in, 121
Carbrooke, John of, 121
– Lucas of, 121
Carleton Forehoe, Karletune, Karltun (Nf.), 121

– church, 27, 121
– *persona* of, see Southwood, John of
– priest of, *see* Thurkil
– Newhage in, 121
Carleville, mr Robert de, official of archdn of Norfolk, 134An
Carlisle, bishop of, *see* Mauclerc, Walter
Castle Acre, Acra, Castelacra, Castellacra (Nf.), Clun. priory, 7–11, 40–8, 60n, 127–8, 152; xliv, xlvi, lvi–lvii, lix
— cellarer of, 127n
— cook of, 127n
— sacrist of, 127n
– vicar of, *see* Walton, John of
Catfield (Nf.), church, Appx II 12
– rector of, *see* Sezze, Berard de
Catton, Cattun', Cattune (Nf.), church, 76, 145; Appx II 21A; lxi
– tithes from, 80
— of demesne of prior and convent of Norwich, 79
Catton (*or* Cotton), Denis of, *see* Denis the clerk
Causton, *see* Cawston
Cavendish, Cavenedis (Sf.), church, Appx I 6–7, 12
– rector of, *see* Leidet, Hugh
– vicarage, Appx I 7
Caversham (Brk.), Appx III (175)
Cawood (Yk. WR), Appx III (176)
Cawston, Causton' (Nf.), church, Appx II 52; xlii
– *persona* of, *see* Brito, R.
– park at, 2
Cerne Abbas (Do.), Appx III (177)
Cerney (Gl.), Appx I 11n
Chedgrave, Chategrave, Chattegrave (Nf.), tithes from, 77, 79, 84
Chedgrave, Philip of, tithes of, 79, 84
Chediston, Chedstane (Sf.), tithes from, 148
Chelebauton, *see* Chilbolton
Cherbourg, Cherburg' (Manche), document dated at, 133, Appx III (181)
Chesney, Robert de, bp of Lincoln, Appx I 3n
– William de, Appx I 5n
Chevere, *see* Chevre
Cheverevill, Chevrevill, William de, bp's attorney, Appx II 13
Chervervilledole, *see* Wiggenhall
Chevre, Chevere, Ascelina, 21
– Hamo, 21n
— son of Hamo, xxxixn
– Robert, 21
Chichester (Sx.), bp of, *see* Neville, Ralph de; Wareham, Ranulf of; Wells, Simon of
– bpric of, custodian of *sede vacante*, *see* Blundeville, Thomas
Chilbolton, Chelebaut', Chelebauton' (Ha.),

John de chaplain, 129W, 145W, 149W; clerk, 128W, 132W, 140W; liii
Chipley (Sf.), Aug. priory, xixn
– subprior of, 99n
Chippenham (Ca.), church, 24–5
– vicarage, 24–5
Cinque Ports, xxv
Cirencester (Gl.), Appx III (175–6)
Clare (Sf.), Gilbert of, earl of Hertford and Gloucester, 112; lvi
– Richard I of, 125n
– Richard of, earl of Hertford and Gloucester, 26, 111; lv
– Thomas of, 58n
– William of, mr, 128W, 135W, 150W; archdn of Sudbury, 129W, 137AW, 145–5W; Appx IV 182; xlvii–xlvii, l, liii; official, 134An, 140; xlvi, liii; rector of Redenhall, xlvin
Claver, Henry le, Appx II 37
— his widow, *see* Joan
– William de, Appx II 37
Claverham (So.), Hardric of, 19W
Clewe, John, 108
Cnoteshale, *see* Knoddishall
Cockfield (Sf.), Nesta of, lady of Lindsay, 71n, 72; Appx II 11
Cockthorpe, Cokethorp, Kokestorp' (Nf.), tithes from, 77–8
Coclesworth, Cukelesword, Cukelesworde (Sf.), tithes from, 49
Coddenham (Sf.), rural dean of, *see* Richard
Cok', *see* Coxford
Cokethorp, *see* Cockthorpe
Colchester, Colecestr', Colecestria (Ess.), Ben. abbey of St John, 49–50, 129; lv, lxi, lxiv–lxv
— abbot of, *see* Adam; William
— precentor of, 50
– castle, custodian of, *see* Blundeville, Thomas de
– document dated at, 50, 109; Appx III (179)
Colet, Richard, 19W
Coletun, *see* Colton
Coleville, Ernald de, 69n
Colton, Coletun (Nf.), church, 121
– priest of, *see* Ulf
Colton, Athelstan of, 121
Colveston, Colvestun' (Nf.), church, 74
Congham, Kangham (Nf.), church, 121
Constantia, widow of William Bataille, xlin
Constantine the chaplain, 98n
Corfe (Do.), castle, constable of, *see* Blundeville, William de
Cornwall, eyre of 1233 in, xxx
Cornwall, earl of, *see* Richard
Cosman, Ralph, 22
Costessy, Costhes' (Nf.), livn
– church, xxixn

INDEX OF PERSONS AND PLACES

– tithes from, 146, 148
Cotton, Bartholomew, chronicler, xxii
– (or Catton), Denis of, see Denis the clerk
Cotun, see Nun Cotham
Coventry (Wa.), Ben. cathedral priory, xxxii, liin
– and Lichfield (St.), bp of, see Muschamp, Geoffrey
Coxford, Cok' (Nf.), Aug. priory, 51–2; Appx I 5; Appx II 50A
Crane, Geoffrey, 149n
Cratfield, Crattefeld (Sf.), church, 102, 104
– vicar of, see Thomas
– vicarage, 102
Creake, Crek (Nf.), hospital, later Aug. abbey, 130; xixn, xxix, xlix
– master of, see Guist, mr William of
Creake, North (Northcrek, Northcreik, Northcreyke (Nf.), tithes from, 77, 79, 84
Creake, South, Sudcrec (Nf.), vicarage, 8–9
– vicar of, see James; Urbe, John Iudicis de
Creake, Bartholomew of, kt., Appx II 54; xlin, lxiii
– Robert of, vicar of West Newton, 43
Creeting St Peter, Creting (Sf.), church, xlin
– separated tithes from, 133
Crek, see Creake
Crekel', see Crichel; Cricklade
Cremplesham, see Crimplesham
Cressi, Creysi, Margery de, 49, 78; Appx II 13, 17
– Roger de, xxxviii
Cressingham, Great (Nf.), church, 76; xlin
– Osegoteshag' in, demesne tithe of, 78
Creting, see Creeting St Peter
Cretingham, Cretingeham (Sf.), church, 69
– persona of, see Alexander
– vicarage, 69; xxix
Cretingham, lady Agnes of, 69
Creysi, see Cressi
Crichel, Crekel' (Do.), ? document dated at, Appx I 12n
Cricklade, Crekel' (Wlt.), ? document dated at, Appx I 12n
Crimplesham, Cremplesham (Nf.), church, 150
– tithes from, 150
– vicar of, see Huntingdon, Thomas of
Croinden, see Croydon
Cromer (Nf.), church, Appx I 8n
Crowland, Criuland, Croiland (Li.), Ben. abbey, Appx I 2; xxxii
Crowland, William son of Goscelin of, Appx I 2W
Croydon, Croinden, Crouwden, Croydein, Croydene, Croyenden (Ca. or Sy.), mr Andrew of, 34W, 66W, 73–4W; lii
– Robert of, 34W

Cruce, Richard de, 108
Cuchewald, see Cuxwold
Cukelesworthe, Cukelesword, see Coclesworth
Curcun, Richard de, 121
– William le, 121
Cuxwold, Cuchewald (Li.), church, Appx I 3

Dalham (Sf.), rector of, 125n
Darel, Thomas, xxxvn–xxxvi
Darley (Db.), Aug. abbey, Appx III (176)
Dauntsey, Roger of, Appx II 44
David son of Llewellyn, Appx III (180); xxxv
Deinardeston', see Denston
Denham (Bk.), rector of, see Ferring, Geoffrey of
Denis the clerk, 49–Aw, 73–4W, 89W, 95W; (of Catton or Cotton), 39W, 93W; bp's clerk, 66W, 78W, 80–2W; liii
Dennington, Dinnevetun' (Sf.), separated tithes from, 133
Denston, Deinardeston' (Sf.), chapel, mills and tithes at, 112
Deopham, Depham', Dypeham (Nf.), church, 38–9
— persona of, see Robert the priest
– vicarage in, 38–9; lviii
– manor, xxv
– tithes from, 38–9
– Sumercroft in, 39
– Tweyt in, 39
Dereham, West, Derham (Nf.), Prem. abbey, 23n, 117–19, 154
— abbot of, See Anger; Ralph
– church of St Andrew, 117 and n, 154
— vicarage of, 117
– church of St Peter, 117n, 154
Dereham, Dierham, mr Geoffrey of, datary, Appx I 10A, 12
Dersingham (Nf.), church, Appx II 27
Devon and Cornwall, sheriff of, see Raleigh, William
Dinnevetun', see Dennington
Diss, Discia (Nf.), persona of, see Ulfketell
– rural chapter of, Appx I 2
– rural dean of, see Walter
Diss, William of, Appx I 2W
Dod, Hugh, Appx II 29; xxxviii
– John, 121
Dodnash (Sf.), Aug. priory, Appx I 38A
Doncaster (Yk. WR), Appx III (176)
Doncheswelle, see Dunkeswell
Donewycum, see Dunwich
Dorchester (probably Ox.), document dated at, 56; Appx III (179)
Dover (Kent), document dated at, Appx III (175)

– Ben. priory of St Martin, 12
— altar of St Thomas the Martyr in, 12
Downton (Wlt.), document dated at, 6, Appx III (176)
Dublin (co. Dublin), archbp of, *see* Luke the chaplain
Dule, son of, *see* Thomas
Dunelm', *see* Durham
Duneton, *see* Downton
Duneswell', *see* Dunkeswell
Dunham, Great (Nf.), church of St Mary, 40
– *persona* of, *see* Walpole, Edmund of
Dunham, Richard of, 121
Dunkeswell, Doncheswelle, Duneswell', Dunkeswell' (De.), William of, clerk, 128–9W, 132W, 140W, 145W, 149W; bp's clerk, 137AW; liii
Dunstable (Bd.), Appx III (177, 179)
– Aug. priory, Appx II 34
— prior of, *see* Richard
Dunwich, Donewycum (Sf.), church of All Saints, 55, 132–3; lvii
— pension from, lvii
— vicar of, see Sunburne, John of
– of St Bartholomew, 133
– of St John, 133
– of St Leonard, 133
– of St Martin, 56, 133
— rector and vicar of, *see* Dunwich, Peter of
– of St Nicholas, 133
– of St Peter, 133
– rural dean of, *see* Philip
Dunwich, John of, 132n
– Peter of, rector and vicar of St Martin's, Dunwich, 56
Durham, Dunelm' (Du.), Robert of, datary, Appx I 11
Dya, mr John de, rector of Thornham, 143n
Dypeham, *see* Deopham

Easton (Nf.), church, xlin
Eccles (Nf.), document dated at, Appx II 55; Appx III (181)
Edingthorpe (Nf.), church, xlin
Edmund, clerk of prior of Norwich, 80W, 89W
Edward, prince, baptism of, Appx III (180)
Eilesham, Elesham, *see* Aylsham
Elham, Kent, church, portioner of, *see* Ferring, Geoffrey of
Ellingham, Elingham (Nf.), rent in, 121
Elmesete, *see* Elmsett
Elmham, North (Nf.) *or* South (Sf.), documents dated at, 43–5, 103, 153; Appx. III (179–81)
– bp's manor at, 43–4, 103
Elmham, North, Elmeham, Elmham, Northelham (Nf.), 146

– bp's manor at, 123; Appx. III (179, 181)
– church, 142; lxii
— vicar of, *see* Hugh
— vicarage of, 142
– demesne of prior and convent of Norwich at, 142
– inhabitants of, *see* Kedere, Elias le; Ringe, Henry; Sparuwe, Richard; Ymein, Simon
– places in:
— Botme, 142
— Stonhull', 142
– tithes from, 77–8
Elmham, South, Helmam, Suthelmam, Suthelmeham (Sf.), 127, 137A, 148; Appx II 54; Appx III (181)
– bailiff of, 134A
– court of, 134A; Appx II 54
– places in:
— Kyndele, 148
— Rothinges, 148
– tithes from, 148
Elmham, Adam of, 34W, 69W
– James of, *see* Ferentino
– Roger of, rector of Barton Bendish, 103
– Simon, prior of Norwich, 128, 130, 139, 142, 144, 152n; bp-elect of Norwich, xxviii
Elmsett, Elmesete (Sf.), tithes from, 49
Elveric son of Thurstan, *persona* of Thornham, 143n
Ely, Elyensis (Ca.), bp of, xlin, xlii, lv; *see also*, Burgh, Geoffrey de; Eustace; Fountains, John of; Northwold, Hugh of; bp-elect, *see* York, Robert of
– Ben. cathedral priory, 13–4, 53–4; Appx I 2A
— prior of, *see* Alexander
– see, custodian of *sede vacante*, see Blundeville, Thomas
Emingestun', *see* Hemmingstone
Emma, son of, *see* Thomas
Emneth, Enemede (Nf.), chapel, 74
– demesne of Lewes priory, 74
Engayne, Viel, xxxii
Enveyse, William l', 19W
Ercall, Alexander of, prior of Haughmond, 134A
Eriswell, Ereswelle (Sf.), church, 49–B
— rector of, lxi; *see also* Peter
– mills in, 49–B
– tithes from, 49–B
Essex, countess of, *see* Matilda
Estfeld, *see* Wymondham
Eudo, abbot of Bon Repos, 140n
– son of, *see* Baldwin
Eustace, bp of Ely, 124A
– the chaplain, Appx I 4W
Eustorgius, prior of Horsham St Faith, Appx II 24

Everard, bp of Norwich, 148n, Appx I 1
Exeter, Exon', Exoniensis (De.), 131, Appx III (177, 181)
– bp of, *see* Apulia, Simon of; Brewer, William; Marshall, Henry
– cathedral church of St Mary and St Peter, 131; lxx
—— treasurer of, *see* Raleigh, William
Exeter, Walter of, chaplain, 145W; clerk, 132W; mr, 128W, 135W, 140W; bp's chaplain and clerk, liii
– William of, chaplain (? *in error for Walter*), 129W
Exning, Ixning (Sf.), church, 30–3
– rector of, *see* Camera, Richard de; Vercelli, George of
– vicar of, *see* Guy; Thomas son of Lambert
– vicarage, 30–1; lviii–liv
Eye, Eya (Sf.), 57, Appx III (179)
– Ben. priory, 55–8, 132–4
—— prior of, *see* William
– Flimsworth, Flemewrd' in, separated tithes from, 133
Eylesham, Eylisham, *see* Aylsham
Eylsi, 121
Eynsham, Heynes (Ox.), document dated at, Appx III (176)

Fakenham, Fagenham, Fakkeham (Nf.), Appx III (180)
– *persona* of, see Wimer
Fakenham, mr Hervey of, official of consistory, Appx II 50A; xl, xlvi, lx
Faldyates (*unid.*), tithes from, 148
Faucunberg, Eustace de, bp of London, Appx II 23
Faversham (Kent), Eustace of, 145B
Fécamp (Seine Inf.), Ben. abbey, custodian of lands of in England, *see* Harpley, Ranulf of,
Felmingham (Nf.), church, xlin
Felmingham (Nf.), William of, Appx I 40; xlii
Felthorpe, Felethorp', Feletorp', Felthorp', Filetorp (Nf.), rector of, *see* Heymer
Feltwell, Feltwelle (Nf.), church of St Mary, 74
– tithes from, 74
Feneberwe, *see* Finborough
Fenham (Nb.), Appx III (176)
Ferentino (Italy), Bartholomew of, rector of St Peter's, Great Walsingham, 26n
– James of (*alias* of Elmham, Romanus), rural dean of Holt, 47, 153; xix, xlviii, lv, lviii
– John of, *persona* of Sproughton, Appx II 1; archdn of Norwich, 47n, 153n; xxviiin, xxx, xlvii; constable of Bristol castle, xlviin
– Sebastian of, *persona* of Westbriggs, 47

Ferring, Fering', Ferinng' (Ess. *or* Sx.), bp's official (Norwich and Winchester dioceses), 130W, 132W; xlvi; dean of St Paul's, xlvi; portioner of Elham church, xlvi; prebendary of Beverley and St Paul's, xlvi; rector of Denham, xlvi
Filby, Filebi, Fileby (Nf.), tithes from, 77, 95
Filetorp', *see* Felthorpe
Finborough, Feneberwe (Sf.), tithes from, 49
FitzGeldewin, Savaric, bp of Bath and Wells, 124A
FitzPeter, Geoffrey, Justiciar, xlviii
FitzWalter, Robert, Appx II 4, 30, 33; xli
Flanders, count of, xxxvii
Flegg (Nf.), rural dean of, 90n; *see also* Ruffus, Walter
Flitcham, Flicham (Nf.), church, Appx I 10a
– demesne tithe of earl of Arundel in, 122
– Aug. priory, xixn
– rector of, *see* Morley, Daniel *and* John of
– tithes from, 121; lx
Flixton (Sf.), manor of, Appx II 54; lxiii
Flowton, Floketun' (Sf.), tithes from, 49
Fontenay (Côte d'Or), Cist. abbey, xlii
Fordham (Ca.), rural dean of, xlivn; *see also* Raveningham, Richard of
Fordham, Fordeham, William of, 39W; clerk, 74W
Foulden, Fueldon', Fugeldon' (Nf.), 41; Appx III (179)
– chapel of St Edmund, 74
– church, 74
Fountains, John of, bp of Ely, xlvn
Framingham, Framingeham (Nf.), mr Nicholas of, 39W
France, merchants of, xxxviiii
Fransham (Nf.), church, xlin
Frederick II, emperor, xxxvn
Frenges, *see* Fring
Fressingfield, Fresingefeud (Sf.), separated tithes from, 133
– Snapes Hall in, separated tithes from, 133
Freton, *see* Fritton
Fring, Frenges (Nf.), William of, tithes of, 78
Fritton, Fritheton' (Nf.), 121
Fritton, William of, 121
Fritton, Freton (Nf. *or* Sf.), Richard of, clerk, 128W, 140W; bp's clerk, liii
Frostenden (Sf.), church, 58A
– rector of, *see* Wenden, Richard of
Fueldon', Fugeldon, *see* Fouldon
Fukeman, William, 37
Fulcher, Robert, 121
Furnival, Basilia de, Appx II 1

Gaiton, *see* Gayton
Gaiwd', *see* Gaywood

INDEX OF PERSONS AND PLACES

Gant, Gilbert de, 74
Gayton, Gaiton, Geytone, Geytun (Nf.), church of St Nicholas, Appx I 4
Gayton, Ralph of, bp's attorney, Appx II 51
– Richard of, clerk, 76W, 78W, 81W, 87W, 89W; bp's clerk, 82W
Gayton Thorpe, Thorpe (Nf.) mediety of church, 154
Gaywood, Gaiwd', Gawdw, Gayod, Gaywde, Geywode, Geywude (Nf.), 7–9, 24, 67, 96A, 139; Appx III (177–8, 180)
– bp's manor at, 46, 48
– bp's park at, xxxv
– land at, 121
Gedding, Geddinges (Sf.), John of, 49
Geistweit, Geistweyt, see Guestwick
Geiton, see Gayton
Geoffrey, archdn of Suffolk, Appx I 4W, 7–8W
– clerk of G. de Montchesney, Appx II 12
– son of Ranulf of Harpley, xliv
– son of Walter, 121
– son of, see Thomas; Walter
German the clerk, Appx I 11W
Gernemuedale, see Wiggenhall
Gernemuta, see Yarmouth, Great
Gernun, William, xlin
Gervase, mr, Appx I 4W, 7W, 9W
Gessinges, see Gissing
Geyste, see Guist
Geystorp, see Guist, Upper
Geytone, Geytun, see Gayton
Geywode, Geywude, see Gaywood
Gilbert, inhabitant of Castle Rising, 74
– prior of Ixworth, 70n
– rector of Withersfield, 125n
– son of Robert, 144
– son of Thomas, Appx II 19; knight, 137A
Gildenegare, Gildenegore, see Wiggenhall
Giles, archdn of Thessalonica, see Verracclo
Gimingham (Nf.), church, demesne and tithes, 74
Gislingham, Gielingeham (Sf.), separated tithes from, 133
Gissing, Gessinges (Nf.), Henry of, 49
Glanvill, Gilbert de, bp of Rochester, 111n, 124A
Glemham (Sf.), 58, 75; Appx III (179–80); xxviii, xlviiin
Glemham, Little (Sf.), tithes from, 49
Gloucester, Glouc', Gloucestr' (Gl.), Appx III (175, 180); xxxv
– Ben. abbey, 59
— abbot of, see Hamelin
– earl of, see Clare, Gilbert and Richard of
Gloucester, mr Robert of, archdn of Sudbury, rector of St Peter Mancroft, Norwich, 59n; Appx I 10AW

Goboy, Alward, 121
Godalming, Godalminges, Godelming (Sy.), Philip of, chaplain, 129W, 145W, 149W; bp's chaplain, liii
Godard, son of, see Silverun
Godesacr', see Wymondham
Godfrey the parker, 34W
Gosewode, see Thrandeston
Goudestorp, see Thorpe Morieux
Gournay (Seine-Mar.), collegiate church of St Hildevert, 137n
Grant, Richard le, archbp of Canterbury, Appx II 32
Gray, John de, bp of Norwich, 5n, 25, 26n, 29n, 35–6, 48, 50n, 61, 63, 77, 81–5, 87–8, 91, 119n, 124A, 139, 143n, 145, 154; Appx I 104–12; Appx II 2, 16, 22, 32; xix, xxi, xliii–iv, l, lvi, lxii, lxv, lxvii, lxix
– Walter de, bp of Worcester, xxi; archbp of York, 1
Gregory IX, pope, 8n, 23n, 37, 58n, 70n; 116n, 145An, 150n; Appx II 41; xxxviii, xix, xxxiin, xxxv
– mr, chancellor of the legate Otto, Appx II 46
– brother of Simon of Huntingdon or Thornham, 143n
Grestain (Calvados), Ben. abbey, xxxii
Grim, 121
Grimston, Grimeston (Nf.), tithes from, 121
Grosseteste, Robert, bp of Lincoln, Appx II 50; xx, xxxi, xxxiv, xxxvn, xlv
Guestwick, Geistweit, Geistweyt (Nf.), church of St Peter, 116, 153
– rector of, see Ralph son of Peter
– vicarage, 116, 153; xxx
Guist, Geyste (Nf.), church, 153
– vicarage, 153; xxx
Guist, Everard son of Ralph of, 116n
– William of, mr, master of Creake hospital, Appx II 21
Guist, Upper, Geystorp (Nf.), church, 153
Gulafre, Gulafr', Roger, tithes of, 78
Guy, Wido, the clerk, Appx I 9W
– vicar of Exning, 30; xlivn
Gypewycum, see Ipswich

Hackford, Hakeford (Nf.), rent in, 121
Haddiscoe, Hadesco (Nf.), tithes from, 146
Hadeston, Hadestun, see Bunwell
Hadstock (Ess.), Richard of, xxxviii
Haganet, see Haughley
Haghman', see Haughmond
Hainford (Nf.), church, 70n
Hakeford, see Hackford
Haketon, see Hapton
Hakun, Richard, 121

INDEX OF PERSONS AND PLACES 193

Halstein, Hauteyn, Robert, vicar of Herringby, 128; lvii
Hambye (Manche), Ben abbey, Appx II 38; lix
– abbot of, see John
Hamel, William de, 112
Hamelin, abbot of Gloucester, 59n
Hampton in Arden, Ardena (Wa.), tithes from, Appx I 10
Happisburgh, Hapesburg, Hapesburge, Hapesburgh (Nf.), church, 121; Appx II 27
– land in, 121
– manor of, 121
– marketplace of, 121
– priest of, see Hugh
Happisburgh, Nigel of, chaplain, 20n, 94
Hapton, Haketon (Nf.), church, 130
Haringeby, see Herringby
Harleston, Herlaveston' (Sf.), William of, attorney, Appx II 16
Harling, Herling (Nf.), demesne tithe from, 74
Harpley, Harpele (Nf.), church, 74
– tithes from, 74
Harpley, mr Ranulf of, rector of Haverhill, 11n; Appx I 10AW xliv; rector of Threxton, xliv; bp's official, xliii–xliv; custodian of English lands of Fécamp, of bpric of London and of Bristol castle, xliv
– his son, see Geoffrey
Hasketon, Haketun' (Sf.), separated tithes from, 133
Haughley, Haganet (Sf.), church, 74
— man of, see Adam
– priest of, see Peter son of Brunsune
– rector of, see Beccles, Alan of; Camera, Richard de
Haughmond, Haghmon' (Sa.), Aug. abbey, 61–2, 134A, 135; lix
– prior of, see Ercall, Alexander of
Hautbois, Great (Nf.), hospital, xixn
Hautesce, Roger, clerk, 145W; bp's attorney, Appx II 51; liii; rector of Thornham, 143; liii
Hauteyn, see Haltein
Haverhill, Haverhille (Sf.), church of St Mary with chapel, 11, 42n; xxixn
– *persona* of, see Bilney, Robert of; Harpley, Ranulf of; Narborough, Walter of
Haywood (St.), Appx III (176)
Hazelwood in Aldeburgh (Sf.), chapel, 129n
Heacham, Helcham (Nf.), church, 74
– rural chapter of, 134A
– rural dean of, 134A
– vicar of, 74
– Bested, Bestede in, tithes from, 74
Heckingham (Nf.), xxxixn
Heckingham, Alan of, xxxixn
Helcham, see Heacham
Helgeton, see Hellington

Helingeya, see Hilgay
Helisham, see Aylsham
Hellington, Helgeton' (Nf.), church, Appx II 24
Helmam, see Elmham
Helmingham (Nf.), church, xlin
Hemesbi, see Hemsby
Hemmingstone, Emingestun', Hemmingestun' (Sf.), mediety of church, 49–50
– Humiliard in, 50n
Hemsby, Hemesbi (Nf.), church, 76
Hengham, see Hingham
Henley, Henleia (Sf.), church, 76
Henry I, king, 66n, 95
— *pincerna* of, see Aubigny, William d'
– II, king, 95; xxvi
– III, 23, 110n, 130n; Appx II 35, 41A; xx, xxii–xxiv, xxxi, xxxiv–xxxvii, xlii, xlix, li
— coronation of, Appx III (177)
— justices of, 97–101
– abbot of Bury St Edmunds, 134
– the chaplain, 39W, 49–AW, 74W, 88W, 95W; bp's chaplain, 76W, 78W, 80–1W; liii
– the merchant, 147n
– rural dean of Burnham, xln
– son of Gerold, Appx I 11
Hereford (He.), Appx III (176)
– bp of, see Maidstone, Ralph; Vere, William de
Herlaveston', see Harleston
Herling, see Harling
Herringby, Haringebi, Haringeby (Nf.), church, 46, 128, lvii
– pension from, lvii
– vicar of, see Haltein, Robert
– vicarage, 46n
Herringfleet (Sf.), Aug. priory, xixn
Hertford (Hrt.), earl of, see Clare, Gilbert *and* Richard of
– Ben. priory, Appx I 6–8, 12
Hervey, prior of Spinney, 107
Hethel (Nf.), church, xlin
– land at, 100n
Hethersett (Nf.), xxxvin
Heveningham (Sf.), church, 102
– benefice in, 102
– rector of, see Nicholas
Heymer, rector of Felthorpe, 92
Heynes, see Eynsham
Hickling, Hikeling' (Nf.), Aug. priory, 63–4; Appx I 8n
Hildebrand, see Wiggenhall
Hildovest', see Hindolveston
Hilgay, Helingeya (Nf.), 121
– fisheries at, 121
Hillington, Hillingtun' (Nf.), mediety of church, xlin
– tithe of demesne of Roger de Staveli at, 74

Hillington, Hillingeton, Anselm of, Appx I 10A
Hindolveston, Hildolvest' (Nf.), church, 81
Hindolveston, John of, 78W
Hindringham (Nf.), church, xxixn
Hingham, Hengham (Nf.), Richard son of William of, 121
Hockering, Hokering', Hokeringg', Hokeryngge (Nf.), lordship of, xxiv
– tithes from, 77–8
Hodierna, 121
Hokering', Hokeringg', *see* Hockering
Holesle, *see* Hollesley
Holkham, Holcam (Nf.), church, 23
— mediety of, 23, 154
– vicarage, 23
Holkham, Henry of, official of archdn of Norwich, 127n; li
Hollesley, Holesle (Sf.), separated tithes from, 133
Holme, Hulme, Hulmo, St Benet of (Nf.), Ben. abbey, 15–6, 65–8, 136–7; Appx II 12; xlin, lv, lxviii
– abbot of, 64n, 101n, 137, xxxvin; *see also* Reginald; Robert
– manors of, 68
Holme, Robert of, demesne tithes of, 95
Holt (Nf.), rural dean of, *see* Ferentino, James of; Robert
Homersfield, Humeresfeld (Sf.), 85; Appx III (178); xxvi
– bp's demesne at, tithes of, 78
– fair at, xxvi
– fishery at, xxxix
– tithes from, 77
Honingham Thorpe, Thorp', Torp (Nf.), demesne tithes from, 148
– park at, 121
Honorius III, pope, 2–8, 8n, 16, 18, 23, 70n, Appx II 8; xxii, xxiv, lii, lviii
Hopton (Sf.), messuage in, 98n
Hormesbi, *see* Ormesby
Horham, mr William of, bp's official, xlvi
Horsey, Horshae (Nf.), John of, *persona* of Orford, 14
Horsham, Horsford (Nf.), Ben. priory of St Faith, Appx II 24
– prior of, 101, lx–lxi; as papal judge-delegate, 37; lxi; *see also* Eustorgius
Horton, Monks, Hortona (Kent), Clun. priory, 75
Houghton, Houthun, Houton, Houtun, Houtune, Hueton, Huetone (Nf.), church, 52
– *persona of*, *see* Houghton, John of
– vicarage, 52
Houghton, John of, archdn of Bedford and *persona* of Houghton, 52
– Nicholas of, mr, 76–7W, 80–2W; lii

Hoxne, Hoxn' (Sf.), 73–4, 134, 137, 151; Appx III (179, 181)
– bp's manor at, xxvi
– market at, xxvi
– rural dean of, l
– synod at, xliii
– tithes from, 77
Hoyland (Li.), rural dean of, papal judge-delegate, 122n
Hubbeston', *see* Ubbeston
Hueton, Huetone, *see* Houghton
Hugh, abbot of Bury St Edmunds, Appx I 3
– mr, *persona* of Mundford, Appx I 11
– priest of Happisburgh, 74
– prior of Lewes, Appx I 10
– son of Ailward, 121
– son of Alexander, 115
– son of John, *persona* of Oulton, 115
– son of Peter, 112
– son of Ralph, 29
– son of Ulf, 121
– son of, *see* Robert; Warin
– vicar of North Elmham, 142
Hukehell', *see* Okenhill
Hulme, Hulmo, *see* Holme
Humeresfeld, *see* Homersfield
Humiliard in Hemmingstone (Sf.), 50n
Humphrey the chaplain, Appx I 10AW, 12W
Hungrilond, *see* Wymondham
Hunstanton (Nf.), chapel of St Edmund in, 62, 135
– church, 61–2, 134A, 135
– vicarage, 61–2, 135
– Redemedewe at, 62, 135
Hunston (Sf.), church, 70n
Huntingdon, Huntendon (Hu.), mr John of, 34W
– Simon, mr, *alias* of Thornham, *persona* and vicar of Thornham, 143n
– Thomas of, mr, vicar of Crimplesham, 150n; liii; bp's attorney, Appx II 41A; liii
Huntingfield, Huntingefeud (Sf.), separated tithes from, 133
Huvewine, Seman, Appx II 36

Iakel', Iakesleia, *see* Yaxley
Ickburgh, Ykeburg (Nf.), church of St Bartholmew, 74
– tithes from, 74
Ickworth, Ikewrde (Sf.), Richard of, 49
Ilketshall, Ilketeleshal', Ilketeshall (Sf.), parish of St Andrew, tithes from, 148
– church of St John, 137A
— rector of, *see* John
– chapel of Gilbert son of Thomas in parish of, 137A; lix
— chaplain of, *see* Bulgeben, Ralph of
Ingelram, bp's marshal, xxxvin, liv

INDEX OF PERSONS AND PLACES

Ingworth, Ingewrth (Nf.), mediety of church, xlin
Ingworth, Richard of, 19W
Innocent III, pope, 124A; xx–xxii
– IV, pope, 70n, 124A; Appx II 6; xxxvi–vii, lxx
Instead, Ystede, see Weybread
Intwood, Intewde, Intewode (Nf.), rector of, 49
– tithes from, 77–8
Ipswich, Gypewycum (Sf.), 54, 87; Appx II 26, 38A; Appx III (178–81)
– archdn of, see Suffolk
– churches in, xlin
– Michelmas synod at, Appx II 39
– priory (Aug.) of Holy Trinity, 53, 97n; Appx II 1, 38A
– priory (Aug.) of St Peter and St Paul, 69
Irmingland, Irmiglond, Irmingefeld, Irminglond (Nf.), parish, 115
– tithes from, 77–8
Irstead, Irstede (Nf.), church, 136
Isabelle, daughter of Robert of Caister, tithes of, 137
Isles, king of, see Reginald
Itteringham (Nf.), third part of church of St Mary, xlin
Iull', Peter de, clerk of Pandulph, IW; l
Ixning, see Exning
Ixworth, Ixewrth, Ixewurd, Yxewrth' (Sf.), 60, 120; Appx III (179)
– Aug. priory, 70; Appx I 9
— prior of, papal judge-delegate, 10; see also Gilbert

James, Iacobus, clerk of Pandulph, vicar of South Creake, 8–9; lii, lxi
Jernegan, Hubert, Appx II 53; his daughter, see Olivia
– Hugh, Appx II 53
Joan, widow of Henry le Claver, wife of Ralph de Sundenlande, Appx II 37
Jocelin the chaplain, Appx II 31; xli
John, 121
– king, 124A; Appx II 32; xx–xxi, xxvi, xliii
– abbot of Hambye, Appx II 38
– cardinal deacon of Santa Maria in Latere, 124A
– the chaplain, 137AW
– the clerk, Appx I 12W
– formerly bp of Ardfert, bp in the universal church, xxixn
– mr, the doctor, 74W
– monk, Appx I 2AW
– rector of Ilketshall St John, 137A
– rector of Worstead, 93
– son of, see Hugh; Walter

Jordan the chaplain, Appx I 10AW
Juliana, widow of William Ruffus, xxviiin

Kangham, see Congham
Karletune, Karltun', see Carleton Forehoe
Kedere, Elias le, 142
Keelby, Keleby (Li.), church, Appx I 3
Kelton, Keletun', see Benhall
Kempstone, Kemestun' (Nf.), church, 41; lvii
– persona of, see Alençon, William d'
– vicarage, 41n
Kenewik, see Tilney
Kenilworth, Kenell', Kenilwurthe (Wa.), Aug. priory, Appx I 10
– prior of, see Robert
Kenilworth, Richard of, vicar, later persona, of Letton, 17
Keningham (Nf.), church, xlin
Kent, earl of, see Burgh, Hubert de
– eyre of, 1232, xxx
Kerdiston, Kerdestun (Nf.), Roger of, 74
Kerebroc, see Carbrooke
Kersey, Kereseye, Kerseye (Sf.), hospital, 71; subsequently Aug. priory, 72; Appx II 11; xixn, xxvii
– parish church, 72
Ketteringham, Keteringham (Nf.), land at, 121
Kettleburgh, Ketilbergh' (Sf.), church, xlin
– demesne tithes from, 148
Kilkenny, mr William of, king's proctor, xxviiin, xxixn
Killingthorp (unid.), Ralph of, xxviii
Kimberley, Kinburle, Kyneburle (Nf.), 121
– church, 121
– priest of, see Thurkil
Kinestorp, see Buxton
King, Coleman le, 121
– Hugh le, 115
Kirby Bedon, Kirkeby (Nf.), church and vicarage, Appx II 43
Kirby Cane (Nf.), two-thirds of church, xlin
Kirkham, mr Richard of, persona of Rushmere, 97
Kniveton, Knyvetone (Db.), Hugh of, rector of Wicken, 108–9
Knoddishall, Cnoteshale (Sf.), church, 37
– inhabitants of, see Kukeman, William; Monastery, Adam of the; Rakebald, Geoffrey and Walter
– tithes from, 37
– places in:
— Buxlow, Buckeslawe, separated tithes from, 133
— Erburestoft, 37
— Grendelheg, 37
— Keleshalelond, 37
— Oldelond, 37
— Radismere, 37

— Stablecroft, 37
— Westhus, le, 37
Knyvetone, *see* Kniveton
Kokestorp', *see* Cockthorpe
Kyneburle, *see* Kimberley

Lambert, mr, Appx I 4W, 6W, 9W
– son of, *see* Thomas
Lando, clerk of Pandulph, IW, 3–4; mr, Appx II 15, 18; li
Langham (Nf.), bp's manor at, xxvi
– chapel, 76
– church, xlin
– market at, xxvi
– tithes from, 77; of bp's demesne, 78, 95
Langley (Nf.), Prem. abbey, Appx II 43; liin
– abbot and prior of, papal judges-delegate, 57n
Langton, Stephen, archbp of Canterbury, 28, 59n, 145A; Appx II 12; xxi, xxv, xlivn
Lanthony of Gloucester (Gl.), Aug. priory, Appx III (175)
Lawrence, clerk of Pandulph, 1W; li
– the shepherd, Appx II 36
Laxfield, Laxfeud (Sf.), church, 133
– separated tithes from, 133
Lecche, Robert de, archdn of Norfolk, keeper of queen's wardrobe, xlix
Lehtlage, Warin, 34W
Leidet, Hugh, rector of Cavendish, Appx I 7
Leiston, Leyston, Leystune (Sf.), Prem. abbey, 37
— abbot of, *see* Philip
– separated tithes in, 133
Leleseya, Leleseye, *see* Lindsay
Lemmer, William, 112
Len, Lenn, Lenna, *see* Lynn
Leominster (He.), Appx III (176)
Leominster, Leomenstr', Leominister, Leoministre, John of, clerk, 128–9W, 132W, 140W, 145W, 149W; liii
Lessingham (Nf.), 125n
Letton, Lettona (Nf.), church, 17, 74
– vicar, later *persona* of, see Kenilworth, Richard of
Leuns, Geoffrey de, tithes of, 78
Lewes (Sx.), Clun. priory, 10n, 17n, 18, 48n, 73–4; Appx I 10; lv, lix, lxxi
– prior of, *see* Hugh
– proctor of, *see* Walpole, Alexander of
Lexington, Robert of, king's justice, Appx II 41A
Leyston, Leystune, *see* Leiston
Lichfield (St.), Appx III (176)
– cathedral church, prebendaries of, *see* Luke the chaplain; Raleigh, William

Lilford (Np.), rector of, *see* Sydenham, Philip of
Limesy, Lymeisi, Lymeysi, John de, Appx I 6–7
Lincoln (Li), Appx III (177)
– bp of, *see* Avalon, Hugh of; Blois, William of; Chesney, Robert de; Grosseteste, Robert
– church of, xlv
– diocese, persons of, 37
— synodal statutes for, xxxix
Lindsay, Leleseya, Leleseye (Sf.), church, Appx II 11
– lady of, *see* Cockfield, Nesta of
Linna, *see* Lynn
Linstead, Linestede (Sf.), separated tithes from, 133
Llandaff (Glam.), bp of, *see* William
Llewellyn, prince of Wales, Appx III (177)
Loddon, Loden (Nf.), Geoffrey of, seneschal of prior of Norwich, 144W
Londe, John de la, 112
London, Londinium, 16–7, 19, 25, 30–1, 38, 59, 89, 111, 116, 125, 138, 145A; Appx II 56; Appx III (175–81)
– bp of, *see* Faucunberg, Eustace de; Sainte Mère Eglise, William de
– bpric of, custodian *sede vacante*, see Harpley, Ranulf of
– cathedral church of St Paul, Appx II 27; Appx III (175, 177, 179–80)
— dean and chapter of, Appx II 23; lix
— prebendary of, *see* Ferring, Geoffrey of; Raleigh, William; Wenden, Richard of
– Charterhouse, Appx I 8n
– council at, Appx III (176–7, 180); xxxi
– collegiate church of St Martin le Grand, dean of, *see* Luke the chaplain
– diocese, persons of, 37
– New Temple at, Appx III (176–7)
— master of, Appx II 35
– Tower of, xxv
— constable of, see Blundeville, Thomas de
London, John of, bp's scribe, lii
– R. of, 66W
– Walter of, *see* Salerne
Longueville, Longavilla (Seine-Mar.), Clun priory, 138; lv
Losinga, Herbert, bp of Norwich, 143n
Lothingland, Ludinglond (Sf.), 121
Louis IX, king of France, xxxvii
Lucas, 121
Lucca, Luca (Italy), Peter de, clerk of Pandulph, 1W; li
Ludham (Nf.), church of St Katherine, 15
— vicarage in, lviii–lix
– chapel of St John, 15
– chapel of St Mary, 15
– inhabitant of, *see* Puncelot, William

INDEX OF PERSONS AND PLACES

– Brunestoft in, 15
– Ridecroft in, 15
Ludham, Stephen of, *persona* of Swanton Abbot, 16
Ludinglond, *see* Lothingland
Luke the chaplain, archdn of Norwich, xlvii; dean of St Martin le Grand, canon of Lichfield, archbp of Dublin, xlvii, lii; *see also* Wissant, Luke of
Lymeisi, Lymeysi, *see* Limesy
Lynn (Bishop's, *now* King's), Len', Lenn, Linna (Nf.), xxxviii–ix
– bailiffs of, Appx II 55
– church of St Margaret, 76
– court of bp at, liii
– customs of, Appx II 55
– dean of, *see* R.
– inhabitants of, *see* Darel, Thomas; Dod, Hugh; Hadstock, Richard of
– land at, Appx II 10
– liberties of, Appx II 15, 55
– mayor and burgesses of, Appx II 41A; xxxviii, lxiii
– piracy at, xxxviii
– St Margaret's bridge at, Appx II 55
– tallage on, xxxviii
– Tolbooth at, Appx II 55; lxiii
– Wyngate in, xlvn
Lynn, West, Lenn' (Nf.), church of St Peter, 74
Lynn, mr Roger of, Appx I 4W
– William son of Deodatus of, Appx II 10

Maidstone, Ralph, bp of Hereford, Appx II 44
Malebiche, Malebyse, Hugh, and Beatrix his wife, 107–9
Malet, Gilbert, 20n; his wife, *see* Riflei, Agnes de
Malmesbury (Wlt.), Appx III (176)
Mandeville, Geoffrey de, 24n
– honour of, Appx I 1n
Mansel, John, king's clerk, *persona* of Bawburgh, 130n; xlii
Manston, Maneston, in Gazely *or* Hundon (Sf.), tithes from, 49
Marlborough (Wlt.), castle, constable of, *see* Bassingbourn, Alexander of
Marsh, Richard, rector of St Peter's, Great Walsingham, 26n
Marshal, Gilbert, 97n
– Henry, bp of Exeter, 124A
– William, earl of Pembroke, xxii
Marsham (Nf.), tithes from, 77; of bp's demesne, 95
Martham (Nf.), church, 76, 90; Appx II 22; lxi
– vicar of, *see* Walsingham, Adam of

Martin, steward of Pandulph, liv
Masca, Pandulph, cardinal deacon of the basilica of XII Apostles, xx
Massingham, Great (Nf.), church, Appx II 38; xxvii, lix
Massingham, Robert of, rector of Little Melton, 70
– mr William of, *persona* of Stoke (by Ipswich), 54A
Matilda, countess of Essex, Appx II 44
– daughter of Basilia, 115
Mauclerc, Walter, bp of Carlisle, xxxvn
Mauger, bp of Worcester, 124A
Mauquinci, Gilbert de, 121
Maurice, mr, vice-official, 122n; l
Meauton, *see* Melton
Melewde, *see* Methwold
Melford, Long (Sf.), two-thirds of church, 36
– vicarage, 36
Melles (Mellis *or* Mells, Sf.), Eudo of, 121
Mellis, Melles (Sf.), church, 133
Melton, Meltun (Sf.), church, 13
– *persona* of, *see* Barking, mr Richard of
Melton Constable (Nf.), constable of, Appx II 45
Melton, Little, Melton, Parva Melton (Nf.), church, 70; Appx I 9
— *persona* or rector of, *see* Calne, William of; Massingham, Robert of
— vicarage in, Appx I 9
– land *or* tenement in, 121; Appx I 9
Melton Mowbray, Meltun (Lei.), church, Appx I 10
Melton, Meauton, Peter of, xxviiin
– Reginald of, Appx II 45
Merdenpaske, Roger, *persona* of Thornham, 143n
Merlay, *see* Morley
Merton, Meretun' (Nf.), church, demesne tithe and lay fee, 74
– inhabitant of, *see* Ulfketel
Merton (Sy.), Appx III (177)
– Aug. priory, prior of, 58A
– council of, xxvi
– Statute of, xxxi
Methwold, Melewde (Nf.), church, 48; lvii
– *persona* of, *see* Brito, Thomas; Vercelli, J. de
– tithes of earl Warenne from, 74
– vicarage of, 48
Meulan, count of, *see* Beaumont, Robert de
Meynilwaring, William de, xlin
Middlesex, archdn of, *see* Reginald
– eyre of, 1229, xxx
Middleton, Midelton (Nf.), church, 35
– vicarage, 35
Middleton, William, bp of Norwich, 61n, 136n
Midland counties, eyre of, xxx

Mildenhall, Mildenhale (Sf.), church of St
  Mary, 6; lvi
– vicarage, 6; lviii–lix
– Bradehowe in, 6
– Cadehowes in, 6
– Fulford in, 6
– Shinemer, Schinemer' in, 6
– Stapehowe in, 6
– Thremhowe, Tremhowe in, 6
Milliers, Miliers, Matilda de, 121
– William de, 121
Missenden (Bk.), Aug. abbey, 114n
Molesfen, *see* Nayland
Monastery, ad monasterium, de monasteriis,
  Adam, 37
– Geoffrey, xlin
– Gilbert, 115
Montchesney, Monte Kanesi, Denise de, 23n
– Ralph de, Appx I 9
– Robert de, 70
– Warin de, 70n
– William de, 23n; Appx II 12
Monte Cassino (Italy), abbey, Appx 14; xx
Monte Kanesi, *see* Montchesney
Morley (Nf.), church, xlin
Morley, Daniel of, *persona* of Flitcham, 122n;
  Appx I 10A
– John of, rector of Flitcham, 122
– Morellus of, Appx I 10A
Morton, John, archbp of Canterbury, xxiv
Moubray, see Mowbray
Mouncy, *see* Munci
Mowbray, Moubray, Nigel de, Appx I 10n
– Robert de, Appx I 10
Muncells, Alan de, Appx I 3n
Munci, mr Alexander de, 76–7W; lii; dean of
  Waynford, liii
Muncorbin, Reginald de, 121
Mundford, Mundeford (Nf.), Appx I 11
– *persona* of, *see* Hugh, mr
Munteny, William de, tithes of, 79–80, 84
Muriel, wife of Simon de Blavigny, xxxixn
Muschamp, Geoffrey, bp of Coventry and
  Lichfield, 124A

Narborough, Nerburg' (Nf.), *persona* of
  Haverhill, 42
Narford (Nf.), Alice of, Appx II 21
– Robert of, knight, 130n
Nayland, Nelande (Nf.), Brakene in, 121
– Molesfen in, 121
Nayland (Sf.), chapel, Appx II 2
Neatishead, Neteshirde (Nf.), church, 136
Nelande, *see* Nayland
Nerburg', *see* Narborough
Netesham, *see* Snettisham

Neteshirde, *see* Neatishead
Nettlestead (Sf.), church, xlin, xlii
– *persona* of, *see* Rupella, William de
Neuton, *see* Newton by Trowse; Newton, West
Neville, Albert de, widow of, *see* Agnes
– Ralph de, royal chancellor, bp of Chichester,
  xxxiv
Newark, Novum Locum (Sy.), 140–1; Appx III
  (181)
– Aug. priory, Appx II 5
Newehage, *see* Carleton Forehoe
Newnham (Wa.), church, liii
Newton Flotman (Nf.), manor, xxiv
Newton by Trowse, Neuton' (Nf.), demesne
  tithe of prior and convent of Norwich at, 95
Newton, West, Neuton (Nf.), vicarage, 43
– vicar of, *see* Creake, Robert of
Newton, Neuton, William, vicar of West
  Barsham, 7
Neylond, *see* Wreningham
Nicholas, cardinal bp of Tusculum, papal
  legate, 23n, 75n; xxi
– the clerk, rector of Heveningham, 102
– mr, Appx I 2W
Nix, Richard, bp of Norwich, xxiv
Norfolk, archdn of, 130; xlviii–l; *see also*
  Bilney, Robert of; Blundeville, Ralph de;
  Buckland, Geoffrey of; Lecche, Robert de;
  Pattishall, Martin of; Roger; Salerne, Walter
  de; Simon the Norman
— official of, *see* Carleville, mr Robert de;
  Ware, mr Peter of
– earl, of, *see* Bigod
Norfolk, Norf', Gilbert of, Appx I 10A
Norfolk and Suffolk, eyre of, 1228, Appx II
  25
– sheriff of, Appx II 42, 49; xxvi–xxvii, xxxv,
  xxxvin, xln
Norham (Nb.), Appx III (176)
Northcrek, Northcreik, Northcryke, *see* Creake,
  North
Northampton (Np.), archdn of, 58An
Northfeld, *see* Wymondham
Northwold (Nf.), Hugh of, bp of Ely, 149n
Northwttune, Northwuutton, *see* Wootton,
  North
Norton sub Hamdon (So.), rector of, *see*
  Raleigh, William
Norwich, Northwicum, Nortwicensis,
  Norwicensis, Norwycensis, Nowicensis
  (Nf.), 47, 51, 54A, 66, 68, 72, 86, 88, 91,
  93, 114, 119, 128, 142, 144, 152; Appx I
  11; Appx III (178–81)
– archdn of, *see* Burgh, Geoffrey de; Ferentino,
  John of; Luke the chaplain
— official of, 67; *see also* Holkham, Henry of
– bp of, *see* Bateman, William; Blundeville,
  Thomas de; Everard; Gray, John de;

INDEX OF PERSONS AND PLACES

Losinga, Herbert; Nix, Richard; Oxford, John of; Raleigh, William; Salmon, John; Scarning, Roger; Suffield, Walter; Turbe, William; Verracclo, Pandulph; Walton, Simon of; bp-elect, *see* Elmham, Simon of; Verracclo, Pandulph
— bailiffs of, Appx II 25, 29, 54–5; xxxviii
— barony of, xxvi
— chaplain of, *see* Breckles, Thomas of; Chilbolton, John of; Exeter, Walter of; Godalming, Philip of; Henry; Sydenham, Philip of; William
— clerk of, *see* Bacun, John; Bilney, Robert of; Chilbolton, John of; Croydon, Andrew of; Denis; Dunkeswell, William of; Exeter, Walter of; Fritton, Richard of; Gayton, Richard of; Iull', Peter de; James; Lando; Lawrence; Leominster, John of; London, John of; Lucca, Peter de; Ringstead, Reginald of; Rusticus; Terry, John; Walpole, Alexander of; William the chaplain; Wissant, Luke of
— consistory court of, 59n; xlvi, lx
— official of, *see* Fakenham, Hervey of
— demesne of, xxxviii, lvi
— marshal of, see Ingelram
— official of, 59n, 137; Appx II 12, 31, 39; *see also* Alvechurch, John of; Beccles, Alan of; Bilney, Robert of; Calne, William of; Clare, William of; Ferring, Geoffrey of; Harpley, Ranulf of; Horham, William of; Shipton, Richard of; Warham, Ranulf of
— proctor of, *see* Lando; *or* attorney, in *curia regis*, see Chevereville, William de; Gayton, Ralph of; Hautesce, Roger; Huntingdon, Thomas of; Ringstead, Reginald of; Rueland, Nicholas; Terry, John
— rights of, reserved, 2, 4, 11, 14, 16–18, 24–5, 27, 29, 34, 38, 40–5, 47–8, 49B, 50–2, 54–6, 58, 60–1, 64, 66, 70, 72, 75, 86, 89, 91–4, 102–4, 107–8, 114–9, 123, 125, 130, 132, 137A, 140–1, 145, 154
— seneschal of, *see* Bassingbourn, Alexander of; Brancaster, Bartholomew of, Wimer
– bpric, xix, xxxvi
— demesne manors of, 84
— in royal custody, Appx II 46; xxxvi
— knights and tenants of, xxvi
– cathedral church and Ben. priory of Holy Trinity, 19–20, 39, 49n, 49Bn, 76–96, 139–45, 152; Appx I 1n; Appx II 2, 21A, 27; xix, xxiii, xxvii, lxi–lxii, lxvi–lxvii, lxix, lxxi
— almoner of, 20n
— almonry of, 79–80, 87, 89, 92
— cellarer of, 78, 81–3, 85, 88, 91
— chamberlain of, 142

— chapter of, 135
— consent of, 2, 6, 15, 18, 23, 39, 116, 128, 130, 142, 153
— seal of, 128, 130, 139, 142, 144, 152
— dean of manors of, 141; lxii
— fine payable to, 49B
— monastery pertaining immediately to jurisdiction of, 15
— oath according to custom of, 2, 6, 15
— precentor of, 88
— prior of, *see* Elmham, Simon of; William
— clerk of, *see* Edmund
— rights of, reserved, 11, 14–17, 25, 27, 29, 31, 34, 38–45, 47–52, 54–6, 58, 60–1, 64, 66, 69–70, 72, 75, 86, 92, 94–5, 102–5, 107–8, 114–8, 123, 125, 130, 132, 137A, 138, 140, 154; Appx I 7, 9; Appx II 2, 25–6, 43
— sacrist of, 83, 127n, 140
– castle, xxii, xxvi
– churches in:
— St George, 76
— St Martin in Coslany, Coselani, 96
— farmer of, *see* Badingham, Richard of
— St Martin-at-Palace, 76
— St Olave, 76
— St Peter Mancroft, Mannecroft, 59
— rector of, *see* Gloucester, Robert of
– citizens of, Appx II 33
– dean (of Christianity) of, 37; lxi
– diocese of, xix
— *matricula* of, 59
— official of, *sede vacante, see* Anger; Beccles, Alan of; Warham, Ranulf of
— persons of, 37
— rectors of, Appx II 56
— visitation of, Appx II 47; xxiv, xxvii
– hospital of St Paul, 95; Appx II 47; lv–lvi, lxi, lxxi
– Jews of, xxxiii
– king's court at, Appx II 15
– schools of, Appx II 50A
— master of, *see* Scarning, Vincent of
– synod at, 8, 10, 91, 96, 128–9; Appx I 4; Appx II 27, 39, 43
Norwich, Robert of, Appx I 11W
Noth, Basilia, 121
– Richard, 121
Nothesdale, *see* Wiggenhall
Notley (Bk.), Aug. abbey, abbot of, 35n
Novum Locum, see Newark
Nuiers, Novers, Nuers, Simon de, 78: xlin
– William de, 121
Nun Cotham, Cotun (Li.), Cist. priory, nuns of, Appx I 3
– canon of, *see* Philip; Walter

INDEX OF PERSONS AND PLACES

Obeston', *see* Ubbeston
Occold, Acolt (Sf.), separated tithes from, 133
Odard, son of, *see* William
Odingselles, Hugh de, Appx I 7n, 8n
Odo, son of, *see* Roger
Offington, *see* Uffington
Okenhill, Hukehell', *see* Badingham
Olivia, daughter of Hubert Jernegan, wife of Robert de Wyndervill', Appx II 53
Omundeswude, *see* Brundish; Tannington
Orford, Oreford' (Sf.), castle, xxii
– church, 14; xlin
— *persona* of, see Horsey, John of
Ormesby (Nf.), churches of St Andrew, St Margaret, St Michael and St Paul, 95
– hall, tithes of, 95
Osbert, priest of Wiggenhall, Appx II 36
– son of, *see* Roger
Osegoteshag', *see* Cressingham
Otto, cardinal, papal legate, 145A; xxix, xxxiin
– chancellor of, *see* Gregory
– court of, xlix
Oulton, Owelton' (Nf.), church, 114–5
— *persona* of, *see* Hugh son of John
— vicar of, 114–5
— vicarage in, lviii
– inhabitants of, *see* Hugh son of Alexander; King, Hugh le; Matilda daughter of Basilia; Monastery, Gilbert of the; Silverun son of Godard; William son of Blacson'
– tithes from, 115
– Blakebrigg' at, 115
Oxeker, *see* Wymondham
Oxford (Ox.), Appx III (175, 177, 181)
– council at, Appx III (175, 177, 181); xxxvn, lvii
– schools *or* university of, xxxi, xxxvi, xliv
Oxford, John of, bp of Norwich, 24n, 34–5, 38n, 41n, 42n, 46, 48, 49An, 61, 63, 69n, 70, 105, 117n, 120, 128 and n, 129n, 143n, 154; Appx I 2n, 4–10, 12; xix, xxxix, xliv–xlviii, lxiii–lxvi

Pagrave, *see* Palgrave
Pailleys, *see* Puleys
Palgrave, Pagrave (Sf.), John, vicar of Wiggenhall St Mary Magdalene, 45
Palmer, Roger, 121
Pandulph, *see* Masca; Verracclo
Panxford (Nf.), church, xlin
Paris (Ile-de-France), university, xliv
Paris, Matthew, monk of St Albans, chronicler, xxxi–xxxiii, xxxv–xxxvi, xliv
Patesley, Patesle (Nf.), Robert of, 34W
Pattishall (Np.), Martin of, archdn of Norfolk, xlvn, xlviii; dean of St Paul's, London, Appx II 15, 26–7; xlvn; king's justice, Appx II 25; xxxi–ii, xxxviii–ix
Paulinus, rector of Threxton, 152
Peasenhall, Pesehal', Pesenhal' (Sf.), chapel, 106
– separated tithes from, 133
Pecham, John, archbp of Canterbury, 25n, 107n, 125n
Pelecoc, Pelecoch, *see* Thornham Magna
Pembroke, earl of, *see* Valence, Aymer de
Penn, Walter son of William of, 114n
Pentney, Pentneye (Nf.), Aug. priory, 96A
Pesehal', Pesenhal', *see* Peasenhall
Peter, rector of Eriswell, 49–B
– son of Brunsune, priest of Haughley, 74
– son of, *see* Hugh; Ralph
Pettistree (Sf.), Byng, Benges in, separated tithes from, 133
Peverel, Piperellus, Matthew, Appx I 1
— Adeliza, wife of, Appx I 1n
— Matthew *and* Mathias, son of, Appx I 1n
Philip, abbot of Leiston, 37
– canon of Nun Cotham, Appx I 3
– the chaplain, 53An, 137AW; *see also* Sydenham
– rural dean of Dunwich, xln
Pickenham, Pykeham (Nf.), house in, 121
– tithes from, 121
Picot, Geoffrey, Appx I 1n
Pincerna, le Butiller, Nicholas, (pretended) rector of Swanton Abbot, 65
– Roger, mr, 128W, 135W, 150W; archdn of Sudbury, 133, 140, 142, 149W; xlvi–xlvii; l, lxix; archdn of Suffolk, 129, 137AW, 144–5W, 151–2; Appx IV (182); xlvi–xlvii, l, lxix
Piperellus, *see* Peverel
Pirnhow (in Ditchingham, Sf.), Pirho, Pyrrehoe, Robert of, knight, Appx II 54
Playford, Pleiford', Pleyford (Sf.), 69; Appx III (180); xxviii
– church, 58, 133
— *persona* of, *see* Bedford, John of; Bech, William de
– land at, Appx II 26
Plumstead, Kent, church, xxvn
Plumstead, Plumstede (Nf.), lxii
– church of St Mary, 76, 88
– wood at, 139
Poitou, Appx III (178); xxii
Ponte Tegle, Robert de, 39W
Pontem, *see* Attebridge
Pontigny (Yonne), Cist. abbey, 145A–B; Appx III (181); xxxvn
Poore, Herbert, bp of Salisbury, 124A
Popi, Bauday, 121
Portsmouth (Ha.), liii
Postwick, Possewic' (Nf.), tithes from, 77–8

Poynnur, William le, rector of Bawburgh, 140
Préaux, Pratell' (Eure), Ben. abbey of St Pierre, 146
Prest, William, 112
Prittlewell (Ess.), Clun. priory, Appx II 2
– prior of, *see* R.
Puleys, Pailleys, William le, 130n
– widow of, *see* Alice
Puncelot, William, 15
Punchard, John, daughter of, *see* Alice
Putehak, Richard, 112
Pykeham, *see* Pickenham
Pyrrehoe, *see* Pirnhow

R., archdn of Norfolk, bp's official, 117; *see also* Bilney, Robert
– dean of Lynn, Appx I 10
– prior of Prittlewell, Appx II 2
Rakebald, Geoffrey, 37
– Walter, 37
Raleigh, Ralegh, William, archdn of Berkshire, xxxii; bp-elect *or* bp of Norwich, 46n, 61n; Appx II 46A–56; Appx III (180–1); xix–xx, xxix–xxx, xxxii–xxxvii, xxxixn, xlii, xlvi–xlvii, liii, lv–lxxii; canon of Lichfield and of St Paul's, xxxii; chief justice of Bench, xxx; elect of Coventry, xxxii; justice *coram rege*, xxx–xxxi; justice in eyre, xxx; keeper of chirographs, xxx; keeper of Rockingham castle, xxxi; king's 'chief minister'; xxxi; postulant of Winchester, xxxiv–xxxvii; rector of Bratton Fleming, xxx; rector of Blatherwyke, King's Somborne, Norton sub Hamdon and Whaplode, xxxii; treasurer of Exeter cathedral, xxxii
— chaplain of, *see* Sydenham, Philip of
— official of, *see* Clare, William of; Ferring, Geoffrey of
– William, kt, sheriff of Devon and Cornwall, xxx
Ralph, abbot of West Dereham, 117n
– clerk of Ailby, Appx I 3
– rural dean of Walsingham, xln
– son of Peter, rector of Guestwick, 116
– son of Simon, tithes of, 78
– son of, *see* Hugh
Randest', *see* Thrandeston
Ranulf the chaplain, vicar of Holy Trinity, Bungay, 29
Rattlesden, Rathlesdene (Sf.), Adam of, 19W
Raveningham, Ravenigham (Nf.), tithes from, 77, 84
Raveningham, mr Roger of, rural dean of Fordham, 31
Raymond, monk of Battle, 32–3
Reading (Brk.), 23; Appx III (175)
Reata, *see* Rieti

Redelingefeud, *see* Redlingfield
Redgrave (Sf.), 36; Appx III (179)
Redenhall (Sf.), rural dean of, l
– rector of, *see* Clare, William of
Redham, *see* Reedham
Redhenfeld', *see* Rotherfield
Redlingfield, Redelingefeud (Sf.), Appx III (178)
– separated tithes from, 133
Redlingtuna, *see* Ridlington
Reedham, Redham (Nf.), marsh at, 121
Reepham, Refham (Nf.), market at, Appx II 49
Reflei, *see* Riflei
Reginald, abbot of Battle, 30n
– abbot of St Benet Holme, 16
– archdn of Middlesex, Appx II 27
– king of the Isles, Appx III (176); li, livn
– son of Roger, 144
– son of, *see* William
Reidon', *see* Roydon
Ressemere, *see* Rushmere
Ria, Henry de, 38n
– Hubert de, xxiv
— tithes of, 78
Rich, Edmund, archbp of Canterbury, 58An, 145A–B; xx, xxxi, xxviiin, xlvi
Richard, abbot of Battle, 30n
– abbot of Bury St Edmunds, Appx II 28
– the cobbler (*sutor*), 112
– earl of Cornwall, xlii
— *persona* of Bacton, Sf., Appx II 39
– prior of Dunstable, papal judge-delegate, 125n
– rural dean of Coddenham, Appx II 20; xln, lxi
– son of Robert, 147
– daughter of, *see* Agnes
– son of, *see* Adam
Richmond, Richmund' (Yk. NR), archdn of, *see* Rotherfield, William of
– earls of, xliii
— demesne tithes of, 148
Rickinghall Superior, Rikingehal' (Sf.), tithes from, 57, 133
– vicar of, *see* Sampson the chaplain; William
Rickinghall, Hugh of, 57
Ridlington, Redlingtuna (Nf.), mediety of church, 74
– demesne tithes from, 74
– land of Alfer at, 74
Ridon, *see* Roydon
Rieti, Reata (Italy), 5; Appx III (178)
Riflei, Reflei, Riffley, Rifle, Rifley, Agnes de, 20, 89, 121
– Eudo de, 121
– Eustace de, 121
– Nigel de, 20n, 121
– Robert de, 121

– William de, vicar of Wicklewood, 20n, 89
Riglonde, *see* Ringland
Rikingehal', *see* Rickinghall
Ringe, Henry, 142
Ringland, Riglonde, Ringelande (Nf.), church of St Peter, 119, 154
– vicar of, *see* Walton, Stephen son of Thomas of
Ringsfield, Ringgesfeld, Ryngefeld, Ryngesfeld (Sf.), mr Michael of, 76–7W; lii; rector of mediety of Scottow, 66; liin
Ringstead, Ringstede (Nf.), Reginald of, clerk, 73–4W; bp's clerk and attorney, Appx II 30; liii
Rising, Castle, Rising', Risinges (Nf.), church, 18, 74
— *persona* of, *see* Rising, Roger of
– inhabitant of, *see* Gilbert
– land at, 74
Rising, Richard of, dean, Appx I 2W
– Roger of, *persona* of Castle Rising, 18
Ristun, *see* Ryston
Robert, abbot of St Benet of Holme, 137
– archdn, 93W; *see also* Bilney; Tew
– the clerk, 73–4W
– the priest, *persona* of Deopham, 38n
– prior of Kenilworth, Appx I 10
– prior of Bath, 124A
– rural dean of Holt, xln
– son of Benedict, 147
– son of Hugh, clerk, 99
– son of Thomas, tithes of, 79, 84
– son of William, Appx II 26; xxviii
– son of, *see* Gilbert; Reginald; Richard; Walter
Roches, Luke des., archdn of Surrey, liin
– Peter des, bp of Winchester, 124A; Appx II 5; xxiin, xxii, xxviin, xxxiv
Rochester, Roffensis (Kent), bp *or* bp-elect of, *see* Glanvill, Gilbert; Wenden, Richard of
— official of, *see* Wenden, Richard of
— subdelegate of, *see* Arches, mr Robert de
– cathedral priory, prior of, papal judge-delegate, 65
— and convent of, 58An
– dean of, papal judge-delegate, 65
Rochester, Rofa, Ralph of, 49–B
Rockingham (Np.), castle, xxx
— custodian of, *see* Raleigh, William
Rode, Richard de, 121
Rofa, Roffensis, *see* Rochester
Roffridus, nephew of Pandulph, vicar of Aylsham, 5; xxiii
Roger, 121
– archdn of Norfolk, I 2W; Appx IV (182)
– archdn of Sudbury, *see* Pincerna
– the carpenter, 112
– the clerk, Appx I 2W

– son of Ansgot, 121
– son of Benedict, 147n
– son of Odo, 112
– son of Osbert, tithes of, 78
Romanus, James, rural dean of Holt, *see* Ferentino, James of
– Peter, *persona* of Bedingham, 113
Rome, Appx III (175, 178); xxi–xxii
– basilica of S. Maria de Palladio, 14; Appx III (178)
– church immediately subject to, 6
Romeb', *see* Rumburgh
Romney, New (Kent), church, pension from, 145A
Ros, mr Jordan de, Appx I 6–8W
– Richard de, 98
– William de, 50n
Rosei, Ralph de, 121
Rotherfield, Redhenfeld' (Ha. *or* Sx.) William of, archdn of Richmond, *persona* of Aylsham, 1; lxi; rector of Walsoken, ln
Rougham (Nf.), church, xlin
Roydon, Reidon', Ridon (Nf.), separated tithes from, 133
Roydon, Richard of, Appx I 2W
Ruddeby, Rudebi, Ruddebi, David of, Appx I 10AW, 11W
Rudham, (Nf.), schools of, Appx II 50A; *see also* Coxford
Rueland, Nicholas, attorney of Pandulph, Appx II 7; lii
Ruffus, Ernald, 50n
– Hamo, Appx II 31; xli
– Walter, rural dean of Flegg, 137n
– William, widow of, *see* Juliana
Rumburgh, Romeb' (Sf.), Ben priory, 109n, 148; lv
Runnymede (Sy.), xxi
Rupella, William de, *persona* of Nettlestead, xlii
Rushmere St Andrew, Ressemere (Sf.), church, 53, 97
– *persona* of, *see* Kirkham, mr Richard of
Russignol, Peter, precentor of York, xxi
Rusteng, Nigel, 121
– Roger, 121
Rusticus, clerk of Pandulph, lW; li
Rybo, Richard de, of Vivonne, king's clerk, *persona* of Blakenham, xliii
Ryburgh, Little, Parva Riburg' (Nf.), church, 34
Ryngefeld, Ryngesfeld, *see* Ringsfield
Ryston, Ristun (Nf.), church, 74; xxv
– rector of, *see* Blundeville, Thomas

Sackeville, *see* Saukevill'
Sadelbowe, *see* Wiggenhall

INDEX OF PERSONS AND PLACES

St Albans, sancto Albano (Hrt.), Ben. abbey, Appx II 27
St Albans, mr Alexander of, Appx I 11W
St Edmunds, sancto Edmundo (Sf.), Alan of, Appx I 10AW, 11–12W
St John, Richard of, chaplain, xlii
Sainte-Mère-Eglise, William of, bp of London, 124A
St Neots (Hu.), Ben. priory, 102–4, 149; lvii
St Omer (Pas-de-Calais), provost of, 8n
Salerne, Walter de (*alias* of London), archdn of Norfolk, 149W; xlix–l
Salisbury (Wlt.), Appx III (176–7)
– bp of, *see* Poore, Herbert
– cathedral church, foundation of, Appx III (177)
– diocese, xxin
Salmon, John, bp of Norwich, 23n; xxxiv
Sampford (Sf.), rural dean of, xl
Samson, abbot of Bury St Edmunds, 35n
– abbot of St Stephen's, Caen, Appx I 4
– the chaplain, vicar of Rickinghall Superior, 57
San Germano (Italy), Appx II 14; xx
Santon, Santona (Nf.), church of St Helen, 74
– church (*another*), 74
– tithes from, 74
Sarneburne, *see* Shernbourne
Satesham, *see* Shottisham
Saukevill', Sackeville, Jordan de, royal justice, 19W
– Robert de, 49
Savoy, Boniface of, xxxv–xxxvi; archbp of Canterbury, xxxvi–xxxvii
– William of, xxxi, xxxiv–xxxv
Saxlingham (Nf.), mediety of church of, xlin
Saxlingham Nethergate (Nf.), church of St Mary, xlin
Scales, Roger de, Appx II 45
Scarning, Skeringe, Skerning', Skerninge (Nf.), church, 153
— vicarage in, 153; xxx
– tithes from, 77–8
Scarning, Roger of, bp of Norwich, 130n
– Simon of, 23n; Appx II 15; bp's servant, liv
– Vincent of, master of the schools of Norwich, Appx II 50A
Scots, king of, *see* Alexander II
Scottow, Scothowe (Nf.), church, 66–7
– rector of, *see* Ringsfield, Michael of; Wyverstone, R. of
Sculthorpe, Sculetorp (Nf.), demesne tithes from, 74
Seething, Seng' (Nf.), Richard of, royal justice, 19W
Selborne (Ha.), Appx III (177)
Selede, John, Appx II 36
Selfhangr', *see* Shelfhanger

Seng', *see* Seething
Sezze, Setia, Berard de, papal writer, rector of Catfield, Appx II 12
Shelfanger, Selfhangr' (Nf.), separated tithes from, 133
Shelland (Sf.), church; subsequently chapel, xlivn
Sherborne (Do.), Appx III (177)
Shereford, Sireford (Nf.), church, 74
Shernbourne, Sarneburne (Nf.), 121
Shimpling, Sympling' (Sf.), Daniel of, Appx I 2W
Shipden, Sipeden', Sipendena (Nf.), church, Appx I, 6, 8
– rector of, *see* Bidun, Walter de
– vicarage, Appx I 8
Shipmeadow (Sf.), Appx II 19
Shipmeadow, Walter son of Batholomew of, Appx II 19
Shipton, Sipton', mr Richard, Appx II 39; official of archdns of Sudbury, 31, 39A; xlv, li; bp's official, xix, xl, xlv; possibly archdn of Norfolk, xlv–xlvi, xlviii
Shotesham, Shotesham, Sotesham (Nf.)
– church of All Saints, 96A
– tithes from, 77–8
Shottisham, Satesham (Sf.), church, 133
Shouldham, Suldham (Nf.), Gilb. priory, Appx II 36
Shrewsbury (Sa.), Appx III (176–7)
Sibton, Sibet', Sibeton, Sybeton' (Sf.), 106; Appx III (180); liin
– Cist. abbey. 105–6
– church of St Peter, 105
— *persona* of, *see* Thomas
— vicar of, *see* Ubbeston, Ralph of
– tithes from, 105
— of demesne, 148
Sibton, Hamo of, 148n
Sideham, *see* Sydenham
Sidestern', *see* Syderstone
Silesfeld, *see* Wymondham
Silverun son of Godard, 115
Simon, knight, 121
– the Norman, archdn of Norfolk, xlix–l
– prior of Norwich, *see* Elmham
– son of, *see* Ralph
Sipeden, Sipendena, *see* Shipden
Sipton', *see* Shipton
Sireford, *see* Shereford
Skekketun', *see* Skeyton
Skeringe, Skerning', *see* Scarning
Skeyton, Skekketun' (Nf.), Guy of, 74
Snape, Snapes (Sf.), Ben. priory, 49
Snapes Hall, *see* Fressingfield
Snettisham, Netesham, Snetesh', Snetesham (Nf.), 118, 121; Appx III (179)
– church, 121; Appx II 27

— vicarage in, 121
- fold at, 121
- le Fresmers marsh, 121
Soisy-en-Brie (Yonne), Aug. priory, 145B
Somborne, King's (Ha.), rector of, *see* Pattishall, Martin of; Raleigh, William
Somerton, mr R. of, (*probably*) episcopal officer, li
Sotesham, *see* Shotesham
Southwood, Sowode, Suthwude (Nf.), land at, 121
Southwood, John of, deacon, *persona* of Carleton Forehoe, 27
Spalding (Li.), Ben. priory, prior of, papal judge-delegate, 122n
Sparham (Nf.), rural dean of, *see* William
- tithes from, 77
Sparham, mr John of, 34W
- William of, tithes of, 78
Sparuwe, Richard, 142
Spinney, Spinetun (Ca.), Aug. priory of St Mary and St Cross, 107–9; xixn, xxvii, lv
- prior of, *see* Hervey
Sproughton (Sf.), church. Appx II 1; xlviii
- pretended *persona* of, *see* Ferentino, John of
Sprowston, Sprouston, Sproustone, Sproustun, Sproustune (Nf.), tithes from, 77, 79–80, 84
Stalham (Nf.), Clement of, *persona* of mediety of Wreningham church, 130n
Stamford (Li.), Appx III (177)
Stanfield, Stanfeld (Nf.), house at, 121
Stanfield, Anketill of, 121
Stangrim, mr, Appx I 2W
Stanhoe, Stanho (Nf.), Hervey of, tithes of, 79, 84
Stanley (Wlt.), Appx III (176)
Stanstead, Stanstede (Sf.), church, 75
Staveli, Robert de, demesne of in Hillington, 74
Stephen, count of Brittany, 148n
Stiffkey (Nf.), portion of vicar of Aylsham in church of St John, 2n
Stockton, Stoketun' (Sf.), tithes from, 49
Stoke Ash, Stok' (Sf.), church, 133
- separated tithes from, 133
Stoke by Clare, Stok' (Sf.), Ben. priory, 36n, 49, 103n, 150–1; Appx I 7n; Appx II 5; liii
- infirmary chapel of, xlv
- tithes from, 49
Stoke by Ipswich (Sf.), church, 54A
- *persona* of, *see* Massingham, William of
Stoke by Nayland (Sf.), church, Appx II 2
Stokesby, Stokeby, Stoqueby (Nf.), church, 138
Stoketun', *see* Stockton
Stow (Sf.), rural dean of, Appx II 39
Stow, Stowe, mr Richard of, 19W; episcopal officer, l

Stradbroke, Stradebroc (Sf.), separated tithes from, 133
- Bradley, Bradel' in, separated tithes from, 133
Stradishall, Stradeshull, Stradeshulle (Sf.), church, 111–2; lvi
- grove at, 112
- inhabitants of, *see* Adam the miller; Alan the clerk; Attebridge, Gilbert; Avelina the widow; Hamel, William de; Hugh son of Peter; Lemmer, William; Londe, John de la; Putehak, Richard; Richard the cobbler; Roger the carpenter; Roger son of Odo; Thomas son of Geoffrey; Trone, Thomas; Underwood, William; Walter the chaplain
- tithes from, 112
Stradsett, Strates', Stratesete, Strattes', Strattesete (Nf.), church, 118, 154n
- rector of, *see* Syderstone, mr Ralph of
- vicarage in, 118; lvii
Stradsett, Osbert of, knight, 118
Stratford Langthorne, Strafford (Ess.), document dated at, 16; Appx III (178)
Stratford St Mary (Sf.), 16n.
Strattes', Strattesete, *see* Stradsett
Stratton, Long, Stratton (Nf.), church, 138
Stuteville, Nicholas de, 113n
- William de, Appx II 13, 16
Suanthun', *see* Swanton Morley
Sudbourne, Suthburne (Sf.), church, Appx I 2A
- *persona* of, *see* William son of Theodoric
Sudbury, Suburiensis (Sf.), archdn of, xl; *see also* Beccles, Alan of; Clare, William of; Gloucester, Robert of; Pincerna, Roger
— official of, 32–3; *see also* Shipton, Richard of; Yaxley, Gilbert of
Sudcrec, *see* Creake, South
Sudwude, *see* Southwood; *see also* Wymondham
Suffield, Sufeud, Walter, clerk, 132W; mr, 126n, 128n; official of archbp of Canterbury *sede vacante*, xxix; bp of Norwich, 41n, 48n, 86n, 89n, 117n, 141n, 150n; Appx II 22, 47–8, 56; xxxvii, xlvi, lxx
Suffolk, archdn of, *see* Geoffrey; Pincerna, Roger; Tew, Robert of; Walpole, Alexander
- synods of, 31, 50, 102, 108, 112; Appx II 39
Suldham, *see* Shouldham
Sumeri, Muriel de, xxviiin
Sunburne (? Somborne), John of, vicar of All Saints, Dunwich, 132
Sundenlande, Philip de, Appx II 37
Susanna, Appx II 36
Sut Elmham, *see* Elmham, South
Suthwude, *see* Southwood; *see also* Wymondham
Suthwuttun', *see* Wootton, South
Swaffham (Nf.), demesne tithes from, 148

Swafield, Swathefeld, Swathefeud (Nf.), William son of Thomas of, 92
Swanetone, Swanetun', *see* Swanton
Swangegeya (*unid., probably in Wymondham*), turbary in, 121
Swanton Abbot, Swaneton', Swaneton' iuxta Scothowe (Nf.), 16
– church, 65
— *persona* of, *see* Ludham, Stephen of
— (pretended) rector of, *see* Pincerna, Nicholas
– tithes from, 65
Swanton Morley, Suanthun', Swanetone, Swanetun (Nf.), tithes from, 77–8
Swathefeld, Swathefeud, *see* Swafield
Swineshead (Li.), Cist. abbey, prior of, papal judge-delegate, 122n
Sybeton', *see* Sibton
Sydenham, Sideham, Sydeham, Sydesham (De.), Philip of, chaplain and kinsman of bp Raleigh, 125, 128, 132, 135, 138, 140–1; liii, lxix; r. of Bugbrooke and Lilford, liii
Syderstone, Sidestern' (Nf.), church, xlin
Syderstone, mr Ralph of, rector of Stradsett, 118
Sydesham, *see* Sydenham
Sympling, *see* Shimpling

Tannington, Thatingetun' (Sf.), separated tithes from, 133
– Omundeswude in, separated tithes from, 133
Tattus, Brumann, 74
Taverham, Thaverham (Nf.), rent in, 121
– tithes from, 148
— of demesne of prior and convent of Norwich, 95
Tefford, Tefordia, *see* Thetford
Terling, Terlinges, Terlingg' (Ess.), 49–A; Appx III (178); xxvin
– church, Appx II 23; xxvii, lix
– vicarage, Appx II 23
Terry, Terri, John, 34W, 39W, 66W, 69W, 74W, 95W; clerk, 93W; bp's clerk, 78W, 80–2W; bp's attorney, Appx II 33; liii
Tettenhall (St.), collegiate church, dean of, *see* Blundeville, Thomas
Tew, Tywa (Ox.), mr Robert of, 88W; Appx I 10AW, 11–12W; archdn of Suffolk, l
Thatingetun', *see* Tannington
Thaverham, *see* Taverham
Thekeston, *see* Threxton
Theldesbothesmede, *see* Wymondham
Thelveton, Theveton (Nf.), demesne tithe from, Appx I 2
Theobald, archbp of Canterbury, 59n
Thessalonica, archdn of, *see* Giles
Thetford, Tefford, Teford, Tefordia (Nf.), 27; Appx III (178)

– Aug. priory of St Sepulchre, 1
– prior of, 1W; ? papal judge-delegate, 10
– Clun. priory of St Mary, prior, xxviii; ? papal judge-delegate, 10; xxvii, xxxvin, xlviiin
– church of St Margaret, 74
– church of St Peter, 74
Theveton, *see* Thelveton
Thomas the clerk, vicar of Cratfield, 104
– clerk of the convent of Norwich, xxixn
– the clerk, son of Lambert of the city of London, 33
– *persona* of St Peter's, Sibton, 105
– rector of St Peter's, Great Walsingham, 26n
– son of Dule, 144
– son of Emma, 144
– son of Geoffrey, 112
– son of, *see* Gilbert; Robert
Thorald son of Baldwin, 49
Thorendis, *see* Thornage
Thorendon, *see* Thorndon
Thornage, Thorendis, Thorn', Thornedes, Thornedis, Thornedys, Thornegge, Tornedis (Nf.), 34, 107, 129; Appx III (179, 181)
– tithes from, 77
— of bp's demesne, 78, 95
Thorndon, Thorend', Thorendon (Sf.), church, 133
– separated tithes from, 133
Thornesdes, Thornedis, Thornedys, Thornegge *see* Thornage
Thornham, Tornham (Nf.), church, 110, 143 and n; xlviii–xlix, lxii
— *persona or* rector of, see Blundeville, Ralph de; Buttamund, Robert; Dya, John de; Elveric son of Thurstan; Hautesce, Roger; Hungtingdon, Simon of; Merdenpaske, Roger; Thurstan the deacon; William son of Elveric
— vicar of, *see* Blundeville, Ralph; Buttamund, Robert
– inhabitants of, *see* Bursemarc', William; Gilbert son of Robert; Reginald son of Roger; Thomas son of Dule; Thomas son of Emma
– land at, lxii
– places in:
— Bradegate, 144
— Chemingrode, 144
— Sloches, 144
— Stuernecroft, 144
— Thornwong, 144
– tithes from, 78
Thornham Magna, Pelecoc, Pelecoch (Sf.), church, 133
– Atburctre in, 134
Thornham Parva, Parva Thornham (Sf.), church, 133
– separated tithes from, 133

Thornham, Simon of, *see* Huntingdon, Simon of
Thorpe, Thorp, Torp' (next Norwich, Nf.), 33, 92, 94, 102, 117; Appx I 10A; Appx III (178–80); lvi, lxii
– assarts by bp at, Appx II 47; lvi, lxii
– bp's bridge at, 139
– church, 76
– heath at, 139
– tithes from, 77
— of bp's manor, 95
– wood, 139
Thorpe, Warin of, tithes of, 78
Thorpe, Honingham, Thorp' (Nf.), demesne tithes from, 148
Thorpe Morieux, Goudestorp' (Sf.), tithes from, 49
Thrandeston, Randest' (Sf.), Gosewode in, separated tithes from, 133
Thrandeston, mr William of, 77W
Threxton, Thekeston, Trecstan', Trecston (Nf.), church, 152
— rector of, *see* Harpley, Ranulf of; Paulinus
– tithes from, 77–8, 152
Thurkil, priest of Carleton Forehoe, 121
– priest of Kimberley, 121
Thurlow, Great (Sf.), church, xlin
Thurstan, Turstin, the deacon, *persona* of Thornham, 143n
– tithes of, 78
Tibura, *see* Tivoli
Tilney (Nf.), Kenewik in, 74
Timworth (Sf.), Ralph of, xlin
– William of, 117n
Tiville, Ralph de, tithes of, 78
Tivoli, Tibura (Italy), 2–3; Appx III (178)
Toft Monks (Nf.), Ben, priory, 146n
Toftrees, Toftes (Nf.), church, 74
Tonbridge, Tonebrige, Tonebrigge (Kent), Aug. priory of St Mary Magdalene, 111–2; lvi
Topcroft (Nf.), chapel of St Giles, 1
Tornedis, *see* Thornage
Tornham, *see* Thornham
Torp, *see* Thorpe (next Norwich); Thorpe, Honingham
Tosny family, patronage of, xlin
Tottington (Nf.), inhabitant of, *see* Brown, John
Trecstan', Trecston', *see* Threxton
Trone, Thomas, 112
Trowse (Nf.), church of St Andrew, 83
Tuddenham, North, Tudneham (Nf.), tithes from, 148
Tuddenham, John of, xlin
Tunstall, Tunstal', Tunstale (Nf. *or* Sf.), Henry of, 81W; clerk, 95W
Turbe, William, bp of Norwich, 38n, 43n, 55–6n, 57, 59n, 73–4, 75n, 136; Appx I 2–3; lv–lvi
Turf, John, 147n
Turkill, William, 29
Turstin, *see* Thurstan
Tusculum, cardinal bp of, *see* Nicholas
Tynemouth, mr John of, 58An
Typford, *see* Wymondham
Tywa, *see* Tew

Ubbeston, Hubbeston', Obeston' (Sf.), church, 102
– vicarage, 102
Ubbeston, Ralph of, chaplain, vicar of Sibton with chapel of Peasenhall, 106
Uffington, Offington, Uffinton, John of, Appx I 11–12W
Ulf, priest of Colton, 121
– priest of Kimberley, 121
– son of, *see* Hugh
Ulfketel, 74
– the priest, *persona* of Diss, Appx I 2
Underwood, sub bosco, William, 112
Unsy the clerk, Appx I 2W
Upton (Nf.), vicarage, 126
Upton, Hugh of, 126
Upwell (Ca.), inhabitant of, *see* Crane, Geoffrey
Urbe, John Iudicis de, vicar of South Creake, 8–9
Uvedale, John de, 121

Valence, Aymer de, earl of Pembroke, 23n
Valle, Guy de, xlin
– John de, demesne tithes of at Withersfield, 125n
Vallibus, Oliver de, tithes of, 78
Valognes, Matilda de, xlin
Veltre, William le, 121
Vercelli, Vercellensis (Italy), George of, rector of Exning, 30
– J. de, *persona* of Methwold, 48
Verdun, Guy de, xlin
Vere, Robert de, 75n
– William de, bp of Hereford, xlivn
Verli, Ralph de, 121
– Roger de, 121
Verracclo, Giles, archdn of Thessalonica, xx, xxiii
– Pandulph, bp-elect *or* bp of Norwich, 91, 113n, 143n; Appx II 1–18; Appx III (175–8); xx–xxv, xxvii, xxxiii, xxxviii, xxxixn, xlii–xlv, l–lii, lviii–lix, lxi–lxxii; papal chamberlain, xxii; papal legate, Appx III (175, 177); xxi; papal nuncio, xxi; papal subdeacon, xx

INDEX OF PERSONS AND PLACES 207

— chaplain of, *see* William
— clerk of, *see* Iull', Peter de; James; Lando; Lawrence; Lucca, Peter de; Rusticus
— seneschal of, *see* Bassingbourn, Alexander of; Brancaster, Batholomew of
Vincent the clerk, Appx I 4W, 8–9W
Vitalis, anchorite of Thornham Magna, 134n
Viterbo (Italy), abbey of S. Martino del Monte, 23

W., prior of Westacre, Appx I 10
Wachesham, *see* Wattisham
Wake, Guy, wife of, *see* Anabel
Walden, Waleden' (Ess.), Aug. abbey, 24–5; lxvii
–abbot of, 58An
Walden, Thomas of, clerk, vicar of Chippenham, 24
Waldingfield (Sf.), William of, widow of, *see* Alice
Waleden', *see* Walden
Walepol, *see* Walpole
Walkelin, archdn of Suffolk, Appx I 2AW
Walpole, Walepol, Walpol' (Nf.), medieties of churches, 73–4
Walpole (Nf. *or* Sf.), mr Alexander of, 69W, 73W; clerk, 93W; ln, lii; archdn of Sf., l
– Edmund of, *persona* of St Mary's, Great Dunham, 40
Walsham le Willows (Sf.), church, 70n
Walsingham (Nf.), rural dean of, *see* Ralph
Walsingham, Great (Nf.), church of St Peter, 26
Walsingham, Little, Wals', Walsingehan, Wausingham (Nf.), Aug. priory, 23n, 26, 113–5
Walsingham, Adam of, vicar of Martham, Appx II 22
Walsoken (Nf.), rector of, *see* Rotherfield, William of
Walter, Hubert, archbp of Canterbury, xlviii
– Peter, 58n
Walter, canon of Nun Cotham, Appx I 3
– chaplain of Stradishall, 112
– rural dean of Diss., Appx I 2W
– son of Geoffrey, rector of Attlebridge, 92
– son of John, 121
– son of Robert, clerk, 99
– son of, *see* Geoffrey
Waltham (Ess.), Appx III (181)
– Aug. abbey of Holy Cross, 116, 153; Appx II 53A
— dedication of, Appx III (181)
Walton, West, Waltona, Waltun', Wautun' (Nf.) mediety of church, 73–4
Walton (Nf. *or* Sf.), John of, vicar of Castle Acre, 127

– Simon, bp of Norwich, xlvi
– Stephen son of Thomas of, vicar of Ringland, 119
Wangford, Wangeford, Wangeforde (Sf.), rural dean of, *see* Munci, Alexander de
– tithes from, 77, 79, 84
Ware (Hrt.), mr Peter of, official of archdn of Norfolk, xxixn, li
Warenne family, earls of Surrey, fee of, 121; patronage of, xlin; tithes of demesne of, in Methwold, 74
Warham (Nf.), mr Ranulf of, bp's official; official *sede vacante*, xxix; royal custodian of, *see* xxiii, xlii; prior of Norwich, xlii; bp of Chichester, xxiii, xlii
Warin son of Hugh, clerk, 99
Wattisham, Wachesham, Wathisham (Sf.), church, 60
Wattisham, Gerard of, 49
Wausingham, *see* Walsingham
Wautun', *see* Walton
Waxham (Nf.), church *or* mediety thereof, 63–4
– vicarage, 63
Wells (So.), Appx III (176, 181)
– bp of, *see* Bohun, Reginald de; Wells, Jocelin of
– dean of, *see* Alexander
— and chapter of, 124A
Wells, Jocelin of, bp of Bath and Wells, 124A
– Simon of, bp of Chichester, 124A
Wells next-the-Sea (Nf.), church, xlii
Wenden, mr Richard of, bp-elect of Rochester, official of Rochester, prebendary of St Paul's, rector of Bromley and Frostenden, 58A
Wendling (Nf.), mr Robert of, episcopal officer, l–li
Wenham (Sf.), Ermeigot of, 49
Wenlock, Much (Sa.), Appx III (176)
Wereham (Nf.), Ben. priory, 61n
Westacre, Westacra (Nf.), Aug. priory, 9; Appx II 36
– prior of, xlin; *see also* W.
Westbarsh', *see* Barsham, West
Westbriggs, Westbrige (Nf.), church, 47
– *persona* of, *see* Ferentino, Sebastian of
Westleton (Sf.), lay fee in, Appx II 31
Westley, Westle (Sf.), Adam of, vicar of Aldeburgh, 129
Westminster (Mx.), Appx II 50; Appx III (178–80)
– *curia regis* convened at, 98n; Appx II 15–7, 26, 31, 37
– St Katherine's chapel, Appx II (178); xxv
Weston (Sf.), church, xlin
Weston, Coney (Sf.), church, xlin
Weston Longville, Weston (Nf.), church, 138

INDEX OF PERSONS AND PLACES

Westwade, Westwde, *see* Wymondham
Wetherden (Sf.), mediety of church, 35
– vicarage, 35
Wetheringsett (Sf.), church, xliii
Weybourne (Nf.), Aug. priory, xliii
Weybread (Sf.), Instead, Ystede in, separated tithes from, 133
Whaplode (Li.), rector of, *see* Raleigh, William
Whitlingham, Witligham, Witlingham', Wythlyngham (Nf.), tithes from, 77–8
Whittingham, Witingeham (Sf.), separated tithes from, 133
Wichingeham, Wichingham, *see* Witchingham
Wicken, Wykes (Ca.), 107, 109
– church of St Mary, 108
— portion of Rumburgh priory in, 108n
— rector of, *see* Kniveton, Hugh of
— vicarage in, 108
– inhabitants of, *see* Clewe, John; Cruce, Richard de
Wickham Skeith (Sf.), church, 49
– manor, 49
Wickhampton (Nf.), church, xliii
Wicklewood, Wicclewde, Wiclewde, Wiclewode, Wyklewude (Nf.), 121
– church of All Saints, 20, 76, 89, 94
— rector of, *see* Brockdish, Robert of
— vicar of, *see* Riflei, William de
– land at, 121
Wicklewood, Eudo of, 121
Wicks Bishop (near Ipswich, Sf.), manor, xxvi, xxviii
Wiclewde, Wiclewode, *see* Wickelwood
Wictone, *see* Wighton
Wido, *see* Guy
Wiggenhall, Wieh', Wigehale, Wigehall', Wigenhale (Nf.), church of St German, 76, 85
— document dated at, Appx III (179)
— tithes pertaining to, Appx II 36; lx
– church of St Mary Magdalene, 44–5
— tithes pertaining to, 44–5
— vicar of, *see* Palgrave, John of
— vicarage in, 44–5
– church of St Mary the Virgin, tithes pertaining to, Appx II 36; lx
– church of St Peter, tithes pertaining to, Appx II 36; lx
– places in:
— Blakenberg, Appx II 36
— Burewenesnewland, Appx II 36
— Chevervilledole, Appx II 36
— Gildengare, Gildengore, 121; Appx II 36
— Hildebrand, Appx II 36
— Maluchil, Appx II 36
— Nothesdale, Appx II 36
— Sadelbowe, Appx II 36

Wighton, Wictone, Wihktun', Withon (Nf.), church, 82, 91; Appx II 3; lxii
– vicarage, 91; Appx II 3; lxii
Wik', Wikes, *see* Wix
Wilby (Nf.), tithes from, 148
William, 121
– abbot of St John's, Colchester, 50n
– bp of Llandaff, suffragan in Norwich diocese, xxiii, xlv
– the chaplain (of Pandulph), 1W; li
– the clerk, 144W
– earl, *see* Aubigny
– *pincerna* of Henry I, *see* Aubigny
– prior of Butley, 37
– prior of Eye, 134
– prior of Norwich, 49n, 66W, 96; Appx II 17
– rural dean of Sparham, xln
– vicar of Rickinghall Superior, 57n
– son of Blacson', 115
– son of Elveric, *persona* of Thornham, 143n
– son of Odard, 121
– son of Reginald, 29
– son of Theodoric, *persona* of Sudbourne, Appx I 2A
– son of, *see* Robert
Willington (Bd., Db. *or* Wa.), Roger of, clerk, xli
Wilton, Wiltona (Nf.), church, 74
Wilton (Wlt.), Appx III (176)
Wimer, *persona* of Fakenham, 89W
– the seneschal, 34W
Wimundeham, Wimundham, *see* Wymondham
Winchelsey, Robert, archbp of Canterbury, 25n; xxiv
Winchester (Ha.), Appx III (177)
– bp of, *see* Roches, Peter des
– postulant of, *see* Raleigh, William
– see of, Appx III (181); xxxin, xxxiiin, xxxiv–xxxvii, lxx
Windsor (Brk.), xxxvii
Wisbech, Wysebeche (Ca.), 40; Appx III (178)
Wissant (Pas-de-Calais), Luke of, bp's chaplain, lii
Witchingham, Wichingeham, Wichingham, Wichlingham, Wychyngham (Nf.), church of St Faith, 138
– church of St Mary, 138; Appx II 48
– tithes from, 77–8
Withersdale (Sf.), Alan of, 58n
Withersfield (Sf.), rector of, 125n; *see also* Gilbert
– tithes from, 125n
Withon, *see* Wighton
Witingeham, *see* Whittingham
Witligham, Witlingham', *see* Whitlingham
Wiverdeston, Wiverdestun, *see* Wyverstone
Wix, Wik', Wikes (Ess.), Ben. priory, nuns, 120

INDEX OF PERSONS AND PLACES

Wixoe (Sf.), land at, 21n
Wooburn (Bk.), manor, Appx II 50
Woking (Sy.), church, Appx II 5
Wolterton (Nf.), Walter of, xlin
Wodbastwick, Bastwick (Nf.), church, 136
Wootton, North, Northwttune, Northwuuttun, Wutton (Nf.), 121
– church, 123
— *persona* of, *see* Bech, Vincent de
— vicarage, 123
Wootton, South, Suthwutton (Nf.), land at, 121
Wootton, Roger of, 121
Worcester (Wo.), Appx III (175)
– bp of, *see* Cantilupe, Walter de; Gray, Walter de; Mauger; Wulfstan
Worlingham (Sf.), church, xlin
Worstead, Worthstede, Wrstede, Wrthested, Wurstede, Wurthstede, Wurtstede (Nf.), church of St Mary, 19, 86, 93
— rector of, *see* John
— chapel of St Andrew, 19, 93
Worstead, Adam of, clerk, 86, 93
– John of, clerk, 86
– John of, lord, Appx II 36
– John of, royal justice, 19W
– Robert son of Richard of, 19
Wramplingham, Wramplyham, Wrapligham (Nf.), 121
– inhabitants of, *see* Eylsi; Grim; Ribald
Wratting, Great (Sf.), rector of, 125n
Wreningham, Wrenigham (Nf.), church of All Saints, xxix, xlix
– mediety of, 130
– rector of, *see* Stalham, Clement of
– Naylond, Neylond in, separated tithes from, 133
Wretham, East (Nf.), 125n
Wretham, (*blank*) de, Appx I 6W
Wroxham, Wrockesham, Wrogesham, Wrogsham, Wrokesham (Nf.), tithes from, 77–8
Wrstede, Wrthested, *see* Worstead
Wulfstan, St, bp of Worcester, Appx III (175)
Wurthstede, Wurtstede, *see* Worstead
Wutton, *see* Wootton
Wycham, *see* Wymondham
Wychyngham, *see* Witchingham
Wygenhale, *see* Wiggenhall

Wykes, *see* Wicken
Wyklewude, *see* Wicklewood
Wymondham, Wimundeham, Wimundham, Wymundham (Nf.), Ben. priory, 27, 121–3; Appx I 1; Appx II 27; lv, lxi, lxiii–lxiv
— prior of, xxvii, lxi
– chapel of St Thomas, 121
– church, 121; Appx II 27
– places in:
— Biskelund, 121
— Estfeld, 121
— Godesacr', 121
— Hungrilond, 121
— Northfeld, 121
— Oxeker, 121
— Silesfeld, 121
— Sudwude, Suthwude, 121
— Swangegeya, 121
— Theldesbotheswede, 121
— Typford, 121
— Westwade, Westwde, 121
— Wycham, 121
— Ydeskestorp, 121
– tithes from, 121
Wymondham, Raymond of, 78W
Wyndervill', Robert de, Appx II 53
– wife of, *see* Olivia
Wysebeche, *see* Wisbech
Wythlyngham, *see* Whitlingham
Wyverstone, Wiverdeston, Wiverdestun (Sf.), separated tithes from, 133
Wyverstone, R., of, rector of mediety of Scottow, 66

Yarmouth, Great, Gernemuta (Nf.), church, 76
Yaxley, Iakel', Iakesleia (Sf.), church, 133
Yaxley, Gilbert of, official of archdn of Sudbury, 32; li
Ydekestorp, *see* Wymondham
Ykeburg, *see* Ickburgh
Ymein, Simon, 142
York, Appx III (177)
– archbp of, *see* Gray, Walter de
– precentor of, *see* Russignol, Peter
York, Robert of, bp elect of Ely, 8n
Ystede, *see* Instead
Yxewrth', *see* Ixworth

SUBJECT INDEX

Advowson (*advocatio, ius patronatus*), 54A, 93, 109–10, 117, 130, 132n, 140, 143n; Appx I 6; Appx II 38; xli–xliii
– claimed by crown, xlii–xliii
– confirmation of, 26, 49
– disputed, 97n; Appx II 16–7, 19; xlii
– grant of, 19–20, 72, 89, 92, 94, 111–2, 113n, 118
– inquisition into, Appx II 22
– of mediety of church, 23
– of third part of church, 38n
– of tithes, 137
agreement (*compositio, conventio*), 49B, 122, 139, 143–4, 152; Appx II 36, 50, 54–5; *see also* concord, final
– before papal judges-delegate, 37, 96, 125n; Appx I 10; Appx II 27
aid, from tenants of bpric, xxvi
ale, assize of, Appx II 54; lxiii
altar, 151n
– dedication of, Appx II 34
– of St Thomas, at Dover, 12
altarage, 2, 6, 15, 29, 31, 39, 44–5, 62, 69n, 104, 115, 117, 127, 135, 153n; Appx II 43
ambassadors, Imperial, Appx III (178)
amercements, Appx II 25, 54; xxvi, xxxvii–xxxviii
– dispute concerning, Appx II 32
anchorite, 134n
appeal, to Rome, xxviii, xxxiv–xxxvi
appropriation (grant *in proprios usus*), xxvii, lvi–lviii, lxi–lxii, lxxvii
– of chapel, 15, 106, 151
– of church, 2–3, 5, 15, 19n, 29–31, 34, 38–9, 41n, 42n, 43n, 44, 51–3, 55, 60, 62, 64, 66, 69, 72, 86, 89–90, 92–4, 96A, 102–3, 105–6, 109, 112–9, 123, 130, 140; Appx I 3n, 4n, 7–9; Appx II 2–3, 22, 24, 43, 48
— by bp's predecessor, confirmed, 35–6, 46, 48, 61, 63, 70, 81–3, 85, 87–8, 91, 102, 128, 129n, 135–6, 145, 153–4; Appx I 12; lvi–lvii
– of mediety of church, 20n, 23, 63–4, 89, 94, 130, 154
– of portion in church, 153
– for increase of alms, 6
– for increase of hospitality, 6, 34, 38–9, 105
– for maintenance of guests, 154
– for relief of poverty of foundation, 130

– for use of pilgrims, 39
– for use of poor, 38, 72, 80, 84, 105, 118n, 134, 154
– for use of sick, 72, 134
– requested by or with consent of patron, 69, 112
– to bp, Appx II 23
– to take effect when vacated by current incumbent, 29–30, 41n, 42n, 46, 48, 52–3, 66, 69–70, 81–3, 85–9, 92, 102–3, 109, 113, 116, 118–9, 123, 140; Appx I 7–9
arable, *see* land
archbishop, *see* Canterbury; Dublin; York
archdeacon(s), xlvii–l
– canonical query concerning, Appx II 8
– grants church *sede vacante*, 130
– jurisdiction of, 141
– vicegerent of, *sede vacante*, 69n, 110n
– *see also* Norfolk; Norwich; Sudbury; Suffolk and (*outside diocese*) Bedford; Berkshire; Richmond; Thessalonica
archdeaconry, dispute concerning, xlviii–l
arenga, 2, 5, 12, 15, 49, 86, 91, 95, 121, 125, 130–1, 133, 140, 148, 150–1; lxv
arms, assize of, xxvi
assarts, 121
– tithes of, 142; Appx II 47; lvi, lxi
assizes, Appx II 25; xxxvii
– *see also* ale; arms; *darrein presentment; mort d'ancestor; novel disseisin*
attachments, Appx II 54
attorney, of bp in *curia regis*, see Boyland, Roger of; Cheverevill, William de; Gayton, Ralph of; Hautesce, Roger; Huntingdon, Thomas of; Ringstead, Reginald of; Rueland, Nicholas; Terry, John; *see also* proctor

bailiffs
– of bp, Appx II 25, 29, 54–5; xxxviii
– of earl of Arundel, Appx II 55
– royal, Appx II 25
barony, of Bury St Edmunds, 134
bastardy, investigation into, 98; xxxix
benediction
– by abbot, Appx II 28
– clause, 74; lxviii

INDEX OF SUBJECTS

benefice
- annual, from church, 53, 69n, 102, 120; Appx II 39
— from mediety of church, 50
- detached, within church, lvi
- in money, from lay fee or ecclesiastical living, 1
- newly created for religious in parish church, 50, 53, 102, 112
- resignation of, 58A
see also appropriation; church, parish; collation; induction; institution; pension; *personatus*; presentation; vicarage
bishop
- consecration of, Appx III (178, 180); xxi, xxv, xxxii
- diplomatic mission of, Appx III (178, 180); xxv
- election of, Appx III (175); xxi, xxv, xxviii–xxix, xxxvi, xxxviii
- in the universal church, xxixn
- of other dioceses, acting in Norwich diocese, xxiii, xxixn
- postulation of, xxxiv, xxxvi
- professional of obedience by, 28, 124
see also Ardfert; Bath and Wells; Carlisle; Chichester; Coventry and Lichfield; Ely; Exeter; Hereford; Lincoln; Llandaff; London; Norwich; Rochester; Salisbury; Tusculum; Winchester; Worcester
books, repair of, 30, 116
Bracton, treastise known as, xxxi
bridge, 139
buildings pertaining to church, 142
burial rights, 151n; see also cemetery

camera, of canons of Langley, Appx II 43
candles, render of, Appx I 3
cardinal, see Bicchieri; Langton; Nicholas; Otto
carpenter, see Roger
carucate, 121
castle, see Colchester; Corfe; London, Tower of; Norwich; Orford; Rockingham
causeway, Appx I 10A
cemetery, 39, 62; Appx II 2; see also burial rights
censure, ecclesiastical, 37; see also excommunication
census, papal, xxi
chamberlain, of Norwich cathedral priory, 142
- see also Ansgot
chancellor, royal, see Neville, Ralph
chancery, royal, xxiii
- rolls of, xxxvii
chantry, lv, lix

- perpetual, 137A
chapel, 11, 15, 19, 62, 69n, 74, 76, 106, 112, 121, 129, 134–5, 151, 153n; Appx II 2
- as part of benefice of canons in church, 112
- domestic, 137A; Appx I 11; xxxiii
- endowment of, 137A; xxxii
- institution to, 137A
- mediety of, 74
- revenues of, as part of vicarage, 129, 153n
chaplain, 34
- of bp, see Breckles, Thomas of; Chilbolton, John of; Exeter, Walter of; Godalming, Philip of; Henry; Sydenham, Philip of; William
- removable, serving churches, 81–2, 85, 87–8, 117n; Appx II 3; lxxii
- to be appointed in church, Appx I 11
- to be properly maintained in appropriated church, 92
- to be provided by patrons, with contribution from rector, 112
chapter, of Norwich cathedral priory, 135
- consent of, to bp's *actum*, 2, 6, 15, 18, 23, 39, 116, 128, 130, 142, 153
chapter, rural, Appx I 2, 27
charter
- of archbp, inspected, 145A–B
- of earlier bp, inspected (and recited), 25, 34–6, 46, 57, 61, 63, 70, 81–3, 85, 87–8, 105, 120; Appx I 12; (but not recited), 74, 77, 84, 128, 135–6, 154; liv–lvi, lxvii–lxviii
- of group of bps, inspected, 124A
- of layperson, cited, 26, 107, 111, 137A
— inspected Appx I 10A
— inspected and recited, 19–20
— lost, 113n
- royal, Appx II 32
chirograph, 49A–B, 134–A, 137, 139, 142, 144, 152; Appx II 50, 55; xxx
- keeper of, see Raleigh, William
church, conventual, dedication of, Appx II 53A; Appx III (181)
church, mother, Appx I 11
— liberty and indemnity of, 109
— rights of safeguarded, 137A
church, parish
— appropriated, 74; lxii; see also appropriation
— building of, Appx I 5
— confirmed to religious house, 34, 49, 72, 74, 95, 111, 121, 133, 145, 150; Appx I 6
— custody of, 65; Appx II 12
— dispute concerning, 1
— farm of, 96
— free land of, 69n, 74, 104, 115, 117
— fruits of, sequestrated, Appx II 52
— grant of, 23, 72, 75n
—— to bp, Appx II 23, 38, 49
— hereditary succession to, 143n

INDEX OF SUBJECTS

—mediety of, 23, 35, 49–51, 63, 89, 94; xlin, lvi
—— pension from, 73–4
— pension from, Appx II 5, 11
— portions of, 39, 69, 73n, 104, 112, 153; xlin
— rights of bp in, Appx II 27
— served by removable chaplain, 81–2, 85, 87–8, 117n; Appx II 3; lxii
— third part of, xlin
— tithes sequestrated from, 77, 84
— two thirds of, 36; xlin
— unification of one to another, xlii
— vacancy of, enquiry into, lx
— *see also* benefice
churchyard, *see* cemetery
clerks
- claimed for bp's jurisdiction, 99, 101; lx
- episcopal, *see* Bacun, John; Bilney, Robert of; Chilbolton, John of; Croydon, Andrew of; Denis; Dunkeswell, William of; Exeter, Walter of; Fritton, Richard of; Gayton, Richard of; Iull', Peter de; James; Lando; Lawrence; Leominster, John of; London, John of; Lucca, Peter de; Ringstead, Reginald of; Rusticus; Terry, John; Walpole, Alexander of; William the chaplain; Wissant, Luke of
clothing of convent, grant for, 121
coal, measurement of, Appx II 55
cobbler (*sutor*), *see* William
collation
- of church by bp, 4; xlii, lviii–lix
— by devolution, 58
- at presentation of patrons, 7, 9, 13, 18
- of vicar to united *personatus* and vicarage, 17
commissary of bp, Appx II 27
compositio, see agreement
concord, final, 69n, 140n, 143n; Appx II 16–7, 26, 41A; xxxviii–xxxix, xliii
- *see also* agreement
confessions, proceeds of, 127n
confirmation
- by archbp of Canterbury, 145A
- by dean and chapter of London, Appx II 23
- papal, 23n, 116n, 145n, 150n
confirmation, episcopal, liv–lv, lxvii
- by *inspeximus, see* charter
- general, 34, 49, 74, 95, 121, 125, 133
- of church, 72, 111, 133, 145, 150; Appx I 6
- of composition, 137
- of concession by rector, 109
- of future acquisitions, 133
- of grant by layman, 19–20, 23, 26, 57, 72, 107, 111; Appx I 1, 6, 10A
- of lease of tithes, 57
- of pension, 49A, 59, 75, 125, 133, 138
- of previous episcopal *actum*, 25, 35–6, 46–8, 61, 63, 70, 77, 81–5, 87–8, 102, 105, 120, 128, 129n, 135–6, 145, 153–4; Appx I 12; Appx II 24; lv
- of surrender of tithes, Appx I 2
- of tithes, 68, 77–80, 84, 125, 133, 146, 148, 150; Appx I 2
convent, clothing of, 121
conventio, see agreement
cook, *see* Alexander
correction, reserved to bp, 141
- and removal of vicar, reserved to bp, 2, 6, 15
corroboratio, lxviii
council
- ecclesiastical, Appx III (181)
- legatine, xxxi, xlix
- papal, xxxvn; *see also* Lateran
- royal, Appx III (175–7, 179–80); xxvi, xxxiii
count, *see* Brittany; Flanders; Meulan
countess, *see* Essex
court
- bp's, Appx II 25, 37; xl
—— accommodation of with royal court, Appx II 25
— of Audience, lxi
— of consistory, lx
—— official of, *see* Fakenham, Hervey of
- ecclesiastical, Appx II 31, 41A, 53; xxxviii–xl, l
— clerks claimed for, xl, lix
- of manor of Flixton, Appx II 54
- of manor of South Elmham, 134A; Appx II 54
- royal, *see curia regis*
- shire, Appx II 32; xxxvii
court, suit of, Appx II 54
cow-pasture (*vaccaria*), 121
croft, 15, 144; Appx II 2
crown, pleas of, Appx II 54
curia, see court; house
curia, papal, xxiii–xxiv, xxviii, xxxv–xxxvi
curia regis, xxiii, xxixn, xxxiii–xxxiv, xxxvii–xliii, xlvi, xlviiin, xlix–l, liii–liv; 21–2, 23n, 26n, 69n, 97n–101n, 110n, 113n, 114n, 130n, 143n; Appx II 1, 7, 13, 16–7, 19–20, 25–6, 29–32, 37, 40, 53
- Bench, xxx
- *coram rege*, xxx–xxxi
- on eyre, xxx
— at Lynn, Appx II 55
customs
- of bp of Norwich, reserved, *see* Norwich, bp of, rights of reserved
- of church of Norwich, *see* Norwich, cathedral church, rights of reserved
- of Lynn, Appx II 51, 55
- of parish church, 2

INDEX OF SUBJECTS

darrein presentment, 50n, 58n, 70n, 97n; Appx II 16; xlii
datary, 128–9, 132–3, 135, 138, 140–2, 151–2; Appx I 10A; lxix
dating clause, lxviii–lxix
deacon, *see* Southwood, John of; Thurstan
dean
– of manors of prior and convent of Norwich, 141
– rural, 31, 47, 49B; Appx II 2, 20, 22, 39; xxxiii–xxxiv, xl
— jurisdiction of, 141
— *see also* Burnham; Diss; Fordham; Holt; Hoxne; Lynn; Redenhall; Samford; Sparham; Stow; Walsingham
debt, 37
– to crown, Appx II 52
– to Jews, Appx II 54
dedication, of conventual church, Appx II 53A; Appx III (181)
demesne, 37, 49, 57, 109; Appx I 1
– of earl of Arundel, 122n
– of Hugh son of Ralph, 29
– of Lewes priory, 74
– of Mildenhall, 6
– of Norwich cathedral priory, 142
– of Snape priory, 129
– of Stradishall church, 112
– tithes of, *see* tithe, demesne
deprivation of vicarage, lii, lix
diplomatic of *acta*, lxiii–lxxii
dispensation, papal, *see* indult
dispositio, lxvi–lxvii
dispute (*causa, contentio, lis, questio*), 1, 10, 37, 96, 122n; Appx I 10A
distraint, of ecclesiastical revenues by royal order, xl, xlii
– *see also* sequestration
ditch (*fossatum*), 6
doctor, *see* John, mr
Domesday, Great, of church of Norwich, lv
dovecote, 6
dower, 21, 29, 100n; Appx II 36–7; xxviiin, xxxix
drove-road, Appx II 36

earl, *see* Arundel; Aumale; Cornwall; Gloucester; Hertford; Norfolk; Warenne
eels, 121
elections, episcopal, 124A; xix, xxi, xxiv–xxv, xxviii–xxix, xxxii, xxxvi, xxxviii
eschatochol, lxviii–lxix
estates, of bp of Norwich, lxiii
exchange of land, 144
Exchequer, royal, Appx II 25; xxii, xxxvii, livn
– barons of, xxvi

– clerk of, *see* Burgh, Goeffrey de; Blundeville, Thomas de
excommunicates, caption of, Appx II 42; xxvii
excommunication, Appx II 41A, 53; xxxviii–xl, liv, lx, lxiii
– absolution from, Appx II 39
– certificate of, 22, 147; Appx II 37
– threat of, 9
exemption
– from episcopal jurisdiction, 141
– from obventions and tithes, 108
expenses, Appx II 39
eyre, general, 19n, 98; Appx II 25; xxx, xxxvii

fair, St Margaret's, Appx II 55
familia, bp's, li–liii
farm
– of church, 96
– of tithes, 49A–B, 57
fealty, Appx II 55
feast day, of St Thomas the Martyr, 38–9
fee, 37, 49, 78
– bp's, Appx II 32
– lay, 74; Appx II 31
field, 2, 6, 37, 39
fine, 49B; Appx II 45; xxxix
– to crown, xxvi, xxxviii
first-fruits (*primitie*), 2
– taken by bp, xxiii–xxiv
fish, prises of, Appx II 55
– *see also* tithes
fishery, Appx II 50
fishing rights, 121; xxxix
fishpond, 121
foldage (*faldagium*), 121
forester, *see* Alexander
format of *acta*, lxxi
foundation of religious house, 71, 107
frankpledge, view of, Appx II 54; lxiii
friars, establishment of, xix

gallon-measures, regulation of, Appx II 54–5
garden, 2, 29, 79
– *see also* tithes
Gospels, oath on, Appx I 3
grange, 37
grant
– by abbot of Bury, 134
– by archbp, 145B
– by bp, Appx II 14, 46–7; lv–lvi, lxi–lxii
— in free, pure and perpetual alms, 144
— of benefice in church, 50, 53
— of mediety of church, 23, 89
— *see also* appropriation
– by king, confirmed by bp-elect and legate, 23

– by layperson, confirmed by bp, 19–20, 23, 26, 57, 72, 107, 111, 151; Appx I 1, 6
– by nuns, Appx I 3
grove (*grava*), 74, 112
guests, grant for maintenance of, 154

habit of religion, granted, Appx II 21
harvest, fruits of, Appx II 56
headgear, secular, worn by bp, Appx II 28
heath, 139
herrings, grant of confirmed, 76
highway, king's, 15, 115
Holy Land subsidy, Appx II 18
homage, 121, 153n
– of church, 115
hospital, Appx II 11, 21
– foundation of, xixn
– *see also* Bury St Edmunds; Creake; Hautbois, Great; Kersey; Norwich; St Paul's
hospitality, grant for increase of, 6, 34, 38–9, 105, 154
house (*curia, domus, mansio, mansiuncula*), 15, 37, 115, 121, 142; Appx I 11
– chapel in, 137A
– newly built, Appx II 14

indenture, *see* chirograph
inscriptio, lxiv
induction into corporal possession, 3, 19n, 33, 67, 90n, 93, 134A; Appx II 22; lx
– into pension, 32
indulgence, 12, 131; Appx I 5; Appx II 9; lxiii–lxv, lxx
indult, papal:
– for appropriation of church, 116n
– for exemption from papal taxation, xxiii
– for plurality, xxxiii, xlvii, xlvi, xlixn, liii
– for recovery of possessions of *see*, xxiii
– to grant benefices to rural deans, xxxiii
– to refuse licence for private chapels, xxxiii
– to remove hereditary incumbents, xxxiii
– to serve parish church by member of convent, 109n
– to take first fruits of churches, xxiii
iniunctio, lxviii
inquisition, 49B, 59n, 90n, 100n; lxi
inspeximus, see charter
institution, xli–xlii
– agreement concerning, Appx II 27
– conducted *sede vacante*, 153n
– of current vicar to *personatus*, 17, 56
– of religious to *personatus*, 117
– refused, Appx II 12
– request from resigning rector for, 58A
– styled collation, 7, 9, 13, 18
– to chantry, 137A

– to *personatus*, 11, 13–4, 16, 18, 27, 40–2, 47, 54A, 110; Appx I 2A, 4; Appx II 1, 4, 19
– to vicarage, 7, 9, 24, 43, 45, 104, 106, 127, 129, 132
interdict, general, 37
intitulatio, lxiii
Italian incumbents, xxi, xxiii, xxxiii, lii
– *see also* Ferentino, James, John *and* Sebastian of; James, mr; Roffridus; Romanus, Peter; Sezze, Berard de; Urbe, John Iudicis de; Vercelli, George *and* J. of

Jews, xxxiii
– debts to, Appx II 54
Judgement by bp, 1, 8, 49B, 122, 152; Appx I 10A; Appx II 20, 36, 39; lx–lxi, lxvii
Judges-delegate, papal, 10, 37, 57n, 58n, 58An, 65, 96, 122n, 125n, 143n; Appx I 3, 10; Appx II 27, 44; xxvii, xl, xlin, xliv, xlvn, xlviii, lxi
– bp as, 37; Appx II 44; lxi
– notification of decisions of, 10, 96
– notification to, 65
– subdelegate of, Appx II 27
– submission to jurisdiction of, 96
judges, ecclesiastical, cited to *curia regis*, xxxiv, xl
jurors, testimony of, Appx II 15
jury, xxxix, lxi
justices, royal, 143n; Appx II 41A; xxvii, xxxvii, lx
– episcopal letters to, 21–2, 97–101, 147; Appx II 37
– in eyre, 19n, 98n, 101n, 132n; Appx II 25–6, 32; xxxviii

knights, *see* Blunt, William le; Creake, Bartholomew of; Gilbert son of Thomas; Narford, Robert of; Pirnhow, Robert of; Raleigh, William; Simon
knight service, Appx II 17

land, 144, 151
– arable, 107, 121, 135, 142
– free, 153n
landsete (*lancettus*), 121
Lateran council, fourth, Appx III (175); xxii, xliii
– canons of, 58; xlii, xlix, lix
laws and constitutions of England, Appx II 54
legacies, 127n
legate, office of, 6
– *see also* Bicchieri, Guala; Otto; Tusculum, Nicholas of; Verracclo, Pandulph

INDEX OF SUBJECTS

legitimate birth, letters testimonial confirming, 98; lx
letters patent
– of bp, 53
– of William of Rotherfield, archdn of Richmond, 1
liberty
– of bp, Appx II 32
– of Lynn, Appx II 15
licence, royal, for election, xxi, xxv, xxviii
litigation, abandoned, Appx I 3
lopcop, Appx II 55

magistri, see Arches, Robert de; Barking, Richard of; Beccles, Alan of; Bech, Vincent of; Bilney, Robert of; Bisacia, Ranulf de; Calne, Walter *and* William of; Clare, William of; Croydon, Andrew of; Dereham, Geoffrey of; Dya, John de; Fakenham, Hervey of; Ferring, Geoffrey of; Framingham, Nicholas of; Gervase; Gregory; Guist, William of; Harpley, Ranulf of; Houghton, Nicholas of; Hugh; Huntingdon, John *and* Simon of; John the doctor; Kirkham, Richard of; Lambert; Lando; Lynn, Roger of; Munci, Alexander de; Nicholas; Pincerna, Roger; Raveningham, Roger of; Ringsfield, Michael of; Ros, Jordan de; St Albans, Alexander of; Shipton, Richard of; Somerton, R. of; Sparham, John of; Stangrim; Stow, Richard of; Suffield, Walter; Syderstone, Ralph of; Tew, Robert of; Thrandeston, William of; Walpole, Alexander of; Ware, Peter of; Warham, Ranulf of; Wendling, Robert of
Magna Carta, xxi
malt, as rent, 74
mandate
– episcopal, lx
— to induct, 3, 32–3, 67, 90
– papal, 37, 65; Appx II 41
manor, 121; Appx II 17, 50
– custody of, Appx II 54
– of bp of Norwich, tithes of, 95
— *see also* Beighton; Blofield; Elmham, North *and* South; Gaywood; Hoxne; Langham; Marsham; Thornage; Thorpe; Wicks Bishop
– of Bury St Edmunds, tithes of, 36
– of Colchester abbey, 49
– of Norwich cathedral priory, 141
– of Wymondham priory, 121
maritagium, Appx II, 36, 53; xxxix
market, xxvi
– in churchyard, prohibited, Appx II 49
– Tuesday, Appx II 55
marketplace, 11, 121

marriage
– annulment of, Appx II 44
– bp's certification of legitimacy of 21, 100; xxxix, lx
– cause relating to, Appx II 14, 37
— reserved to bp, 141
– custody of, of heiress, xxvii–xxviii
marsh, 6, 15, 74, 107, 121
marshal, bp's, *see* Ingelram
mass, payments for, 127n
matricula, of church of Norwich, 59; lv, lxvii
mayor, making of, Appx II 41A
meadow, 15, 62, 69n, 74, 112, 121
– *see also* tithe
measures, false, Appx II 54
mediety, *see* church, parish
merchants, Appx II 55
– of France, xxxviii
messuage, 98n, 121, 143n, 144; Appx II 2
mill, 29, 49, 69n, 74, 104, 112, 121
– pond, Appx I 10A
– *see also* tithe
miller, *see* Adam
moor, 115
mort d'ancestor, 98n; Appx II 25–6; xxviii, xxxvii, xxxix
mortmain, 23n

narratio, lxvi–lxviii
nomination, episcopal, to vicarages, *see* vicar
Norwich, Valuation of, lvi, lviii
notificatio, lxvi
notification
– in association with chapter of Norwich, 96
– of decisions of papal judges-delegate, 10, 96
– to papal judges-delegate, 65
– to royal justices, 21–2, 97–101, 147; Appx II 37
novel disseisin, Appx II 25; xxxvii–xxxviii

oaks, covert of, 139
oath, 1–2, 6, 15, 49B; Appx I 2, 11; Appx II 27, 41A; lxiii
– corporal, Appx II 55
– on Gospels, Appx I 3
– *see also* pledge; profession
obedience, canonical, Appx II 27
– *see also* profession
oblations, 2, 15, 37, 62, 105, 115, 127n, 142
– personal, to vicar, 127n
obventions, 15, 37, 39, 105, 112, 142; Appx II 27
– exemption from, 108
– of chapel, Appx I 11
oculus episcopi, archdn as, Appx II 8

INDEX OF SUBJECTS

officers, episcopal, *see* Somerton, R. of; Stow, Richard of; Wendling, Robert of
official, archdn's, xix
– mandate to, 32–3
– of archdn of Norfolk, *see* Carleville, Robert de; Ware, Peter of
– of archdn of Norwich, 59n, 127n; *see also* Holkham, Henry of
– of archdn of Sudbury, *see* Shipton, Richard of; Yaxley, Gilbert of
official, bp's, 105, 122n, 137; Appx II 31, 36, 39, 53; xxxix–xl, xliii–xlvii, lx, lxv
– cited to *curia regis*, xl
– mandate to, 3–4
– *see also* Alvechurch, John of; Beccles, Alan of; Bilney, Robert of; Calne, William of; Clare, William of; Ferring, Geoffrey of; Harpley, Ranulf of; Horham, William of; Shipton, Richard of; Warham, Ranulf of
– of consistory, *see* Fakenham, Hervey of
– vice-, *see* Maurice
ornaments, repair of, 30, 69n, 116

pannage, 121
parish
– delineation of, 37; Appx II 36
– establishment of, xix
– religious house founded in, 109, 117n
– *see also* church, parish
park, 2, 121
– *see also* tithe
parochia for 'diocese', 74
parsonage house, 6
– *see also* vicarage house
pasture, 49, 121
– common, 121
patron
– consent of, to appropriation, 69
— to benefice within church, 120
– of monastery, 108
peace, provisions for, Appx II 15
penalty, for non-payment of pension, 49B, 132
pension, lv, lxi, lxvii
– from church, 32, 56, 59, 69, 75–6, 83, 87–8, 91, 102n, 103, 109, 138; Appx I 3–4; Appx II 5, 11; lv
— to rector, 110; lvi–lvii, lix
– from issues of bpric, Appx II 46
– from mediety of church, 73–4
– from vicar to monastic rector, 127–8
– in grain, 143n
– in lieu of tithes, 49A–B, 152
– in wax, 127
– paid between obedientiaries, 83, 87–8
perambulation of parish boundaries, 37
persona, 48, 62, 89, 97, 105, 113; Appx I 9, 11; Appx II 39

– instituted, 11, 13–14, 18, 27, 56, 58, 110
– religious house described as, 117
– vicar described as 5, 15, 29, 52, 61, 66, 102, 109, 115–6, 118, 132; Appx II 24
– *see also* rector
personatus
– as a money payment, xlviii
— by vicar to monks, 132
– united with vicarage, 17, 56
– valuation of, 142
– *see also* church, parish; institution
Peter's Pence, xxi
pilgrims, grant for use of, 39
pincerna regis, *see* Aubigny, William I d'
piracy, xxxviii
pleas, crown
– of lands and fees, Appx II 25
– relating to Lynn, Appx II 29, 55
pleas of strangers, Appx II 55
pledge of faith, Appx II 26
– *see also* oath
Poitevins, fall of, xxxi
poor, grant for use of, 38, 72, 80, 84, 105, 118n, 134, 154
pope, bp's letter to, Appx II 8
– mandate of, ordering provision to benefice, 58A
– *see also* judges-delegate; *and* Alexander III *and* IV; Gregory IX; Honorius III; Innocent III *and* IV
portion, *see* church, parish
prebend, daily, of vicar, 127n
presentation to benefice
– rejected by bp, Appx II 40
– royal, xl, xlii
– *see also* institution; nomination, episcopal
prior, appointment and dismissal of
– reserved to abbot of mother house, Appx II 27
– reserved to bp, 49
prise, Appx II 55
prison, royal, Appx II 42
proctor
– appointment of, Appx II 15
– of abbot and convent of Battle, 33
– of abbot and convent of Colchester, 49B
– of bp, *see* Lando; *see also* attorney
– of James, papal scribe, 9
– of prior and convent of Canterbury, 39
procurations
– of archdns and deans, 30, 116
– of earl of Warenne, 74
profession, of bp to archbp, 28, 124
prognostic, xxxii
prohibition, writ of, 147n; Appx II 20, 31, 53; xxxviii, xl, xliin, l
protection
– archiepiscopal, 145B

INDEX OF SUBJECTS

– episcopal, lv
provision, papal, xlviii
pulses (*haraciis*), tithe of, 121

quitclaim, 20n, 38n, 70n, 132n, 139; Appx II 16–7, 26
– payment for, Appx II 10
quo warranto, Appx II 32

rector, 30, 49, 112
– claim to be, 65
– consent of, to creation of benefice within church, 120
—— to exemption of religious house from tithes, 108
– to bear ecclesiastical burdens of church, 112
– testament of, Appx II 56
– *see also persona*
religious house
– foundation of, 107; xix, xxvii, lv
– immediately subject to Roman church, 6
– statutes for, Appx II 6; lxi
– *see also* church, conventual; *and also under individual houses*
render, annual, Appx II 55
rent, 29, 49, 69n, 112, 115, 121, 151
– assised, 2
– quitclaimed, Appx II 10
rolls, of royal government, xxxvii
Rule of St Augustine, 108

salt, measurement of, Appx II 55
salutatio, lxv
salvation of souls, grant for, 19–20
sanctio, lxviii
scholars, of Bury, 35n
schools, Appx II 50A
scribe
– legate's, *see* London, John of
– papal, *see* James; Sezze, Berard de
script of *acta*, lxxi
seal
– of bps, lxii, lxviii
– of consistory of Norwich, Appx II 50A
see
– temporalities of, *sede vacante*, xxi, xxv, xxvin, xxxii, xxxvii, xliii
– vacancy of, 110n; xxi, xxviii–xxx
seneschal
– of bp, 143n; *see also* Bassingbourn, Alexander of; Brancaster, Bartholomew of
– of prior, *see* Loddon, Geoffrey of
sequela, 108, 121
sequestration, of fruits of church, Appx II 52; xl, xlii

– *see also* distraint
servant
– bp's, *see* Scarning, Simon of
– lay, 37
sheriff
– of Bedfordshire and Buckinghamshire, Appx II 44
– of Norfolk and Suffolk, Appx II 42
sick, grant for use of, 72, 134
sokeman, 74
Statute of Merton, xxxi
statutes
– for religious house, Appx II 6; lxi
– synodal, Appx II 46A; xxxiv
steward, legate's, *see* Martin
stream, Appx I 10A
Sunday pennies, 127n
synods, Appx II 56; lii, lx
– of Norfolk and Norwich archdeaconries, 10, 91, 96, 128–9; Appx I 4; Appx II 39, 43
—— Easter, 8; Appx II 27
– of Sudbury and Suffolk archdeaconries, 31, 50, 102, 112; Appx II 39
—— Easter, 109
synodals, vicar to pay, 23

tallage, xxxviii
taxation
– papal, xxi–xxiii
– royal, xxxi
temporalities, *see* see
tenants, granted to church, 108
tenements, 121
testaments, last, Appx II 18, 53
– cases relating to, reserved to bp, 141
– of rectors, Appx II 56
theam, 121
tithes, 10, 15, 37, 39, 74, 78–9, 84, 95, 105, 117, 146; lv, lxvii, lxi
– allocated to parishes, Appx II 36
– appropriated to monks, 106, 121
– confirmation of, 68, 77–80, 84, 125, 133, 146, 148, 150; Appx I 2
– demesne, 29, 49, 57, 65, 74, 78–80, 84, 95, 104, 121–2, 125n, 129, 137, 142, 148, 152; Appx I 2, 10
—— leased, 57
—— payment in lieu of, 137
– farmers of, 68, 122
– great, 29, 39n, 49–B, 69n, 79–80, 106, 108, 112, 115, 122, 129, 137, 152
– lesser, 2, 29, 37, 44–5, 49, 62, 79, 108, 112, 115, 122, 135, 142
– litigation concerning, 49B; lxi
– *novelle*, 29
– separated, 133
– sequestrated from parish churches, 77, 84

218   INDEX OF SUBJECTS

– of assarts, 74, 142; Appx II 47
– of beans, 142
– of cheeses, 74
– of corn (*bladi*), 104
– of crofts, 31
– of flax, 15, 29, 127
– of geese, 15
– of grain, 74, 142, 153
– of hall, 6, 95
– of hay, 29, 44–5, 69n, 74, 104, 142, 153
– of hemp, 15, 29, 127
– of hens, 15
– of lambs, 15, 74, 127
– of manor, 36, 68
– of meadows, 121
– of milk, 15
– of mills, 29, 49–B, 69n, 74, 104, 112, 121, 127, 135
– of oxen, 15
– of parks, 121
– of peas, 142
– of piglets, 74
– of pulses, 121
– of rents, 74
– of sale of woods, 121
– of the sea, 62, 135
– of sheep, 74, 95
– of tofts, 6
– of turbary, 142
– of vegetables, 44–5, 105–6, 115, 153
– of wood, 105
– of wool, 15, 127
tol, 121
toll, Appx II 51; xxxviii
– of boats, Appx II 55
toll booth, Appx II 55
tournament, xlii
trentals, payment for, 127n
tronage, Appx II 55
turbary, 121, 142

university, *see* Cambridge; Oxford; Paris

valediction, 65, 96
vicar, 5, 15, 25–31, 34–6, 39, 44, 51, 57n, 60–3, 70, 74, 89, 91, 96A, 105, 108, 110n, 113, 128, 142; Appx I 7–9; Appx II 3, 27
– appointed by advice of bp, 39
– collation of, 4
– correction and removal of, reserved to bp, 2, 6, 15
– deprivation of, 8
– institution of, 7–9, 24, 45; lix
– perpetual, 38, 48, 86, 115, 117, 119, 123, 129, 132; Appx II 27

— institution of, 43, 104, 106, 127, 129, 132; lix
– portion of, 2, 126
– provision for maintenance of, 49, 51–2, 60–1, 63, 70, 74, 86, 96A, 105, 108, 127; Appx I 7–9; lv–lvi
– tithes leased to, 57
– to be nominated by bp, 2, 5, 15, 29–30, 52, 61, 66, 103, 114–6, 119, 132, 135; Appx I 2; Appx II 24; lviii
– to bear ecclesiastical burdens of church, 2, 15, 29–30, 39, 44–5, 62, 116, 127–9, 132, 153n
– to bear one third of costs of repair of books and ornaments, 30, 39, 116
– to bear canonical burdens of mediety, 23
– to bear extraordinary burdens *pro rata*, 62
– to bear proportion of burdens on church, 2, 119
– to keep residence, 153n
– to minister in person, 23, 129, 132
vicarage, 2–5, 15, 30–1, 33, 39, 41n, 44–5, 48, 61–2, 66–7, 69, 76, 91, 102–3, 110n, 114–6, 118–9, 121, 123, 126–8, 140, 142, 150n, 153; Appx II 2–3, 23–4, 27, 43; lvii–lix, lxvii
– farm of, 8–9, 114, 117–8
– perpetual, 23, 29, 30n, 104, 106, 127, 132, 135; lviii
– to be leased, 114
– united with *personatus*, 17, 110n; xlviii–xlix, lix
– united with pension, 56
vicarage
– buildings, 29, 62
– house, 15, 142
– messuage, 31, 39
vicegerent of archbp of Canterbury and archdns, *sede vacante*, 69n, 110n
vidimus, 19–20, 25; lv
– see also *inspeximus*
visitation
– agreement concerning, Appx II 27
– episcopal, Appx II 41; xxvii
– reserved to bp, 141

wardrobe
– queen's, keeper of, *see* Lecche, Robert de
– royal, liii
— clerk of, *see* Luke the chaplain
wardship, Appx II 31, 45; xxvii–xxviii
warranty, Appx II 1, 17
– grantor not to be vouched to, 134
warren, 139; Appx II 50
wax, as pension, 127
widowhood, grant in, 72

INDEX OF SUBJECTS

will, *see* testament
wine, prise of, Appx II 55
wine-casks, empty, Appx II 55
witnesses, produced before bp, 138
wood, 37, 121, 139
– holly, 139
– sale of, 121

wrek, 121
writ, royal, Appx II 1, 25, 42, 44, 46, 49, 52; xli–xlii, xlv, xlix

year, calculation of, lxix–lxx